The Fear Brokers

The Fear Brokers

by

Senator Thomas J. McIntyre

with

John C. Obert

The Pilgrim Press

New York

Philadelphia

Library of Congress Cataloging in Publication Data

McIntyre, Thomas J   1915–
  The fear brokers.

  Includes bibliographical references.
  1. United States—Politics and government—
1945–   2. New Hampshire—Politics and government—1951–   3. Conservatism—United States.
4. Conservatism—New Hampshire. 5. McIntyre,
Thomas J., 1915–   I. Obert, John C.,
1924–   joint author. II. Title.
E839.5.M33   320.9′73′092   79-4255
ISBN 0-8298-0357-2

The Pilgrim Press, 287 Park Avenue South, New York, New York 10010

*For my wife, Myrtle, and our
daughter, Martha
For my coauthor's wife, Natalia,
and their children, Tom, Gretchen,
Christopher, and Cameron
And for Kenneth M. Birkhead
and all the members
of my staff who served
so loyally and so well
for sixteen years*

Contents

Part II

A Commentary

It was never Senator McIntyre's intention to have *The Fear Brokers* published before the general election of 1978. He felt that preelection publication would make the book's message suspect in some eyes by tying it to his own political ambitions. Thus, no account of his campaign for reelection or of the outcome of that campaign appears in the body of the text.

A commentary is now in order, however, because the central message—that liberals and moderates who discount the appeal and the formidability of the New Right do so at their own and the nation's risk—gained unforeseen and ironic emphasis on November 7, 1978. On that day Senator McIntyre, a native son of New Hampshire and heavily favored to win a fourth term, was narrowly defeated. The winner, Gordon Humphrey, is an airline copilot, who moved to the state only four years before. He prepared for his candidacy by serving as field coordinator for the Conservative Caucus, one of the largest and fastest growing New Right organizations.

The irony in Senator McIntyre's defeat lies in the fact that few, if any, political figures understand the right wing as he does. Few were as well prepared to do battle with it and survive. He had done so on other occasions. This time, though prepared as never before, he could not counter the depth and the skillful exploitation of the fears, the grievances, and the resentments that feed the New Right movement.

Humphrey campaigned hard and relentlessly for many months. He hammered at emotional single issues—the Panama Canal treaties, welfare statism, public funding of abortion, the alleged decline of U.S. military strength—and he tapped resentment over taxes, government spending and regulation. Late in the campaign he launched an expensive but highly effective television blitz over Boston stations, targeting the heavily populated southern tier of New Hampshire counties. He promised repeatedly that if elected he would be the "biggest skinflint" in the U.S. Senate. Fifteen days before the general election, opinion polls showed Senator McIntyre holding a commanding two-to-one lead over his opponent. But on election day Gordon Humphrey won by a margin of 5,800 votes.

Analysts differ in their explanation of how the McIntyre lead evaporated in so short a time. Some fault the polls. Others credit the Humphrey television blitz. Still others say that after sixteen years in office the senator fell victim to "incumbency disease" or was finally defeated by his political arch-enemy, William Loeb, whose right-wing newspapers dominate New Hampshire's publishing scene.

But we who know Senator McIntyre—we who have worked with him through the years and love the man—take solace and pride in our belief that he fell victim to his own political integrity.

In what may well be the most tax-conscious state in the nation he refused to exploit the tax revolt. While his opponent enthusiastically championed the Kemp-Roth tax reduction bill, Senator McIntyre voted against it and called it what it was—inflationary and a cynically expedient betrayal of the Republican party's traditional commitment to fiscal integrity. Of Proposition 13 the senator said there were sounder ways to provide property tax relief than adopting a measure that was inherently discriminatory, fiscally irresponsible, and that promised in the long run to cost the people local autonomy.

On the matter of government spending, he called for reasoned judgment, noting on a number of occasions that thrift was an admirable goal so long as it did not make the helpless the first, foremost, and perhaps the only victims of spending cutbacks.

It is clear now that the senator's attempt to bring balance to the public dialogue over taxes and spending may have hurt him.

The most dramatic evidence of the potency of the dollar issue in this election was the defeat of Republican Governor Meldrim Thomson Jr. Thomson, perhaps the most conservative governor in the nation, had been elected three times, with growing majorities, on his staunch opposition to broad-based taxes. This time, however, he was challenged by an attractive Democrat, Hugh Gallen, who not only pledged the same opposition to a state sales or income tax but capitalized on Thomson's first serious miscalculation of a pocketbook issue. In his zealous support of nuclear power for New Hampshire, Thomson backed Construction Work in Progress (CWIP) charges—a 9-percent surcharge on electric bills to finance part of the New Hampshire Public Service Company's cost of building a huge nuclear power station at Seabrook. Gallen said CWIP was, in effect, a hidden and costly tax on electricity users, and when it was revealed that the public service company intended to increase stockholder dividends at a time when it was arguing it needed the CWIP charges to afford the Seabrook plant, Thomson found himself politically embarrassed. Most observers are convinced that while Thomson's bizarre right-wing activities, described in detail in this book, cost him some support in this election, the decisive issue was CWIP and Gallen's skillful use of it.

If Senator McIntyre's approach to taxation and spending hurt him, he was also hurt by the balanced positions he took on defense and foreign policy questions. While his opponent was demanding unquestioned U.S. military superiority and decrying efforts to reach a SALT II agreement, Senator McIntyre, a veteran member of the Armed Services Committee, repeatedly expressed his conviction that this country remains the strongest on the face of the earth and that in its strength it should not fear to negotiate a meaningful strategic arms limitations agreement with its major adversary.

Finally, there was the issue that prompted the senator's celebrated speech on the Senate floor on March 1, 1978, that in large part inspired the writing of this book and that in the judgment of many was the single issue that hurt his candidacy most—his vote to ratify the new Panama Canal treaties. A year before the election—indeed months before the vote on the treaties—the New Right had promised that this was the issue it would use to defeat Tom McIntyre. And in the aftermath of the election, spokespersons for the movement made it clear that his defeat pleased them more than the outcome of any other race.

Senator McIntyre's concession statement on election night acknowledged the impact of this issue.

> Over the years I tried my best to give our state a moderate, a civil, and a responsible voice in Washington. On the tough issues, I called them as I saw them, and I could do no more than that. Some will say that my votes on issues like the Panama Canal treaties cost me this election. And they may be right. But when I voted for the treaties I said I did so because I believed they were in the best interests of our country. I still believe that, and I am confident that time will prove me right.

We who worked as members of his staff share his sadness at leaving the office he loved. But we take comfort and great satisfaction in the knowledge that we worked for a good and decent man, who chose to risk that office rather than compromise respect for truth and reason.

We also share a common fear—the fear that what happened to Tom McIntyre on November 7, 1978 will make other good officeholders and candidates afraid to risk the same fate. It is the senator's hope—and our hope—that what he has written will convince other moderates and liberals that, notwithstanding his own defeat, the drift to the right in this country is no more inexorable than it is desirable. *The Fear Brokers* argues that the direction this country takes will be largely determined from this point on by the level of courage and integrity and intelligence displayed by those who understand the ultimate consequences of what the New Right has in mind for America.

John C. Obert
Arlington, Virginia
November 20, 1978

Foreword

by
Senator Mark O. Hatfield

The Panama Canal debate was droning on. There was little interest in what was being said on the Senate floor; the arguments, pro and con, were being endlessly repeated, usually in the presence of just a handful of senators. Attention was focused on how undecided senators would cast their votes.

I went to the Senate chamber on the first day of March to take care of some customary business. Senator Thomas McIntyre of New Hampshire was just beginning his speech on the Panama Canal. Assuming it would be like most others—a reiteration of familiar points in favor of the treaties, which I had long since decided to support—I did not intend to pay close attention to all that was being said. Suddenly, however, it became clear that this was no ordinary senatorial rhetoric. Rather, it was one of those rare, extraordinary speeches, marked by a penetrating discernment of the American political climate and characterized by a stalwart display of political and moral courage.

Senator McIntyre confronted squarely an issue far more crucial than the outcome of the Panama Canal treaties, namely, the atmosphere of poisonous intimidation and vengeance of the New Right, which had come not only to dominate the Panama Canal debate, but today threatens to permeate the American political climate with calumny and fear. "My concern," he said, "is the desperate need for people of conscience and good will to stand up and face down the [bullies] of the radical New Right before the politics of intimidation does to America what it has tried to do to New Hampshire."

This was no safe and generalized warning about the perils of the New Right. Tom McIntyre faced and condemned idols close to his home. Courageously, he spelled out the roles of William Loeb, publisher of New Hampshire's largest newspaper, and of Meldrim Thomson, governor of New Hampshire and chairman of the Conservative Caucus, in fomenting "the politics of threat and vengeance." He did so at a substantial political risk; his concern was that truth, in an atmosphere of civility, tolerance, and mutual trust, remain the guiding qualities of American political debate.

This book has flowed forth from that historic Senate speech. With a fearless honesty, Tom McIntyre unveils the forces and personalities of the emerging New Right across the nation and focuses particularly on that struggle in his own state. His perspective is not limited to politics. Rather, he makes illuminating observations about the psychological, religious, and social dimensions of the New Right's appeal.

Tom McIntyre's words bear the stamp of credibility, for he has known, like few other members of Congress, the relentless assaults of the right wing in his native state on his politics, his personality, his wisdom, and his character. He has experienced those things which he writes about, and that gives a special urgency to his warnings and an authenticity to his perspectives.

When I listened to Senator McIntyre's words in the Senate in March of 1978, and as I later read over the chapters of this book, I reflected on my own encounters with elements of the extreme right wing. I can still vividly remember, as a young person in Oregon, seeing members of the Ku Klux Klan parade openly through the streets of Oregon's cities. Their racist ideology was directed then not toward the repression of Blacks—there were few black people in Oregon during that time—but toward Jews. It was an ugly eruption of anti-Semitism that spawned the open emergence of the Klan in my state during those years, and that continues to lurk beneath the surface of portions of the extreme right wing today.

Years later in my political experience, I condemned extremism of all kinds, but especially the extremism of the Right, when I keynoted the Republican National Convention in 1964. What I remember most was the frightening and scornful tones of the hisses and boos evoked by that sentence in my speech. It spoke to me not merely of strong political disagreement, but of a spiteful kind of enmity waiting to be unleashed to destroy anyone seen as the enemy—domestic or foreign.

A few years later I encountered this vilification more personally. During my opposition to the Vietnam War, the religious segment of the Radical Right attacked not only my patriotism, but the authenticity of my personal Christian faith. It is a tactic of the Radical Right to impugn the personality and the character of its foes. And I can testify that these kinds of attacks are the most difficult for the politician to absorb.

From my own experience, I have observed three traits that seem most to typify the thinking of the extreme right wing, and that are much in evidence today in the ideology of the New Right as it attempts to gain contemporary converts.

First is a hypernationalism which is so accentuated that it can only be called an idolatry. Loyalty to the nation becomes equated with the political agenda of the right wing—to be for escalating our production of nuclear arms, to be against any SALT agreement, to oppose the ERA, and so forth. To take a different side on any of the issues means, in the eyes of the New Right, that you are against the nation, that you are unpatriotic, that you are a disloyal citizen. Historically, the more such a version of national righteousness gains political power, the greater is the extent of political repression that inevitably follows.

Second is the manipulation of religion to ordain the cause of the New Right. In essence, this frequently translates into meaning that opposition to their political agenda proves not only that you are un-American, but that you are ungodly. A civil religion is employed, which declares—in direct contradiction to biblical truths—that our nation carries a divine privilege, and that if we embrace the political dogma of the Right we will be turning to God's true purposes for the nation. A national religious and political chauvinism is thus promulgated by the false purity of the New Right. They and a nation transformed in the New Right's image are declared to possess divine sanction.

As a Christian, there is no other part of the New Right ideology that concerns me more than its self-serving misuse of religious faith. What is at stake here is the very integrity of biblical truth. The New Right, in many cases, is doing nothing less than placing a heretical claim on Christian faith that distorts, confuses, and destroys the opportunity for a biblical understanding of Jesus Christ and of his gospel for millions of people.

. Finally, persistent threads of racism lie right below the surface of the New Right's ideology. From the earliest days of the nation onward, elements akin to the right wing have attempted to prey upon prejudice toward foreigners, toward Blacks, toward Jews, toward Native Americans, and toward other religious minority or alien groups. These sentiments continue to be subtly seized upon and inflamed by the extreme right wing.

Our nation is in an era of political mistrust and uncertainty. Fundamental questions—and I think healthy ones—are being raised about the purposes of government, the quality of our lives, and the values that are to guide us. But it is always in such a time that people become vulnerable to having their legitimate questions manipulated into hysterical fears. That is the intention of the New Right today, in our country, in order to increase its political power.

I stand with Senator Thomas McIntyre, who warns us of the dangers inherent in today's political climate with the rise of the New Right. His words and his own political stance are an example of how fear can be met with hope, how hysteria can be answered by discernment, and how intimidation can be overcome by courage.

Acknowledg- ments

I thank Senator Mark O. Hatfield for his gracious foreword to *The Fear Brokers* and for his understanding and support of its message.

I express my gratitude, too, to everyone who contributed to the research, organization, writing, editing, and publication of this book. Some can be named; others, for regrettable reasons inherent in the theme of the book, cannot.

Coauthor, John C. Obert, my long-time special assistant, continued to meet his staff responsibilities while devoting early mornings, late nights, weekends, holidays, and his annual leave to the preparation of the manuscript. When concluding the project demanded almost full-time attention, his Senate salary was reduced to the minimum required to keep his insurance protection in force. Approval of this arrangement was obtained from the Senate Ethics Committee, which was apprised from the outset of the nature of the project.

Resource material for *The Fear Brokers*, much of it gathered over a period of years, was augmented by previously published material cited in the text, collected in further research by Nancy Wilder, provided by Wesley McCune's Group Research, Inc., or obtained from Diane Fairbank, Scott Wolf, and Greg Denier.

Special mention must be made of the invaluable help provided by Robert Hoyt, of *Christianity and Crisis*, in editing and revising the manuscript, and by my legal counsel, Alan Novins.

Finally, there is the matter of acknowledging inspiration. For me, it was the memory of two men of gallant spirit, consummate decency, and boundless faith in our country and in its institutions—the late senators Hubert H. Humphrey and Philip M. Hart. For my coauthor, it was the patient understanding of his wife, the encouragement of his friend Charles J. Freeman, and the lasting influence of his longtime political mentor, Byron G. Allen. And both of us drew additional inspiration from our retired colleague, Kenneth M. Birkhead, who has spent so much of his life doing battle with the Radical Right.

Author's Note

This is not a book about American conservatism, an old and honorable political philosophy I do not share but hold in high esteem.

Rather, it is a book about the Radical Right, about people who profess to love America more and understand it better than you or I do but whose words and deeds belie this claim.

To be more precise, it is about the exploitation of genuine and widespread anxieties by political leaders who preach passionate certainties but whose chauvinism about America masks their own deep-seated reservations about the Grand American Experiment—about our basic values, traditions, and institutions; about the Bill of Rights and the Constitution itself—and whose shrillness reveals their profound fears about our strength as a nation, our character as a people.

It is a book about spokespersons for a movement which has no confidence that truth will prevail in the open market of ideas, which chafes under the necessary disorderliness of democracy, and which neither understands nor tolerates diversity and dissent.

In sum, it is a book about frightened would-be tyrants, about leaders whom Hannah Arendt characterized in another but not so different context as "sheep in wolves' clothing."

I hope that what I have set down, along with the public record of their own words and deeds, proves them to be what they truly are.

If I bring to this task a particular credential, it is this: Unlike the social historian, whose study of political extremism is, for the most part, consideration in the abstract, I have had to cope with the Radical Right, personally and directly, almost every day of my public life. From the time of my first campaign for the U.S. Senate (1961), it has been my lot to fend off attacks from this element while trying to bring some semblance of reason and perspective to the public dialogue.

So I know the Radical Right. I know what they are and how they function.

I know that when *you* say you are for peace, *they* will say you are for appeasement.

I know that when you say you are for an end to the arms race, they will say you want to leave America helpless before its enemies.

Further, if you speak of protecting the environment, they will say you want to destroy free enterprise; when you defend the First Amendment, they will say you favor the spread of pornography; if you argue that all our liberties depend on preserving due process of law, they will say you are for coddling criminals; and if you support carefully circumscribed handgun legislation to protect citizens who live in high-density crime areas, they will say you are part of a Communist plot to take away the rifles and shotguns of law-abiding persons who shoot for sport.

And now I know also that when you say the Panama Canal treaties are in the best national security interests of the United States and that they serve the cause of justice, they will say you have betrayed your country and have sold out to its enemies.

Some may think that these attacks are my own inventions, mere parodies of respectable political arguments. Not at all; they are accurate paraphrasings of slogans in recent or current use. One cannot caricature a caricature, nor is it possible to oversimplify the oversimplifications that constitute the standard armamentarium of the Radical Right.

The reader may question whether such transparently ad hominem devices can be effective with an electorate as literate and relatively sophisticated as the American public. But along with many others who are active in public life, I can testify that these techniques can be powerful. They can force rational and decent public servants into a falsely defensive stance. They can determine the agenda for the public dialogue, ensure that the dialogue will be more divisive than constructive, distract us from the essence of critical issues, and sidetrack every effort made by reasonable people to reason together.

Finally, it may seem that my response is rooted in partisan concerns. In truth, some moderate Republican colleagues are discovering now what I had occasion to learn long ago as a middle-of-the-road Democrat in the special circumstances of New Hampshire: The Radical Right has no more tolerance for mainstream political thought than it has for the liberal left. To be a moderate these days—to address issues on their merits, to support what you believe to be practical and sensible policies—is to invite not only disagreement but the most relentless harassment. It is that simple and that alarming.

For many years my concern about the Radical Right was narrowly focused: I was preoccupied with its manifestations in my home state of New Hampshire, and I found it difficult to believe that such an alien philosophy could attract a national constituency. Thus, my direct experiences with this brand of political extremism were limited to those on home grounds, most especially in the persons of William Loeb and Meldrim Thomson Jr.

This book contains a good deal of information about Loeb and Thomson—more perhaps than some readers may care to have. However, I have come to feel that it is important for Americans generally to acquire some sense of these men. Sinclair Lewis wrote *It Can't Happen Here* to show clearly that, in truth, it *can* happen here—there is no cosmic law forbidding the triumph of extremism in America.[1] What has happened in New Hampshire through the influence of Thomson and Loeb is not a final victory for the philosophy of the Far Right, but it has gone far enough in that direction to be frightening. And it is not fiction.

William Loeb is the publisher of New Hampshire's largest and only morning and statewide daily newspaper, the *Manchester Union Leader,* and of its only statewide Sunday newspaper, the *New Hampshire Sunday News.* His links to the Radical Right go back many years, and his newspapers have trumpeted its bellicose message ever since he burst upon the New Hampshire publishing scene thirty-two years ago.

Meldrim Thomson Jr. has been the governor of New Hampshire since 1972. Like Loeb, who has never even lived in New Hampshire, Thomson is not a native of the state; his roots are in Georgia. And while a fellow Georgian brought the best of the enlightened New South to the White House, Meldrim Thomson —with Loeb's enthusiastic support—brought the worst of the benighted Old South to New Hampshire.

In sharp contrast to President Carter, who says racial integration was the best thing that ever happened to the South, Meldrim Thomson says that Martin Luther King Jr. "did great harm to the American way of life through his association with Communist-inspired organizations"; that our black ambassador to the United Nations, Andrew Young, is a "kook" who supports "Communist butchers and terrorists"; and that John Vorster, the former leader of South Africa's apartheid government, is "a courageous statesman."

Publisher Loeb champions Stanford engineering professor William Shockley, who contends that Blacks are genetically inferior to Whites. Loeb chaired a national lobby against passage of the 1963 Civil Rights Act and has said he hopes "the black population of New Hampshire will never increase from its present minimal figure." In his view, the celebrated television drama *Roots* was not only a "wild exaggeration" but a "Russian"-inspired attempt to brainwash the American people into feeling so guilty about slavery that they will sit by and do nothing "when the Russian Communists lead hordes of black terrorists to slaughter whites in South Africa."

If this were the only attitude shared by Loeb and Thomson it would be discomfiting enough for a state with such a historic commitment to freedom. But it is not. This book shows how they also mirror each other in their scorn for civil liberties, the First Amendment, academic freedom, due process of law, and women's rights; in their intolerance of dissent; in their flouting of New England's home rule tradition; in their unconcern for the helpless and the disadvantaged; and in a mutual propensity for cloaking their purposes in the mantle of God-fearing *real* Americanism.

By the rigid Loeb-Thomson standards of orthodoxy, even their own party is suspect of heresy. Nominally they are Republicans, but in practice they are disdainful of the party. They seem determined to purge it of moderation and to remold it to their own image.

Finally, William Loeb and Meldrim Thomson preach a common gospel about the collapse of America. They speak of a nation that has lost its will and its way, a nation morally and economically bankrupt, a nation that has forfeited military supremacy and global influence, a nation that has degenerated into a second-class power. But oblivious of the inconsistency, both would have our allegedly irresolute and impotent nation plunge into war over the slightest provocation.*

During the time I mistakenly believed that these bizarre distortions of America and Americanism were the exclusive province of William Loeb and Meldrim Thomson, I confined my counterefforts to New Hampshire. But in the spring of 1975 I learned that they were not; that they do indeed exist throughout the nation. I became aware of it as a result of a speech I made in which I said that serious consideration of George Wallace for the Presidency was "incredible and appalling."

I had expected attacks from Loeb and Thomson, for Loeb had already endorsed Wallace's candidacy and Thomson had once sought the governorship, unsuccessfully, as a candidate of Wallace's American Independent party. What I had not anticipated was the avalanche of messages from all over the country that crashed down on me. Telegrams, postcards, letters inundated my office. Those from Wallace defenders outnumbered those from Wallace critics by at least ten to one.

A common theme was present in the mail from Wallace people. Whether neatly typed, grammatically correct and on letterhead stationery, or crudely scrawled on a postcard, the communications conveyed (1) an obsessive fear of Communism; (2) hatred of liberals, liberalism, and the federal government; and (3) a total conviction that they were the *real* Americans and I was not. The most superpatriotic messages carried the most dismal assessment of America's strength and character and evidenced the most inflamed and deep-seated bigotry. Although many expressed vicious anti-Black sentiments, even more were anti-Semitic and anti-Catholic.

It was then that I realized how much fear and hatred existed

* See chapter 17.

throughout this land of the free; how ready the frightened and hate-filled are to express themselves and how easily they could be exploited by the expedient or the unscrupulous.

That lesson was confirmed and reinforced three years later, when the U.S. Senate focused its attention on ratification of the new Panama Canal treaties. Before voting on the treaties, senators were subjected to threats of massive political retribution if they voted for ratification. After the vote, those who supported the treaties were roundly castigated as tools of the Communist conspiracy and as "Benedict Arnolds."

In September 1977 I had promised the people of New Hampshire I would not be stampeded into a judgment on the canal treaties. For the next six months I studied the history of the canal, the original treaty, and the provisions of the new treaties. I consulted with those whose opinion I respected and carefully heeded the New Hampshire people who had considered the issue with their intellect as well as their emotion.

I concluded that, on balance, the new treaties not only did American justice to a lesser nation, but they were in our own national security interests. I also decided that rejection of the new treaties was precisely what the Communist powers wanted.

While I was in the process of forming a judgment on the treaties, the Radical Right exerted intense pressure on me to vote against ratification. The pressure reached outrageous proportions. And so, when I took the Senate floor on March 1, 1978 to announce how I would vote on the treaties, I coupled that announcement with a strongly worded condemnation of the politics of threat and vengeance that was carried out in the campaign against the treaties. That campaign, I said, "has impugned the loyalty and the motives of too many honorable Americans to be ignored or suffered in silence a minute longer."*

Within forty-eight hours a torrent of mail and phone calls began to flood my office. Although the messages from New Hampshire were gratifying in that they ran three to two in support of my statement, the mail from outside New Hampshire ran twenty to one against. While a reassuring few took issue in civil and rational terms, most of the opposition mail was vitriolic and abusive; it charged me with treason and promised retribution.

* See chapter 7.

Even though these messages bore remarkable resemblance to the letters from Wallace supporters received three years earlier —particularly in their impassioned jingoism—there were several noticeable differences. The first was in their relative boldness. In 1975 a great many letter writers did not sign their names; in 1978 nearly all did. Clearly, the intervening years had seen a rapid growth in the confidence and assertiveness of these people.

The second difference was more subtle. In 1975 the bigotry was plainly evident; in 1978 it was masked, albeit often crudely. What was formerly described as "the international conspiracy of Jewish bankers" had now become "an international bankers' conspiracy," which, in the letter writers' view, cynically promoted the new treaties in order "to bail out bad investments." (Many times Sol Linowitz, one of the negotiators of the new treaties, was linked to this alleged conspiracy and his name was pointedly underlined.)

The increasing assertiveness of ultraconservative extremists would seem to be tied to the rapid development of a number of lobbying and fund-raising organizations that are now grouped under the umbrella title of the "New Right." Because many of these organizations attempt to project an image of respectability and indeed have respectable names on their organization letterheads, ultraconservatism has assumed a more benign appearance.

As for the playing down of bigotry and even labor-baiting, this could be accounted for in part by the fact that some of the leaders of the New Right are not truly racist nor vehemently antilabor. This point should be carefully noted and underscored.

There is at least one other reason for the change I observed: the indisputable fact that broadening the base of the Radical Right *demanded* a mellower approach. Hard-shell bigots and labor-baiters have never constituted a substantial constituency, and any radical movement that counts on them alone will always be of limited membership and influence.

Thus, out of conscience and/or out of political perspicacity, the New Right eschews several old hard-line approaches as they set about wooing the worried American who is neither bigoted nor paranoid.

This lone evidence of benignity, however, should not obscure the essential nature of the New Right. It is still—by its own admission—a *radical* movement. It is alien to mainstream political thought. It remains ideologically extreme, even if tactically more pragmatic, and, like its organizational forebears, it relies on superpatriotism, militant anti-Communism, and the exploitation of highly divisive issues as its primary stock in trade. The most significant resemblance to its predecessors is the movement's ready resort to impugning the loyalty of those who stand in opposition to its goals.

Moreover, I have seen little evidence that the New Right discourages support from the bigots and the paranoid, favors labor's goals, or is particularly fastidious about the people it chooses as leaders. The national chairman of the Conservative Caucus, the New Right's grass-roots political operation, for pointed example, is Meldrim Thomson Jr., the selfsame governor of New Hampshire. He not only heads this nationwide operation but serves as "secretary of state" in the conservatives' shadow cabinet. In this capacity he has become a national figure by addressing right-wing audiences from coast to coast, and he has become an embarrassment overseas, where he periodically travels to denounce U.S. policy while lauding the authoritarian regimes of the nations he visits.

It is one thing for the governor of a small state in the northeast corner of the country to say the Carter Administration is following a pro-Communist course; or to proclaim the President's declaration of amnesty a "Second Day of Infamy"; or to demand the impeachment of UN Ambassador Andrew Young; or to impugn the Americanism of National Security Council Director Zbigniew Brzezinski and former Secretary of State Henry Kissinger by pointedly noting that they are foreign-born*; or to call for gutting the Fourteenth Amendment and for training the National Guard in nuclear weaponry. It is another for him to do these things as the chairman of a national organization that has the means to spread his views the length and breadth of the land.

It was these actions, in company with the New Right's self-professed character and purpose and the politics of threat and vengeance the movement pursued in its efforts to defeat the

* See chapter 17.

Panama Canal treaties, that prompted me to make my March 1, 1978 Senate speech. Knowing what I do of Meldrim Thomson Jr. and his mentor, William Loeb, and of what they have done to one small part of America since fate brought them together, I closed that speech with the following words:

> My political fate is not my concern here today. My concern is the desperate need for people of conscience and good will to stand up to the bully boys of the radical New Right before the politics of intimidation does to America what it has tried to do to New Hampshire.
>
> So I say to my colleagues:
>
> If you want to see the reputations of decent people sullied, stand aside and be silent.
>
> If you want to see people of dignity, integrity, and self-respect refuse to seek public office for fear of what might be conjured or dredged up to attack them or their families, stand aside and be silent.
>
> If you want to see confidential files rifled, informants solicited, universities harassed, enemy hit lists drawn up, stand aside and be silent.
>
> If you want to see dissent crushed and expression stifled, stand aside and be silent.
>
> If you want to see the fevered exploitation of a handful of highly emotional issues distract the nation from problems of great consequence, stand aside and be silent.
>
> If you want to see your government deadlocked by rigid intransigence, stand aside and be silent.
>
> If you want this nation held up to worldwide scorn and ridicule because of the outrageous statements and bizarre beliefs of its leaders, stand aside and be silent and let the Howard Phillipses,* the Meldrim Thomsons, and the William Loebs speak for all of us.

In a sense, this book flows out of that speech, out of the need I felt to document for a wider public the concerns that I expressed in the Senate. My purpose is to illustrate by the public record what could lie in store for America if a movement led by the likes of Meldrim Thomson and William Loeb should ever achieve the influence and power that—to my everlasting regret —it achieved in my beloved New Hampshire.

This book is divided into two parts: Part I deals with the nature, growth, and impact of the New Right on the national political scene. Part II focuses on the extremist views of William Loeb and Meldrim Thomson Jr. By reporting how the political implementation of those views has affected New Hampshire, I

---

* Howard Phillips is national director of the Conservative Caucus.

hope to point up the warning for the nation implicit in that state's experience.

The reader is cautioned not to expect an examination of the scope or in the depth of such seminal works as Richard Hofstadter's *The Paranoid Style in American Politics*, Daniel Bell's *The Radical Right*, or Theodore W. Adorno's *The Authoritarian Personality*.[2] *The Fear Brokers* is not intended to be a work of scholarship, nor a presentation of exclusively original reflections. I have drawn from the works cited above, however, in order to bring historical perspective to a contemporary assessment of the Radical Right and to provide authoritative insights into the psychology of extremism.

In like manner, I have relied upon disinterested reportorial accounts in newspapers and other periodicals in order to chronicle the development of the New Right, to describe its organizations and leaders, and to note its accomplishments and failures. For deeper analysis of the New Right's significance, I have looked to commentators and editorialists of varying political persuasions, as well as to Wesley McCune's Group Research, Inc., the perennial monitor of right-wing activity.

Some explanatory comments may help to keep the plan of the book (especially Part II) and my purpose in writing it in perspective. First, I do not wish to suggest, by what has already been said or what is to come, that the Radical Right totally controls my state. (If that were the case, neither I nor John Durkin, a Democratic colleague, would be representing New Hampshire in the U.S. Senate; nor would Democrat Norman D'Amours be serving in the House of Representatives.) The message of Part II, however, is that even with partial control the Radical Right can wreak a great deal of havoc.

Second, readers from outside New Hampshire should understand that this situation would probably not be *exactly* duplicated elsewhere in the Union. This is the story of one state, with its own history and culture. To point up its unique nature and what has happened there, I have recorded the events in concrete detail. I ask that readers use their imaginations to penetrate these particularities in order to get at the essence of the reactionary Right. For, in other settings, it will appear in different guises and make use of different bases of power.

Third, I want to make explicit what has been obvious all

along: I am hardly a detached observer. It would be idle and dishonest to affect neutrality or the kind of pure objectivity sought by a scientist in testing hypotheses. But I can attest that the facts related are all matters of public record, easily verifiable by anyone with sufficient interest. My interpretation of that record must stand or fall on its merits.

And last, although even as I write I am engaged in a campaign for reelection to the Senate seat I now hold, this book is not a campaign document. It was my choice that the publication date be set for *after* the November 1978 balloting. Thus, my personal interests are satisfied only to the extent that this book may advance the cause of sanity and civility in the political processes of our nation.

PART I

Introduction

There are Americans among us, not all of them professional doomsayers, who believe that the dilemmas our country faces have at long last surpassed our vaunted genius for problem-solving. That is a judgment no one can disprove, but which I do not share. What I do fear is our fading capacity to cope with one another.

After sixteen years in the U.S. Senate—difficult years that have tested our institutions and our social fabric as rarely before —I believe I understand something of the dimensions of our problems. I do not question their seriousness.

We do have adversaries in the world, powerful adversaries whose ideologies and ambitions are at risk-filled variance with our own. Both we and our potential antagonists deploy weaponry so fearfully destructive that the dangers attending a major conflict are far greater than any that previous generations have known.

And the cost we must bear for our uneasy security is proportionately huge. It not only burdens our economy, but conditions our hope of relieving grinding hunger and poverty in the world —and thus our hope of helping to create a stable international order.

At home we are confronted by a critical energy dilemma born of the impending exhaustion of domestic sources of oil and natural gas. Our growing dependence on cartel-controlled imports

imposes another heavy charge on the economy that seriously ex-
acerbates our other economic problems, most notably inflation.
This crisis—and that is its proper name—is further com-
pounded by the clash of regional interests in the nation; by the
risks, known or feared, of converting to a coal and/or nuclear-
based economy; and by the political, technical, and commercial
obstacles that hinder rapid development of nonpolluting, re-
newable energy sources.

In the meantime we are experiencing a dramatic middle-class
taxpayers' revolt directed, legitimately enough, against government waste and ineffectiveness but also capable of creating new
social tensions by crippling responsible measures to promote
equity and equality among our people. In the very midst of that
revolt there are signs that the Kerner Commission's warning
about "two Americas" is still valid. The week Proposition 13
was adopted in California, unemployment among the black
youth of Washington, D.C. climbed to nearly 45 percent.

These are great problems, perhaps unprecedented in their
scope and in their interlocking complexity. Not all of them can
be "solved"; it is hard, for example, to foresee an end in our
generation to the dangerous tensions between the West and the
Soviet bloc. Nevertheless, all these problems demand a response at once vigorous and careful; if they are left untended or
are handled impulsively, the consequences could be formidable indeed. Clearly, these unprecedented challenges make unprecedented demands upon our will and our resources.

In my view, however, our ability to meet such challenges
from year to year, from decade to decade, depends most centrally upon a prior condition: the maintenance among our citizens of a certain degree of mutual respect. My recent experience suggests that this quality of comity is at risk today.

This may seem a thesis more appropriate to a book of sermons
than to a discourse on political life. Not so. In my reading of history (especially American history), it is not the genius or inadequacy of certain leaders or programs but the health or the pa-
thology of the entire body politic that has most strongly affected
our ability to cope with critical issues. Nations, like families,
thrive on trust and founder when trust is gone. Any nation, but
particularly a democracy, is able to preserve its essential character when its people can achieve enough in the way of consensus

and commonality of purpose to harmonize their inevitable differences. When the social atmosphere of an era is parched by the heat of incivility, when epithets replace evidence and accusations are substituted for reasonable argument in public discourse, the very being of a nation is under threat.

If we are entering such an era—and there are alarming signs that we are—then the burden of our already-awesome problems may indeed exceed our strength.

It is hard to propound a thesis like this without sounding like Cassandra on the one hand or Pollyanna on the other. Let it be clear that when I speak of our need of trust, civility, and mutual respect, I do not rule out the clash of differing beliefs, interests, or even prejudices. Such conflicts occur in the healthiest of families. Indeed, the family that never experiences open conflict is probably in trouble. The genius of our political system has resided in its capacity to resolve conflict by encouraging its expression in a way that leads (however slowly at times) toward pragmatic compromise, not by repressing it.

But our system is something more than a set of operating rules. It has an inner life. It exists within and draws its strength from a context of human attitudes. Although our political mores permit strong advocacy and sharp, even angry criticism, yet the system requires—as a matter of its own survival—a certain level of patience and tolerance, a certain element of restraint in our rhetoric, an ultimate reliance on the power of reason. These qualities are never more needed than when, as today, we must make difficult choices in situations that test the limits of our knowledge and comprehension.

Yet, as we look about us we see more and more persons embracing what Eric Sevareid calls "dangerously passionate certainties." And not only are they embracing these "certainties," but they are using the most intemperate and uncivil means of forcing them on others. This spirit is dangerous. It alienates us one from the other. It polarizes issues beyond hope of resolution. And it is infectious, for it invites responses in kind.

To be sure, the dogmatic espousal and forceful imposition of "dangerously passionate certainties" are hardly unique to our own time. Nor are the consequences that follow: bitter disharmony and paralysis of the national will. But consider the differences between the present and previous periods especially marked by discord. In earlier times there were frontiers to push back in order to give society breathing space, to give more people a chance for their own place in the sun. Seemingly limitless resources and power were available to throw at problems—and at adversaries—until they were vanquished. And the tools of science and technology that would make us healthier and wealthier had just begun to be deployed.

Today there are no westward frontiers. Increasingly, we see that the liberating power of applied science often brings new dangers, from pollution to depersonalization, rising out of technology itself. Then, just as we learned through the oil embargo and the preachments of Earth Day and of Sun Day that our resources are finite and precious, we also discovered through the Vietnam War that even our vaunted power can be circumscribed by conditions beyond our control . . . and that even the brightest and the best can make tragic mistakes when their intellectual integrity is compromised by political loyalties and misdirected fervor.

Our geopolitical situation has changed as well. In this age of ICBMs and nuclear-powered submarines, the oceans that once gave us a sense of unassailable security have shrunk to mere moats. Reluctantly, we have come to realize that our superpower ranking does not mean that we can have our will wherever and whenever we wish, but that the very reach of our influence subjects us to the impact of events in every corner of the globe.

For some of us it has been a sobering quarter century. For others it has been disorienting, the more so because during this same period there have been political, economic, social, and, yes, moral upheavals that seemed to ensure that we would never again be quite the same people or quite the same nation.

There is no need to recite that history in detail. To reexperience the shock, the poignancy, the troubling yet partially valid disillusionment many of us have suffered through, one need only reflect on words and phrases that might serve as chapter headings for a chronicle of our time:

—John Kennedy and Lee Harvey Oswald; Robert Kennedy and Sirhan Sirhan; Martin Luther King and James Earl Ray; "Bull" Conner, police dogs, and firehoses on the streets of Birmingham; riots in Newark, Detroit, Washington;

—Lyndon Johnson and the "light at the end of the tunnel"; My Lai, the "Christmas bombings," and the "incursion" into Cambodia; gunfire at Kent State and at Jackson State; marches, sit-ins, riots at Columbia and at Berkeley;

—the generation gap and the sexual revolution; hippies, yippies, Weathermen, and flower children; pot, grass, and smack;

—Watergate, the Nixon tapes, the "smoking pistol"; abuses of civil liberties in the name of security; the birth of OPEC (Organization of Petroleum Exporting Countries); "stagflation"; the women's movement, Gay Pride, and the rebirth of ethnicity;

—ecology, the limits to growth, pro and antinuclear power; terrorism in the skies and on the streets. . . . The list goes on and on.

We have survived, but the strain has been immense and it has taken a toll. As this book is written, a new President is completing his first year and a half in office. There were no wars, no major catastrophes, no truly traumatizing incidents. Yet, by early summer of 1978 there were unmistakable signs of an impending crisis in public confidence.

There are thoughtful people who survey the times and the challenges, who counsel patience and listen to other analyses even as they present their own. They understand that problems of unprecedented complexity can be solved only with time and painstaking care; that there are linkages between problems, so that precipitous action in one arena will exacerbate difficulties elsewhere. They understand, too, that this is a new President working with a different, more independent and willful Congress than we have known for a century, and that the establishment of a new balance may take more time.

But there are others who, out of zealotry or expedience, are eager to prey upon the frustrations and anxieties of a nation strained by a generation of disenchantment. They would relieve those frustrations through the sacrifice of scapegoats. They would ease anxieties with absolutes and certainties, with the promise of decisive action and magic elixirs. And they would do all this in the name of "real Americanism."

We have heard voices like these before, uttering the same extremist denunciations and offering the same simplistic nostrums. Today, however, their techniques are more polished and their influence threatens to become pervasive. There is a temptation—it is part of the threat they pose—to respond to their shibboleths with the same kind of apocalyptic rhetoric: to say that because they intend to reshape America out of any resemblance to the heritage we know, they must somehow be silenced. Paradoxically, were we to adopt any such course we would accomplish their goal, even if at their expense. In my view, no such option is open to us.

Yet, I believe with all my heart that the forces of moderation must identify this threat and find a means to cope with it. From recent memory we ought to know that our liberties are not self-enforcing. The Bill of Rights, after all, is only a set of ideas. So is the very notion of freedom under the rule of law, of law for the sake of freedom. Ideas like these, however noble, are perishable. They will control our political life only as long as we understand them and insist upon their preservation, only if we are able to recognize when they are being undermined, as I believe they are today.

I do not minimize the task. The moderate is at an immediate disadvantage in this kind of struggle because the very nature of moderation is antithetical to the passion that must be brought to it.

Like most moderates, I am beset by doubts, torn by countervailing influences, often plagued by a maddening inclination to see elements of worth on all sides of an issue. At times I am genuinely envious of the zealot's unwavering self-certainty.

There was a time when this was a source of confidence-shaking concern for me; after all, no one wants to think of himself or herself, or be thought of by others, as being irresolute or devoid of principle or lacking conviction. But now I take solace in the wisdom of Eric Sevareid's valedictory challenge to retain "the courage of one's doubts as well as one's convictions." In recent days I have come across the same reassuring thought expressed by two significant thinkers of our time, Jacob Bronowski and Learned Hand.

In his classic work *The Ascent of Man*, Bronowski considers physicist Werner Heisenberg's Principle of Uncertainty and suggests it might better be called the Principle of Tolerance.

> The Principle of Uncertainty or, in my phrase, the Principle of Tolerance fixed once for all the realisation that all knowledge is limited. It is an irony of history that at the very time when this was being worked out

there should rise, under Hitler in Germany and other tyrants elsewhere, a counter-conception: a principle of *monstrous certainty*. When the future looks back on the 1930s it will think of them as a crucial confrontation of culture as I have been expounding it, the *ascent* of man, against the *throwback* to the despots' belief that they have *absolute* certainty.[1]

Not long ago someone refreshed my memory of what Judge Hand had said in his celebrated "I Am an American" Day speech at Central Park in New York City on May 21, 1944.

What then is the spirit of liberty? I cannot define it: I can only tell you my own faith. The spirit of liberty is the spirit which is not too sure that it is right: the spirit of liberty is the spirit which seeks to understand the minds of other men and women; the spirit of liberty is the spirit which weighs their interests alongside its own without bias; the spirit of liberty remembers that not even a sparrow falls to earth unheeded; the spirit of liberty is the spirit of Him who, near two thousand years ago, taught mankind a lesson it has never learned, but has never quite forgotten.

Later, in the reinforcing testimony he subsequently offered before a Senate committee, Judge Hand quoted Oliver Cromwell, the unlikely source that Jacob Bronowski also cited in *The Ascent of Man,* and both to the same effect. Alluding to Cromwell's historic image of ruthless despotism, Judge Hand noted that there were times when even Cromwell acknowledged the dangers of passionate conviction.

It was just before the Battle of Dunbar; he [Cromwell] beat the Scots in the end, as you know, after a very tough fight; but he wrote them before the battle, trying to get them to accept a reasonable compromise. These were his words: "I beseech you, in the bowels of Christ, think it possible you may be mistaken." I should like to have that written over the portals of every church, every school, and every court house, and, may I say, of every legislative body in the United States. I should like to have every court begin, "I beseech you, in the bowels of Christ, think it possible we may be mistaken."

The wisdom of those words will be forever lost upon those zealots of the political extreme who never harbor a self-doubt. But it behooves all of us who call ourselves moderates to preach that lesson whenever we can, wherever we can, to whomever we can. Only in this way can we validate the crucial premise that humankind is, as Jacob Bronowski said, "nature's unique experiment to make the rational intelligence prove itself sounder than the reflex."[2]

CHAPTER 1

Target: Home-town America

There is a great social upheaval at the heart of America that now finds an expression in the constellation of traditionalist, individualist and fundamentalist movements. It feeds the established politicians and practitioners of the Right, and is well-fed by them. But to disregard its authentic roots in home-town America is to misread the new national mood, and to become its vulnerable victims.
—ANDREW KOPKIND[1]

My roots are in home-town America. I was born and grew up in Laconia, New Hampshire, and I took my values and many of my attitudes from the local community and my morals and ethics from the faith into which I was born and which I still profess. I respect my roots because I understand them.

To know home-town America is to know the people whom the New Right sees as most susceptible to its appeals. Without a clear, indeed an empathetic understanding of the hopes, fears, and aspirations of heartland America, liberals and moderates cannot mount a persuasive rebuttal to the New Right's delusive tenets or a telling counter to its tactics.

Later chapters draw upon the observations of sociologists, political scientists, and opinion analysts to consider in dispassionate detail the vulnerability of home-town America to the blandishments and fear-mongering of the New Right, but in this opening chapter a brief synopsis is offered to preface a personal commentary.

If public comity is indeed the crucial precondition for solving great national problems, then it would be a mistake for liberals and moderates who agree with that conjecture to counter in kind the divisive tactics of the New Right. To preserve what remains of comity, liberals and moderates would be better advised to confront the New Right with arguments based on fact and reason. They need also a clear understanding of the nature of the adversary and of the constituency under courtship.

With regard to the adversary, it is important for liberals and moderates to recognize at once that the leadership of the New Right, although often messianic in its zeal, is nevertheless calculating, resourceful, and above all perceptive, and that its battle plan is carefully drawn.

The prime target in that battle plan is the Middle American who either lives in home-town America or whose attitudes and life-style are "home-town" rather than metropolitan. Characteristically, it is likely that he or she descends from latter-day immigrants. It may also be assumed that many Middle Americans (particularly ethnics of Catholic persuasion) feel a continuing need, as Pulitzer prize-winning historian Richard Hofstadter contends, to achieve middle-class respectability and to demonstrate their loyalty and patriotism.[2]

These people more often than not meet the definition of "cultural fundamentalist" coined by Joseph R. Gusfield.[3] Cultural fundamentalists, Gusfield said, take their values from the traditions of local society, in contrast to cultural modernists, who are more cosmopolitan and attuned to mass society's more transient values. Cultural fundamentalists, he said, are therefore more inclined to bring moral and religious attitudes to bear on social and economic problems. Gusfield also postulated that cultural fundamentalists have a character more rigidly and exclusively oriented toward production, work, and saving, while modernists are more concerned with consumption and enjoyment.

In sum, the hypothetical Middle American being wooed by the New Right is probably a cultural fundamentalist in that he or she either lives in or follows the life-style of home-town America, is a descendant of latter-day immigrants, a seeker of status (however modest), and a person highly motivated by the spirit of patriotism.

It is also likely that this hypothetical Middle American is a Democrat, because the Democratic party holds majorities, often heavy, in virtually every definable grouping. The paradox of cultural fundamentalists affiliating with what traditionally has been the more liberal of the two major parties is dealt with in detail in chapter 3, but in sum it is explained by the long-time dominance of what is called "interest politics" over "status politics."

Interest politics, as defined by Hofstadter, is based upon economic needs and expectations—farm prices, wage rates, job security, old-age assistance, bargaining power in the marketplace. Lasting Democratic loyalties were achieved not only through the party's skillful exploitation of interest politics issues, but by their implementation into law under Democratic administrations.

Nevertheless, there was and is an inherent conflict between the social conservatism espoused by the cultural fundamentalists and the votes they cast for liberal Democratic candidates and programs. This element of conflict is identified by Hofstadter in his definition of status politics as opposed to interest politics.

> Besides their economic expectations, people have deep emotional commitments in other spheres—religion, morals, culture, race relations —which they also hope to see realized in political action. Status politics seeks not to advance perceived material interests but to express grievances and resentments about such matters, to press claims upon society to give deference to noneconomic values. As a rule, status politics does more to express emotions than to formulate policies. It is in fact hard to translate the claims of status politics into programs or concrete objectives (national Prohibition was an exception, though ultimately an unsuccessful one); and for the most part the proponents of such politics, being less concerned with the uses of power than with its alleged mis-

use, do not offer positive programs to solve social problems. The operative content of their demands is more likely to be negative; they call on
us mainly to prohibit, to prevent, to censor and censure, to discredit, and
to punish.[4]

Midway through the seventies the leadership of the New
Right sensed that the time had come to challenge interest politics with status politics, judging that inflation, taxes, and disenchantment with Great Society programs had eroded the effectiveness of the former, while uncertainty, apprehension, and
resentment were energizing the latter.

New Rightists sensed that many Americans were beginning
to see the lack of spending restraint at all levels of government
as evidence of a mass collapse of discipline, order, and purpose
and as a threat to what they long believed was the right and respectable way to perform as citizens and parents.

They sensed that a substantial, growing number of people
saw permissiveness as the malady weakening the entire moral
structure of the nation, from the highest echelons of government
down to the individual family structure. It had become plausible to blame permissiveness for a rich roster of evils: corruption
in high office; government waste and inefficiency; lack of courage and purpose in foreign policy; a denigration of patriotism;
an excess of costly frills and a paucity of standards in public
education; welfare cheating; and a social atmosphere that encouraged youth rebellion, the generation gap, the counterculture, the drug culture, sexual promiscuity, disdain for the work
ethic, disinterest in religion, and a disinclination to marry and
procreate within the sanctions of church and state.

The Rightists calculated that these same Americans saw abortion on demand, easier penalties on marijuana use and possession, First Amendment restraints on suppressing pornography, the Equal Rights Amendment, Gay Rights, school busing
to achieve racial balance in the classroom, and even gun control
and the new Panama Canal treaties, as threats to long-held standards and values. They proceeded to exploit these issues with
vigor, determination, articulate and charismatic representatives,
and a sophisticated direct mail program that circumvented the
media and the political Establishment, and they achieved nota-
ble and alarming success.

Having established a political beachhead through the adroit

use of status politics, the New Right then decided it was time to turn its attention to interest politics as well. In the late winter and early spring of 1978 the movement gave inspiration and support to taxpayer revolts, which crested in California on June 6 with the overwhelming adoption of Proposition 13, a measure that cut property taxes by 57 percent, put stringent restrictions on future rate increases, and seemed certain to hurt some essential human services.

The impact of New Right incursions has prompted a distressing reaction among some liberals and moderates. Instead of focusing their indignation on the leadership of the New Right, they have turned their scorn on the followers of the movement, frequently alluding to the home-town Americans who are electing or nominating New Right candidates or voting for drastic measures like Proposition 13 as "ignorant," "selfish," "short-sighted," and "bigoted."

I find these words unthinkingly harsh. I also find them politically obtuse, because the meld in home-town America is too complex for blanket judgment. I know there are determinedly ignorant, mean-minded, bigoted provincials on every Main Street in the country. But I know, too, that there are wise and caring people of broad vision. What makes this mix even more intriguing is the manifestation of contradictory characteristics in the same people at different times. This, in turn, makes home-town America an arena where transient exigencies and influences determine whether the noble or the base will prevail in any given period. Indeed, it was the mix and flux of contradictory attitudes that made it possible, and to some observers confounding, for home-town America to look upon such disparate political figures as George Wallace and Robert Kennedy with simultaneous and equal favor.

By mid-1978 the exigencies that determine the political mood were working to the advantage of the New Right, in no small part because the New Right made the effort to understand the pysche of home-town America and to fashion its blandishments accordingly. One may find, as I do, an unconscionable expedience in those appeals, but that is all the more reason why liberals and moderates must make an equal effort to understand the milieu and to develop an effective and responsible counter to the Right. Because I come from Main Street culture, perhaps my personal experiences can offer certain insights.

Earlier I referred to Richard Hofstadter's hypothesis that the descendants of latter-day immigrants, particularly ethnics of Catholic persuasion, persist in striving for middle-class respectability and feel a constant need to reaffirm and demonstrate their patriotism.

My father was a modestly successful merchant who cared generously for his family. He had economic status in our community. But we were Catholic and Irish, albeit lace-curtain Irish, in a state long led by old-line Protestant Yankee families. The New Hampshire Constitution, for instance, was drafted by Anglo-Saxon Protestants and contained a specific provision barring non-Protestants from holding the governorship. It was not until the late 1930s that the state elected its first Irish-Catholic governor, and he, not surprisingly, was a Republican. Thus, we McIntyres felt obligated to seek respectability, that is, social status, by strict conformity with community mores, a staunch provincialism, and perfervid patriotism.

An editorial that appeared in William Loeb's *New Hampshire Sunday News* a few days after my reelection in 1966 demonstrated the social forces that were at work. My opponent in that election was Harrison Thyng, a retired air force general.

> From Senator McIntyre we can look for six years of continued servility to the Democratic Administration—if it remains in power—tempered by his notorious obsequiousness to Bobby Kennedy and the Irish Mafia. . . .
>
> Senator McIntyre, arrogant in victory . . . promises to eliminate not only his political rivals, but his newspaper critics as well. To hear him tell it, he is going to drive them all out of the state, notwithstanding that some of us—including most eminently Harrison Thyng himself—have roots in this granite soil which considerably antedate the extrication of Mr. McIntyre's forebears from the bogs of Old Erin.

It is ironic that the editorial was written by B.J. McQuaid, associate publisher of Loeb's newspaper, who is also of Irish descent. Note that in the line "notwithstanding that some of *us* . . . have roots in this granite soil which considerably antedate the extrication of Mr. McIntyre's forebears from the bogs of Old Erin," McQuaid was laying claim to an American heritage that was deeper than mine because his ancestors supposedly came to this country before the first McIntyre arrived.

As I look back over the years and note how my attitudes and positions on issues have changed or moderated, I realize that it may well have been the unconscious defensiveness of being new-family American that made me waffle at first on McCarthyism ("his goals are good, but I don't like his tactics"); that kept me too long a hawk on Vietnam; that early on often persuaded me to "err on the side of caution" in the Armed Services Committee by voting for weapons systems I suspected might be wasteful, unnecessary, or provocative; and that kept me from recognizing the validity of the arguments advanced first by the antiwar factions and later by activists in the environmental movement because the conduct and attire of so many representatives of both movements did not reflect what I had grown up to believe was "respectable."

It is not easy to admit to these flaws in reasoning and judgment, but I do so to make the point that in America there are millions of people—the sum products of their heredity and environment and of the influences that have shaped them from birth—who are basically decent and honest, neither paranoid nor bigoted, but who are anxiety-ridden over what frequently appears to them to be an inexorable assault on their total personal value system. If they are to be reached by moderates and liberals and are to be discouraged from succumbing to the fear-mongering and the simplistic arguments of the New Right, then first it behooves us to understand them, to understand that behind each anxiety is a reason, perhaps exaggerated, but nevertheless a reason grounded in *some* element of truth and fact.

These people are too valuable to America to forfeit them to the extremist cause, but they *will* be forfeited if we look upon them as the New Right looks upon us—with derision and contempt. This caution, I believe, is particularly in order for my own Democratic party, because the changed complexion of the party makes it more likely that the new liberals of the party could make this crucial mistake.

In relatively recent times the Democratic party—long the comfortable home of both the workingperson and the cultural fundamentalist—has also become the comfortable home of the rich, the highly educated, the sophisticate, the social elite, the radical chic, the cultural modernist. There are now within the party many who, as someone has put it, drive BMWs and Saabs, wear Earth shoes, do organic gardening on their patios, and drink piña coladas. All these people tend to read the same books, magazines, and newspapers, talk only to one another, and thus reinforce the comfort of their own biases and convictions. That kind of intellectual inbreeding can produce a moral smugness disturbingly akin to that of the extremists on the Right.

I do not always agree with columnist Michael Novak, but no other media figure, to my knowledge, has his insights into the mind and heart of the working-class American, and particularly the ethnic American. A few years ago Novak wrote what I feel is a proper remonstrance to all political parties, movements, and leaders.

> There are many different moral systems among a diverse citizenry like our own. It makes a moral difference whether one is a Protestant, a Jew, a Catholic, a non-believer. It makes a moral difference whether one is from the Northeast or the Southwest. It makes a moral difference whether one tends toward "idealism" or toward "realism." No one of us adequately represents the full moral range of all the American people. No one of us has a set of principles, however deep or broad, adequate for approaching the multiple moral systems of all the others around us. No one of us is perfectly suited to defining the common good. In an important sense, therefore, the deepest moral principles in each of us are partially a danger to all those others, whose principles are different. Consequently, many rightly fear leaders who are merely principled. We know that we need leaders whose principles are tempered by respect for *pluralism*. We value a certain *humility*.
>
> A wise and good political leader in a democracy must (1) distrust his own moral principles, even when he is faithful to them, aware that they may unduly blind him to other aspects of reality. He must also (2) be humbly alert to the fact that, however right he thinks he is, he may be wrong. So complicated are most judgments in the public sphere that no one knows for sure which course of action is right, which wrong.[5]

What Novak wrote applies equally well to the extremists of the New Right, to the cultural modernists and the new liberals of the Democratic party, to all of us.

Smugness and condescension no more build bridges between people than zealotry in obsessive pursuit of mission. Neither approach encourages understanding or tolerance. Both serve only to polarize.

The Vietnam War is the most dramatic example of polarization in our time, for zealotry on both sides of the issue drove people into corners where they would not or could not open their minds to a different viewpoint.

I offer a personal anecdote as a case in point: Antiwar demonstrations peaked in the spring of 1971, with thousands of protesters gathering for marches and rallies in Washington and in San Francisco on April 24. These demonstrations came on the heels of the most effective antiwar protest up to that time—the lobbying efforts of the Vietnam Veterans Against the War that were carried out the previous week.

I had long since joined the ranks of those who wanted to set a firm date for withdrawal of American troops from Indochina, but four veterans who paid a visit to my office opened my eyes (indeed, brought tears to them) to an aspect of the war I had resolutely kept out of sight and mind—its brutalizing effect upon some Americans who had to fight it. To this day I can see and hear that tortured young man who leaned over my desk and asked, "Senator, I know that you saw combat in World War Two, but did you ever see an *American* put a bayonet in the belly of a woman and rip her open to her chin?"

The Vietnam Veterans concluded their week-long demonstration by holding a candlelight parade in front of the White House and then ritually ripping off their medals and decorations and throwing them over the fence in the direction of the Oval Office. The consensus was that this expression moved the Congress as no other demonstration had.

But within the week a new group of protesters—for the most part college and high school students—descended on the nation's capital and threatened to undo all the good. The slogan for this group was "If the government of the United States does not stop the war in Vietnam, we will stop the government of the United States"—and they almost did. Senate floor proceedings were interrupted with shouts of "Stop the War!"; demonstrators roamed the halls of Congress wailing and moaning; "killer" squads were sent to individual senators' offices in simulated search and destroy missions; sit-downs and lie-downs were staged throughout Capitol Hill.

One morning in the midst of all this, as I was returning from a Banking Committee meeting, accompanied by Federal Reserve Board Chairman Arthur F. Burns, and was preparing to enter my reception room, I glanced down the corridor and caught a glimpse of a woman, somehow familiar, striding toward us in an obvious state of outrage. I turned away and invited Chairman Burns to go into my office. But that was easier said than done.

The reception room floor was covered wall to wall with people who were lying side by side and shouting up at us to sign their Vietnam Manifesto. Chairman Burns and I picked our way through the bodies to the entryway of my private office, only to be brought up short by the commanding voice of the woman I had seen marching down the corridor a few minutes earlier.

"Get out! Get out!" she demanded of the demonstrators. "Don't you people know you're undoing all the good the veterans did last week?"

A bearded young man jumped to his feet and waved a printed broadside in her face. "Read our manifesto!" he shouted. "Read it! Read it! Read it!"

The woman drew herself up, glowered at him, and said, with withering sarcasm, "Read it? Young man, I *wrote* it."

None of the demonstrators had recognized Mary McGrory, Pulitzer prize-winning columnist for the *Washington Star* and one of the most effective antiwar voices in the nation.

What some of the young antiwar zealots would not or could not admit was that there *were* mature men and women working quietly, effectively, and responsibly to bring U.S. involvement in the war to an end. Nor were they able to understand how counterproductive their own excesses were to the cause.

Most centrally, they did not understand that it is impossible to change the collective mind of America by peremptory demand and provocative action, that people need leeway to think, to weigh old opinions against new evidence, to allow themselves to be persuaded it is time to change their minds.

The same applies today. Moderates and liberals alarmed over the seeming effectiveness of the New Right's appeal cannot, *must* not, counter by ridiculing the targets of that appeal, or by trying to force upon them the very attitudes they find so threatening to their life-style and value system. Let us not emulate the Radical Right by making blanket assumptions and categorical judgments that slide over the facts and offend against civility.

We must keep in mind that

—not every opponent of school busing is a bigot. Some who resent the practice believe that it inconveniences or disadvantages their children and that it is counterproductive to other efforts to improve race relations.

—not everyone who is offended by pornography is a prude,

nor everyone a hopeless square who waits for the final verdict
on whether marijuana and cocaine are indeed less dangerous to
one's health and the public safety than tobacco and alcohol.
There is something to be said for taste and prudence.

—not everyone who champions jobs and economic development is against a clean environment. Some try to draw a realistic
balance. Environmental chic notwithstanding, there is no way a
nation of 218 million people can survive on organic garden plots
and the barter of clay pots and macrame.

—not every person who owns a gun is compensating for phal-
lic inadequacy or unrequited aggressions, as some gun control
advocates suggest. Many gun owners spend as much time and
money promoting conservation and restoring endangered spe-
cies as they do hunting.

—not every housewife is enslaved by male chauvinism and
crying out for liberation. Many are housewives by personal and
happy choice and subscribe wholeheartedly to the goals of the
Equal Rights Amendment.

This is not to imply that liberals and moderates must compromise their own principles. To do so would only fuel the New
Right's rapacity. Rather, it is to suggest that if we truly want to
advance the cause of peace and of social justice we must temper
our approach with understanding. If the New Right's stock in
trade is polarization, then ours must be accommodation in order
to achieve necessary consensus.

We cannot accommodate the leadership of the New Right.
They are beyond the reach of reason and of compromise. Our
efforts, then, must be directed toward those to whom the New
Right is beginning to appeal in this era of dizzying change and
social upheaval.

Can it be done? I believe it can.

Let me cite one issue in which it *seems* that there is no middle ground—abortion. I am convinced that much of the bitter
divisiveness over this issue can be attributed to misconceptions
about the real feelings of those on either side. Are those who
favor legalized abortion totally insensitive to the act or to its
wholly innocent victim? Are those who oppose abortion totally
insensitive to the plight of women who feel driven to it?

Were one to listen only to the shouts of "Murderer!" and
"Bigot!" flung about at confrontations, one would think so. But
my experience with the people who favor legalized abortion

convinces me that the thoughtful among them are not enthusiastic advocates of the practice, but consider it an option of last resort. They do appreciate the awesomeness of the act. They understand that few women who have abortions and few physicians who perform them are left unmarked by the experience, even when they have satisfied their consciences that a higher right and a greater good were served.

A Washington obstetrician who performs legal abortions and says he does so in good conscience nevertheless calls it "a lousy answer to a terrible problem." And so it is. For no matter how one looks upon the personhood or lack of personhood of a fetus, its humanhood cannot be denied.

I will not believe that any humane person "likes" abortion. Nor will I believe that any humane person prefers aborting an unwanted pregnancy to avoiding an unwanted pregnancy.

By the same token, my experience with antiabortion people convinces me that the thoughtful among them appreciate that it is far easier to moralize in the abstract than it is to confront the problem directly when it strikes one's own family. Contrary to widespread belief, they *do* have compassion for women who feel driven to abortion as the sole remaining answer to their dilemma.

My feelings reflect those of most opponents of abortion. Although I am committed by conscience and by creed to the fetal right to life, I cannot remain unmoved by the dilemma of a woman physically drained and mentally distraught from bearing and caring for a dozen children, with a thirteenth on its way; I cannot remain unmoved by the predicament of a woman pregnant at the close of her reproductive years, confronted with a dangerous delivery and the sharply increased chances of bearing a mongoloid child.

I cannot be indifferent to the plight of a twelve-year-old impregnated by her own father or brother, of mentally ill or retarded girls and women made pregnant by the sexually depraved, or of rape victims who conceive. Nor can I turn my conscience away from the undeniable fact that even if many of the children so conceived are carried to term and delivered, their chances for adoption are as remote as their chances for love, security, and happiness in the circumstances in which they are born.

What I am saying is this: If each side on the abortion issue could look into the other side's true heart, perhaps the bitterness would ease. Perhaps there would be hope for mutual understanding if not agreement, for good will if not consensus. An issue so personal, so intensely emotional, cries out for humility and compassion—not self-righteousness.

In her wise and humane book, *In Necessity and Sorrow: Life and Death in an Abortion Hospital*, Magda Denes writes, "Abortions reside in the realm of individual struggle, personal defeat, private hell. *The enemy is embedded in being human.*"[6] But perhaps an answer to the abortion issue is *also* embedded in being human . . . in being *more* human to one another, in trying to understand one another, in agreeing that we have a common goal if not common means. There may be disagreement about whether a fetus is a person. There may be disagreement over who has the paramount right—the fetus or the already-born. But few persons, if any, believe abortion is a desirable answer to the problem of unwanted pregnancies.

The rending difficulty rises when those on either side of the issue focus solely on their differing perceptions of the "absolute values" that are in contention. Granting that this is not a meaningless battle over abstractions, I am still disturbed by the often venomous character of the dispute. Much energy has been spent by some people on both sides in blackening the character and motives of those on the opposite side—energy that might have been better spent if either side could listen to the other.

The truth is that both sets of absolutes are worthy of respect and that neither *absolutely* precludes the other. I suspect also that if both sides insist on total victory, neither will achieve as much progress toward its own goal as could be brought about by mutual recognition of the values both share.

As long as we persist in debating the abortion issue in the narrow terms of whether it should be eliminated or reduced by legislation or by constitutional amendment, we will remain at bitter odds, and the common goal will be lost in self-righteous and self-indulgent rancor and acrimony.

Far better that we join hands and broaden the field of endeavor, turning our mutual efforts to means we can all live with —education in family planning; expanded options in birth control methods that are safe, effective, and religiously acceptable; enhanced opportunities for adoption of unwanted children. In this way we who object to abortion would honor our commitment to fetal rights by reducing the incidence of abortion through means that are not perceived as infringing upon the rights of the already-born. In this way those who support legalized abortion—but who concede it is an undesirable last resort —could work with us to encourage development of a wider range of more desirable alternatives.

I am encouraged, for example, by the promise of research into new "natural" methods of birth control that may turn out to be more reliable than either the rhythm system or the temperature system.

The Department of Health, Education and Welfare has a three-year study under way in Los Angeles on what is called the ovulation or the Billings method of natural birth control. If such natural contraception proves to be as effective and reliable as it is hoped, it would not only offer Catholic women an alternative to artificial contraception, but would provide a safe alternative for any woman who fears medical complications from the use of oral contraceptives or intrauterine devices.

Obviously, the expansion of the range and availability of birth control options that are safe, effective, reliable, and consonant with religious scruples will reduce the number of unwanted pregnancies *and* the incidence of abortion.

In selecting a topic to illustrate the thesis of this chapter, I could hardly have picked an issue more difficult than abortion. Further, the one certainty about the approaches I have outlined is that they will not satisfy either faction in the dispute. And that, of course, is the point. We live in a free, open, and pluralistic society, the kind of society in which issues of profound meaning to many citizens must be resolved in the public forum. We have methods of problem-solving, but if they are to work well we must also have a problem-solving spirit. One ingredient of that spirit is an understanding that solutions to real problems that are defined differently by different groups within our society will rarely, if ever, wholly square with the views of any one group.

If we accept such disappointments, it is not because we are willing to abandon our own principles merely for the sake of togetherness. Rather, it is because we place a high value indeed, comparable even to the value we place on human life, on the democratic process. Speaking—proudly—as an American politician, I can testify that despite its imperfections, the workings of that process call forth all the ingenuity of the human mind toward reaching accommodations that respect, *as much as possible*, all the differing values of all the differing moral systems within the community.

This American heritage is at least as important to me as my Irish genes. Therefore, it appears to me that any who are willing to alienate half the citizenry of the country by insisting that their own truth must prevail in all respects do not assess the gift of freedom at its true price.

CHAPTER 2

Sharp Turn to the Right?

There's definitely a conservative majority in the country today . . . people who are conservative in their premises if not in all their conclusions.
—HOWARD PHILLIPS
National Director,
Conservative Caucus[1]

To many liberals and moderates, myself included, that confident assertion by Howard Phillips in the late spring of 1975 seemed to ring more of wishful thinking than of fact. Just three years later liberal columnist Marquis Childs would write that "the tide is moving to the right so rapidly that the wisdom of the past may no longer prevail."[2]

Is Childs' assessment valid? Is he correctly reading the political mood and direction of the country? The evidence is confusing and often contradictory, but if his reading is indeed accurate, then the potential consequences ought to give troubling pause to all Americans who cherish the right to think and to speak as they choose and who understand the overriding impor-

25

tance of civility, mutual respect, and good will in the decision-
making process of a free, pluralistic society.

There is no denying the multiplying signs of a political turn to
the Right, but enough questions remain about the exact nature
of the trend—and about its depth, breadth, and staying power—
to guide a telling counter to those who would push it beyond
the bounds of reason and of responsible restraint.

Childs made the above statement on June 15, 1978, only days
after California voters sent a political shock wave rolling across
the country by mandating a drastic cut in property taxes, inviting an inevitable reduction in essential government services,
for a time casting doubt upon reelection prospects for Democratic Governor Jerry Brown and a long shadow over his Presidential aspirations.*

On that same primary election day antitax sentiments were
dramatically expressed elsewhere in the country. In Ohio, for
instance, voters rejected more than half of nearly two hundred
school-tax and bond issues, leaving it uncertain whether schools
in Columbus and Cleveland would open in the fall.

Ultraconservatives found other reasons to cheer the results of
the June 6 balloting. In New Jersey, Republican voters rejected
veteran liberal Senator Clifford Case's bid for renomination and
turned instead to a young, New Right candidate to be the party's
standard-bearer. Republican voters in Iowa also chose a candidate from the Far Right to challenge Democratic Senator Dick
Clark in the November general election.

In the September primaries, political convulsions shook two
of the most liberal states in the Union—Massachusetts and Minnesota. Massachusetts Governor Michael Dukakis, described by
the *Boston Globe* as "a good governor who had the misfortune
of alienating one constituent group after another," suffered a
stunning upset at the hands of conservative Democrat Edward
J. King. King's well-financed campaign hammered at government spending, high taxes, inflation, and crime. On the other
hand, Republican voters rejected the New Right candidacy of
Avi Nelson, in his bid to take the Senate nomination away from
moderate incumbent Senator Edward W. Brooke.

In Minnesota, millionnaire businessman Robert E. Short, for-

* See chapter 8.

mer owner of the Minneapolis Lakers basketball team and the Washington Senators baseball team, upset highly respected liberal Congressman Don Fraser in the Democratic primary to decide the party's candidate for the late Hubert Humphrey's Senate seat. Short spent heavily to win the nomination, inviting Republicans to cross over and vote for him, and campaigned hard against government spending, taxing, and regulating; against abortion; and against environmentalist concern over the potential despoliation of the state's Boundary Waters Canoe Area. He portrayed Fraser, whom he had supported in the congressional race only two years before, and other liberals as villains and criticized both the White House and the Congress with such phrases as "those nuts who are taxing hell out of us." Short advocated a 20-percent across-the-board cut in federal spending. At this writing, the Minnesota Democratic-Farmer-Labor party, created in Senator Humphrey's liberal image, was still withholding party endorsement of Short's candidacy in the general election. One veteran D-F-Ler expressed Humphrey loyalist anguish over the situation by saying, "How can I possibly support a Democratic candidate who thinks like Ronald Reagan, talks like Spiro Agnew, and campaigns like Richard Nixon?"

In my own state of New Hampshire, New Right candidate Gordon Humphrey, former field director for the Conservative Caucus, trounced two moderate Republicans in the primary to determine my opponent in the general election, and incumbent Republican Governor Meldrim Thomson Jr., national chairman of the Conservative Caucus, won renomination over the surprisingly strong challenge of former Governor Wesley Powell. Powell, buoyed by his primary showing, then filed as an Independent candidate in the general election, making for a three-way race with Thomson and Democratic candidate Hugh Gallen. (NOTE: An analysis of the general election of 1978 appears in an addendum at the close of this chapter.)

The evidence of a turn to the Right is not restricted to the election results of 1978. There were earlier manifestations.

The seed money from "The New Right" has enabled a number of otherwise hopeless or faltering candidates even to get into the race, ideologue or not. Party financiers are slower with this kind of help or cannot even get involved in a primary contest. The gung-ho conservatives had, indeed, supplied many non-cash services. They put on many

campaign seminars around the country, they have an effective network
for turning up potential candidates, they provide expertise in the nuts
and bolts of campaigning—and they are zealous. Also, they are sticking
together more than ever. And they are beginning to reach out for new
constituencies. Moreover, they have been successful. Their money and
staff assistance helped substantially in the election of conservative Congressmen in four of five special elections last year.[3]

And there are other manifestations of a conservative revival.
The attention paid to the California vote on Proposition 13, for
instance, obscured the fact that twenty-six states were already
considering or adopting measures to grant tax relief or to put
limits on taxes, spending, or state indebtedness. Also little no-
ticed is the fact that twenty-four state legislatures have already
passed resolutions calling for a constitutional convention to prohibit federal budget deficits. If ten more legislatures pass this
resolution, it will trigger the process of calling the first such convention in history.

In addition to the ballot box manifestations of a growing conservatism are the signs of a turn to the Right in social views. Demands for the restoration of the death penalty, for example, appear to be growing in volume and are falling on receptive ears.
In recent months ordinances ensuring the civil rights of homosexuals have been struck down in Dade County, Florida, in St.
Paul, Minnesota, and in Eugene, Oregon. The right-to-life
movement has grown in numbers and in effectiveness, mustering an impact at the polls not readily perceived in elections held
as recently as 1976.

More directly apparent to me has been the influence of conservative forces on the deliberations of the Congress.

A Citizens Guide to the Right Wing, published by Americans
for Democratic Action, said of the New Right: "In Congress,
their associates, a small group of extreme conservatives, have
frightened and harassed what was expected to be the most
progressive Congress in our recent history into a state of political shock."[4] The ADA guide notes that extreme conservatives
beat back in the last Congress a number of pieces of progressive
legislation, including new voter registration, public financing of
elections, and the Consumer Protection Agency, and, in party
politics, have succeeded in installing their people in dozens
of key local, state, and national party positions.

Moreover, on at least two significant occasions when the New Right did not succeed in achieving its primary purpose, it did succeed in delaying and nearly derailing important national legislation. Senate heroes of the New Right seized upon two issues to monopolize virtually all the chamber's time and attention through the first six months of 1978. These two issues were the Panama Canal treaties, which locked up the Senate in sustained debate from January until mid-March, followed immediately by labor law reform, which a determined filibuster by New Right advocates forced back to committee in mid-June after repeated attempts to invoke cloture fell short of the necessary votes. In both instances, it must be noted, the majority of the Senate was denied the opportunity to work its will, meanwhile leaving other important legislation for delayed and foreshortened consideration.

Sensing that Vietnam had become a festering sore in national pride, the New Right took its campaign against the Panama Canal treaties to home-town America, making effective use of such slogans as "There Is No Panama Canal . . . There Is an American Canal in Panama" by teaming up with national and local veterans' organizations and retired military officers' associations to pound home the message. On the Senate floor, however, the New Right antitreaty forces muted the hyperpatriotic rhetoric of their public and direct mail campaign, concentrating their arguments on supposed dollar costs and security risks of the treaties and on such legal nuances as the House's alleged right to vote on the treaties because they involved transfer of American properties (an argument rejected by the courts). Coupled with this was the calculated projection of an image of reason. Opponents repeatedly stated that they had no objection to new treaties, but that the treaties under consideration were simply not the right treaties.

On the heels of the treaties debate, which climaxed in ratification of each document by the margin of a single vote, the Senate took up labor law reform and debated this measure for five more weeks.

This was the first major attempt to update basic labor law in many years, and proponents of the measure considered it a modest proposal. Briefly, the legislation would make it generally easier for employees to unionize and win contracts by imposing

stiffer penalties on illegal attempts to block organizing or bargaining efforts.

Again the New Right took its case to home-town America, rallying the active lobbying support of local small businesses and
chambers of commerce as well as that of national business
groups. Once more there was a marked difference between the
hyperbole of the public and the mail campaign—which featured such perennial right-wing canards as "Big Labor will take
over the country!"—and the debating techniques on the Senate
floor. New Right filibuster leaders, for example, sometimes
stressed the point that they themselves had belonged to labor
unions and were not antilabor but sincerely believed this particular legislation was tilted too far in labor's favor. After repeated
efforts to cut off the filibuster failed and the bill was remanded
to committee, Richard Lesher, president of the U.S. Chamber of
Commerce, described the action as confirmation of "a strong in-
stinctive feeling among Americans that labor unions already are
too powerful" and said it was "a resounding victory for the
American people." The real significance of the New Right's
ability to frustrate this legislation lay in the fact that it could line
up impressive support to revive the perennial bogey of union
power at a time when both membership and influence of organized labor are in demonstrated decline. Without the intense
lobbying by business groups the New Right could not have accomplished its purpose.

With regard to the New Right's recent successes in nominating and electing candidates, it should be noted that most of
these victories were achieved in contests where there either
was no incumbent, or a decidedly vulnerable incumbent, coupled with low voter interest. Jeffrey Bell's primary victory over
Senator Case in New Jersey is a good example of the latter
point. Only 10 percent of the eligible Republican voters went to
the polls in this primary, the lowest turnout since the 1920s, re-
flecting apathy over the outcome rather than enthusiasm for the
victor.

It may also surprise some readers to learn that for all the ce-
lebrity attaching to the Proposition 13 victory in California, that
primary drew fewer numbers to the polls than the primary of
1976. Indeed, referenda on the hot tax question are generally at-
tracting less voters than normal elections.

Moreover, not all the candidates backed by the New Right in the spring of 1978 won nomination. Republican Congressman John B. Anderson of Illinois handily beat back a right-wing primary challenge; California voters nominated all incumbent U.S. representatives and chose a relatively moderate Republican over a Far Right candidate to oppose Governor Brown in November; and in Virginia two right-wing candidates failed in their respective bids for House and Senate nominations.

As to the New Right's recent exploitation of tax resentment, a significant question remains here too. Are taxes really the hottest focal point of public resentment? Or are they the most convenient target for expressing an accumulation of grievances, some of which are even more compelling? A Gallup poll conducted only weeks before the Proposition 13 vote in California revealed that by a margin of nine to one, Americans believe it is more important to control inflation than to cut taxes.[5] Indeed, slightly more poll respondents favored working toward a balanced federal budget than favored a tax cut, ostensibly because they believe the former holds some promise for reducing inflation. The same poll reflected still another indication of how seriously Americans view inflation. By a margin of 50 to 39 percent, respondents favored wage and price controls, compared with a margin of 44 to 40 percent only two months earlier.

And just a month after the vote on Proposition 13 was being interpreted as a sign that the public was turning selfishly inward and away from social concerns and responsibilities, a nationwide Harris survey indicated that "the major concerns of Americans in the latter part of the 1970's are by no means centered on the physical acquisition of goods."[6] Instead, Harris said, "they focus on the improvement of the environment in all its varied aspects." He noted also that the survey made it apparent "that many of the concerns of young people in the 1960's have been translated into broader objectives for society in the 1970's."

The Harris survey found heavy majorities for conserving energy, curbing air, water, and noise pollution, protecting the privacy of the individual, strictly enforcing safe working conditions, making products and services safer, better nutrition, improving the quality of products and services, adequate public housing, improved public transportation, and better employment opportunities for minorities.

In sum, election results thus far would seem to be more a measure of the New Right's pragmatic political skills in choosing particular battlefields and issues and in motivating conservative voters to go to the polls than a sure measure of the overall public mood. Nevertheless, the New Right's accomplishments are real and impressive and cannot be attributed solely to political acumen, organization, and skill.

As the *Washington Post* put it six days after the June 6 primaries:

> It's rash to read too much from these early returns. New Jersey doesn't prove that GOP conservatives are ascendant everywhere. . . . Still, something's stirring. Public disgruntlement over inflation, high taxes and bloated government was plain before last week. So, in a larger framework were the breaking down of old political hierarchies and coalitions and the surge of young candidates and special-interest and single-issue action groups. . . . The only thing that's obvious is that the season of upsets and unsettledness has really just begun.

Addendum

Since the body of this manuscript was written before I undertook my unsuccessful campaign for reelection, I have to resort to an addendum to consider the results of the general election of 1978.

Before the midterm elections, columnist David Broder anticipated that no clear trend would emerge. He was right. Nevertheless, a general rightward movement is evident in the overall results.

Seventy-seven new House members and twenty new senators are to be seated in the new Congress, but despite the large turnover, party ratios changed only slightly—the Republicans gaining three Senate seats and twelve House seats but the Democrats retaining overwhelming margins in both Houses.

Republicans gained six governorships, achieving significant victories in Tennessee, Wisconsin, Texas, and Pennsylvania, but sustained stunning losses in New Hampshire and in Kansas.

Postelection attention focused on three Senate races where right-wing candidates upset liberals or moderates—my loss to Gordon Humphrey in New Hampshire, William L. Armstrong's defeat of Senator Floyd Haskell in Colorado, and Roger Jepsen's win over Senator Dick Clark in Iowa—the collapse of the late Senator Hubert Humphrey's Democratic-Farmer-Labor party in Minnesota, where Republicans took both Senate seats and the governorship, and the election of a right-wing Democrat to the governorship of Massachusetts.

There were, however, some offsetting gains by liberals and moderates. Liberal Democrat Carl Levin defeated conservative Republican Senator Robert P. Griffin in Michigan; Alabama populist, internationalist Democrat Donald Stewart defeated James D. Martin for the late conservative Senator James B. Allen's seat. And in New Jersey, where New Right candidate Jeffrey Bell had upset veteran Senator Clifford Case in the Republican primary, Democrat Bill Bradley scored a smashing victory over Bell in the general election.

Moreover, the November elections did not show a consistent pattern of voter support for Proposition 13-type tax-cutting measures. Voters approved state spending limitations in four states but defeated similar measures in three others. Measures to cut or limit taxes were passed in three states but lost in two others.

Of particular importance to the subject of this book, however, is how the New Right fared in midterm voting, and here we find some significant statistics.

The Gannett News Service analyzed campaign contributions by seven large political action committees, representing the major areas of special interest donations. On November 10, Gannett's Pat Ordovensky wrote that this analysis "shows that the activist New Right, which has been making steady gains in both Houses of Congress, got by far the most for its money in Tuesday's voting."

Ordovensky reported that the Committee for the Survival of a Free Congress, which he described as the "backbone of New Right Congressional activities," helped thirteen candidates who unseated incumbents. "It was the only committee," he wrote, "that supported Gordon J. Humphrey, the little-known airline pilot who upset Senator Thomas J. McIntyre (D-N.H.). At the same time the right-wing group lost only one incumbent, freshman Rep. John E. Cunningham of Seattle. That gives it a net gain of an even dozen seats in the next Congress."

The Gannett analysis also indicated that the AFL-CIO fared

poorly in the midterm elections, backing three winning challengers and nineteen defeated incumbents for a net result of minus sixteen.

The *National Journal* of November 11, 1978 commented: "The Committee for the Survival of a Free Congress, a 'new right' political action committee, gave substantial support to twenty-six non-incumbents seeking House seats, twelve of them challenging incumbents. The result was sixteen victories and ten defeats." In twelve other House races where the committee endorsed nonincumbents but gave them less support, eight ended in committee victories.

In contrast, the liberal counterpart to the Committee for the Survival of a Free Congress, the long-standing National Committee for an Effective Congress, endorsed or gave major financial support to twenty-eight House incumbents, all Democrats. Twenty-one of them won, but of the twenty-five nonincumbents the liberal committee endorsed only nine won.

In practical terms, the net gain of one ultraconservative vote in the U.S. Senate does not look significant until one recalls that ratification of the Panama Canal treaties was accomplished by the margin of a single vote. In 1979 the New Right has made SALT II its target, and that one-vote gain by the movement could be crucially important.

One other result of the midterm elections seems certain to work to the advantage of the New Right. One of every six House members and one of every five senators will be a newcomer, and as the *National Journal* of November 11 pointed out, this high turnover could accentuate the lack of party discipline, especially among the Democrats, that has characterized recent Congresses.

> In recent years, many new Members have been reluctant to go along with the tradition that congressional advancement requires them to march in step with their party leaders. They have been less willing to be led and—perhaps because they feel more vulnerable politically than many of their seniors—less willing to support party positions that clash with the views of their constituents. The sheer number of new Members will inevitably add to the uncertainty of those—both within the Carter Administration and in the private sector—who must deal regularly with the Congress.

When the 96th Congress opened in January 1979, a majority of the House of Representatives had been serving only since January 1975. And in the Senate, forty-eight members—nearly half the total membership—were serving their first term.

CHAPTER 3

Something's Stirring

Behind the seeming summer torpor of the capital, there is drama of great fascination taking place. It is the internal struggle of the governing Democratic Party to adapt its historically liberal premises and programs to the conservative forces now dominant in America—and to do so without breaking apart at the seams.
—DAVID BRODER[1]

To put the political drama David Broder finds so fascinating into proper perspective, it is first necessary to consider why the Democratic party became the governing party and why the overwhelming majority of Americans call themselves Democrats.

If one accepts the conventional wisdom that the Democratic party is the more liberal of the two traditional party organizations, then a superficial appraisal of its membership advantage and the offices held by party members at all levels of government would encourage one to conclude that the nation is turning liberal, not conservative.

A Gallup poll determined that in 1977 Democratic party

affiliation was then near its historic peak. At 49 percent, it was only four points under the high of 53 percent recorded in early 1964. At the same time, Republican party affiliation had fallen to 20 percent, its lowest point in forty years, with only one person in five classifying himself or herself as a Republican. The proportion of independents, Gallup reported, has remained the same in recent years—about three in every ten, or 31 percent. Moreover, the decline in Republican affiliation has been across the board. It has dropped equally among men and women and among the various educational groups. Contrary to what might have been expected, it has declined somewhat more in the Far West than in any other region.

These statistics tell only part of the story. In a *Fortune* magazine article Everett Carll Ladd Jr. noted that "so many Americans now vote so often for Democratic candidates that the G.O.P. has been consigned to half-party status, and the Democrats have become the established governing party to a degree unequaled by any other alliance since the Jeffersonians."[2]

Ladd pointed out that Democrats are well ahead of Republicans in every age group, from the youngest segment to the oldest; that while wage workers are more Democratic than businesspersons and executives, a majority of even the latter now identify with the Democrats and vote for Democratic congressional candidates; that all educational groups show a Democratic margin as do all income levels, including the very prosperous. Indeed, Ladd noted, people who come from very wealthy backgrounds prefer the Democrats by a two-to-one margin. Beyond this, Democrats lead Republicans in every region, among all religious groupings, and among virtually all ethnic groups.

> Perhaps most striking of all, the Democrats lead not only among voters who think of themselves as liberals and moderates, but even among self-described conservatives. A majority of such conservatives voted for Democratic congressional candidates in 1976, and more of them identify with the Democrats than with the G.O.P.[3]

To explain why all this is so, Ladd referred to a number of polls taken over the previous five years and particularly to a celebrated survey conducted in 1976 by Potomac Associates, a respected Washington-based research group. These surveys found that the basic reason for Democratic predominance is "the almost universal acceptance among Americans of the general policy approach of the New Deal."[4]

"Consider, for example," Ladd wrote, "the issue of public spending for social services. People may complain today that taxes are too high, that bureaucrats intrude too much, that the 'government wastes money.' But ask them what they want to do in each specific policy sector, and they reply, 'Keep going.'"[5]

Senator Gary Hart (D-Col.) has coined a phrase to point up this paradox: "If you want government to get off your back, get your hand out of the government's pocket."

The Potomac Associates survey asked whether "the amount of our tax money now being spent" for federal programs should be increased, cut back, kept at the current level, or cut out entirely. Before answering, each respondent was advised to "bear in mind that sooner or later all government spending has to be taken care of out of taxes you and other Americans pay." Even with this caution, the survey found that the public "favored at least some increase in spending on the fifteen programs at the top of the list." These programs included helping the aged, the unemployed, black Americans, and the poor; developing self-sufficiency in energy; providing adequate housing; improving medical and health care; supporting and improving public schools; rebuilding rundown sections of cities; providing better mass transportation; coping with drugs and addicts; reducing air pollution; and making college possible for deserving young people.

In his analysis of the Potomac survey data, Ladd noted that support for such programs was spread across the social spectrum.

> The proportion of people from families earning $25,000 a year and higher who think government should spend more to improve education is almost identical to that for persons with annual family incomes of $7,000 and under. College graduates and those with less than a high school education are about equally supportive of greater federal expenditures on health services. Professionals and managers on the one hand, and unskilled workers on the other, give *equal* backing to increased spending on urban problems.[6]

Most surprising, the survey data showed that overwhelming majorities of self-proclaimed conservatives wanted either to increase government spending in most of the principal policy areas, or at least to maintain existing programs.

One might immediately conjecture that in the two years since this survey was made a drastic change in attitude must have taken place in order to account for the taxpayers' revolt of 1978. The *Washington Post* conducted its own poll in late spring 1978 to determine whether the nation was turning Right, and its findings were essentially the same as those of the Potomac Associates survey. The *Post* poll found that long-standing support of New Deal-type federal programs was unchanged.

Beyond the seeming consensus on New Deal-type programs, there is polling evidence that the American people give broad support to other positions more often, although surely not exclusively, identified with liberalism. A Harris poll taken in 1977 showed the people favoring racial equality by a margin of 88-7, desegregation of housing by 77-14, desegregation of schools by 75-7, and a U.S.-Russian agreement to end war by 95-2.

All this considered, why, then, the persistent talk that the nation is moving to the Right? Why does the New Right say it with such conviction? Why do so many Democrats—including President Carter's own pollster, Patrick Caddell—think they discern a decided drift toward conservatism?

The answer is not to be found in self-definition as such, for even though a September 1978 Gallup poll found nearly half the people identifying themselves as conservative as against less than a third who called themselves liberals, this has to be measured against a Gallup poll taken in 1939, at the cresting of the New Deal, which found 52 percent of the people calling themselves conservatives. Yet, one year later Franklin D. Roosevelt swept to his third term.

The two polls already mentioned do offer a hint of why something's stirring. The *Washington Post* poll that showed continued approval of New Deal-type programs also revealed that disenchantment with government performance "has risen dramatically in all groups." The *Post* also cited surveys conducted by the University of Michigan which showed that the number of Americans who said they did not trust the federal government to do what is right had more than doubled from 1966 to 1976, rising from 30 percent to 63 percent.

These findings point up the need to consider now a sociopolitical phenomenon that does not lend itself readily to the statistical yardstick, yet is of crucial importance in determining whether conservatism is indeed on the rise.

"The older conception of politics," Richard Hofstadter pointed out, "was that it deals with the question: Who gets what, when, how? Politics was taken as an arena in which people define their interests as rationally as possible and behave in a way calculated to realize them as fully as possible."[7] Hofstadter credits Harold Lasswell with a new conception that questions the adequacy of this rationalistic assumption and points up the need to take the emotional and symbolic side of political life into account as well.

The new question thus becomes:

> Who perceives what public issues, in what way, and why? To the present generation of historical and political writers it has become increasingly clear that people not only seek their interests but also express and even in a measure define themselves in politics; that political life acts as a sounding board for identities, values, fears, and aspirations. In a study of the political milieu these things are brought to the surface.[8]

The same point is made in different terms by Hadley Cantril and Lloyd A. Free in *The Political Beliefs of Americans.*[9] In this book they discuss what they call the Ideological Spectrum vis-à-vis the Operational Spectrum, explaining that the first referred to people's abstract beliefs and the second to their practical attitudes. Considering the Cantril-Free definitions in a *Wall Street Journal* article on February 21, 1978, historian Arthur M. Schlesinger Jr. stated that the Ideological Spectrum would include people's beliefs about the proper role of government in economic and social life, whereas the Operational Spectrum consists of their attitudes toward specific government programs affecting their daily lives.

It is only when we grant proper significance to the Cantril-Free concept of the Ideological Spectrum that we can begin to understand why the New Right can be so confident of its assessment of the public mood. We find, for example, that while most Americans say things are not bad for them personally, in part because of what federal programs have meant for their well-being and quality of life, at the same time, many are deeply concerned about what inflation, the growing tax burden, changes in cultural mores and value systems, the Soviet arms buildup, and the newly learned limits to our own resources and power portend for themselves and their children, and they see themselves as alienated, unheeded, and helpless to influence the course of events.

When these Americans—their confidence in the integrity, the foresight, and the ability of their elected officials already shaken by the Vietnam, Watergate, and energy-inflation crises—watch today's decision-making process snarled by intransigence, regional rivalries, petty politicking, and, not least, by the very number, size, and complexity of our problems, their instincts are to turn against those who have disappointed them and to redirect their own attention to causes that are closer to home and to heart and to issues ostensibly simpler to define and resolve.

The New Right sees this as fertile ground. In explaining the purpose of the Conservative Caucus, National Director Howard Phillips said,

> The theory of the Caucus is that there are those conservative Democrats and independents out there and they have long since ceased to perceive that the party system out there is relevant to their concerns. So they have expressed themselves in other ways, like in Right to Life, in American Legion posts, Sons of Italy chapters, the Kiwanis Club and in sportsmen's groups. That's where they've shown their leadership. . . . We have to go to these institutions to find our non-Republican new majoritarians.[10]

It is here, then, that we find the real source of the New Right's confidence. It is betting high stakes that in the conflict between old political loyalties and new anguishes and resentments, it is anguish and resentment that will prevail and ultraconservatism that will reap the political benefits.

In sum, the New Right is counting heavily on the intense yearning of millions of Americans to return to a simpler, more innocent time when there were no limits to America's resources, power, and influence; when conformity prevailed and there were few challenges to value systems and to authority; when the sanctity and the integrity of the family seemed more secure; when one could walk the streets in safety; when the dollar was sound, taxes were low, and everything in the universe appeared to be in its right and proper place. In a malapropism more poignant than laughable, Archie Bunker said, "The world was better when it was the same."

Considering the clash between ideological and operational spectra as it manifests itself within the Democratic party,

Everett Ladd noted that to date this has posed a serious problem only in Presidential elections, especially in recent ones in which a new factor, which he calls "the New Liberalism," has emerged.

> The New Liberalism's attitudes are very different from—indeed, often at odds with—those of the New Deal liberals. For example, the New Liberals support the busing of schoolchildren to achieve racial integration; they reject "equality of opportunity," insisting instead, upon "equality of result"; they want to extend civil liberties, notably the rights of the accused in criminal trials; and they sharply question the value of economic growth, believing that it damages the "quality of life." The New Liberalism also differs from the New Deal ethos in the matter of personal morality; it takes a libertarian stance on such matters as abortion, legalization of marijuana, homosexuality, and racial intermarriage.[11]

Ladd accurately noted that the New Liberals are a minority within the party and in the nation as a whole; that their view is intensely controversial among the large traditional and working classes who have now become bourgeois and "therefore anxious to protect a status gained at considerable effort and often held tenuously"; and that because of this the old New Deal Democratic Presidential majority is gone. "The New Liberalism impacts too strongly on the national stage and it is too divisive for the Democrats—however skillful their candidates —to be able to package a ticket that leaves both New Liberals and Old Liberals comfortably allied."[12]

Although this impact has not as yet been felt so strongly at the level of congressional elections, the New Right intends to make its impact because the contrast between the New Liberals and the New Right on so many social issues is too inviting not to be exploited when it promises, as it seems, to divide the Democratic party and win support for Rightist candidates.

Moreover, although the Harris survey of July 3, 1978 showed a sharp drop in public support for a wider range of life-styles, the *Washington Post* canvass of the political mood in the spring of 1978 indicated that some social views espoused by the New Liberals, although still held by only a minority of the general populace, are growing in public acceptance, further alarming the constituency already being ardently courted by the New Right.

After citing the increase in public disenchantment with government performance, the *Post* reported:

> In only one [other] area do the *Post*'s polls and other polls suggest significant change over the last decade, and that is in a liberal direction on what might be called lifestyle questions. On how severe penalties should be for the use of marijuana, on the right of newsstands to sell pornography, on the role of women in society and on several other such issues there has been unmistakable movement toward a more tolerant or "liberal" point of view.

It must be noted, however, that whatever movement there has been toward a more liberal point of view has been hesitant and tentative, a fact pointed up by the discrepancy between the findings of the Harris survey and the *Post* poll. For example, many Americans believe that homosexuals should have the same rights, employment opportunities, and job security as heterosexuals, but they are not so committed in that belief as to help brace the barricades against Anita Bryant and company.

The New Right, in contrast, shows no such hesitancy or ambivalence, portraying righteous anger and passionate certainty as it warns its followers of the consequences of liberalized social views.

Witness the contents of the first mailing to solicit memberships and money for Meldrim Thomson's Conservative Caucus. Using words like bullets, this letter was fired off in November 1974:

> Dear Friend:
> Are you as sick and tired as I am of liberal politicians who: Force children to be bused; appoint judges who turn murderers and rapists loose on the public; force your children to study from school books that are anti-God, anti-American, and filled with the most vulgar curse words; give your tax money to communists, anarchists and other radical organizations; do nothing about sex, adultery and homosexuality and foul language on television?
> Are you tired of feeling no power to change things? If so, why don't you join the Conservative Caucus?

In the next seven months appeals such as this brought in $524,387 from 36,840 people, according to Caucus Director Howard Phillips.[13] And by the spring of 1978 the caucus had become the largest and fastest growing of all New Right grassroots lobbying organizations, attesting to the organization's ability to capitalize on the uneasiness aroused by New Liberal social views in home-town America and among cultural fundamentalists everywhere, including many older-generation New Deal Democrats.

But the views of the New Liberals within the Democratic party are not the only source of internal tension for the party. In relatively recent times a distinctive challenge to traditional Democratic policies has been mounted by respected figures who were once part and parcel of the Old Liberal Establishment but who are now called neoconservatives. These include such renowned academics and social theorists as Irving Kristol, Daniel Bell, Edward Banfield, Nathan Glazer, Seymour Martin Lipset, Norman Podhoretz, and James Q. Wilson; author and political activist Ben J. Wattenberg; and Democratic senators Daniel Patrick Moynihan of New York and Henry M. Jackson of Washington, honorary chairman of the centrist Coalition for a Democratic Majority. Podhoretz edits *Commentary* magazine, and Glazer and Kristol *The Public Interest*. Many neoconservatives write articles for these two publications expressing their growing skepticism about the efficacy or the desirability of government programs to solve social problems. Instead, they seem to argue, the solution lies in the free market system. So they advocate such alternatives as housing vouchers for the poor instead of building government housing projects; pollution taxes rather than environmental protection regulations; a negative income tax for the poor instead of welfare programs; an end to affirmative action quotas and the restoration of meritocracy.

Some vigorously espouse moves to restore what they see as traditional social values. In an essay titled "The Limits of Social Policy" Harvard's Nathan Glazer conjectured that welfare programs tended to perpetuate the social dependency they were designed to resolve, because they usurp responsibilities that properly belonged to the family, the church, the school, and neighborhood organizations. "I am increasingly convinced," Glazer wrote, "that some important part of the solution to our social problems lies in traditional practices and traditional restraints."

But the neoconservatives themselves are not left unchallenged. Many liberals within the Democratic party do not share their faith in the free market's conscience or capacity to address and alleviate social problems, denouncing this approach as little more than a sophisticated presentation of the old trickle-down theory. Others directly charge the neoconservatives with buckling under to pressure from the Right and retreating under fire. Still others, like Harvard's Kenneth Arrow, think conservatives and neoconservatives alike are wrong in their negative appraisal of programs launched under the aegis of the Great Society. They say the Great Society was oversold and underfinanced but nevertheless accomplished some noteworthy goals in health care for the elderly, housing for the poor, and college for Blacks. "It was not Utopia," says Arrow, "not a revolutionary transformation of society. But it represents genuine progress, and underselling the achievements as though nothing happened is perverting reality."

But the strain on the Democratic party created by the competing presence of New Liberals and neoconservatives, even though significant and trying, nevertheless could be accommodated by the party's traditional elasticity. One of the enduring strengths of the party has been its capacity to tolerate ideological diversity and somehow put together a "sellable" platform its members can support.

A more critical challenge to the party today, as David Broder has pointed out, is adapting its historically liberal premises and programs to the dominant conservative forces without losing its philosophical integrity and without self-destructing. Broder defines those dominant conservative forces in terms of shifts in foreign policy, economic policy, and social policy. "In foreign policy, Soviet expansionism in Africa and its arms buildup in Eastern Europe have shifted the focus of American diplomacy from the pursuit of détente to an updated version of the containment doctrine. The shift is pushing defense spending higher, delaying arms-control agreements and sharpening the exchanges between Moscow and Washington."[14]

In economic policy, he contends, inflation has shifted the focus from reducing unemployment, where the Carter Administration was quite successful, to restraining prices, where success to date is no more than minimal.

And in social policy, he says, "the rising chorus of complaints about the costs and inefficiency of government has driven officials in Washington, as elsewhere, to seek to constrain government, rather than expand and improve its benefits."[15]

Broder contends that if the Republicans were the governing party, they would have little difficulty adapting their rhetoric or their programs to the prevailing mood. "But, the Republicans are suffering the after-effects of a decade of their own leadership failures and are exiled from power. So these shifts are taking place at a time of extraordinary Democratic dominance at all levels of government. The tensions they are producing inside that party are growing."[16]

In sum, these tensions within the Democratic party and the general debilitation of the Republican party provide the New Right with a choice of targets.

The evidence to date would indicate that the movement's main objective is to take over the Republican party or to replace it with a new conservative party. A secondary—but simultaneous—objective is to push the Democratic party to the Right while weaning away the cultural fundamentalists within the party and enlisting them in the New Right cause.

CHAPTER 4

The New Right— Substance and Strategy

It's a new dimension of conservative activity . . . an explosion of new, aggressive and effective conservative organizations that have put aside their differences and jealousies and are working together for a broader constituency.
—PHILIP M. CRANE
Chairman, American
Conservative Union

We are different from previous generations of conservatives. We are no longer working to preserve the status quo. We are radicals working to overturn the present power structure in this country.
—PAUL WEYRICH
National Director,
Committee for the
Survival of a Free
Congress

47

We organize discontent. . . . We must prove our
ability to get revenge on people who go against
us. . . . We'll be after them, if they vote the
wrong way. We're not going to stop after the
vote's past.
—HOWARD PHILLIPS
National Director,
Conservative Caucus

To attempt to define the New Right in a single phrase would
be as futile as trying to clutch quicksilver in the palm of one's
hand. The movement's blending of zealotry with pragmatism
marks a significant departure from traditional right-wing movements in America. That difference and others demand a comprehensive consideration of its ideology, composition, strategy,
and tactics.*

The following examples show how single-factor analysis is in-
adequate to capture the true character of the movement:

William Lanouette, writing in the *National Journal,* made it a
matter of dating. "The New Right is 'new' because its most active members trace their present activities to about 1974. Then
their impatience with the shambles of the Nixon-Ford Administration led a few behind-the-scenes technicians and subalterns
to resort to political activism and to assume leadership roles for
themselves."[1]

It is true that 1974 was a significant year for the development
of the movement, but the ideology of the New Right was born a
decade before—in the Goldwater campaign of 1964. The *Journal* definition also fails to take into account that the movement
includes such potent organizations as the American Conservative Union, founded the same year as the Goldwater campaign;
or that it amplifies its effect by working in close concert, when
their purposes coincide, with such long-established groups as
the U.S. Chamber of Commerce, the National Association of

---

* For the sake of completeness this chapter details the principal leaders of
the New Right, the organizations they guide, and the remote and recent history of the movement. Some readers may find it preferable to scan the material
first and then to use it later as a reference source.

Manufacturers, the American Legion, the Veterans of Foreign Wars, and the National Right to Work Committee.

Thomas S. Winter, editor of the conservative political weekly *Human Events*, offers an even simpler, more misleading definition, saying the New Right describes "those people who use Richard Viguerie's services."[2]

Direct mail wizard Richard A. Viguerie,* does indeed serve the communicating, mail lobbying, and fund-raising needs of such major New Right organizations as the National Conservative Political Action Committee, the Committee for the Survival of a Free Congress, the Conservative Caucus, Americans Against Union Control of Government, a number of candidates backed by the movement, and such ancillary groups as the Right to Keep and Bear Arms Political Victory Fund, Gun Owners of America, and the Public Service Research Council.

However, another major direct mail firm closely tied to ultraconservative politics—Bruce W. Eberle and Associates, in Vienna, Virginia—performs the same function for Ronald Reagan's Citizens for the Republic, the American Conservative Union, Fund for a Conservative Majority, additional New Right candidates, and the Committee to Defeat the Union Bosses' Candidates.

A broader, more accurate characterization is provided by Kevin P. Phillips, conservative political analyst. Phillips defines the New Right as "social issue" conservatives, in contrast to older "business" conservatives, and goes on to say the movement is non-Republican—or on-again, off-again Republican; noncommittal about whom it will back for the Presidency in 1980; and anti-elitist. Phillips also sees the growth of populist conservatism as evidence that "a new party might be emerging, somewhat in the way the Republican party did in the 1850's. Any such new party would come from the insurgent South and West and be heavily anti-establishment in nature."[3]

To put the ideology of the New Right into perspective, and to understand more precisely what it is that distinguishes the movement from its predecessors, requires a brief consideration

---

* Chapter 5 describes Viguerie's operations and their importance to the movement.

of the history of the right wing in America.* Late in the eighteenth century many Americans were persuaded that an Aus-
trian secret organization called the Illuminati was controlling
the American colonies (and later the new American nation)
through the Order of Free Masons. In 1796 a book exposing this
alleged plot gained considerable currency, partly because it was
endorsed by some prominent clergy and educators. One of the
chief targets of the movement was Thomas Jefferson, whose international contacts and reputation made him suspect among
those who were determined to "protect" America from foreign
influences.

This particular conspiracy theory died for lack of evidence
that the Illuminati had ever existed—but not before it provided
fuel for passage of the Alien and Sedition Acts.

> The influx of immigrants into the new country fed many opposition
> movements, especially as Jefferson and Andrew Jackson appealed poli-
> tically to the new citizenry. In the late 1820's, the Anti-Masonic move-
> ment gained such a foothold that a modern historian has described it as
> "a sociological precursor of movements such as the Ku Klux Klan and
> McCarthyism."[4]

Anti-Masons held conventions, published tracts, fielded candidates, and ultimately elected two governors and many state
legislators before the movement was absorbed into the Whig or
Republican parties.

> But out of the conservative ideology came the Native Americans and
> the Know-Nothing Party, aimed against the massive immigration of poor
> Catholics from Ireland and Europe. The Know-Nothing Party (so called
> because members were instructed to reply to inquiries: "I know noth-
> ing") scored major victories in the mid-1850's and in 1856 its candidate
> for President was Millard Fillmore, the former Whig President of the
> United States.[5]

After the Civil War, right-wing extremism took on a more
overt anti-Catholicism. President Ulysses S. Grant, briefly a
member of the Know-Nothings, proclaimed that the next issue
capable of dividing the country might be Protestants versus
Catholics. Like the Know-Nothings before them and the Ku
Klux Klan, which was to follow, the American Protective Asso-

---

* An analysis of the psychology of right-wing extremism is presented in
chapter 9.

ciation, the next manifestation of extremism, began as a secret society that drew its main strength from a working class, "still fearful of the immigration from Catholic countries."[6]

But it was during the period after World War I "that the pattern of right-wing extremism took on some of its particular twentieth-century characteristics, partly as a result of America's new involvement in the world and the changing nature of that world."[7]

The Ku Klux Klan was on the rise outside the Deep South in the 1920s. It dominated the politics of Oregon, Oklahoma, Texas, Arkansas, Indiana, Ohio, and California as well as other northern states during that period and peaked at a membership of between three million and six million.[8] This group was to collapse as a significant political force, but in the mid-1970s there were signs of renewed life in the movement in parts of the Deep South and in border states such as Maryland.

In the early and midthirties a number of neofascist groups became active, among them William Dudley Pelley's Silver Shirts. Dominating the era, however, was Father Charles E. Coughlin of Royal Oak, Michigan, described as the leader of a right-wing movement that "broke with the old, more simplistic movements." The "radio priest" at first "parlayed anti-Communism and anti-capitalism into a fascistic appeal with anti-Semitic thrusts, later broadening his attack into a full-scale assault on the Roosevelt New Deal. His listeners ran into the millions, even in those days, and he stimulated floods of mail—much as the modern right wing exhorters do."[9] In 1936 Coughlin supported William Lemke for President on a Union ticket and gained the support of Gerald L.K. Smith, one of the most notorious anti-Semites of the time, and of Huey Long.

Dale Kramer, in an article written for *Harper's Magazine*, discussed Coughlin's ultimate fall from power and pointed up two historic weaknesses of right-wing extremism—political naiveté and ineptitude, and frightening overzealotry.

> Contrary to the view of his admirers, Coughlin is no student of political and economic affairs. His economic arguments defy analysis and his political naiveté has been little short of astounding. Not only is he plainly unfamiliar with American history and politics, but he suffers from a chronic inability to take the advice of anyone who does; or, equally disastrous, he takes the advice, generally contradictory, of everyone.[10]

In October of 1936 Coughlin confidently predicted he could deliver nine million votes to Lemke, his personally nominated and manipulated candidate for President. Indeed, he was so confident that he said he would retire from radio if his prediction were not realized.

Kramer recounted a conversation Coughlin had with the press shortly before the election in which he said the United States was seeing its last election. "We are at the crossroads. One road leads to Communism, the other to fascism. I take the road to fascism." This quote, published in many newspapers and featured on the *March of Time* radio broadcast, may have signaled the beginning of the end for Coughlin; that and the outcome of the 1936 election. Instead of getting nine million votes, Lemke got only 800,000.

Coughlin was not the only Far Right foe of Roosevelt's New Deal. The American Liberty League, which was created by wealthy persons who had worked together to repeal Prohibition, was "so patently conservative that the Democrats actually welcomed its opposition. It banged away at what it characterized as government intervention and the welfare state, but petered out after a splash of publicity."[11]

Some of the organizations that were spawned to fight New Dealism endured, however.

—The Committee for Constitutional Government, headed by the late Frank Gannett and Dr. Edward Rumley, published a stream of right-wing propaganda in the 40s and into the 50s.

—The Foundation for Economic Education was set up as a high-tone chamber of commerce type of intellectual center for free enterprise, and is still active.

—Freedoms Foundation at Valley Forge, Pa., was started in 1949 by three conservative businessmen to "undergird our constitutional Republic and combat the increasing threat of Socialistic Communism to the American Way of Life." It still bestows more than a thousand awards a year for success in advancing its credo.

—At Harding College in Searcy, Ark., Dr. George S. Benson started a free enterprise, anti-government crusade that still goes by the name of the National Education Program.

A little later, these were joined by a plethora of right-wing operations: H.L. Hunt's "Life Line" radio program; Dr. Billy James Hargis' Christian Crusade, which dabbles in politics and economics; the Rev. Carl McIntire's Twentieth Century Reformation Hour, which evangelizes on issues other than fundamentalist religion; and scores of others with stranger names, such as the National Indignation Convention.

Riding this big wave—and zeroing in on organized labor—was the National Right to Work Committee, now a multi-million dollar force. And a unique addition, in 1958, was Americans for Constitutional Action, which grew out of a plan by a few reactionaries to realign the major political parties into conservative and liberal polarities.* ACA is very much alive and helping conservative candidates—nearly all Republicans.[12]

In the Truman years the most visible new manifestations of the movement were the China Lobby and McCarthyism.

D.W. Brogan explained the phenomenon of the China Lobby in terms of "the illusion of American omnipotence," which he defined as the "illusion that any situation that distresses or endangers the United States can only exist because some Americans have been fools or knaves."[13] Under this illusion, the "loss" of China to Communism could not possibly be seen for what it really was—the result of massive strategic and economic realities and forces largely beyond our control—but as evidence that this enormous country had been "lost" or "stolen" because of mistakes or treachery on the part of American leaders.

Richard Hofstadter expanded this consideration: "Moreover, the persistent faith that American intervention could have changed Chinese history was accompanied by the faith that this involved nothing more than the choice of a few sound alternative policies, without demanding of the American people the massive sacrifices necessary to sustain a major commitment in China."[14]

Although the China Lobby per se is no longer the potent political force it once was, its lingering effects are apparent in the heated opposition to any moves to broaden U.S. relations with the People's Republic of China.

The motivation and the support for McCarthyism are dealt with later in this book. Suffice it for now to note that the ideological base for McCarthyism was extremely narrow, embracing as it did the single issue of anti-Communism. McCarthy did not— or could not—convert his crusade into a cohesive reactionary political movement. Nevertheless, McCarthyism did provide an opportunity for pseudoconservatives to express their disen-

---

* *Union-Leader* Publisher William Loeb wholeheartedly subscribes to this political realignment plan.

chantment with traditional Republicanism. To many of these people

> the Eisenhower administration was worse than a disappointment, it was a betrayal. It did not repeal the New Deal reforms, do away with high taxes, kill foreign aid, or balance the budget. In fact, its primary historical function seemed to be to legitimate what had been done under Roosevelt and Truman: when it left certain domestic and foreign policies intact, it made them more generally acceptable by passing them, so to speak, through the purifying fire of eight years of Republicanism and thus confirming that they represented, after all, a bipartisan consensus. The right-wing minority saw all this not as a clue to the nature of our national problems but as further evidence that the conspiracy originally set in motion by the Democrats was being carried on by the Eastern Republicans behind Eisenhower. McCarthy, for example, had been quick to strike at Eisenhower and to change his slogan, "Twenty years of treason," to a more inflammatory one: "Twenty-one years of treason."[15]

What made Eisenhower Republicanism even harder for the right wing to swallow was the realization that things would not have been *that* much different had Robert A. Taft been in the White House. Taft, "Mr. Republican," provided a definitive contrast between traditional economic and political conservatism and right-wing extremism. It is true he was a fiscal conservative and an opponent of federal expansionism, but he knew the federal government had to play a significant role or society would not be able to honor certain responsibilities to all its members.

For example, Taft said that the federal government should concern itself with "seeing that every family has a minimum standard of decent shelter" and should assist those states that wanted to put a floor "under essential services in relief, medical care, in housing, and in education." Moreover, Taft thought the federal government should underwrite the states in providing "a basic minimum education to every child" and should sustain minimum wage laws "to give the unorganized worker some protection" comparable to that achieved by unionized workers. He also favored retention of a steep graduated income tax, programs to maintain farm prices, and, through the social security program, the assurance of a living wage to every citizen sixty-five years of age and over.

So, the right wing chafed in frustration and bitterness through eight years of Eisenhower rule, followed by four years of Democratic rule, before it had its collective opportunity to express itself in Barry Goldwater's campaign of 1964. Pseudoconservatives had waited a long time to hear a Presidential candidate say, as Goldwater reportedly said on various occasions:

Governmental activities in "relief, social security, collective bargaining, and public housing" have caused "the weakening of the individual personality and of self-reliance."

Farm subsidy programs deserve "prompt and final termination."

The graduated income tax is "confiscatory."

The country has "no education problem which requires any form of Federal grant-in-aid programs to the states."

The government "must begin to withdraw from a whole series of programs that are outside its constitutional mandate," including "social welfare programs, education, public power, public housing, urban renewal."

"My aim is not to pass laws but to repeal them."

"I fear Washington and centralized government more than I do Moscow."

These statements spoke to the pseudoconservatives' worship of economic individualism.

On other occasions Goldwater appealed directly to the cultural conservatism of his followers, notably in his opening campaign speech in Prescott, Arizona. It was there that Goldwater struck this particular theme: "There is a stir in the land. There is a mood of uneasiness. We feel adrift in an uncharted and stormy sea. We feel we have lost our way."

In later speeches Goldwater cited evidence of "this drift and decay" that had overcome the country: "Wave after wave of crime in our streets and in our homes . . . riot and disorder in our cities . . . a breakdown of the morals of our young people . . . juvenile delinquency . . . obscene literature . . .

corruption." All these evils had mounted because "the moral fiber of the American people is beset by rot and decay."

Goldwater declared that "something basic and dangerous is eating away at the morality, dignity and respect of our citizens —old as well as young, high as well as low." He suggested that this was a poor time in the nation's history "for the Federal government to ban Almighty God from our school rooms." The Republican candidate pointedly took note that the Democratic party platform was silent on the question of a constitutional amendment allowing the restoration of prayer in the classroom and added, "You will search in vain for *any* reference to God or religion in the Democratic platform."

He played, too, to the superpatriotism of the pseudoconservatives, saying, "Are you proud of our fight for freedom? Are you proud of Panama? Are you proud of the burned effigy in Greece? Are you proud when no country is too small to pull Uncle Sam's whiskers and get away with it? Are you proud of wheat deals with the destroyers of liberty?"

Most importantly, Goldwater preached the hardest of hard lines on the issues of military strength and of coexistence with our adversaries.

Hofstadter, interpreting Goldwater's view, said the Arizonan looked upon the Cold War as a series of relentless confrontations between ourselves and the Communists on various fronts throughout the world.

> If we maintain superior strength we can emerge victorious from all these confrontations, and in time the whole Communist world (which should be treated uniformly as a bloc, whatever its apparent internal differences) will crack under the stress of repeated defeats. The goal of our policies cannot be limited to peace, security, and the extension of our influence, but must go on to ultimate total victory, the ideological and political extermination of the enemy. "Our objective must be the destruction of the enemy as an ideological force possessing the means of power. . . . We will never reconcile ourselves to the Communists' possession of power of any kind in any part of the world."[16]

When Goldwater was pressed on whether such an approach would trigger a general war, he promised that, faced with U.S. superiority in weapons, the Soviets would never strike. But, Hofstadter noted, this is a promise no *American* can deliver, and for whose fulfillment we must depend upon Moscow.

Moreover, there is a curious passage in *Why Not Victory?* [Goldwater's book] in which Goldwater flatly admitted that such fulfillment is not to be expected. The Communist world, he said, is likely to resort to general war only under one of two conditions. One, of course, is if we invite their attack by political weakness and military disarmament. But the other is "if there is a decisive switch in world affairs to the point where it is obvious they are going to lose." And it is, of course, precisely to this point that Goldwater has always urged that they be pushed. The central dilemma of total victory, as expounded by Goldwater, is thus made to seem more ominous and insoluble than the many perplexing dilemmas of coexistence.[17]

Goldwater's rhetoric may have thrilled his followers, but it alarmed the majority of Americans. Some saw his views on economic individualism as threats to government programs under which they had greatly benefited. Even more saw his hawkishness on military and foreign affairs matters as risking their very survival. The notorious line from his acceptance speech—"I would remind you that extremism in the defense of liberty is no vice"—dismayed a great many traditional conservatives as well as liberals and moderates, and it was to dog him throughout the campaign.

The Goldwater campaign's dramatic departure from traditional Republican ideology and rhetoric was not its only distinguishing feature. Constituency, human resources, and strategy were also decidedly different from prior Republican campaigns. Goldwater appealed most to those Republicans whose discontent with the party was keenest and whose ideological fervor was the strongest. Highly motivated by what he had said and written in the months and years before the convention, they took over the party at the grass-roots level in 1964 and won delegate spots to the nominating convention.

Hofstadter singled out another key difference in that campaign.

Goldwater's zealots were moved more by the desire to dominate the party than to win the country, concerned more to express resentments and punish "traitors," to justify a set of values and assert grandiose, militant visions, than to solve actual problems of state. More important, they were immune to the pressure to move over from an extreme position toward the center of the political spectrum which is generally exerted by the professional's desire to win. Their true victory lay not in winning the election but in capturing the party—in itself no mean achievement—which gave them an unprecedented platform from which to propagandize for a sound view of the world.[18]

Take over the party the Goldwater "true believers" did, but they also went down to thundering defeat in the November election. By the time voters went to the polls, many were saying, "He's too radical for me." For the first time in modern history, the Democratic candidate was endorsed by newspapers with greater total circulation than those endorsing the Republican candidate. Indeed, Goldwater was to be the first Republican candidate for President ever to lose the State of Vermont.

Many of the ideological characteristics that surfaced in the Goldwater campaign were common to earlier right-wing movements: cultural fundamentalism, economic individualism, obsession with conscious or inadvertent "treason" or "disloyalty," the absolutist's embrace of passionate certainties, and the apocalyptic view of political events and issues. In character, too, was the campaign's negativism. Virtually everything was opposed. Virtually nothing of specific substance was *proposed* beyond more military weaponry.*

The legacy of 1964 is clearly apparent in today's New Right. The same ideological characteristics are there and so is the negativism—anti-Salt II, anti-Panama Canal treaties, anti-traditional Republicanism, anti-Communism, anti-Equal Rights Amendment, anti-taxes, anti-regulation, anti-gun control.Whatever positive face they put on their endeavors is couched in general value terms few can dispute: "freedom," "individualism," "family," "enterprise."

Where the New Right departs from Goldwaterism is not in ideology but in strategy and tactics. Its leaders are no less convinced than Goldwater was in 1964 that there is "a conservative majority out there," but they seem determined not to make the mistakes the Goldwater campaign made in trying to court that majority.

Today's New Rightists saw in that campaign how true believers could be mobilized at the grass-roots level to give a conservative the nomination. They also saw how political amateurism and rampant, highly exposed overzealotry can destroy a campaign once the nomination is won.

Some drew still another lesson from the Goldwater debacle

---

* There is nothing personal in my criticism, direct or implied, of Barry Goldwater's campaign; in truth, I like the senator from Arizona. I find his politics appalling, but his personality winning and delightful.

and from the collapse of the Nixon Presidency. It was concluded that the Republican party need not be the only vehicle for their cause. Indeed, some believe the Republican party is dead and should be replaced by a third party, or should be rebuilt from scratch under New Right dominance. Others see the cause as being better served by seeking majorities in *both* political parties and electing one of its representatives President.

In 1974 the people destined to be leaders of the New Right—for the most part young enough so that some came out of William F. Buckley's archconservative Young Americans for Freedom—began to organize new groups, enlist existing groups (like the American Conservative Union), lay out strategy, cross-pollinate ideas, coordinate their efforts, and build up mailing lists of thousands of like-believers, ready lobbyists, and willing contributors of money.

Early in 1978, Scott Wolf wrote in the *Democratic Viewpoint:*

> In 1978, the Democratic Party and its major candidates for federal and statewide office will be facing a better organized, better financed, and more politically astute right wing movement than at any time in recent memory. Possessing the latest in direct mail technology, and energized by new innovative leaders, the right wing movement will help train, staff, finance and guide literally hundreds of 1978 Republican campaigns. Moreover, the right wing will undoubtedly continue through 1978 a direct mail blitz which reportedly accounted for 75 million mail messages in 1977.
>
> Despite the ambitiousness of its future goals and magnitude of its past accomplishments, the national right wing movement is currently dominated by perhaps a dozen organizations and individuals. In the sphere of electoral politics, the major organizations include the following:
> —The National Conservative Political Action Committee
> —Citizens for the Republic (headed by Ronald Reagan)
> —The Committee for the Survival of a Free Congress
> —The Gun Owners of America
> —The Fund for a Conservative Majority
> —The Conservative Victory Fund
> Arch-conservative organizations dealing primarily in lobbying activities and public relations rather than electioneering include the National Right to Work Committee, the Conservative Caucus, the American Conservative Union, the Eagle Forum (Phyllis Schlafly's anti-ERA, anti-feminist organization), and the Young Americans for Freedom (the training ground for many of the right wing movement's current leadership).[19]

Wolf noted how the leaders of recently organized New Right

groups serve essentially as technicians and organizers, for the most part shunning any visible role. "But," he wrote,

despite their anonymity, they exert influence at least comparable to, if not greater than, that of such more visible conservative spokesmen as Barry Goldwater, Strom Thurmond, William Buckley and John Tower. The small roster of "New Right" leaders is headed by Richard Viguerie, the leading direct mail expert of the right. . . . Closely aligned with Viguerie are Paul Weyrich, the director of the Washington-based Committee for the Survival of a Free Congress, Howard Phillips, the director of the Conservative Caucus (an organization seeking to set up grass roots conservative organizations in most of the nation's 435 congressional districts), and Philip Crane, Republican Congressman from Illinois with 1980 presidential ambitions, who currently controls the American Conservative Union.[20]

He cited three other developments of recent years that have helped strengthen the influence of the right wing:

First, through the vehicle of direct mail, the Right can carry its message to between six and seven million people. Not long ago, the conservative message was carried almost exclusively by such elitist publications as *The National Review* and *Human Events* and rarely reached the lower-middle-class citizen.

Second, the Federal Election Campaign Act of 1973, by prohibiting domination of any single federal election by a small corps of contributors, forced the right wing to seek a broader market for contributions. Thus, the direct mail operation developed by the movement solicits more money from more people and, at the same time, gives much more extensive distribution to the movement's messages. *Congressional Quarterly* noted that as recently as 1972, conservative groups contributed only $250,000 to candidates for federal office. Presently, direct mail solicitation is expected to provide millions of dollars in contributions to federal candidates, as well as to support campaign services.

Finally, Wolf pointed out how the New Right has been blessed with a political environment in which all the emotional issues are natural "conservative" issues that it has exploited with vigor and skill.

To round out the characterization of the New Right, a detailed consideration of several major organizations representative of the movement is in order. As examples, I have chosen the National Conservative Political Action Committee; two organiza-

tions that still exhibit some fealty to the Republican party—
Ronald Reagan's Citizens for the Republic and Philip Crane's
American Conservative Union; and two groups that indicate
more willingness to seek conservative followers and conservative candidates from both parties, or which in time could become the base of a third political party—Paul Weyrich's Committee for the Survival of a Free Congress and Howard Phillips'
Conservative Caucus, chaired by Meldrim Thomson Jr.

The National Conservative Political Action Committee was
established in March 1975. The chairman of NCPAC is John T.
Dolan, who served as the organization's executive director until
April 1977. In a prospectus of limited circulation Senator Jesse
A. Helms (R-N.C.) expressed its goals.

> The idea is to pool the resources of the best people we've got all across
> the country. Experts in campaign strategy, political polling, press rela-
> tions, voter registration drives, campaign management, etc. We're put-
> ting them all under one roof called the National Conservative Political
> Action Committee. Then, when it's really rolling, we can (a) coordinate
> the efforts of these specialists, and send them where they'll have the
> greatest impact, (b) help underwrite their expenses, and (c) use them to
> train youth and top campaign staff members. I'm personally convinced
> that this will be far more effective than simply throwing money at a cam-
> paign and hoping something happens.

Organized ostensibly to counter the AFL-CIO's Committee
on Political Education (COPE), NCPAC performs much the
same function for conservative candidates as COPE does for
prolabor candidates. It encourages conservative aspirants to
run, lines up supportive commitments from other political
groups and individuals, and refers campaign staff and consultants. NCPAC recruits, trains, and places campaign staffers and
has established a résumé collection service of conservative personnel.

NCPAC's 1978 regional training seminar, the Conservative
Campaign College, was held in Arlington, Virginia, over a four-
day period. What was significant was not only the breadth and
depth of the training, which embraced every facet of campaign
management, but the striking evidence of how New Right organizations operate as a mutually supporting network. Sponsors of
this NCPAC seminar included Morton Blackwell, Committee
for Responsible Youth Politics; John Buckley, Fund for a Con-

servative Majority; Gregg Hilton, Conservative Victory Fund; Andy Messing, American Conservative Union; Howard Phillips, Conservative National Committee; Ron Robinson, Young Americans for Freedom; Paul Weyrich, Committee for the Survival of a Free Congress; and John Snyder, Right to Bear Arms Political Victory Fund.

Most of NCPAC's funds are raised through direct mail solicitation carried out by Richard Viguerie companies. The Federal Election Commission files show that in 1975, NCPAC took in $443,370; in 1976, $2,561,921; and in 1977, $1,328,841. In contrast, the AFL-CIO's COPE collected only about a third as much in 1977, listing receipts of $458,323.

NCPAC also seems to be adhering to the goal Senator Helms set for it, that is, using much of the money for activities tangentially supportive of political campaigns. For example, of the $2.6 million raised in 1976, only $386,862 went to candidates, and in 1977, only $20,316 out of $1.3 million. The *Washington Post* of March 20, 1978, quoted Chairman Dolan as explaining the fund division in these words: "It was meant to be this way. We didn't raise it for candidates. We planned most of it to go to research, lobbying, surveys and other activities to build the conservative base."

In the 1976 congressional elections, NCPAC supported 150 candidates, among them 124 Republicans, twenty-one Democrats, two conservatives, one independent, one libertarian, and one affiliated with George Wallace. Of particular importance here was the NCPAC's crucial role in electing New Right candidates in three special congressional campaigns—including two to fill the vacancies resulting when Washington Congressman Brock Adams became Secretary of Transportation in the Carter Administration and Minnesota Congressman Bob Bergland became Secretary of Agriculture. NCPAC contributed $6,552 to help elect Arlan Stangeland* to Bergland's House seat and $9,000 to elect John E. "Jack" Cunningham to Adams' seat. In

---

* In the spring of 1978, Stangeland, identified as a former district director for the Conservative Caucus, was presented with a plaque by the caucus "for the work he did in arousing nationwide resistance to President Carter's proposal for election day voter registration" (Conservative Caucus Member's Report, June 1978).

its 1978 Annual Report, NCPAC said Stangeland, Cunningham, and the third successful candidate it backed, Louisiana Republican Robert L. Livingston, all credited the organization with making "the winning difference" in their campaigns. NCPAC called Cunningham's "a smashing NCPAC victory" and acknowledged that it had helped his campaign in other ways. For example, Merrill Jacobs, NCPAC director of research, was given a leave of absence to work as Cunningham's campaign coordinator, and the organization said it also referred a direct mail program to handle fund-raising and "introduced Jack Cunningham to other conservative groups and encouraged them to support his effort."

How Cunningham thanked the New Right for its help in electing him is recounted in chapter 5. It should be noted here, however, that it was legislation introduced by Cunningham that largely inspired thousands of Native Americans to conduct their "longest walk" protest in Washington in the summer of 1978. This legislation, the Native Americans Equal Opportunity Act, would, in effect, direct the President to abrogate all treaties entered into by the United States and Indian tribes.

In 1977, when NCPAC spent nearly a million dollars in staff time, in-kind service, and cash contributions to candidates and programs, the organization concentrated on helping to elect conservatives in state and local elections. NCPAC claimed its candidates were successful in eleven of fourteen races in New Jersey and in 62 percent of the contests in Kentucky.

The liberal Republican Ripon Society took the NCPAC to task, however, for supporting too many conservative Democrats in Virginia.

> NCPAC could write a primer on how to undermine the Republican party and anyone requiring enlightenment on NCPAC's political sagacity has only to look as far as NCPAC's role in its home state: Virginia. NCPAC and its Virginia offshoot, VCPAC, are truly bipartisan. In 1975, they supported a conservative Democrat against a conservative Republican for a State Senate seat from Alexandria. The Republican won. ("I think we support too many Republican candidates," NCPAC official Terry Dolan told *U.S. News & World Report* earlier this year, noting that about half the candidates it backed in Virginia were Democrats.)[21]

This would seem to be in violation of Ronald Reagan's eleventh commandment: Thou shalt not campaign against fellow Republicans. Indeed, it is the observance of this commandment that distinguishes Reagan's Citizens for the Republic from many other organizations in the New Right.

Formerly Citizens for Reagan, Citizens for the Republic (CFTR) was established under its new name early in 1977. Its purpose, according to Richard Viguerie's *New Right Report*, is "to concentrate on electing conservative Republicans. It will publish a hard-hitting twice-monthly newsletter which will go to contributors and to the press. They start with a bankroll of about $1,000,000, the best fundraising name around (Reagan), and the largest contributor list (183,000) of any conservative political action committee."

According to the *Democratic Congressional Campaign Committee Report* of January 1978,

> Citizens for Reagan raised about $18 million during the 1976 Presidential campaign. It received $5 million in taxpayer-financed federal matching funds. After the Presidential campaign, Citizens for Reagan had $1.6 million, most of which was the final payment the Citizens for Reagan Committee received from the Federal Election Commission in Presidential campaign matching funds. These funds were the starting balance for Citizens for the Republic, and the name was formally changed on January 31, 1977. Pursuant to the FEC ruling that a Presidential candidate is required to return to the United States Treasury an amount proportional to the public share of the overall unused campaign receipts, CFTR returned $611,141 to the Federal government in unused matching funds on November 28, 1977. According to its quarterly report ending September 30, 1977, CFTR had raised $664,205 and spent $790,785 in 1977 and had a cash balance of $1,434,205. It has raised most of its money from direct mail. During the first six months of operation, CFTR sent more than three quarter of a million pieces of mail from which it received more than $300,000 in contributions. . . . CFTR maintains a full-time staff of 13 persons and a monthly payroll of from $30,000 to $40,000. [Franklyn C.] Nofziger, as Executive Vice Chairman, receives $45,000 a year.

Reagan serves as chairman of CFTR, and Senator Paul D. Laxalt (R-Nev.) is chairman of the steering committee.

The *Democratic Congressional Campaign Committee Report* states that CFTR's bimonthly newsletter, sent to all twenty-five-dollar contributors and to the press, had a circulation of about 12,000 at the start of 1978. Reagan writes a feature article for each newsletter on issues ranging from the Panama Canal to the Occupational Safety and Health Administration (OSHA) to social security to changes in the election laws to the Allan Bakke case to the Humphrey-Hawkins full employment bill.

Like NCPAC, Citizens for the Republic also conducts regional seminars that have featured, besides Reagan, such speakers as Paul Laxalt, Jesse Helms, and Reagan's running mate in 1976, Senator Richard S. Schweiker (R-Pa.).

Reagan has maintained a heavy speaking schedule. Jack Germond and Jules Witcover, columnists for the *Washington Star*, have noted that Reagan's standard speaking fee is $5,000 but reported in their January 8, 1978 column that he no longer charges that fee for party fund-raisers. As the inheritor of much of the Goldwater legacy of the sixties, in 1976 Reagan came within an eyelash of taking the Republican nomination from an incumbent President, and there is every sign that he is reserving his options for making another run in 1980. Meanwhile, he is working hard to move the Republican party to the Right in order to accommodate his views and his candidacy.

Reagan's biggest political problem is his age; he will be seventy on March 11, 1981. Reports have appeared in the press about reservations some of his backers are having because of the age issue. Alert to this, and also to the possibility that Reagan may elect not to run in 1980, are several rising young stars from the New Right, not the least of whom is photogenic and personable Congressman Philip M. Crane (R-Ill.), chairman of the American Conservative Union.

Established in 1964, the American Conservative Union has taken on a more decidedly New Right cast in recent years under Crane's chairmanship and his reportedly close relationship with Viguerie. One indication is the leadership overlap from other New Right organizations. According to COPE, Alan M. Gotlieb, an ACU director, is also a director of the Committee to Defeat the Union Bosses' Candidates and is chairman of the Citizens Committee for the Right to Keep and Bear Arms. Phyllis Schlafly, another director of the ACU, chairs the Eagle Forum and is a director of STOP ERA. Still another director is John Buckley, chairman of the Young Americans for Freedom. A member of the ACU advisory assembly is Joseph Coors, president of Coors Brewery, sponsor of Heritage Foundation, and business adviser for the Committee for the Survival of a Free Congress.

COPE lists other leaders of the ACU: senators Edward Jacob "Jake" Garn, Orrin G. Hatch, Barry Goldwater, Jesse Helms, Paul Laxalt, Carl T. Curtis, and Robert J. Dole; and congressmen John M. Ashbrook, Lawrence P. "Larry" McDonald, and William L. Armstrong.

ACU, COPE says, functions as a coordinating body for the Right, providing research, publications, and policy papers to a wide variety of right-wing leaders and groups.

The Conservative Victory Fund, a political action committee connected with the ACU, raises and distributes money during election years.

The American Conservative Union reportedly helped finance Ferrol G. Barlow's Supreme Court challenge to OSHA and claimed a "great victory" when the court ruled that an employer can bar from a workplace a federal safety and health inspector who does not have a search warrant. Barlow is a leader of the John Birch Society in Pocatello, Idaho.

The ACU also established a task force, headed by Orrin Hatch of Utah, to defeat labor law reform in 1978. Hatch's filibuster efforts succeeded in blocking passage and forced the measure back to committee.

ACU publishes *Battle Line*, a monthly magazine; *Public Monitor Report*, a bimonthly report for "taxpayers and businessmen" on government regulations; and issue analyses. It also conducts a yearly conference in Washington to help coordinate the activities of New Right and Old Right groups.*

Chairman Philip Crane, forty-seven, the son of a physician turned conservative newspaper columnist, a former university professor, author of three books—the latest *Surrender in Panama*—is considered certain to win reelection to his House seat in 1978.

But Crane has much higher political aspirations. In August 1978 he became the first announced candidate for the Presidency, challenging Ronald Reagan's presumptions of solid conservative support for the Republican nomination in 1980. Crane's frequent trips to New Hampshire in the spring and

* The ACU's role in the campaign against the Panama Canal treaties is detailed in a later chapter, as is its most recently launched campaign against SALT II.

summer of 1978 seemed designed to lay the groundwork for a campaign in the nation's first Presidential primary of 1980.*

This examination of organizations representative of the New Right would be incomplete without a consideration of the Committee for the Survival of a Free Congress (commonly considered the right-wing counterpart of the twenty-nine-year-old National Committee for an Effective Congress) and of the Conservative Caucus, the right-wing's response to Common Cause.

In an article published in June of 1975, the *Washington Star* described Paul Weyrich, director of the Committee for the Survival of a Free Congress, as a New Right leader whom Richard Viguerie admires. For his part, the *Star* reported, Weyrich "does not beat around the bush about differences between traditional conservatives and the 'new right' emerging around Viguerie."

The *Star* quoted Weyrich to this effect: "I sat in meetings with these guys [the traditional conservatives] for years. They would come up with actually brilliant ideas. Then the question would come up, 'What should we do about it?' And then nobody would seem to know." Weyrich views the New Right as the conservative element that knows what to "do about it" and can get it done.

> We are different from previous generations of conservatives. We are no longer working to preserve the status quo. We are radicals, working to overturn the present power structure in this country. . . . Our enemies are not encroaching socialists [who are] taking away what's there. They have already succeeded. We are not in power, *they* are.[22]

Weyrich, former president of Heritage Foundation and one-time aide to Senator Carl Curtis (R-Neb.) and to former Senator Gordon Allott (R-Colo.), says the 1978 Senate race in Colorado

---

* Crane, whom William Loeb calls his favorite young Republican, nevertheless was chastised by the publisher. Loeb said Crane's candidacy would divide the conservative vote in the New Hampshire Presidential primary and thus make it possible for a moderate Republican like Senator Howard Baker or George Bush to win that primary. Loeb suggested that Ronald Reagan should announce that if he is nominated and elected in 1980 he will serve only one term (because of his age) and that Reagan should make Crane his 1980 running mate.

is "the number one interest in the country" for his group. It happens that Floyd K. Haskell, the Democrat who defeated Allott in 1972, is up for reelection.

After directing a volunteer force of congressional staffers in several congressional elections, Weyrich put together his plan for the Committee for the Survival of a Free Congress, established it in July of 1974, and took the concept to Senator Curtis. In a fund-raising letter of early May 1975 Curtis reported that

> in less than 120 days before the 1974 elections, CSFC raised and distributed $194,000 to 71 conservative Congressional candidates in 37 states, many of whom would have lost to liberals and labor unions without CSFC emergency help. . . . If we don't act now, liberal pro-union legislation could severely cripple our free enterprise system. Your contribution is needed now to help save our country from this liberal threat.[23]

The present chairman of CSFC is Addah Jane Hurst of Arlington, Virginia. Eli Howell is vice-chairman; Dr. George Hajjar, secretary; Dr. Charles Moser, treasurer; David W. Troxler, assistant director. The organization's board of advisers lists some of the most conservative members of Congress, including Republican senators Clifford P. Hansen of Wyoming, Jesse Helms of North Carolina, James A. McClure of Idaho, Orrin Hatch of Utah, Paul Laxalt of Nevada, and William K. Scott of Virginia; and representatives Robert K. Dornan of California, Mickey Edwards of Oklahoma, Trent Lott of Mississippi, Dan Marriott of Utah, and Larry McDonald of Georgia, the last a National Council member of the John Birch Society.[24] Its business advisory committee includes such ultraconservatives as Joseph Coors of the Coors brewing family of Golden, Colorado. Coors, who gives financial backing to several conservative organizations, reportedly provided the start-up money for Weyrich's CSFC, just as he did for the Heritage Foundation, which Weyrich earlier served as president.[25]

According to the December 1977 *Democratic Congressional Campaign Committee Report,*

> CFSC relies on the majority of its contributions through direct mail efforts. For direct mail printing, postage and mailing, it has expended over half its total receipts for 1977, the majority of accounts which are contracted through firms owned by Richard A. Viguerie. . . . FEC records indicate that the Committee received $421,248 in 1974; $586,802 in 1975; $1,688,533 in 1976; and $757,559 as of October 31, 1977. Expendi-

tures for those three years were $381,354 in 1974; $525,129 in 1975; $1,738,498 in 1976; and $736,466 as of October 31, 1977.

The *National Journal* of April 8, 1978 reported that

the Committee for the Survival of a Free Congress will contribute about $400,000 to candidates this year, according to Paul Weyrich, its director. The group has a $1.2 million budget and spends much of the rest on strategy sessions, lobbying and direct mail. Most of the campaign money will go for services rather than for direct cash contributions because "we find this has a greater influence on the direction of the campaign," Weyrich said. About 80 percent of the $400,000 will go to Republicans and nearly all of that to challengers. (The National Committee for an Effective Congress, which supports liberal candidates, hopes to raise about $1 million this year. About three-fourths will go directly to candidates.)

Weyrich early on established how CSFC's money would be distributed. In a *Conservative Digest* interview in August 1974 he said, "We are attempting to work with local people to recruit conservatives, to go into primaries where necessary, and to elect them. But not just to give them money. We give them expertise, tools with which they can be elected."

In its promotional material, CSFC emphasizes that its contribution to conservative candidates is more than financial. It offers to determine which liberal candidates are vulnerable and whether any conservative candidates have announced. If no conservatives have announced, CSFC will try to recruit such candidates. When candidates who seek CSFC's blessing and support have been personally interviewed and selected for support, they must attend a three-day training seminar to learn a prescribed precinct organization method. Candidates for the House must adopt this method before they can get any funds from CSFC.[26]

The CSFC declares itself willing and able to back conservative Democrats and conservative independents as well as conservative Republicans. But in the 122 congressional races where CSFC involved itself in 1976, the organization backed 105 Republicans and only fifteen Democrats and one conservative.

One of CSFC's functions is to prepare a target list of incumbent liberals it deems necessary to defeat and/or vulnerable. This list is compiled by matching the incumbent's voting record against the CSFC's standards of true conservatism. Ratings range from "staunch conservative" to "radical"—here used in a pejorative sense.

For the 1978 congressional election year, CSFC had identified 137 House members as "radical" and had targeted thirty-five of these for defeat. Among them were such prominent Democratic names as Morris K. Udall, Patricia S. Schroeder, Claude D. Pepper, Abner J. Mikva, John Brademas, Robert F. Drinan, Helen S. Meyner, Thomas J. Downey, Joseph L. Fisher, Mike McCormack, Thomas S. Foley, and Les Aspin.

According to the *Democratic Congressional Campaign Committee Report* on CSFC, the thirty-five targeted liberals were chosen on the basis of five votes that CSFC considered to be classical liberal-conservative confrontations.

—Roll Call No. 98, March 23, 1977. Common-site Picketing. Passage of the bill to permit a labor union with a grievance with one contractor to picket all contractors on the same construction site and to establish a construction industry collective bargaining committee.

—Roll Call No. 265, May 18, 1977. Hatch Act amendments. Ashbrook (R-Ohio) amendment to prohibit a federal employee organization from coercing, threatening, or intimidating its workers into participating in any form of political activity and to prohibit the organization from using dues or fees for political purposes.

—Roll Call No. 317, June 7, 1977. Hatch Act amendments. Kindness (R-Ohio) amendment to add language to define the term extortion as an attempt to obtain property from another person by the use of threatened force or fear with reference to labor.

—Roll Call No. 365, June 22, 1977. Foreign Assistance Appropriations for Fiscal 1978. Young (R-Fla.) amendment to prohibit the use of any funds contained in the bill for direct or indirect assistance to Uganda, Cambodia, Laos, or Vietnam.

—Roll Call No. 384, June 27, 1977. Legal Services Corporation Act. McDonald (D-Ga.) amendment to prohibit legal assistance in cases arising out of disputes or controversies on the issue of homosexuality or gay rights.

CSFC considered a "No" vote on common-site picketing and a "Yes" vote on the other four items to be the proper votes.

The Ashbrook amendment to the Hatch Act, the Young

amendment to the Foreign Assistance Appropriations bill, and the McDonald amendment to the Legal Services Corporation Act were all agreed to by the full House, which rejected the common-site picketing bill and the Kindness amendment to the Hatch Act. Thus, the CSFC position prevailed on four of the five measures.

If Richard Viguerie likes Paul Weyrich and his Committee for the Survival of a Free Congress, he is ecstatic about the Conservative Caucus and its leadership—and with reason. National Director Howard Phillips and its national chairman, New Hampshire's Governor Meldrim Thomson Jr., talk Viguerie's language.

One day in 1958, shortly after completing high school, Phillips picked up the phone, dialed the local Republican organization, and said, "Hello, I think I'm a Republican.* What can I do to get active?" According to a profile in the *Washington Star* of June 24, 1975, Phillips is the son of an insurance broker in Ward 22, a working-class neighborhood in Boston. His parents were New Deal Democrats. "But his grandfather," the *Star* said, "was a Russian immigrant, who started out as a taxi driver, driving the Cabots and the Lodges around Beacon Hill, was an intensely patriotic man who had instilled in his grandson a strong feeling of self-determination, patriotism, a willingness to work for a cause."

At Harvard, Phillips rose to the presidency of the student council and helped found Young Americans for Freedom, the group organized by conservative columnist William F. Buckley in 1960 as a counterforce to Left-liberal youth movements. He grew tired of the YAF, saying, "After a while the internal disputes within that organization led me to think it had ceased to be an instrument of change. I got tired of going to meetings where conservatives fought one another."

Phillips became a strong supporter of Richard Nixon, and when the Californian became President, Phillips was chosen to

---

* Phillips still exhibits either uncertainty or cynicism about his political identity. In the spring of 1978 he changed his registration in Massachusetts so that he could seek the Democratic nomination for the U.S. Senate seat held by Republican Edward Brooke. In the September primary Phillips ran fourth in a field of five candidates.

dismantle the Office of Economic Opportunity, a Great Society antipoverty program that had long been a favorite target of conservatives. He gave it every effort, but the Congress refused to let him complete the demolition job. Later Phillips called the experience "radicalizing." He claimed that big business did not help him, contending that it was interested in funding even the most hokey poverty groups as long as the cities were quiet during the summer.

Frustrated, Phillips left OEO in 1973 but kept it a prime target after he joined the American Conservative Union as a "public monitor." The record is not clear on why Phillips elected to leave the American Conservative Union, then the largest of the New Right political activist groups, in July of 1974, but shortly thereafter he took up the task of organizing what is now the Conservative Caucus, a group that nearly matched the ACU's membership (in '75) less than a year after it was founded.

It seems the idea for the Conservative Caucus was first raised by conservative Republican Jesse Helms. Helms, said the *Washington Star,* "apparently misread a May 1974 poll taken by the Gallup organization." John Carbaugh, an aide to Helms, recalls the senator's reaction. "He just sat down and looked at the poll and said to himself, 'conservatives are fools.'"

The poll that so intrigued Helms said that while most people would prefer the traditional Republican and Democratic party labels, when they were asked to say whether they were conservative or liberal, 36 percent said they would choose the conservative label, 26 percent said liberal, and 36 percent said they were undecided. Helms then fastened on Gallup's breakdown of the undecideds and jumped to a conclusion that was later challenged.

Gallup proportioned the undecided in a way that reflected the 36-to-26 ratio of those who chose to label themselves. But in a speech Helms delivered he said that when Gallup then

> asked the undecideds to choose—*forced* them to choose between conservative and liberal party labels, the overall breakdown of all respondents rose to 59 percent conservative and 41 percent liberal. . . . Imagine that. This year, 1974, the conservative percentage is the highest ever, at 59 percent! Even after Watergate, and I believe because of the anti-conservative campaign of the media, the people are more conservative than ever before.

Calling this the "real political news story of the year," Helms castigated the press for ignoring it.

"One reason the press may have overlooked it," the *Washington Star* noted, "is that it is a spurious number." Asked about the 59 percent speech, George Gallup Jr., president of the polling group, said, "That's clearly not the situation. He [Helms] obviously neglected to put in that we arrived at that in terms of a ratio. We could never *force* undecideds to make a choice."

But the Gallup disclaimer notwithstanding, the 59-percent claim gained a life of its own, was repeated in speeches throughout the country, and was widely publicized in conservative publications. It lent validity and impetus to Phillips' promotion of the Conservative Caucus.

Nevertheless, it took two more actions to move the idea for the Conservative Caucus past step one; both occurred in November 1974. Phillips first persuaded Governor Meldrim Thomson Jr. to accept the national chairmanship of the movement and then flew around the country recruiting state chairpersons.

> But lightning didn't strike until Nov. 6, when Richard A. Viguerie . . . sent out the first of more than 2 million letters soliciting caucus membership contributions, using lists of known conservative sympathizers.*
>
> Phillips had office space [rented] from Viguerie and a list of 11,200 names, provided by Viguerie. . . . Viguerie says he has advanced at least $100,000 worth of services to Phillips to "front end" the operation. "It's a business where you are not afraid to pay $12 to get a $10 contribution," says Phillips, "because the rule of thumb is you'll get at least seven times that much back from him in future contributions." Phillips says he has been awed by the response. "There's no doubt about it," he told a reporter, "Viguerie really is the godfather."[27]

There was reason for Phillips' awe. He told the *Star* that the direct mail appeal sent out through Viguerie's network brought in more than a half million dollars from nearly 40,000 new members in less than eight months. By mid-1978 membership in the

---

* This was the letter quoted in chapter 3, which asked if the recipient was sick and tired of liberal politicians who force children to be bused, appoint judges who turn murderers and rapists loose on the public, force children to study from school books that are anti-God, anti-American, and filled with the most vulgar curse words, and so on.

Conservative Caucus was believed to have risen as high as 300,-
000, thereby equaling or even surpassing the American Conservative Union and making it the fastest growing and perhaps
the largest of the New Right grass-roots lobbying organizations.

In addition to Chairman Meldrim Thomson Jr. and National
Director Howard Phillips, the Conservative Caucus, as of Au-
gust 1977, listed the following trustees on its letterhead: J. Alan
McKay, Lawrence J. Straw Jr., Peter J. Thomas, and Lyle Ryter.
Like Phillips, McKay and Straw came out of the Massachusetts
branch of Young Americans for Freedom.

Besides the workhorses in the organization, the Conservative
Caucus needed names. To get them, the caucus stole a march on
the Republican National Committee by organizing its own
shadow cabinet early in 1977, designating Chairman Thomson
as "Secretary of State" and stacking other "cabinet" posts with
some noted ultraconservatives. In its February 28, 1977 issue,
Group Research Report reviewed the selections. "The Conservative Caucus has announced a 'shadow cabinet' to counter
the Carter cabinet and seek public exposure for the conservative point of view. In doing so, the right-wingers who lean toward a third party jumped ahead of the orthodox Republicans,
such as John Connally of Texas, who has advocated such a
ploy."

The first year of its existence, the shadow cabinet was chaired
by "Attorney General" William Rusher, publisher of *National
Review* and one of the leaders of the 1976 explorations of a third
party for conservatives. When the Caucus announced its
shadow cabinet for 1978, however, Rusher was gone from the
roster; the attorney general's position had not been filled.

The new shadow cabinet listed Meldrim Thomson as "Secre-
tary of State"; Hans Sennholz as "chairman of the Council of
Economic Advisers"; Richard A. Viguerie as "Secretary of Com-
merce"; California State Senator H.L. "Bill" Richardson as
"Secretary of the Interior"; Carl Curtis as "Secretary of the
Treasury"; Larry McDonald as "Secretary of Defense"; Dr.
Howard Hurwitz, former superintendent of Long Island City
High School, as "Secretary of Health, Education and Welfare";
Texas State Representative Clay Smothers as "Secretary of
Labor"; Barbara Keating as "Secretary of Housing and Urban
Development"; Representative Steven Symms (R-Idaho) as

"Secretary of Agriculture"; former Texas Congressman Ron Paul as "Secretary of Energy"; Robert K. Dornan as "U.S. Ambassador to the United Nations"; Lt. Gen. Daniel O. Graham (USA-ret.) as "director of the Central Intelligence Agency."

Something can be learned about the interlocking relationships among New Right organizations and leaders by noting the organizational ties of some shadow cabinet members.

—Viguerie, of course, is called "godfather" of the New Right;

—Barbara Keating, unsuccessful candidate for the Senate in New York on the conservative ticket in 1974, is a member of the board of directors of the American Conservative Union and chairs the Consumer Alert Council. The latter reportedly raises money to end "unneeded regulation" by government "which denies the public its inherent right to free choice."

—H.L. "Bill" Richardson is chairman of Gun Owners of America, a Viguerie-served organization ostensibly dedicated to electing politicians who oppose any form of gun control.

—Daniel O. Graham, former director of the U.S. Defense Intelligence Agency, was listed as co-chairman of the Organizing Committee of the Emergency Coalition Against Unilateral Disarmament in full-page newspaper ads that appeared on February 22, 1977, the day before Paul C. Warnke came before the Senate Armed Services Committee. Graham's Organizing Committee spearheaded opposition to Warnke's nomination as U.S. Arms Control and Disarmament Agency director. John M. Fisher, president of the American Security Council—a conservative organization that has been called the "voice of the military-industrial complex"—was listed as Graham's co-chairman.

—Congressman Larry McDonald has been identified as a Birch Council member by *Group Research Report*.

—Hans Sennholz was identified by *Group Research Report* as "a professor of economics at Grove City College, who, for about nine years, was editor and speaker for the John Birch Society."

Further evidence of the linkage in the mutually supportive New Right network is found in the list of the Citizens Cabinet Organizing Committee members who participated in the cabinet selection. In addition to Howard Phillips, that list included Edwin Feulner, president of the Heritage Foundation, the Joseph Coors-funded conservative think tank; Morton Blackwell, chairman of the Viguerie-served Committee for Responsible Youth Politics and editor of Viguerie's magazine, *Conservative Digest;* Paul Weyrich, director of the Committee for the Survival of a Free Congress; Richard Dingman, director of the House Republican Study Committee; Representative Bob Stamp (D-Ariz.); Fran Watson, head of Conservative Democrats of America and of Citizens for Judicial Restraint; Joseph Coors; and Louisiana State Representative Louis "Woody" Jenkins, president of the American Legislative Exchange Council, an organization dedicated to electing conservative legislators and lobbying for conservative legislation.

A *Citizens Guide to the Right Wing*, published and distributed by Americans for Democratic Action in the spring of 1978, features an exhaustive analysis of New Right organizations and leaders and their ties to Richard Viguerie's operations. This linkage has prompted some observers to conclude that the primary purpose of the New Right political apparatus is to create a third political party. They have noted that the New Right groups (1) often capitalize on the same issues and support the same candidates when their by-laws allow candidate support; (2) that at times they assist one another in fund-raising; (3) that leaders serve on more than one organization board; (4) that many owe their existence and continued operation to Richard Viguerie.

Observers have noted, too, that Viguerie once offered himself to the American Independent party as a Vice-Presidential candidate. He withdrew after AIP nominated Lester Maddox for the Presidency.

ADA's *Citizens Guide to the Right Wing* made this comment on Viguerie and the AIP:

> Viguerie's attempt to seize the AIP ticket in 1976 was no frivolous or ego-inflating interlude. It was part of a long-range plan to draw conservatives away from the Republican party, destroy that party, and create a "new majority" of alienated blue-collar workers, urban ethnics and right-wingers. "I get up in the morning and that's my goal until the sun sets," says Viguerie. "I don't believe in my lifetime you will ever again be able to successfully market the word Republican. You could as easily sell the Edsel or Typhoid Mary. The Republican party is like a disabled tank on the bridge impeding the troops from crossing to the other side. You've got to take that tank and throw it in the river."[28]

Speculation about the New Right's alleged determination to form a third political party appears to focus on the Conservative

Caucus as the primary vehicle for accomplishing this goal. Observers have cited the philosophical similarities—as expressed in their respective platforms—between the caucus and the National Organization of State Conservative Parties, a coalition established, according to one of its mailings, to bring the respective state organizations together "under the banner of a single, new, national party."

The "planks" in the Conservative Caucus "platform" are the Right to Enjoy the Income from One's Own Labor, the Right to Religious Liberty, the Right to Life, the Right to National Sovereignty, the Right to Economic Justice, the Right to Be Individually Judged, the Right to Political and Economic Liberty, and the Right to Self-government.

Whether the speculation about third-party aspirations of the New Right is accurate remains to be seen. There is abundant evidence, however, to indicate that some New Right leaders are restive under the banner of the GOP. For example, the national chairman of the Conservative Caucus, Meldrim Thomson, has not been steadfast in his loyalty to the Republican party. When he lost the GOP nomination for governor in 1970, he bolted the party and ran as a third-party candidate.

It must be said for Howard Phillips that, from the outset, he has made no secret of his goals for the Conservative Caucus. Alan L. Otten, writing in the *Wall Street Journal* for May 29, 1975, said Phillips told him his goal was to construct "reinforcing coalitions" to build the local caucuses from men and women already organized behind specific causes which they care deeply about, for example, people fighting busing or gun control, Equal Rights Amendment, easy abortion, amnesty, liberal textbooks.

Otten quoted Phillips, in part: "Right now it's easier for a Congressman to vote liberal than conservative. The teachers or labor unions or big business firms that will benefit from a program keep very close tabs, and if he doesn't vote their way, he hears about it. . . . We want to make it at least as painful for him to vote for it as to vote against it."

Later in the interview Otten learned how Phillips felt about the Republican party as the vehicle for conservatism. He described Phillips as feeling that "the Republican Party just won't do."

In the June 1975 *Washington Star* article referred to earlier,

Phillips is described as the one who tried to dismantle OEO but who "is now after bigger game. He is trying to abolish the Republican party."

One Conservative Caucus membership mailing characterized Phillips in these words:

> For more than 14 years, Howard Phillips has fought uncontrolled power in the hands of bureaucrats, special interests, and the liberal media. In 1973, as acting Director of the U.S. Office of Economic Opportunity, he led a courageous fight to stop Federal funding for forced busing, "welfare rights," abortion on demand, quotas for jobs and schooling, and all the other liberal causes which the American taxpayer is required to subsidize.

Today Phillips not only serves as national director of the Conservative Caucus, but also serves as president of the Conservative Caucus Research, Analysis and Education Foundation and as chairman of the Conservative National Committee.

The CC Foundation, like the Conservative Caucus itself, is headquartered at Richard Viguerie's central address—7777 Leesburg Pike, Falls Church, Virginia—and calls itself "a nonprofit, non-partisan, tax deductible organization working to prepare and widely disseminate at the constituency level information concerning the Federal operations and policies authorized and proposed by members of Congress."

Some might question the "non-partisan" nature of the foundation after reading the phrasing of certain questions put to a mailing list of potential contributors. Respondents were asked to rate:

> —President Carter's relationship with Big Labor.
> —How you feel about the Administration's efforts to cut our ties with Taiwan, while cozying up to Red China.
> —Whether you think Carter's plan for increased socialization of medicine makes sense.

Trustees of the foundation feature some familiar names. Representative Louis Jenkins, for example, is secretary and one of the trustees is William Rusher.

Phillips' Conservative National Committee, with offices listed at 1721 DeSales Street in Washington, has a separate purpose: to raise funds for conservative candidates. An October 1, 1977 mailing said the committee had set a goal of $175,000 to be raised by October 25, with some of the money to be used for conservatives in the November elections of that year and some to be used for conservatives running in primary elections in 1978. Again, the trustees of this organization are familiar New Right names: among them John T. Dolan, Louis Jenkins, and Paul Weyrich.

The key to Phillips' strategy for the Conservative Caucus can be found in these paragraphs from an essay he wrote (and copyrighted in November 1977) titled "The Crisis of Accountability and Its Cure":

> By penetrating pre-existing circles of influence and identifying key contacts therein, conservatives can multiply their influence times the resources of those whom they persuade to join with them.
>
> Conservative issue groups (e.g. single purpose organizations set up to fight busing, promote textbook reform, cut taxes, or what have you) exist in almost every major community.
>
> Influence can also be increased by mobilizing occupational interests affected by Congressional action (there are more than one thousand realtors in the average Congressional district, hundreds of law enforcement personnel, doctors, and so forth). Institutions (whether factory, university, Rotary Club, VFW post, or barbershop) can be searched for like-minded persons of leadership potential.
>
> Issues, interests and institutions are all fertile sources for conservative recruitment. Political movements thrive on discontent.

His attitude that this strategy will prevail is expressed in these two lines from a June 30, 1977 mailing of the Conservative Caucus: "Our job is not merely to slow down socialism, but to fulfill an alternative vision of America's future. Start thinking about what we should be doing *when we take power*" (emphasis mine).

His confidence conceivably stems not only from the growth in Conservative Caucus membership, but from the unified and closely meshed efforts of the entire New Right apparatus. This unity and singleness of purpose was not, however, present from the beginning of the movement. Articles about the New Right written in 1975 speculated on whether the movement would focus around George Wallace. The *Washington Star*'s analysis followed that pattern.

> There is still considerable debate over whether Wallace would be the best leader for the new party, but he has certainly become the conservatives' weather vane, pointing the way to the new masses they will have to enroll to emerge as a majority. It is the little guy, the blue-collar

worker, who—according to the polls—is becoming alienated from the
old "New Deal" Democratic coalition and now seems to be drifting in a
kind of limbo between old trade union rhetoric and the new Wallace
populism. Conservatives are out to exploit this limbo. Phillips is a good
example of the change. He has enjoyed traditional conservative creden-
tials that rival the Buckleys'. He has supported big corporations and
global enterprise with the leading rhetoricians of the Nixon Administration. He still wears his pin-stripe suits, but now he identifies with the
little guy. "I think George Wallace has a very good ear for political feeling in the country."

Before Wallace's candidacy collapsed in 1976, the New
Right's tactics and its tilt toward the Alabaman were reportedly
disturbing some members of the American Conservative Union
and of Young Americans for Freedom. Both organizations, the
Washington Star reported, were "split down the middle" over
the impact of Wallace, Viguerie, and "the New Right." The *Star*
went on to say that

> many of the "New Right" opponents are libertarians, men who see Wal-
> lace as an authoritarian figure who would use government to repress
> those who disagree with him on social issues. Others, so-called "fiscal
> conservatives," could not co-exist with blue-collar workers because they
> disagree with laws protecting labor unions, Social Security, unemploy-
> ment compensation, Federal health insurance, and other programs that
> the blue-collar voters are likely to cling to.

Still another element reportedly was concerned about the possible stigma of racism and anti-intellectualism.

There was also evidence in 1975 that there was some organizational jealousy at work. The *Star* noted that "the American
Conservative Union was once by far the largest, most powerful
conservative organization, with over 40,000 members. Now it is
rivaled by Phillips' Conservative Caucus. The ACU's Congressional campaign fund-raising unit, the Conservative Victory
Fund, is mirrored by Weyrich's group."

The *Star* quoted Tom Winter, editor of the conservative
weekly *Human Events* and vice-chairman of the American Conservative Union: "The general feeling of ACU's board is that
Conservative Caucus is duplicative of ACU's programs. ACU
has been working for years to set up state organizations and continues to do so." The article later referred to Arthur Finklestein,
described as the favorite pollster used by conservative candidates, and noted that Finklestein believed "the assault by Vi-

guerie and his allies could not split the conservatives away from the Republican party. Conservatives, Finklestein told a recent meeting of the Florida branch of the American Conservative Union, are strongly attached to their traditional institutions. 'They identify with Ford as a conservative.'"

By 1978, however, there were few signs of internal friction in the New Right. Under Phil Crane's chairmanship, the American Conservative Union was enjoying the same remarkable surge in membership as the Conservative Caucus. *Newsweek* of June 5, 1978 reported that the ACU's membership was up to 300,000. Moreover, Crane seemingly had brought the ACU into a closer relationship with the Viguerie organizations.

So compatible had the various group leaders become that *The New York Times* was able to say of them: "Over cocktails and, sometimes, dinner, they map nationwide campaigns against busing, racial quotas, publicly funded abortions, homosexual rights and other things that they believe are contributing to the disintegration of the American family and way of life."[29]

This much seems certain: Although the right-wing movement of today is much more pragmatic than it was in 1964, it is not a whit less committed to extremist views. Thus far it has avoided the kamikaze strategy of the Goldwater campaign. It confines its shrillness and stridency to direct communication with the true believers, while appearing much more restrained in the public arena. Moreover, it has learned well the importance of tightly knit organization and the efficient focusing of effort and money. Beyond this, of course, it has available computerized direct mailing for soliciting support and contributions. Such a service did not exist in 1964.

The New York Times reported that total fund-raising by the right wing in 1977 came to between $25 million and $30 million, of which more than $3.5 million was raised by conservative political action committees for electoral purposes.[30] This made possible the mailing of millions of pieces of direct mail to congressional offices opposing such Carter proposals as the nomination of Paul Warnke to be chief arms negotiator, the Universal Voter Registration Proposal, labor law reform, the Panama Canal treaties, and other issues.

The New Right's program for 1978 was even more ambitious, targeting the election of archconservatives to the Senate, the

House, and to state and local office; the defeat of many progressive Democrats; and the stimulation of millions of pieces of congressional mail on such points of debate as SALT II, taxes, and welfare reform.

Looking two years ahead, William Lanouette, writing in the *National Journal*, considered another New Right goal: "The acquisition of such tight control over the Republican Party that the party's 1980 Presidential nominee will have to come from the extreme conservative wing of the Republican Party, a prospect which seems increasingly likely at this early date."[31]

That nominee could be Ronald Reagan. It could be Philip Crane. Or it could be one of the other rising young stars of the New Right—Orrin Hatch of Utah, who defeated veteran consumer advocate Senator Frank Moss in 1976 and who led the Senate fight against labor law reform; or Congressman Jack Kemp (R-N.Y.), former pro football star and sponsor in the House of the bill to cut federal income tax rates by 30 percent, on the assumption that the resulting stimulus to the economy will result in no loss in tax revenue.

Hatch's victory was considered one of Richard Viguerie's biggest successes that year.

> In his race against Senator Moss, Hatch was the recipient of the valuable Washington-honed technical and financial assistance from five groups affiliated with Richard Viguerie. In the general election campaign alone, the Committee for the Survival of a Free Congress, the National Conservative Political Action Committee, the Committee for Responsible Youth Politics, the Employees Right to Work Committee, and the Public Service Political Action Committee collectively gave $22,000 to Hatch's campaign. Hatch also received thousands of dollars from such other right-wing groups as the Conservative Victory Fund, the Free Enterprise Political Action Committee, and the Young Americans Campaign Committee. Ultra-right fat cat Joseph Coors and his political action committee donated $6,000 to the Hatch race.[32]

Group Research Report of February 28, 1978 described Jack Kemp as

> an up and coming member of the conservative Congressmen who are active in causes. In 1965—five years before he was elected to Congress—Kemp was a member of the Executive Committee of District Speakers, Inc., a network organized by the late oil billionaire and ultra-conservative propagandist, H.L. Hunt, "to alert and activate those who can speak

or learn to speak fluently in the cause of preserving the freedom and sovereignty of our nation."

Kemp, the *Report* said, has appeared on programs of the Young Americans for Freedom and "in 1972 boasted that he owned a copy of every selection of the Conservative Book Club."

It should be evident, then, that the New Right will not be without a candidate for President in 1980, even if Ronald Reagan elects not to run.

CHAPTER 5

Tactics and Techniques

*Those who do not care for our cause we don't
expect to enter our ranks in any case.*
—Barry Goldwater
1964 Republican
National Convention

*Most conservatives have always run on the theory
that you should maximize the good
areas . . . and don't split your time by
campaigning in the bad, strongly Democratic
areas. We're opposed to that kind of thinking. We
think no area, black, labor, etc., should be
ignored.*
—Paul Weyrich
National Director,
Committee for the
Survival of a Free
Congress

We have to break down their [labor's] assumption
that conservatism equals Republicanism, and
Republicanism equals big business.
—HOWARD PHILLIPS
National Director,
Conservative Caucus

The reality is that the labor movement and the
women's movement are embattled against a
common enemy. If any rank and file union
members fall for the Radical Right's overtures,
they will inevitably find themselves the victims of
one of the oldest con games in the world, "bait
and switch"; the bait may be one of the so-called
"life-style" issues, but the switch will unfold on a
bread and butter issue.
—National NOW Times,
June 1978

If any one event served to draw the distinction between the New Right and the Goldwater Right of the 1960s, that event occurred on February 4, 1978, in Youngstown, Ohio. What took place that day clearly demonstrated how the two movements differ in character, strategy, and tactics . . . and why a union official was to tell columnist Jack Anderson later, "We are very concerned about the New Right's political effectiveness and sophistication. . . . They have more money, they're more intelligent in the approach to our people, and they have a better degree of organization than any right-wing organization that we've seen before."

On that winter day in 1978 seven leaders of the New Right attended a confidential meeting, organized by Philip Crane, with five union leaders representing steelworkers, building trades, and carpenter locals. In Crane's words,

our paramount motive for the meeting was to learn from them—to determine what they saw as the major factors behind the recent closing of the Youngstown Sheet and Tube plant with the consequent loss of 4,000 jobs. We also wanted to explore the possibility that we might have more in common with labor than we realize—especially on economic issues. . . .

The analysis of the union leaders as to the reasons behind the closing of Youngstown Sheet and Tube brought up some amazing similarities between their views and those of any card-carrying conservative. They spoke of injury to the investment climate because of our country's tax laws; of the inability to absorb mounting production costs imposed by government regulations; of the unfair trading practices of some of our nation's foreign competitors; of the lack of a coherent energy policy designed to provide abundant resources; and of inflation dictated by uncontrollable deficit spending. In short, they articulated the very concerns shared and articulated by conservatives in Congress.[1]

Joining Crane in that meeting were Richard Viguerie, the direct mail linchpin of the New Right; Howard Phillips, national director of the Conservative Caucus; Paul Weyrich, national director of the Committee for the Survival of a Free Congress; and Texas Republican Committeeman Ernest Angelo, Massachusetts Republican Chairman Gordon Nelson, and Representative Mickey Edwards (R-Okla.)

Accounts of the meeting that appeared in the *Washington Post* and in other publications produced these revealing comments to the press from the New Right participants:

According to the *Post,* Crane expressed confidence

that the New Right has the money, the expertise, and the issues to put to use the discontent and restlessness of a potential union constituency that feels betrayed by both the Democratic and the Republican parties. This place is one of the first warning bells of the death of the American dream, unless somebody does something. What's plaguing Youngstown is plaguing Johnstown, Gary, Buffalo, and many other cities. Why shouldn't we, as conservatives, appeal to people in these kinds of straits?

Congressman Edwards: "What they [the labor union officials] talked about was jobs—tariffs, trade agreements, protectionism and environmental laws that hurt industry. The fact that they are basically conservative doesn't surprise me."

Weyrich said the New Right leaders at the meeting dissociated themselves from the Old Guard Republican Establishment and concentrated on gut issues. "It nearly blew my mind," he said. "I've never heard anyone in the New Right movement talk as harshly about environmental law as these guys [the union officials] did."

Phillips said he had urged other New Right leaders "to avoid treating unionists as one-dimensional people" and advised capitalizing on such issues as gun control and abortion.

The Youngstown meeting clearly pointed up differences between the substance, strategy, and tactics of the New Right and those of the Goldwater movement.

As indicated by the quote from Goldwater's acceptance speech cited at the beginning of this chapter, the Goldwater movement adopted a defiant "take it or leave it" approach to politics that delighted the true believers but circumscribed its constituency.

By going to labor union officials the New Right showed its willingness to woo every group of Americans.

A second difference is evident in the New Right's deliberate attempt to shed the elitist stigma of conservatism. While Goldwater's core support came from middle- and upper-class ultraconservatives, including well-educated John Birch Society members, the New Right senses there is untapped ultraconservative sentiment among blue-collar workers.

Moreover, the anti-big bank and anti-big business feeling expressed by New Right leaders is not necessarily feigned to win labor support. It stems from the movement's inherent right-wing, anti-Establishment "populism." Like the anti-Illuminati conspiracy theory of colonial times and other earlier right-wing extremist movements, the New Right is essentially nationalistic; hence its antipathy toward American-based multinational banks and corporations that, they suspect, enhance foreign influence in this country. In sum, the New Right, while solidly pro-business, is not pro-*all* business.*

Third, the Youngstown meeting illustrated the New Right's pragmatism, as opposed to the kamikaze instincts of the Goldwater movement.

Press reports indicate that by mutual consent the New Right and the labor union officials avoided specific areas of disagreement—right to work, common-site picketing, and labor law reform legislation—and concentrated on issues where they might find common ground.

---

* The New Right also resents big business contributions to liberal and moderate candidates. *Congressional Quarterly* of August 5, 1978 quotes Robert K. Dornan as saying, "Corporate managers are whores," and Paul Laxalt as saying, "Our natural constituency are the taxpayers and producers in the middle. Not big business."

In contrast, Barry Goldwater seemed to go out of his way to seek confrontation with those whose votes he was ostensibly seeking. Thus, on October 9, 1964, in the midst of his campaign, he went on national television and told of how he had gone into the heart of Appalachia and "deliberately" attacked the "phony war" on poverty; how he had gone into the heart of Florida's retirement country and had "deliberately" warned against the "outright hoax of this administration's medicare scheme"; and how he had gone into the heart of the farm area and had "deliberately" called for the transition from a controlled to a free agriculture.

On these points, then, the New Right has shown itself different from the Goldwater movement—and, potentially, a far more formidable political force.

But on one count it suffers in comparison.

Barry Goldwater, for all the extremist rhetoric, for all his reckless bravado, for all the impetuosity and impracticality, was honest in the presentation of himself and his politics. The people knew where Barry Goldwater stood. They admired his candor, but they did not accept his views. What is important is that the voters had a right to know what Goldwaterism was and Barry Goldwater told them.

What the New Right is depends upon what is being said by whom to whom—and how and when it is said.

It is little wonder that the New Right leaders eschewed the subject of labor legislation at the historic meeting in Youngstown. One year before, to the month, the organizer of the meeting, Philip Crane, had introduced in the House of Representatives a right-to-work bill, the most feared and hated of all anti-union legislation. And one must speculate as to whether the New Right leaders told the union officials that, even as they talked, the Radical Right was cranking up Richard Viguerie's big mail machine to pump out a torrent of antilabor propaganda aimed at defeating the centerpiece of organized labor's 1978 legislative program—labor law reform.

True, Viguerie's efforts were strongly assisted by the most formidable anti-union force in the country—the twenty-year-old National Right to Work Committee—and by a number of corporate political action groups. What is central to the consideration here, however, is that the New Right's campaign against labor law reform was perfectly consistent with the anti-union views it has expressed since the movement's inception.

I call attention again to the letter signed by incoming New Right Congressman Jack Cunningham of Washington, which, in effect, was his thank-you to the movement for the help it gave his campaign. That letter, mailed to the true believers through Viguerie's National Conservative Political Action Committee, indicated the real feelings of the New Right toward organized labor, especially this passage attacking the labor movement for its support of election-day registration at the polls.

> The union bosses will have their troops out election day digging up derelicts, vagrants and anyone else who will take a dollar to cast a vote. . . . George Meany's henchmen will just drive them to the polls like a herd of blind cattle. . . . We must stop these villains from seizing total and final control of our elections.

The AFL-CIO lists among the most anti-union members of the Congress and the most anti-union organizations a number of individuals and groups generally considered to be important components of the New Right: senators Jesse Helms, Carl T. Curtis, Jake Garn, Orrin Hatch, and Strom Thurmond (R-S.C.); congressmen Larry McDonald, Steven D. Symms (R-Idaho), Robert E. Bauman (R-Md.), Philip Crane, and Mickey Edwards; the National Conservative Political Action Committee, the Committee for the Survival of a Free Congress, the Conservative Caucus, the American Conservative Union, the Committee to Defeat the Union Bosses' Candidates, Young Americans for Freedom, and the Heritage Foundation.*

Here are some excerpts from anti-union letters distributed by New Right organizations:

> With access to millions of union dollars, the liberal Big Union bosses can and do buy elections. That's why we have forced busing, government subsidy of "Gay" liberation, food stamps for students and strikers,

---

* Some New Right leaders, Congressman Jack Kemp for one, deplore "union baiting" as unfair and counterproductive, according to *Congressional Quarterly* of August 5, 1978. But *CQ* says others continue doing it because "it brings in a terrific amount of money." *CQ* quotes Robert K. Dornan as saying, "Even the word 'union bosses' makes me antsy. But maybe we need one more go-around on this to get some people elected. It's a hell of a money-raising issue."

furloughs for convicted rapists and murderers, higher taxes, and more inflation.

—Letter signed by Mickey
Edwards in behalf of the
Conservative Caucus, which he
serves as congressional adviser

Please send a check to the Committee for the Survival of a Free Congress today. We can't delay any longer if we are to defeat the Big Labor politicians in time for the 1978 elections. If we don't act now, liberal pro-union legislation could severely cripple our free enterprise system.

—Letter signed by
Congressman George Hansen
(R-Idaho) in behalf of the
Committee for the Survival of a
Free Congress

There is much more than a battle between the parties going on here in Washington. It is a struggle between Conservatives and Big Labor bosses. Big Labor has already "bought" the Liberals in Congress—and the result is more and more pro-Big Labor legislation—at any price.

—Letter signed by Philip
Crane in behalf of the
American Conservative Union

When a bill to reform U.S. labor law was passed by the House of Representatives late in 1977, the New Right, the National Right to Work Committee, and the corporate political action committees targeted the Senate, where the measure was to come up in late spring 1978, immediately after the long debate over the Panama Canal treaties.

The labor law reform bill, backed by the Carter Administration, was aimed at alleviating delays in National Labor Relations Board processes and discouraging deliberate flouting of existing labor law by strengthening penalties. With floor amendments proposed by the Senate Majority Leader, the measure represented a reasonable approach which law-abiding employers need not have feared.

Its passage would have affected only a handful of employers, like the J.T. Stevens Company, who have refused to follow labor laws that have been on the books for more than forty years, preferring instead to pay their fines and repeat their offenses.

But somehow, as Helen Dewar wrote in the *Washington Post*, this issue suddenly assumed a symbolic and political importance "transcending the likely impact of its provisions." Dewar reported that the estimated total cost of lobbying for and against the measure ran upward of $8 million. She noted that in less than half a year the National Right to Work Committee alone had sent out twelve million pieces of mail.

The mail generated by the Right to Work Committee, the National Association of Manufacturers, the U.S. Chamber of Commerce, and a bevy of corporate political action committees began to flood Senate offices. Labor, suddenly aware of the all-out effort to defeat the bill, responded with a postcard campaign that added to the deluge.

Over a twenty-seven-week period in 1978 that included the weeks when a filibuster against the bill was conducted by Orrin Hatch and other conservatives, my own mail averaged 440 pieces a week and totaled 12,340—with 8,956 against the bill and 3,384 in favor. Senators from larger states could not keep up with correspondence on this issue, particularly since many of them had a backlog of letters from the Canal treaties issue. (Ward Sinclair, writing in the January 29, 1978 *Washington Post*, said Richard Viguerie had sent out some three million appeals for money and for letters to Congress opposing the treaties.)

There has been considerable discussion and debate over the impact of generated mass mail. For my own part, I believe that the development and widespread use of this technique by countless special interests has changed not only the face but the very character of the American political process. Today, the political process is very nearly dominated by the computer. The New Right pioneered and mastered the technique of computerized mass mailings to generate letters and postcards and to raise political money, but its practices have been adopted by the national Republican party and by corporate political action committees that are proliferating almost daily.

The *National Journal* of April 8, 1978 reported that by using computerized direct mail techniques, the Republican congressional campaign committees took in $10.3 million in 1977, sixteen times what the Democrats raised. The *Journal* also noted that from 1975 to 1978 the number of corporate, trade association, and ideological political action committees doubled to more than 1,000, and that business political action groups alone expected to triple in 1978 the $5.8 million they spent on congressional candidates in 1976.

As to the amount of congressional mail generated by the New

Right and all other political action committees using computerized direct mail communication to solicit support for or against issues, a few statistics tell the story:

One hundred million pieces of mail a year are delivered to the House of Representatives, a figure that has tripled from 1972 to 1978. Senate mail in 1977 totaled forty-one million pieces, eight million more than the year before. Senator Alan Cranston of California averages 10,000 letters a week and uses half his office budget to pay staff members who handle the mail and arrange responses.

In his January 29, 1978 article in the *Washington Post,* Ward Sinclair said, "It has come to this: One of the American political system's simplest exercises, the letter to your representative or senator, has become a monster of sorts. Computers are talking to computers." He quoted Congressman Romano L. Mazzoli (D-Ky.) to this effect:

> This mass mailing is about to wipe us out. It is easy to poke fun at, but I don't know how to respond. They go computer. We go computer. We've reached the crazy point of 1984 already. It is weird, upside down, expensive and almost not productive at all. It is wasteful, debilitating and time consuming. We go in smaller and smaller concentric circles, and one of these days we will eat ourselves.

But does it have a measurable effect on the process? I believe the evidence answers "Yes."

There is no doubt in my mind that the mail generated over the Panama Canal treaties had an effect. If it did not sway many votes, it surely encouraged the prolongation of the debate and invited the near-destruction of the treaties by reckless amendments.

And surely the storm of mail over labor law reform contributed to blocking passage of the bill.

Many believe the mail campaign against common-site picketing forced Gerald Ford to rescind his endorsement of the measure, thereby prompting Labor Secretary John T. Dunlop to resign, and that it contributed significantly to the bill's defeat in the House in 1975 and again in 1977.

Explaining this, Henry Walther, who heads the National Right to Work Committee's direct mail operations, told Sinclair: "A politician will say he does things because of the facts. In Congress you have people who are solid for or against an issue and maybe a third who flop around and make political choices to vote for the people they represent. By targeting these people, we are trying to hold them accountable to what the people at home think." This, however, presumes that people like Walther always know precisely *how* the "people back home" feel. The evidence indicates that the majority of generated congressional mail comes from the *conservative* side of the political spectrum.

What this has done to the character of American politics was analyzed by William Schneider in *Politics Today.*

> What is going on here is not the tyranny of public opinion, but black-mail by private opinion. . . . Single-issue constituencies can blackmail politicians "democratically," without resorting to intimidation or finan-cial pressure. It doesn't even matter that a majority of public opinion is on the other side. They need only be so committed that their vote is swayed by one issue, and well enough organized to communicate that fact to politicians. Any survival-oriented politician will not want to of-fend such a constituency.[2]

Schneider recalled Congressman Paul N. "Pete" McClos-key's response when he was asked why so many members of Congress were reluctant to take sides on Watergate. "Politi-cians," McCloskey said, "will not take sides on a controversial issue until it becomes clear to them that they will lose more votes by *not* taking a side than they will by taking a side."[3]

Single-issue constituencies, Schneider said, exercise an effec-tive veto by whipping up controversy. He cited ERA as an ex-ample.

> The Equal Rights Amendment sailed through 35 state legislatures and then abruptly stalled, three states short of ratification. Public opinion did not suddenly shift against ERA. What happened was that Phyllis Schlafly and her supporters got organized and turned ERA into a contro-versial issue.[4]

A Harris survey conducted in January 1978 showed ERA fa-vored by a margin of fifty-one to thirty-four, yet Schlafly and her Eagle Forum continue to call ERA's backers—which include Rosalynn Carter, Betty Ford, Lady Bird Johnson, and Mary Crisp, cochairperson of the Republican National Committee— "Libs and Lesbians, Frauds and Follies."

Schneider concluded his column with comments which, I be-lieve, get to the heart of the problem.

While the moral fervor of veto groups is certainly not new, their technology is. We are facing what *Politics Today* editor Alan Baron calls a new era of machine politics, where the machine is a computer. Political consultants and direct mail specialists are able to target those voters most likely to respond to a specific issue appeal. In other words, votes are "bought," not with jobs or favors, but with personalized issue campaigns.

Veto groups also add an element of unpredictability to political life. In the past, partisanship gave a degree of coherence to our politics. The only controversial issues on which politicians did risk taking a stand were partisan issues. The voters most likely to be offended by a partisan appeal were partisans of the other side, and their votes were lost to begin with. The documented decline of partisanship in the electorate means that voter loyalties are no longer so easily predicted. Veto groups see the electorate as an unlimited resource for building ad hoc coalitions, whereas politicians must continue to operate under the constraints of partisanship. "We have one advantage over the president," Richard Viguerie, the New Right's leading direct-mail strategist, said earlier this year in discussing the campaign against Senate approval of the Panama Canal Treaties. "He can't campaign against a member of his party just because of one vote, but we intend to field a candidate against everyone who votes for the treaty."[5]

Viguerie's was no idle threat. As we have seen, the New Right succeeded in taking the Republican nomination away from Clifford Case in New Jersey in the spring of 1978 and has put up primary challenges to treaty supporters in other states.

The willingness of the New Right to attack Republicans as well as Democrats if those Republicans do not measure up to their test of conservatism is what prompted eight Republican senators to write to National Republican Committee Chairman Bill Brock and protest that this practice "is not the kind of healthy competition we should encourage within the Republican Party. It is cannibalism."

Brock himself also sees a danger. *The New York Times* headlined a story "G.O.P. Chairman Says Single Issue Groups Imperil Political System." The story quoted Brock as saying single-issue political activism by right-wing committees was creating financial problems for his party and governmental problems for the nation.

The Republican leader contended that efforts by such groups to elect or defeat candidates on one or two polarizing questions, such as abortion and gun control, were "hazardous for the political system" because they tend to "reduce the quality" of the officials who are elected.

Asked specifically about the impact on the party of Richard A. Viguerie, a professional direct-mail expert who works primarily for conservative causes, Mr. Brock replied, "I can't believe that draining our resources is helpful."

National officials in the Republican Party have been privately complaining for some time that the multiple Viguerie fund-raising efforts have siphoned off a good deal of money that otherwise would have gone to the party and a somewhat broader range of ideological support. Mr. Viguerie maintains that his direct-mail campaigns raised $25 million last year.

"There are hundreds of these single-issue constituencies, and they create a very serious problem," Mr. Brock told reporters at a breakfast meeting. "Any voter who follows their instructions is not going to be judging the candidates broadly as they should."[6]

None of this criticism seems to bother Richard Viguerie, who has been called the "godfather" of the New Right, the "founding father" and the "guru" of the movement, and the vital link in the entire coalition of relatively new right-wing political activist organizations. Whatever he is called, this much is certain: To know Richard Viguerie is to know the New Right. And to know how effective he is in raising money, soliciting support for or against legislation, finding ultraconservative candidates, and exploiting emotional issues is to understand why he angers and deeply concerns the AFL-CIO, Americans for Democratic Action, and loyalist Republican leaders at one and the same time.

Born in Texas in 1934, Viguerie is the son of a middle-management executive of a petrochemical firm. He was graduated from the University of Houston in 1958 and attended the university's law school for a year and a half before dropping out in what he describes as a "joint decision by my law professors and myself."[7] While on campus, however, Viguerie got caught up in something far more to his interest and liking—the first stirrings of ultraconservatism following the Eisenhower era. He became active in Young Americans for Freedom, and by dint of hard work and a talent for organization, he was named executive secretary and national financial secretary of the organization in 1961 and moved to its national headquarters in New York City. There Viguerie discovered that his most onerous task was raising money to pay off the organization's $20,000 in debts. The usual way to go about this was to make personal calls on wealthy conservatives. Whether he found this personally demeaning or simply not a quick and effective way to raise money is not known, but Viguerie began casting about for an alternative. Four years later, Viguerie—who had come to Washington with Young Americans for Freedom—left the organization and became a political consultant. He also went to work for Conservative Books by Mail, Inc., which published such titles as *Religion Can Conquer Communism.*

In 1965 he "stumbled" into the business of direct mail fundraising, a business which by now has made him a wealthy man and has given the New Right the fiscal impetus it needed. "Without direct mail," Viguerie says, "the conservative cause would not exist today."[8] Five years after founding his own company, Viguerie ran a direct mail campaign for G. Harrold Carswell, Richard Nixon's derailed Supreme Court nominee, in Carswell's equally unsuccessful effort to become a U.S. senator from Florida. The same year he also handled direct mail efforts in behalf of Republican senators Barry Goldwater and Howard Baker in their campaigns for reelection. Two years later Viguerie was responsible for the fund-raising appeal for Congressman John Ashbrook's Presidential campaign. Ashbrook, it should be noted, was William Loeb's choice that year.

According to Viguerie, his real activation as a militant conservative occurred the moment he learned that Gerald Ford had picked Nelson Rockefeller as his Vice-President. "That did it," Viguerie said. "I got on the phone, invited fourteen conservative friends to dinner and started scheming about how we could stop Rockefeller from becoming Vice-President. Of course, we didn't stop him, but it gave us a feeling, a sense that we could take charge if we just wanted to. I began to play a more active role in conservative politics from then on."[9]

Today, Viguerie is not only the fulcrum of much of the New Right's efforts, he is unquestionably the premier direct mail political fund-raiser in America. From a $400-investment in January 1965, he has built a private conglomerate with annual billings of millions of dollars and has at least forty clients, including such New Right organizations as the Conservative Caucus, the Committee for the Survival of a Free Congress, the National Conservative Political Action Committee, as well as the National Tax Limitation Committee, Gun Owners of America, and the Second Amendment Foundation, also a gun owners' alliance.[10]

In 1968 Richard Viguerie was a one-man operation headquartered in a room over a Capitol Hill drugstore. By 1978 he had a headquarters in Falls Church, Virginia, printing and mailing facilities in Maryland and in Washington, D.C., and 350 employees.

> Viguerie's company also has subsidiaries. His Diversified Mailing Services Inc. processes direct-mail appeals. His Diversified Printing Services Inc. produces brochures and letters for clients. And Viguerie Communications Corp. publishes *Conservative Digest* and *The Right Report* and will add new newsletters on gun ownership and other topics this year. He also talks of syndicated radio and television programs and syndicated political columns . . . , but boasts that he is flooded with work right now and turns away "98 per cent of all the people who come to me." He maintains lists with about five million names of "right of center" people and as many as 20 million others who might respond to a variety of conservative appeals.[11]

As his business and profits grew, Viguerie was able to "seed" new business, reportedly advancing clients front-end money in the form of postage, mailings, and other services in order to get the money coming in. Each new client may bring in additional names of prospective donors and Viguerie then can assume "ownership" of the new names and add them to his own lists.[12]

In a June 23, 1975 *Washington Star* article it was reported that Viguerie had front-ended the last George Wallace Presidential campaign, advancing Wallace more than $100,000 worth of mailing services.[13] Jules Witcover writes in *Marathon,* his book on the 1976 campaign, that over a three-year period Viguerie raised $7 million for Wallace.[14]

Viguerie mailed about seventy-five million letters in 1977, some fifty million of them political, and raised about $25 million for political and other causes. He says:

> It looks like direct mail costs a lot, but you've got to remember that this is how conservatives communicate with each other. I think you will find that a large number of conservative PACs [political action committees] have come to realize that giving money to a candidate is not necessarily the best way to support a candidate. Giving cash to candidates has to be fourth or fifth down the line. . . . It doesn't make much sense to give cash to a candidate if he doesn't know what to do with it.[15]

Whether cost effective or not, Viguerie's operation knows how to raise money and raises it in awesome amounts. One comparison in fund-raising effectiveness is enough to show why lib-

erals and moderates are worried. Two thirds of the way through
1977 one of Viguerie's New Right clients, the National Conservative Political Action Committee, had already raised more than
a million dollars, while the largest liberal political action fund-
raising group, the National Committee for an Effective Congress,
had raised only $229,825.

What else do we know about Richard Viguerie? What is he
like? An account appearing in *The New York Times* sought to
describe him.

> A lean, intense 43-year-old, who keeps a Bible on his desk and an
> electric golf putting game in a corner of his office, Mr. Viguerie talks pas-
> sionately and openly about his ambitions for the New Right.
>
> "We want to turn the thinking of this country around," he told a visi-
> tor. "We have a chance to bring a conservative to power, to the White
> House, not just delay socialism for a few years." . . .
>
> His target in 1978, he says, is to replace as many liberals of both par-
> ties as possible with "leverage conservatives, men who can influence
> policy and help elect other conservatives." These include such right-
> wing favorites as Senators Helms, Orrin G. Hatch of Utah, Paul D. Laxalt
> of Nevada and Strom Thurmond of South Carolina.
>
> "The New Right is moving," Mr. Viguerie says with a broad grin.
> "They're organized, they've got talent in spades and they're going to
> have an impact."[16]

In 1975 Richard Viguerie told the *Washington Star* that he
had "burned his bridges" with the Republican party and would
like to build a conservative party on social issues, "something
that is much broader than the conservative movement you might
normally think of." He believes such a new third party will, in
time, replace the Republican party. His theory is that people
have become so alienated by the Left-ward drift of both political
parties that if someone were able to put together a "new majority" out of one-issue people—linking those opposed to busing,
those to gun control, opponents of abortion and of the Equal
Rights Amendment, together with the anti-obscenity faction, for
example—it would make a powerful base.[17]

He is not particularly enamored of either Barry Goldwater or
Ronald Reagan, maintaining that neither man tried hard enough
to win the Presidency. And, although he would like to have had
George Wallace spearhead a third-party movement, he had
some reservations about the Alabaman even before his Presi-

dential campaign collapsed in 1976. "Quite frankly," Viguerie said of Wallace early in 1975, "the governor has never indicated an interest in leading a strong third-party movement. His interests have always been in himself running for office. . . . He's been trying to feather his own political nest but not a movement. He hasn't been trying to bring like-minded groups together in a permanent way."[18]

Viguerie speaks of the "massive, major, big effort" it's going to take "to restore freedom in this country"[19] and tells visitors he works twelve hours a day to "save the western world." There is evidence, too, that he lives by his rhetoric. A June 1975 profile in the *Washington Star* included these revealing passages:

> Viguerie admits he has had trouble fitting into the Washington community, for he practices what he preaches. For example, he lives next to one of the most prestigious high schools in the Washington area, Walt Whitman in Bethesda, Maryland. But he took his two daughters . . . out of Whitman recently and now buses them many miles every day to a Christian fundamentalist school that includes an hour of Bible reading every day in its curriculum.
>
> "They [the public school] took out world history and substituted something about life in a remote Eskimo village and the life cycle of the salmon," he grumbles. He is opposed to busing, too, but in his case it is the lesser of two evils. "It is a good feeling in the evening to know I don't have to spend the next three hours undoing what the school system has done to my children."
>
> He took them out of his Catholic parish's catechism classes, too, after he discovered they were being shown films on ecology. Then, after hearing a number of sermons on the plight of Cesar Chavez and the California farm workers he quit the parish altogether. "You know," Viguerie explained to a reporter, "I think there is something to be said about sin in our life. There is sin in the world and you should talk about it and I would like to hear about it on Sunday morning instead of about how Cesar Chavez needs my support and love and all."[20]

A number of New Right leaders contend they are "religious" and often open their strategy sessions with a prayer. Viguerie is no exception, saying, "We believe we should be in politics as a way of improving the world from a religious concept."[21] Sin, in Viguerie's view, is not only to be talked about, it is to be punished in the temporal as well as in the eternal realm, and he includes what he views as "political" sins. Hear him on what the New Right contemplated for senators who supported ratification of the Panama Canal treaties:

We're going to look *very* carefully at the votes when all this is over and do an *awful* lot of punishing next election. We're going to oppose people in the primaries, Republican or Democrat, if they come down on the wrong side of this issue. We're going to oppose 'em in the general election, and in some cases we're maybe going to be running third-party candidates.[22]

CHAPTER 6

Religion and the Far Right—Salvational vs. Social Gospel Politics

*Man cannot keep religion and politics separate.
This is not a life option. The only choice facing
him is whether to relate his real religion to the
social scene in a critical or redemptive way, or to
refuse to do so and see a pseudo-religion sucked
in to give authority without judgment to the
demands of the state. State religions do not rise
out of the cross-fire of socially-relevant
theologies. They spring, rather, from the failure
of traditional faiths to apply themselves vitally to
the real world. The surest defense against a
preferential status for any particular institution
is a vigorous program of social and political
analysis on the part of all Christian
denominations, and all Christian men and
women.*
—WILLIAM MUEHL
Professor of Practical
Theology, Yale Divinity
School

101

No examination of the causes and potential consequences of the rise of the contemporary Radical Right can ignore the concurrent rise of evangelical religion and born-again Christianity. Although there are few, if any, direct organizational links between the two movements, a significant element within the body of evangelicalism reinforces the Radical Right in its collective mind-set and tactics. Both groups show a strong tendency toward absolutism, authoritarianism, and apocalypticism.* Both are given to simplistic slogans. Both trade heavily in emotions, and both regularly issue fierce condemnations of those they oppose, often picturing them not as simply mistaken, but evil.

It is important, however, to acknowledge several reasons why it is as unfair as it is difficult to make a blanket characterization of evangelicalism. The first is the problem of defining what constitutes an evangelical. The word is ordinarily used to refer to people who make a literal interpretation of the Bible, who accept its authority without question, who believe in salvation through faith in Jesus Christ, and who are committed to converting other people to the same set of certainties.

But as Donald Dayton of *Sojourners* magazine has pointed out, the word evangelicalism has been used to define everything from pop religion to rigid confessionalism to the born-again movement. Sometimes, he claims, it is used to mean little more than a religious resistance to modern cultural currents.

If it is difficult or impossible to offer a single definition of evangelicalism, it is equally difficult to characterize the movement's politics. Clearly, there is a difference between the political and social views of an evangelical like Senator Mark Hatfield, for instance, or former Senator Harold E. Hughes of Iowa, and those of someone like Robert Welch, founder of the John Birch Society. And surely the progressive views of such evangelicals as Martin Luther King Jr. and President Carter contradict any delusion that all evangelicals are stamped from the same ideological mold.

Further evidence of the social and political bifurcation of the evangelical movement can be found in the thriving existence of publications like *Sojourners* and *The Other Side*. Even though both periodicals adhere to a conservative, if not fundamentalist,

* See chapter 9.

theology, their social views are progressive and their political judgments range from liberal to libertarian to Gandhian nonviolence. Articles in the July 1978 issue of *Sojourners,* for example, dealt sympathetically with the "longest walk" campaign, which sought to rally public opinion against legislation that would abrogate or limit certain long-established rights of Native Americans. The same issue of this journal claimed that the tax revolt spreading across the country "threatened to speed up the division between the haves and the have-nots"; staunchly supported nuclear disarmament; and criticized U.S. policy in Zaire. The May 1978 issue of *The Other Side* was devoted almost exclusively to a compassionate examination of the plight of Blacks in South Africa.

Some point to the astonishing growth of both magazines—*Sojourners* circulation went from 5,000 to 35,000 in just two years —and to the revival of Evangelicals for Social Action* as evidence that liberalism within the evangelical community is gaining. President Carter's election not only gave impetus to the entire evangelical movement, they say, but gave specific incentive to the activist element within evangelicalism committed to social and economic justice. Others attribute the liberalizing influence to the influx of young members into the movement. Richard Quebedeaux, in *The Worldly Evangelicals,* describes these young evangelicals as "a highly literate, zealous elite" most of whom were "active in civil rights struggles, the counterculture, the Jesus movement, the anti-war protests, even the New Left."[1]

Vital as this movement is within evangelicalism, and important as its influence may become, for the moment it remains a minority deviation from "the long-time partnership between conservative religion and right of center politics."[2]

There is a third element within the evangelical movement— the politically inactive and uncommitted. Richard Hofstadter acknowledged the existence of this group when he wrote, "There are large numbers of fundamentalists who interpret their religious commitment as a reason to withdraw from

* A coalition of several religious communities that espouse an all-encompassing religious life-style embracing the social as well as the salvational gospel.

worldly politics, in which they see no more hope than they do in the other things of this world."[3]

More recently, Barbara Hargrove of Yale Divinity School alluded to these people as "encapsulated." Nevertheless, she said, their self-insulation from social realities "has tremendous political effects." To be born again, Dr. Hargrove contended, should mean to reenter society with a sense of meaning and purpose, a total commitment toward all aspects of the society that one lives in.

> But the increase in religiosity that one finds in today's society, the hundreds of thousands of people following cult leaders, is neutral. These people don't represent a liberal or conservative faction. They only lose their political voice. They become amenable to outside political direction, because they feel that their religion ultimately sustains and supports them in their private lives. They don't care about the rest of the world. When people don't care, it obviously becomes easier for an individual politician to assume power. It's a lot easier to take over a flock of sheep than an aware group of human beings.

If Dr. Hargrove's conjecture is valid, these "encapsulated" evangelicals can indeed have a "tremendous" effect on the political process. In one respect, their retreat from social and political realities contributes to the overall decline in political participation and election day turnouts. As we have seen, the New Right has used low voter-turnouts to advantage in both primary and special elections. In another respect, the encapsulated evangelical, devoid as he or she is of a cohesive political philosophy or party allegiance, is particularly vulnerable to the highly personal single-issue politics practiced so assiduously by the New Right. And in still another respect, these essentially apolitical, self-insulated evangelicals, who number in the millions, may be motivated to support candidates solely on the basis of a candidate's expressed born-again Christianity. This may account in part for Richard Viguerie's interest in finding and encouraging religious fundamentalists to run for public office.

Of most relevance to this examination, however, is the historical existence within the evangelical movement of right-wing political activism inspired by an extreme cultural fundamentalism. Hofstadter noted that the ascendancy and prominence of this element is cyclical, and that it seems to be tied to those periods of history where relative economic prosperity dulled the impact of interest politics and sharpened the impact of status politics.

> It is significant that the election campaign which, of all the campaigns in our history, was most completely dominated by status politics was the Smith-Hoover campaign of 1928, conducted when the ill-fated boom of the twenties was nearing its peak. In 1964, again under prosperous conditions, the issues of status politics once more played an unusually significant part.[4]

Hofstadter described the 1920s as a time when small-town and rural Protestants were waging a vigorous defense of their cultural values against "their rapidly gaining foes—the advancing Catholics and minority ethnic groups on one side and the modernists in religion and secularists in intellectual culture on the other."[5] The Ku Klux Klan, Prohibitionism, the campaign in the schools against evolution, anti-Catholicism, and the whispering campaign against Al Smith were all aspects of this struggle. In successfully pressing for legislation restricting immigration, they scored a permanent and significant victory, Hofstadter noted, and registered another important, but temporary, victory in achieving Prohibition. But on other issues they continued to lose ground—notably, their campaign against the teaching of evolution in the public schools; the fight against modern laxity in manners, morals, and censorship; and the effort to contain the influence of immigrants in politics.

> The rural Protestant Democrats fought in 1924 to keep their party free of urban ethnic domination, and the two factions nearly tore the Democratic party apart at its 1924 convention. By 1928 the enemy was in control and Smith was nominated. He paid a heavy price for his religion and his defiance of establishment manners and morals, but he did succeed, partly by mobilizing the ethnic Catholic vote, in rehabilitating his party and raising it from the desperate condition it had reached in the two previous elections. The Democratic party became the coalition party of the new urban polyglot America. What Smith had begun, Roosevelt completed; F.D.R.'s consolidation of the ethnic and working-class elements in the country into an effective political force was almost as important as his economic reforms.[6]

The cycle that brought status politics to the fore in the 1920s waned through the Depression years and the years of World War II, but the Cold War pressures of the early 50s, again a time of relative prosperity, evoked another resurgence. This time the focus of attention was Joseph R. McCarthy of Wisconsin. By this time many Protestant fundamentalists were able to overcome their historic antipapist sentiments enough to accept McCarthy, a Catholic, as their leader in a crusade against what was perceived as a common foe. This single-issue alliance remained more or less intact for the next two decades.

> Above all, they have found a fighting issue that helps them to surmount their previous isolation, an issue on which at last they have common ground with all America: they are implacably and consumingly anti-Communist, and in the grand ecumenicism of their anti-Communist passion they welcome all allies. They are particularly happy to have made terms with the Catholics and to accept members of minority ethnic groups as comrades-in-arms.[7]

Hofstadter noted, however, that this ecumenical crusade focused more of its efforts and most of its vehemence against imagined foes at home than it did against undeniable adversaries abroad. "Those who look at the world in this way see their fundamental battle as one to be conducted against other Americans at home, and they respond eagerly to the notion, so pervasive in the right wing, that the worst enemy of American liberties is to be found in Washington."[8]

Still another factor contributing to the Rightist inclination of some evangelicals is today's flouting of the "protestant ethic."

> One strain in Protestant thinking has always looked to economic life not just for its efficacy in producing goods and services but as a vast apparatus of moral discipline, of rewards for virtue and industry and punishments for vice and indolence. . . . Today these assumptions have been flouted. The modern economy, based on advertising, lavish comsumption, installment buying, safeguards to social security relief to the indigent, government fiscal manipulation, and unbalanced budgets, seems reckless and immoral, even when it happens to work. In the intellectual synthesis of contemporary ultraconservatism, the impulses of Protestant asceticism can thus be drawn upon to support business self-interest and the beautiful mathematical modes of neo-classical economists.[9]

It is evident, then, that the contemporary Radical Right, in the persona of a constellation of relatively new political action organizations, has a triple appeal to the evangelicals described above. Not only does the New Right appeal to them in terms of cultural fundamentalism and vigorous anti-Communism, it mixes those appeals with the promise of more economic freedom for business and individuals if the New Right cause can prevail.

An example of the melding of evangelical preaching and right-wing politics can be found in this paragraph from a fund-raising mailing sent out by Billy James Hargis' Christian Crusade Ministry on July 14, 1978:

> Oh, believe me, dear friend, the problems that are facing Billy James Hargis and the Christian Crusade Ministry in Tulsa are the same problems that are facing hundreds of our Christian Crusade supporters around the country. There is not enough money to go around. Inflation has just about ruined our country and all of our people, while our politicians are giving more and more money to Communist countries like those terrorists in Africa that Andrew Young and President Carter are supporting, yet our people can't afford meat and fresh fruit and vegetables at these high prices. Carter's economic policies are just ruining our country.

In the spring of 1976 *Sojourners* warned that the evangelical Far Right was engaged in a nationwide effort to organize a massive evangelical, conservative political movement. The magazine stated that the plan is "to begin at the ground level and organize a massive, grass roots, evangelical conservative political movement. Because of a late start, however, the effort will be limited this year [1976]."

By January 1978 the political pressures of this movement—organized or spontaneous—prompted Iowa state legislator Gregory Cusack to stand up at an interdenominational Legislative Day gathering in Des Moines and express his fears that right-wing politicians were "using Christianity" to lead the United States toward fascism. "I am sick and tired of people using the cross to beat me over the head. They are always so darn sure they know what Christ would say." The way they use the Bible, said Cusack, "is enough to make you throw up." He objected to people "who use the cross as a club to tell you how to vote" and who use the Bible to buttress their own views. "Christ used the Scriptures to *free* people."[10]

Right-wing evangelicals, he said, have "codified" their views and make it clear to a legislator that if he doesn't agree with them he isn't a Christian.

This Iowa legislator, a Roman Catholic who once thought of entering the priesthood, said that when a caller starts out by saying he or she is a Christian, "it gives you a clue in advance" about the caller's outlook; it is likely to be a person "who says no money for abortions for poor women, calling them 'sluts';

who wants to keep homosexuals 'in their place'; and who wants to kill people in the name of Christ. It is that kind of mixing of church and state that I protest," Cusack said. "It results in laws that are spiteful and hateful."[11]

Fascism, he observed, always starts by attacking "the most vulnerable groups. Who cares about welfare? Who cares about homosexuals? Who cares about criminals?"

To recognize the frightening character of fundamental extremism is not to measure its impact. As Hofstadter noted in 1965, we have always known more about the role of fundamentalist leaders in right-wing groups than we do about followers. The John Birch Society's Robert Welch, for example, was brought up as a pious fundamentalist Baptist and named his organization after a young fundamentalist Baptist preacher who was killed by the Chinese Communists. Hofstadter pointed out, too, that Billy James Hargis moved on from evangelism to right-wing politics in the same way as such predecessors as Gerald L.K. Smith, Gerald Winrod, and J. Frank Norris. The Rev. Carl McIntire was expelled from the General Assembly of the Presbyterian Church before he opened his own Bible Presbyterian Church. Today he reaches a large audience with radio broadcasts that not only attack modernist Christianity and ecumenism but embrace Far Right politics.

Although evangelical leaders have often been numerous and prominent in right-wing politics, it remains difficult to measure follower participation precisely. Further complicating any attempt at an accurate assessment is a more basic question about the dimensions of evangelicalism itself: Is today's apparent growth in the movement real or is it a media creation?

Writing in the March 1978 issue of *Sojourners,* Jim Stentzel said,

> Part of the problem is definitions. As a percentage of the population, the numbers of born-again evangelicals may not be significantly greater than during the church boom of the 1950's.* The millions labeled

---

* Between 1936 and 1962 membership in the Southern Baptist Convention, for example, grew from 2,300,000 to 10,000,000. Comparable growth occurred in the conservative Churches of Christ. Richard Hofstadter pointed out that the increase in these two groups "far outstripped that of more moderate Protestant denominations in the same period."

merely pious then now register as "born again" in the Gallup polls. The difference today may be that, with a born-again President and media assurances of acceptability, the evangelicals who were there all along are not only coming out of the woodwork but getting on page one.

Harvey Cox of Harvard Divinity School recently expressed the same reservations.

> People like Anita Bryant, these celebrity evangelists, have much more influence on the purported growth of the movement today than they would have, say, thirty years ago. Today when someone like Anita makes a declaration, the Associated Press immediately picks it up and everyone in the country knows about it. The subject then becomes a household conversation, and we end up having more people exposed to evangelism—Anita's version, at least. Is this alleged growth simply a media event? Has it been invented by the press? Or does it have some real quality?

Others, however, see the growth in the movement as genuine. The Rev. Charles Adams of Hartford Avenue Baptist Church in Detroit, for example, says, "There are people marching down the aisles by the hundreds of thousands, claiming that they've had a personal experience with God."

Peggy Shriver, a staff member of the National Council of Churches, not only seems to agree with this assessment, but undertook to explain it at an Interchange on the New Right held in April 1978 in Washington, D.C.

> That an evangelical conservatism should flourish in the religious community is also not surprising. When you live in a time of uncertainty, hunt for the group of Christians who are most sure of the truth and where they stand. When values are under strain and authorities are not respected, find a group of religious people who know exactly what the source of authority for their lives should be and have agreed on the message. The simpler the better, actually, in a time of confusing complexity. A few key affirmations and truths, not to be contradicted or qualified, can assure you that you are on solid ground when you have experienced an earthquake. Find a group that does not jar you or challenge your pet assumptions about your standard of living, your sense of justice, your concept of patriotism.[12]

This comment was tempered with an appeal for empathy and understanding.

> There are some upsetting events taking place that make us all scurry for religious cover: new technologies related to sex and reproduction that raise questions, new freedoms, challenges to tradition, and social

dilemmas for which the society is ill-prepared to cope, including changing roles of women and men, as motherhood becomes an option for
the first time in our cultural history.[13]

Along with new social and ethical issues, Shriver noted there
are also upsetting political and economic factors: the U.S. hu-
miliation in Vietnam; the power of OPEC; apparent Communist
advances in Italy, Africa, and France; and, at home, unemployment and inflation—an array of strains and anxieties that inevitably make political and religious fundamentalism attractive to
those looking for simple, authoritative answers. Unfortunately,
the answers are often profoundly negative in character. Echoing
a concern expressed by many main-line religionists, she
warned:

> A Christianity which exaggerates the evil of the world, neglecting God
> as creator of his good creation, falls prey to other exaggerations also. Sin-
> fulness is so condemned that salvation, about which much is said, loses
> its joy in the anger of judgment. A rigid sense of what is pure and right
> increasingly limits the number of persons who are "acceptably" saved.
> Pride easily dominates when one adopts a stern authoritarian position
> that knows itself to be pure in judgment and action. . . . Aggressive ac-
> tion or aloof alienation are the likely responses of the evangelical funda-
> mentalist to the political scene.[14]

In a book coauthored by Donald W. Shriver Jr., president of
Union Theological Seminary in New York City, and Karl Ostrom four characteristics of "ethical maturity" in political life
are examined: (1) "basic trust"; (2) a high level of integrity between what one believes and the actions one takes; (3) openness—to other points of view and to people quite different from
one's self; and (4) public regard, through which one is willing to
sacrifice self for the public good.[15]

Religious Radical Rightists (and sometimes Leftists too),
Peggy Shriver said, may be very strong in at least two of these
characteristics but weak in the other two. A high level of integrity between what one believes and how one acts and a willingness to sacrifice for the public good are two characteristics of
many Right extremists, and religion reinforces them. "But a lack
of basic trust in the world, the society, the institutions of that
society," she said, "makes activism and sacrifice serve some
strange purposes. And a lack of openness to people with differing points of view, backgrounds, religious perspectives, race,

or ideology may strongly limit the size of the public for which they are willing to sacrifice."[16]

The question is how does lack of these characteristics of "ethical maturity" among certain fundamentalists translate into political significance?

One example, which provides a certain ominous déjà vu, is the "Christian Yellow Pages," a yellow-paged telephone directory, similar in format to the regular directory, that lists only born-again Christians, with whom one is asked to do business.

The General Assembly of the Presbyterian Church in the United States adopted a resolution asking denominational members not to patronize the directories because they are "divisive among Christians" and "discriminatory in relation to the Jewish Community."

Conservative columnist George F. Will concluded that the "Christian Yellow Pages'" rhetoric about "not doing business with the anti-Christ system" was "hostile talk." He said it was "an act of aggression against a pluralistic society" and added, "Discrimination condoned—indeed, incited—in commerce will not be confined to commerce."[17]

I experienced the "ominous déjà vu" while doing research for this book. In "The American Fascists," an article written by Dale Kramer for *Harper's Magazine*, I came across a chilling description of a meeting of the Christian Mobilizers, one of the most belligerent and anti-Semitic of the native fascist organizations of the late thirties and early forties. "Inside the hall are tables laden with Pelley's *Liberation*, Coughlin's *Social Justice*, Bund speeches, Winrod's *Defender*, the Mobilizers' own literature, and various independent anti-Semitic tracts. On the walls are heavy black slogans: 'Buy Christian' and 'Jobs for Christians.'" Kramer noted that the chairman of the meeting "takes time to sell little books containing slips reading 'Mr. Christian Merchant, the Christian Mobilizers' slogan is *"Buy Christian"* and that is why I bought here,' to be handed to merchants after purchases."[18]

Another example that may hold political significance is the remarkable growth of evangelical radio and television broadcasting. According to the National Religious Broadcasters, some 850 religious organizations and groups now reach 115 million people via radio and fourteen million via television; one new radio station is being added each week and one new television station each month either through construction or a change in the orientation of an existing station.

In the June 4, 1978 issue of the *Washington Post Sunday Magazine*, William Martin considered the phenomenal growth of M.G. "Pat" Robertson's Christian Broadcasting Network. Martin reported that Robertson, who founded CBN in 1960 with capital assets of less than $70 and a vandalized and deteriorating UHF television station in Portsmouth, Virginia, "now oversees four television stations, six radio stations and is attempting to form a Fourth Network that will serve as a genuine alternative to the Big Three, which he sees as dominated by sex, violence and secular humanism."

Martin said CBN's flagship program, *The 700 Club*, is received in all fifty states and in more than a dozen foreign countries over approximately 130 television stations and a like number of radio stations, and is also carried into 4,000 communities via cable TV. By the end of 1977, Martin said, CBN had established itself as the largest syndicator of satellite-transmitted programs in the U.S. "and in January of this year [1978] held its first live nationwide telethon, raising $750,000 in gifts and pledges in a seven-day period."

Moreover, Martin noted, the budget for CBN operations reached $1 million in 1971, an estimated $10 million in 1975, and $20 million in 1977, and that in January 1978 Robertson had said that year would be "a year of doubling."

This phenomenal success has inspired Robertson to build CBN University, a graduate institution offering master's degrees in communications and theology, at CBN Center, a twenty-million-dollar complex under construction in Virginia Beach, Virginia.

However, even Pat Robertson, whose public image is as cool and restrained as McIntire's is fervent, has come under criticism for his unrelenting promotion of conservative political views. In his *Washington Post Sunday Magazine* article, Martin cited as examples Robertson's opposition to gay rights legislation and his suggestion that the plight of Blacks in Rhodesia may not be as bad as some have said.

As for any direct ties between militant evangelism and the New Right, some illumination is provided in this passage from *Sojourners:*

The Christian Freedom Foundation was founded in 1950 to further right-wing economics, with substantial backing from J. Howard Pew's Glen Meade Trust. Third Century Publishers need a non-profit administrative organization, which Christian Freedom Foundation now provides, and Third Century publishes all materials. The new purpose has become the national effort to elect "real Christians" to government, though that could jeopardize their tax exempt status if it were too overtly acknowledged. Christian Embassy is located in Washington, D.C. and is an outgrowth of Bill Bright's* (of Campus Crusade) vision for evangelizing government officials. There is no legal or organizational link between Campus Crusade and Christian Embassy, but there is continuity of leadership and staffing.[19]

Richard Viguerie, a Catholic, had moved his family from their neighborhood parish because the priest had preached a sermon on Cesar Chavez, and he had taken his two daughters out of Catholic catechism class because "ecology" was discussed. Viguerie also took his children out of public school because he objected to the way history was being taught and transferred them to an alternative Christian day school.

This has double significance in view of the fact that Viguerie told *Sojourners* that there "was an excellent chance his firm would be involved in doing so [raising money to support campaigns by conservative evangelicals] for at least a few." *Sojourners'* description of and quotes from one such candidate, the Rev. Bob Thoburn of Virginia, follow:

> Rev. Thoburn . . . is an archetype of an extreme right-wing evangelical candidate for Congress. He operates an alternative "Christian" school in the Virginia suburbs of Washington attended by the children of both Rus Walton and Richard Viguerie. Thoburn is using all the Third Century's materials, which he is sending to "every pastor in Northern Virginia." According to Thoburn, "the liberal voting records of some men like Hatfield [Republican Senator Mark Hatfield of Oregon] are not Christian."[20]

Thoburn informed *Sojourners* that he is not only a born-again Christian, but he will "vote Christian." "What's the use of hav-

---

* *Group Research Report*, January 31, 1978: "Bill Bright, the Protestant evangelist who runs the *Campus Crusade for Christ*, has announced plans for a $1 billion campaign to carry his 'I Found It' crusade worldwide. Working with him to raise the money are such financiers as actor Roy Rogers, motel mogul Wallace E. Johnson, and Texas oilman Nelson Bunker Hunt, a Council member of the John Birch Society."

ing some evangelical Christians in office if they don't vote like Christians?"

And what does voting "like Christians" mean? Here are some of Thoburn's views:

> The welfare state is contrary to the Bible. The purpose of civil govern-
> ment is to punish criminals, protect our property rights, and maintain a
> strong defense. The government's function is not to redistribute wealth;
> the income tax is unscriptural. . . . The free market is the biblical ap-
> proach to economics. . . . We should have let the military win in Viet-
> nam in a couple of weeks. The most powerful nation in the world could
> have easily licked a fourth rate power like them.[21]

It is tempting to scoff at such political primitivism, but there are evidences of the appeal of such simplistic approaches, as we have already seen. Moreover, the opposition of main-line politi-cal leaders and main-line religious leaders has been ineffective in some recent instances.

In late spring 1978, for example, C. Conoly Phillips, an elder in the First Presbyterian Church of Norfolk and a self-described "evangelical Christian," surprised everyone with the support he was gathering as a candidate for the U.S. Senate among dele-gates to the Virginia Democratic state convention. After being in the race only eight weeks, running primarily on religious grounds, Phillips had already claimed a significant bloc of con-vention delegates. Newspaper accounts at the time indicated that some of the delegates pledged to Phillips had never been politically active before but were moved to support their candi-date by his theology, not his politics.

This phenomenon inspired Virginia Presbyterian leaders to pass a resolution warning their congregations that candidates like Phillips, whose candidacy was self-described as a call from the Lord, encourage bigotry and threaten the traditional separa-tion of church and state.

The Rev. Michael H. Hall of Richmond, who wrote the reso-lution, said: "I became more and more alarmed. I was amazed at the naiveté of people who would go along with this type of per-son, who claims to have a call from God, without questioning anything further. . . . This type of campaign would wreak havoc on our system by concentrating on what religion a person is rather than his ability in government or position on the issues." [Note: Phillips said in interviews that he had not taken positions on most issues because he had "not had time to study them."] Hall went on to say that one of the reasons for his alarm was that he sees parallels between the credulousness of the Phillips supporters he has seen and the rise of Nazism in prewar Germany.

> One aspect is this Superman concept, that he's been called by God. This superiority concept, that he has a 100 percent pure pipeline to God, has parallels to the rise of Nazism. . . . He apparently feels that he is totally God's agent. . . . I find this at best naive and at worst ridiculously hypocritical, as well as insulting to my profession and to those who are trying to be Christians.[22]

C. Conoly Phillips did not win the Senate nomination at the Virginia Democratic convention, nor did the Rev. Bob Thoburn win the Republican nomination for the Eighth Congressional District seat in Virginia. However, rejection of one evangelical candidate with extreme political views and another with virtually no political views is not a definitive measure of the impact of fundamentalist conservatism on the political process.

Anita Bryant was denied the vice-presidency of the Southern Baptist Convention at its 1978 convention, but there can be no minimizing the effect her "call from God" campaign has had upon the issue of homosexual rights. Her successful drive for the repeal of a Dade County, Florida ordinance prohibiting discrimination against homosexuals was followed by the repeal of similar ordinances in St. Paul, Minnesota, in Wichita, Kansas, and in Eugene, Oregon. In St. Paul almost the entire Establishment of political leaders, business and civic leaders, labor leaders, and main-line religious leaders was positioned against repeal of the ordinance and for protection of homosexual rights, but a campaign led by an evangelical minister beat the Establishment by a vote margin of two to one.

Moreover, one may assume that the historic asceticism of fundamentalists regarding economic freedom, government spending, and taxation was tapped to advantage by the proponents of Proposition 13 in California and will continue to be tapped in similar referenda in other states. And surely the superpatriotic, anti-Communist mind-set of right-wing evangelicals was fully exploited in the campaign against ratification of the new Panama Canal treaties. My own mail offered at least surface evidence that this was the case. Without exception, every letter, card, or telegram I received from what appeared to be an evangelical minister or church member expressed opposition, often heated, to the treaties.

Why is this disturbing? Not because religion is irrelevant to politics; not because religiously motivated people have no business bringing moral judgment to bear on politics, "speaking truth to power." To me, as to most Americans, religion remains the ultimate guarantor that human life has meaning. It also remains the principal historic font of our broad consensus in matters of justice and of public morality[23] and the surest source of respect for the worth of every human person.

It should be noted further that fundamentalism as a *religious movement* is not properly subject to a *political* critique, and that even one who does not share fundamentalist beliefs may recognize—indeed may well admire—the simplicity, zeal, confidence, and peaceful joy so often evident among "true believers."

It is another matter altogether, however, when the fundamentalist *mind-set* becomes operative in political affairs. Politics is inescapably the realm of contingencies and ambiguities, of difficult choices among unsatisfactory alternatives, of melding into workable consensus the conflicting values within a pluralistic society. Citizens are cruelly deceived when they are led to believe that it is possible, on the basis of some higher revelation as interpreted by adamantly righteous religious leaders, to transcend the need for study and reasoned debate about political issues or to invest their political judgments with the same passionate certitude they may have about the nature of God and the ultimate destiny of humankind.

It is altogether right and fitting for religionists to seek justice and to resist evil out of fidelity to God's commands. But God has not told us—we must discover for ourselves—*how* God's commands are to be carried out in the political order. One cannot find in any sacred book direct or detailed guidance about the proper size of the defense budget, the appropriateness of national health insurance, the best means of slowing inflation, or —needless to say—the legal and human rights of Panamanians vis-à-vis Americans in the Canal Zone.

In short, fundamentalist fervor translated into political crusading, especially of the condemnatory, single-issue variety, is not, in my judgment, sound religion or good politics. To the extent that New Right leaders are encouraging this all-too-easy blurring of essential distinctions, our political life is further deprived of that restraint and rationality we so badly need.

CHAPTER 7

The Hyperpatriots

*Now conservatives can get excited about the
Panama Canal giveaway and they can go to the
polls, look for a person's name on the ballot who
favored these treaties and vote against him. . . .
Conservatives have one weapon the White House
really doesn't have—the ability to* punish. *. . .
We're going to look* very *carefully at the votes
when all this is over and do an awful* lot *of
punishing next election. We're going to oppose
people in the primaries, Republican or Democrat,
if they come down on the wrong side of this
issue. We're going to oppose 'em in the general
election, and in some cases we're maybe going to
be running third-party candidates.*
—RICHARD VIGUERIE[1]

*We must create total uproar over the Carter
Administration's plan to give away the Canal.
The enclosed bumper strip for your car can help
alert* All *Patriotic* Americans *to the problem!*
—Mailing from REP. LARRY
McDONALD (D-GA.) in behalf of
the Conservative
Caucus' campaign
against ratification of the
Panama Canal treaties,
May 7, 1977*

*When did the people give you the right to make
deals with a two-bit Communist, and an alien
people beside? We have a flood tide of aliens as it
is—Jews, blacks, take your pick. . . . Concerning
your weasel-words, such as "Bully Boys of the
Radical Right"—let me tell you that I don't need
or desire any Jew-contrived labels such as
"conservative," "leftist," "extremist," ad
nauseum. . . . I am content to be called an
American patriot, thank you. And as for your
remarks concerning that fine Christian American,
Meldrim Thomson—may I say that I'm very happy
that New Hampshire has a* MAN *in high office.*
—Letter I received
protesting my intent to
vote for the canal treaties

When George Wallace's Presidential star flamed out in 1976,
it was tempting to believe that what he stood for died with his
White House aspirations. In truth, however, Wallace's candidacy succumbed to a number of causes, and public dissatisfac-
tion with his ideology was not the major factor. Questions about
his health and physical capacity for the job played a part, along
with the rise of Southern-born Jimmy Carter, whose primary
campaigning presented a more palatable populism, untouched
by the taint of racism.

But the basic elements of Wallace's appeal, that crude but at
the same time skilled and calculated blend of interest politics
and status politics, highly seasoned with flaming pro-American-
ism, remained intact and ready to be tapped in the historic clash
over the Panama Canal treaties.

---

* McDonald, a member of the John Birch Society Council, sent out this
mailing on his congressional letterhead stationery, noting it was not paid for at
taxpayers' expense. The quote above was handwritten at the bottom of the letter. The mailing included a petition to be signed and sent to the President, a
postcard to mail to a senator, an appeal for contributions to the Conservative
Caucus of up to $1,000, an opportunity to earmark $5 of the contribution for a
subscription to the Conservative Caucus members' report, and a picture of
Fidel Castro and Senator George S. McGovern (D-S.D.) captioned "Bosom
Buddies: Communist Premier Fidel Castro and ultra-liberal Senator George
McGovern are both working to force the United States into surrendering the
Panama Canal."

The *Washington Star*'s Mary McGrory says she was present at
the birth of the Panama Canal as a potent political issue. "I saw
it born in New Hampshire in the Presidential primary of 1976. I
watched Ronald Reagan say 'We built it, we paid for it, it's
ours' . . . and I saw the response of the audience . . . and I
saw Reagan's reaction to that response. He looked stunned. He
stepped back from the microphone, blinked . . . and then he
smiled. He *knew* he had an issue."

Reagan's realization that the new treaties were a potent issue
was to be substantiated by the early polls in 1977, all of which
showed a heavily lopsided proportion of Americans opposed to
the ultimate transfer of the canal to Panamanian hands.

In hindsight, this should not have been a surprise, for the
Panama Canal treaties encompassed the entire spectrum of
emotional political appeals—not only to the existing Far Right
but to that great mass of Americans who are unhappy and unsure about the state of the nation and its future and about their
own identity, status, and personal security.

In an article on the apparent trend to the conservative,
Terence Smith notes:

> Regardless of how they characterize the trend, most politicians concur
> on two basic explanations for it. On domestic issues, they generally be-
> lieve the public has been disillusioned by the cost and relative ineffec-
> tiveness of the big-budget social program of the "Great Society." On for-
> eign issues, most of them believe that the final debacle in Vietnam
> created a deep-seated concern about the country's image as a world
> power. This, they feel, lies behind a new hawkishness that finds expres-
> sion today in the opposition to the Panama Canal treaties, the cancella-
> tion of the B-1 bomber, and, to a lesser extent, the proposed withdrawal
> of United States troops from South Korea.[2]

One of the letters I received protesting my vote for the treaties said it all. I was advised not to misjudge the issue: "It is not
just the treaties that we object to. The treaties give us a chance
to get everything off our chest in one big, dramatic protest." The
treaties are a symbol, a rallying point for the expression of a
whole range of grievances by Middle and blue-collar America.

The letter writer then proceeded to tick off inflation, high
taxes, and the national debt, all charged to the "big spenders" in
government; income redistribution that gave nonproducers
more than they were entitled to at the painful expense of the

producers in society; social engineering that upset communities and schools and made the streets too dangerous to venture forth upon after dark; the remoteness and aloofness of government and its arrogant unconcern for the legitimate complaints and the real needs of decent citizens. Capping the letter was an emotional outburst over the alleged withering of American status and influence around the world, diminution of national pride, and the national security risks the writer believed were inherent in the new canal treaties. An undertone apparent in this letter, as in so many others I received, hinted of a deep-seated suspicion that the Panamanians are inferior beings, lacking the "American" skills and energy needed to maintain the canal efficiently and keep it secure and open to all nations. (That is not surprising, in view of the unconscious racism that infects so many of us. Most Europeans, as well as Americans, were astonished when it turned out that Egyptians were capable of operating the Suez Canal efficiently.)

In virtually every instance the canal issue contained both status and interest politics ingredients that were made to order for exploitation by the New Right. And the New Right went to work with skill, organization, dedication, and money and invited other conservative organizations to join them. It will be helpful to review the tactics and to recall the rhetoric that went into this campaign.

Two major coalitions were quickly formed. The Emergency Coalition to Save the Panama Canal included the American Conservative Union, the American Security Council, Citizens for the Republic, the Conservative Caucus, the Committee for the Survival of a Free Congress, the Council on National Defense, the Council on Inter-American Security, the National Conservative Political Action Committee, the Campus Republican Action Organization, and the Committee for Responsible Youth Politics.

Most of the same organizations, plus the Young Republicans, made up the Committee to Save the Panama Canal.

The Emergency Coalition, initiated by the American Conservative Union in August 1977, held a rally on the Capitol steps on September 7, the day the treaties were signed, and carried out united efforts to block ratification. The Committee to Save the Panama Canal, chaired by Paul Laxalt, sponsored a Truth Squad, which was originally scheduled to visit seven cities ir five days in mid-January 1978. Laxalt said the Truth Squad was to be made up of "a cross section of experts" on different questions raised about the treaties. "We hope," he said, "to arouse the public to tell the Senate clearly and convincingly that it will not stand still for ratification of any document which gives up control of the canal."

Besides Laxalt, the Truth Squad included senators Robert Dole, Jake Garn, Orrin Hatch, Jesse Helms, and William Scott and congressmen Robert Bauman, Mickey Edwards, George Hansen, Larry McDonald, and John Rousselot. Adm. John McCain and Lt. Gen. Daniel O. Graham were among the retired military leaders who took part.

The seven cities on the original schedule were all designated as stops because of their location in states where senators were thought to be wavering on the treaties. However, Senator Humphrey's funeral and inclement weather forced cancellation of visits to Nashville, Atlanta, and Cincinnati. The Truth Squad did hold scheduled rallies in Miami, St. Louis, Denver, and Portland.

The *Miami Herald* of January 18 said Larry McDonald "drew sweeping applause from the partisan crowd" when he said the treaty giving the canal to Panama would be "a giant step in America's retreat from greatness."

Two rallies were held in Denver on January 19, with Ronald Reagan addressing 1,000 at the first; five hundred turned out for the second.

The January 20 *St. Louis Post-Dispatch* reported that Senator Garn "brought the crowd to its feet" when he shouted, "We are going to look after American interests first. And if you [the Third World] don't like it, that's just too damn bad!"

In the *Oregon Journal* of January 21 Conservative Caucus Director Howard Phillips was quoted as saying at the Portland meeting, "Our message is that only one amendment to the treaties will be acceptable. The amendment is one that assures the United States continued sovereign control of the Canal Zone."

The American Conservative Union and the Conservative Caucus made particularly substantial contributions in the effort to defeat the canal treaties. The American Conservative Union already had spent $600,000 on the issue.

Approximately two million pieces of direct mail have been sent urging defeat of the treaties. In May of 1977, Senator Strom Thurmond (R-SC) agreed to head the Panama Canal Task Force at which time ACU began mailing a letter over his signature encouraging people to write to their Senators and Representatives and to raise money to place newspaper advertisements. . . . The ACU staff has conducted three polls of Congress on the Panama Canal issue: a poll of Senators' constituent mail; a survey of House Members' attitudes on treaty ratification and a House vote on the Panama question; and a poll of Senate members.

The ACU Executive Director, F. Andy Messing, in a release dated Dec. 30, 1977, reaffirmed that the ACU "is spending every available penny to defeat these one-sided treaties" and announced that "ACU is leading the opposition forces on the Panama Canal Issue." The major efforts of ACU since November [of 1977], according to Messing, have concentrated on the marketing of the 30-minute ACU television film, "There Is No Panama Canal . . . There Is an American Canal in Panama." By the end of February, the program will have been shown in 48 states on 193 television stations. Featured on the program are U.S. Senators Jake Garn, Jesse Helms, Paul Laxalt, Strom Thurmond; ACU Chairman Philip Crane; retired Canal Zone Federal District Judge Guthrie F. Crowe; Director of National Security and Foreign Affairs for the Veterans of Foreign Wars, Phelps Jones; and Executive Director of the Reserve Officers Association, Major General J. Milnor Roberts, Jr. ACU pays individual stations for air time. The program is interrupted several times to cut to a slide which displays the toll-free number which viewers may call to pledge a contribution to ACU. Those who pledge then receive a mailgram from Congressman Crane with a return envelope for their checks. The program has produced 50,000 pledges and contributions totalling $240,000, according to [Richard Viguerie's] *The Right Report* [February 16, 1978].[3]

(According to the January 31, 1978 edition of Wesley McCune's *Group Research Report*, "At the core of the operation [against the canal treaties] were the American Conservative Union, which is chaired by Congressman Philip Crane [R-Ill.] and the fund-raising genius of Richard A. Viguerie, the leader of the New Right. Viguerie has sent out nearly four million letters, generating some $1,400,000 in contributions, in behalf of just two groups—ACU and the Conservative Caucus. Estimates of the total to be raised and spent run as high as $2,000,000.")

The Conservative Caucus mailed more than two million fund-raising letters urging defeat of the Panama Canal treaties, which raised in excess of $800,000 by early 1978.

The caucus' neopopulist approach to the issue is exemplified in these excerpts from a letter the organization mailed out over the signature of ultraconservative Larry McDonald:

> Nearly two-thirds of the members of the Senate have concluded that they have more to fear from the vested interests pushing the canal surrender and $80 million per year payoff than they have to fear from you. . . . Big Labor, Big Business, Big Media, Big Banks and Big Government are all putting on the pressure in favor of the sellout. . . . The Big Boys are more concerned with getting their loans paid off and their investments returned than with the national security of the United States. . . . The Big Boys believe that it is more important to avoid conflict in the short run, than to preserve, protect and defend the United States of America in the long run. . . . It's our jobs—yours and mine—to make Senators know that hundreds of thousands of patriotic Americans will pledge now to vote forever against any elected official who supports the Panama Canal sellout.

The caucus letter contained a pledge, described as the recipient's "first step." "I pledge allegiance to the United States of America. I pledge never to cast my vote for any elected official who supports the surrender of U.S. sovereign jurisdiction and control over the American Canal and Zone at the Isthmus of Panama."

The recipient was asked to sign the two enclosed pledge cards and to send them to his or her U.S. senators. A symbolic penny was attached under slogan "Millions for Defense, Not One Cent for Tribute."

The letter requested that a maximum contribution be sent to the Conservative Caucus to help it reach its goal of obtaining at least three thousand signed voter pledges in every congressional district in the United States. Each person who contributed $25 or more was to be sent a copy of Crane's book *Surrender in Panama: The Case Against the Treaty*.

Other antitreaty activities carried out or at one time planned by the caucus included "Keep Our Canal" days, observed in nearly every state; fifty-three statewide training conferences to organize activity at the congressional district level; marches and demonstrations in Washington, D.C., on the day President Carter signed the treaties; "Keep Our Canal" mailings to more than two million citizens; financial support for and participation in the Truth Squad; close coordination with other antitreaty groups, retired military leaders, and elected officials; radio and television spots sent to nearly five hundred stations, featuring

Ronald Reagan's antitreaty testimony to the Senate Judiciary Subcommittee on Separation of Powers; a fact-finding mission to Panama in June 1977 by Conservative Caucus Chairman Meldrim Thomson and Louisiana Republican State Representative Woody Jenkins, president of the American Legislative Exchange Council, "whose members," the caucus letter said, "have promoted anti-treaty resolutions in state legislatures."

The caucus also planned a nationwide "Keep Our Canal Day" and a "Headlights On to Save the Canal," whereby all Americans were urged to turn on their car lights all day February 22 to indicate opposition to the treaties. (When the Headlights On gimmick flopped dismally in New Hampshire, Meldrim Thomson said it was because the state had become so energy conscious.) Public rallies against the treaties were staged in Miami on January 8 and in Concord, New Hampshire on January 14. The caucus said it planned to distribute cassette tapes developed by Orrin Hatch, "so that every citizen can hear the whole story about why turning over the Canal to a Castroite Dictator—and paying him $80 million a year to boot—are bad for America."

The antitreaty campaign launched by the New Right proved an immediate problem for the national Republican party.

In November 1977 Ronald Reagan sent out a fund-raising letter that read:

> I'm convinced nothing short of a full-fledged nationwide citizens' campaign can defeat these Carter-negotiated treaties. That's why Citizens for the Republic, of which I am Chairman, and I personally are supporting an all-out grass roots "Campaign to Defeat the Treaty." Without equivocation, I am going to do everything I can to win this fight and keep our Canal!

One month before Reagan sent out this letter, the Republican National Committee voted to oppose ratification of the treaties. This put the RNC on Reagan's side and against the proratification stance of former President Gerald Ford and former Secretary of State Henry Kissinger. With both Reagan and Ford possible candidates for President in 1980, Republican National Committee Chairman Bill Brock was caught in the middle. Even though he arranged for Reagan to sign an RNC fund-raising letter that stated, "I am convinced the only way to defeat the Carter-negotiated treaty is to conduct a full-fledged campaign to alert citizens to the dangers Republicans see in this Treaty," Brock did not develop a campaign plan to defeat the treaties and refused RNC funding of half the cost of a charter plane for a congressional tour to discourage ratification. When Reagan learned of this, reportedly he asked that the mailing of this letter be discontinued.

Conflict within the Republican leadership over this issue peaked when Meldrim Thomson's Conservative Caucus announced that it was considering filing a major lawsuit against Brock. That such an action could be even contemplated points up how sharply the treaties separated the New Right from mainline liberal and conservative thought.

Six consecutive American Presidents had advocated revision of the original treaty to make it fairer to Panama and to ensure the canal's security and accessibility.

In the U.S. Senate the new treaties had the support of Minority Leader Howard H. Baker Jr. of Tennessee and Majority Leader Robert C. Byrd of West Virginia.

Moreover, the treaties were backed by the Joint Chiefs of Staff, by almost every major religious denomination, by virtually every major daily newspaper in the country, by the AFL-CIO, by the National Jaycees, by the president of the National Association of Manufacturers and the president of the prestigious Business Roundtable, by countless other executives of major corporations, and by fifty-six other nations, including all major allies of the United States.

Not only did many key figures in the business community part company with the New Right over the treaties, but so did a number of conservative intellectuals; columnist William F. Buckley upheld the treaties and so did the newest star in the conservative intellectual constellation, columnist George F. Will.

Given the impressive body of treaty support, the fact that the New Right could hold the documents hostage for as long as it did—and come within a single vote of denying ratification—attests to the effectiveness of the campaign it waged. Indeed, had the votes been cast a few weeks earlier, the New Right might have won the battle.

As it was, the backing given the treaties by established elements in political, economic, and religious circles had begun to tip the public opinion polls. When the issue first surfaced in 1977, a lopsided majority of Americans were staunchly opposed to ratification, but by midspring 1978 sentiment was almost equally divided. Since a key argument in the New Right's campaign against the treaties was the alleged denial of the public will, this shifting of opinion threatened to file away the firing pin on the movement's big gun. This inspired antitreaty forces to heat up the campaign, and Congress was suddenly flooded with mail solicited and directed by New Right groups.

Because my own mail became so voluminous, so abusive, and so widespread in origin, it was now clear that the kind of antitreaty campaign being conducted in New Hampshire by Meldrim Thomson and William Loeb* was of a nationwide pattern, a fact I was able to confirm in conversations with a number of Senate colleagues.

By the end of February I had decided it was time to speak out against the New Right's tactics. I reserved time on the Senate floor for the morning of March 1 to announce my support of the treaties and, at the same time, to denounce the way the issue had been politicized by the radical opponents of ratification.

This speech marked the first time the subject of the New Right and its tactics was discussed in the Panama Canal debates. My words were heard by millions of Public Radio listeners and therefore drew almost immediate nationwide response. The speech and the response—positive as well as negative—are at the heart of this book.

I began by discussing the treaties themselves. It was clear to me that there were considerable risks in rejecting them out of hand simply because Panama's form of government and negotiating tactics were not to our liking. Refusal to ratify for that reason alone would play into the hands of our adversaries, would offend most of our neighbors in this hemisphere, might trigger a political upheaval in Panama that would replace Torrijos with a regime even more nationalistic and possibly more oppressive, and could cripple President Carter's capacity to conduct foreign policy for the remainder of his time in office.

> I do not like doing business with dictators of either the left or the right, and I have been struck by the irony that many of those who are in

* See chapter 17.

such public high dudgeon over the repression of human rights in Panama ignore or even excuse the same repression of freedom in South
Korea, for example, or South Africa.*

The hard truth is that there are times when diplomacy, like politics,
forces unfastidious bedfellows upon us whether we like it or not. Omar
Torrijos is a diplomatic fact of life who at the moment cannot be wished
away. . . . What I am saying is that I have never believed that offended
sensitivities and ruffled chauvinism were sufficient grounds for sum-
marily rejecting the new treaties. We are too big to be that petty.

The provisions of the treaties, I said, should be measured on
their merits by putting them to the test of three questions: First,
are they in the best national security interests? Second, are they
consistent with U.S. commitment to justice and to the right of
self-determination for all nations? Third, are there omissions or
ambiguities in the documents that could, in time, surprise
and/or embitter either signatory? I stated that I had sought positive answers and firm assurances from both the Pentagon and
the State Department, and that while some were slow in coming, they had been provided. I would vote for ratification because "after six months of hard study, I have concluded that on
balance the new treaties are the surest means of keeping the
canal open, neutral and accessible to our use—and are in keeping with our historical commitment to deal fairly and justly with
lesser powers."

As to the dollar costs of a new treaty arrangement, my studies
had persuaded me that in sum the American people might have
to pay more than they expected, and the Panamanian people
might have to settle for less than they anticipated. "What is important, however, is that all of this is known before the final
vote."

At this point I turned to the matter of the New Right's manner
of campaigning against the treaties.

I want to express myself on the way the issue of the canal treaties has
been politicized, and I will do so with no little anger and resentment.
Perhaps what I am going to say is not precisely germane to the question
before us, but I believe with all my heart that it must be said and said
now.

The campaign waged by certain opponents of ratification—in my state
and throughout the nation—has impugned the loyalty and the motives of
too many honorable Americans to be suffered in silence a minute longer.

* See chapter 16.

I believe the techniques used to exploit the issue of the canal treaties are the most compelling evidence to date that an ominous change is taking place in the very character and direction of American politics. . . . I see abundant evidence everywhere that dangerously passionate certainties are being cynically fomented, manipulated, and targeted in ways that threaten amity, unity, and the purposeful course of government in order to advance a radical ideology that is alien to the mainstream of political thought.

I spoke of the zealousness of this campaign, contrasting its perfervid recklessness with responsible commitment to principle.

I would make a distinction between commitment that is rooted in reality—commitment, for example, that recognizes the linkage between problems and the consequences of ignoring that linkage when applying solutions—and commitment that denies reality and is, in truth, but the blind and obsessive pursuit of illusion.

Extremists who deny reality in the pursuit of illusion deny something else, something of fundamental importance in our republic of free men and women. They deny the differences that distinguish one human being from another. They deny the indisputable fact that each of us is the result of a unique combination of genes and chromosomes, of influences and impressions, of training and of faith, and of the milieu from which we sprang. In short, they deny everything that science and simple observation tell us about human nature and individual capacities and limitations.

By proceeding from the flawed premise that all of us are alike, it is easy for ideologues to conclude that we must see every issue as they see it—unless there is something sinister in our motivation. And they proceed from that flawed premise with an arrogance born of the conviction that they and they alone have a corner on patriotism, morality, and God's own truths, that their values and standards and viewpoints are so unassailable they justify any means, however coarse and brutish, of imposing them on others.

Although I was referring to the politics practiced by "what has become known as the New Right," I also noted that the record of extremists on the ideological Left bore "a remarkable and regrettable similarity. There have been times when some of us have felt the wrath of the purist Left. And now—today—many of us are feeling the wrath of the New Right because we will not bow to their threats against ratification of the canal treaties."

I went on to describe the differences between traditional conservatism and the radicalism of the New Right.

I know the traditional conservatives of my own state. I have competed with them in the political arena. I have worked with them in behalf of our state. I know them to be people of honor, civility, and decency. The New Right cannot comprehend how people of opposing viewpoints can find common ground and work together. For them, there is no common ground. And this, in my judgment, is the best indication of what they truly are—radicals whose aim is not to compete with honor and decency, not to compromise when necessary to advance the common good, but to annihilate those they see as enemies.

The beliefs and the tactics of the Radical Right are nothing new to those of us who call New Hampshire home, I indicated, so it was no surprise to see Governor Thomson, Mr. Loeb, and the Conservative Caucus team up to threaten John Durkin (who had announced earlier that he would vote for ratification) and Tom McIntyre for supporting the treaties.

I am certainly not sanguine about such powerful and ruthless opposition, but after sixteen years of weathering the sustained attacks of Mr. Loeb and his ilk neither am I anguishing over the outcome. My political fate is not my concern here today. My concern is the desperate need for people of conscience and good will to stand up and face down the bully boys of the radical New Right before the politics of intimidation does to America what it has tried to do in New Hampshire.

I then ticked off a litany of what the Radical Rightists had tried to do in New Hampshire* and concluded with these words:

I cannot believe that the loutish primitivism of Meldrim Thomson and William Loeb is what the American people want in their leaders, no more than I can believe that the American people want the divisive politics of the New Right to determine the course of the nation.

On two occasions in the past several years we witnessed dramatic evidence that the American people desperately want to put acrimony and division aside, to heal the wounds, and to come together again as a people. The first was that brief and shining moment on Independence Day of our Bicentennial Celebration, a moment when all at once we were again united in the pride of our heritage, our esteem and affection for one another, our confidence in the future. The second occurred but a few short weeks ago when the entire nation paused to pay its final respects to that most beloved of Americans, Hubert Humphrey.

The outpouring of affection for Senator Humphrey was proof

* See Author's Note.

that most Americans want their leaders to be healers—not haters; that most Americans want the politics of mutual respect and good will—not the politics of threat and vengeance; and that most Americans want to be asked for the best that is in them —not the worst.

> In the long run I am confident that the forces of decency and civility will prevail over the politics of intimidation, just as I am confident that reason and commitment rooted in reality will prevail over extremism in the pursuit of illusion.

I knew when I made that speech I would be in for heavy and sustained fire from the Right, and for the next six weeks it was unrelenting. But what I did not anticipate was the support and encouragement the speech drew from so many quarters. That response proved to me that a great many people not only had concluded that ratifying the treaties was the responsible thing to do, but that the campaign waged by the New Right was indeed reprehensible because it was such a violent distortion of traditional politics.*

The measure of the New Right as a force to fear is not to be found, then, in the movement's inability to secure antitreaty votes from one third plus one of the membership of the U.S. Senate. The proper measure is that it bucked the political, economic, and religious Establishment and came within a single vote of blocking ratification, that it did indeed achieve the goal of creating a public uproar over the issue and that its techniques, however successful, were so repugnant they would move as mild-mannered a person as Mark Hatfield to issue a scathing denunciation.

Beyond all this are the potential life-and-death consequences of such political techniques when they involve issues of delicate international import. I do not know what would have happened had the canal treaties been rejected. Perhaps no more

---

* I have been asked on a number of occasions precisely what it was that distinguished the New Right's campaign against the treaties from lobbying campaigns conducted by labor unions, for example, or by other organizations on other issues. Robert Abernathy put the question to me on the *Today* show the morning I made the speech. I felt at the time that my answer was neither sharply focused nor especially persuasive, and it remained for a Republican colleague in the Senate, Mark Hatfield of Oregon, to articulate the definitive difference. Some of his remarks will be found in chapter 19.

than a burst of anti-American demonstrations in the streets of
Panama. But the possibility is undeniable that armed conflict
could have erupted and that once again we would have to send
Americans to fight and die in another jungle, this time in our
own hemisphere.

That the reckless jingoism displayed by the New Right in its
campaign against the treaties could someday prevail in another
critical global issue is the thought that troubles me most. Indeed, it fills me with the gravest fear.

Even as I write this, one of the key organizations in the movement—the American Conservative Union—is launching a new
campaign, a campaign to destroy public confidence in the ability of the United States to reach a meaningful arms limitation
agreement with the Soviets *before* that agreement is even finalized.

The ACU has prepared a television documentary, *Soviet
Might/American Myth: U.S. in Retreat,* which it hopes to tele-
cast nationwide if test screenings in California, Texas, and Florida raise enough money through viewer contributions to buy air
time.

At a June 15, 1978 news conference featuring a preview of the
film, ACU Chairman Phil Crane said, "We intend to do everything possible to warn the American people of the pernicious
nature of these SALT treaties and of the hypocritical rhetoric of
the U.S.S.R. on defense."

On this issue, in contrast to the canal treaties, the New Right
started its campaign at sharp odds with public opinion. A Harris
survey released less than a week before the ACU unveiled its
anti-SALT film showed that 72 percent of the American people
"favor the U.S. and Russia coming to a new SALT arms control
agreement." The survey noted that

> the single most important finding from this poll is that the American peo-
> ple are far more sophisticated in their views on American-Soviet rela-
> tions than the country's leaders apparently realize. Above all else, this
> poll demonstrates that the public does not buy linkage as a predication
> for dealing with Russia. A sizable majority holds the view that the canvas
> of U.S.-Soviet problems covers a wide assortment of areas, and that it is
> possible to relieve tensions in nuclear arms control while at the same
> time facing up to dealing with Russian military adventures in Africa with
> tough countermeasures. It is evident that the American people want the
> U.S. to be tough in its response to Cuban and Soviet incursions in Africa.

But, at the same time, the desire for reaching basic accords with the Soviet on arms control runs even deeper.

In midsummer of 1978 it was apparent that many Estalish-
ment politicians, as well as the New Right, did not recognize
the American people's simultaneous desire for an arms control
agreement and a firmer stand against Soviet expansionism, Soviet suppression of human rights, and Soviet persecution of
"Refuseedniks" such as Anatoli Shcharansky and Alexander Ginz-
burg, nor do they acknowledge the priority the public assigns
arms control.

Joining New Right advocates in calling for suspension of
SALT talks and trade agreements to voice American displeasure
over Soviet actions were key representatives from the neocon-
servative element in the Congress and some surprising liberal
voices as well. Yet, as the *Washington Post* editorialized on July
12, 1978,

> Negotiating an arms-control treaty is in no sense a one-sided affair. It
> is a process promising advantage to the United States. . . . For Ameri-
> cans to imagine they can reduce the risks and costs of life in the nuclear
> age without some adjustment to their most dangerous adversary is an
> exercise in escapism.

The case the American Conservative Union is trying to make
against SALT is—like the campaign against the canal treaties—
predicated upon simplification and distortion of a highly complex issue, hyped up once again by unrestrained jingoism. Witness these words spoken by retired Gen. John Singlaub in the
ACU's television documentary against SALT II:

> For years I have anguished, as have most of my fellow officers and
> most of you, as the United States of America retreated from the front
> ranks of Free World leadership.
> Korea was a heartbreaking stalemate—because we have refused to
> make it our policy to win. The loss of Cuba to communism was a defeat
> in our hemisphere—because we turned the Monroe Doctrine into a
> meaningless piece of paper. Vietnam was a defeat, because, repeating
> our Korean blunder, we refused to win. The American canal which this
> administration would abandon to Panama is our first retreat from United
> States soil—because we buckled under the psychological warfare of our
> own State Department and the pressure from New York bankers who
> wanted the American taxpayers to bail them out of their bad loans to the
> Panamanian dictator.

The reader may recall that President Carter removed General Singlaub from command in South Korea after the general took public issue with the Administration's proposal to reduce American troop presence in that country over an extended time period. Under our Constitution, determining such policy is the province of the civilian leadership of the country, not the military, and General Singlaub, while still in uniform and on active duty, chose to flout that critical provision by injecting his own views into a matter of the greatest delicacy.

There is a disturbing similarity between General Singlaub's impropriety in Korea and the brazen indiscretion of the American Conservative Union in delivering a videotape of its anti-SALT II documentary to the Soviet Embassy in Washington before the American people had had an opportunity to pass judgment on the validity of the film's message.

CHAPTER 8

June 6, 1978—A Political Benchmark?

People don't know the bastards we've been electing. They didn't know they elected people who were evil, 90 percent immoral. They want to take everything we have—but now we're giving them an enema.[1]
—HOWARD JARVIS,
Co-sponsor of
California's Proposition 13

By limiting property taxes through the state constitutional amendment, the proposition in a broad stroke slashed the total income of local governments by more than 22 percent on the average. And for some communities and school districts that depend heavily upon the property tax, it reduced income by as much as 70 percent.
—ROBERT LINDSEY[2]

Within six months they'll be banging on the White House door for emergency relief.
—A high-ranking
Administration official[3]

135

*There is no doubt that it [passage of Proposition
13 in California] is a landmark in American
federalism.*
—RICHARD P. NATHAN,
Senior Fellow,
Brookings Institution,
and authority on federal
grant programs

The elections held on June 6, 1978 did little either to dampen
the enthusiasm or shake the growing confidence of the New
Right. Again mustering its boldness, zealotry, organization, and
fund-raising expertise, the movement pulled off some impressive victories by skillfully exploiting the festering resentment over taxes and government.

Key figures and organizations in the movement made valuable contributions toward upsetting veteran liberal Republican
Clifford Case in his bid for nomination to a fifth term and to the
nomination of an ultraconservative Republican to oppose
Iowa's Democratic Senator Dick Clark. The New Right also
played an important role in bringing about passage of California's initiative to slash property taxes by some 60 percent. In
two of the three instances, taxes were a primary focus; in the
Iowa primary, taxes were a factor but only one of a number of
others.

In New Jersey thirty-four-year-old Jeffrey Bell won a hairline
primary victory over Clifford Case, thus ending the career of
one of the most liberal Republicans to serve in the U.S. Senate
in recent times. Analysts differ on why Case lost: some point to
the age differential (Bell was born the year Case first entered
Congress); others cite the alleged complacency of the Case
campaign; still others note conservative Republicans' traditional lack of enthusiasm for the senator.

Nevertheless, negatives alone may not have been enough to
defeat Case. Bell himself had to offer something. And what he
offered was a platform based on a pledge to support a tax-cutting
proposal advanced by conservative Republican Congressman
Jack Kemp of New York and conservative Republican Senator
William V. Roth Jr. of Delaware. Their plan would reduce federal income tax rates almost a third.

Bell argued, as did Kemp and Roth, that such a tax cut would stimulate the private sector, spur the general economy, and, in the long run, generate more tax revenue.

It was not a contrived issue for Bell; he came to it naturally. Described as a "serious-minded philosopher of the right" in the *Washington Post* of June 8, 1978, Bell was Ronald Reagan's staff idea man in the latter's bid for the Presidential nomination in 1976 and the originator of Reagan's proposal for a ninety-billion-dollar reduction in federal spending. That proposal drew some ridicule and raised some fears two years before, but Bell claims it would have been "a winner" had it been explained properly at the time.

Although the extent of New Right backing of Bell's candidacy was not known at the time of this writing, it already was apparent that he relied heavily upon carefully pinpointed direct mailing to like-minded Republicans whose names were screened from lists painstakingly copied from election books in each courthouse.

According to *The New York Times* of June 11, 1978, Bell spent $100,000 of his $500,000 campaign war chest to obtain the names for his mailing list. The *Times* also reported that 80 percent of the half million dollars Bell spent on the primary campaign came from outside New Jersey.

The young challenger won by 3,500 votes out of more than 230,000 cast, one of the lowest turnouts for a Republican primary in New Jersey history. Bell went into the primary campaign a distinct underdog. He was bucking not only a veteran of the Senate, but the Republican state organization as well. On election day he was still considered a short-ender and his victory has to be seen as an upset.

In the Iowa Republican primary for the Senate, the New Right—in the persons of Meldrim Thomson Jr. and Richard Viguerie—injected itself directly into the campaign. Indeed, in the days immediately before the election, Thomson's name was featured in major Iowa newspapers almost as often and as prominently as the names of the candidates—former Lieutenant Governor Roger Jepsen, State Commerce Commissioner Maurice Van Nostrand, and lawyer Joseph Bertroche.

The controversy broke on May 8, 1978, when a letter signed by Meldrim Thomson Jr., as governor of New Hampshire (and not as chairman of the Conservative Caucus), was mailed to 100,-

000 conservatives throughout the country by Richard Viguerie's direct mail firm. The full text of the letter appears here, despite its length, since in its own way it is a classic of New Right litera-ture, because of its tone and rhetorical tactics and also be-cause—even though it contained serious factual errors that were thoroughly exposed in the media—it seems to have worked.

Dear Friend:

You and I have the best opportunity this year to defeat a Senator who voted to give away the Panama Canal. I'm referring to the campaign in Iowa against Senator Dick Clark.

A good conservative friend of mine, former Lt. Governor Roger Jep-sen, is running against Dick Clark. And there's no doubt in my mind Roger Jepsen can win provided good conservatives like you and me will help him.

Roger has the advantage of running against Dick Clark's ultra-liberal voting record. Clark's liberal record includes votes to:

• use taxpayers' money to finance Federal elections.
• Federally subsidize abortions.
• delay construction of the B-1 bomber and make major slashes in the defense budget.
• give food stamps to strikers, repeal Right to Work laws, repeal the Hatch Act, permit Common Situs picketing, and other power grabs.
• continue Federal court-ordered busing of our school children.

And Dick Clark voted to give away taxpayers' money to Marxist dic-tator Omar Torrijos to take away our Panama Canal.

One of the reasons why Roger Jepsen can win is because the cam-paign to beat ultra-liberal Dick Clark is in the rural and conservative state of Iowa. Roger Jepsen can win because he is a dynamic conserv-ative candidate. He's a former state senator who knows how to win elections. He was elected Lt. Governor of Iowa twice. In 1970 he was reelected with the highest plurality of any Republican in Iowa's his-tory.

The best way for Roger to win is to expose Dick Clark's ultra-liberal voting record. Too many people in Iowa think Clark is a conservative because he talks conservative in Iowa. The trouble is his liberal votes in Washington aren't publicized back home.

Clark is one of the most liberal Senators in Congress. Every major lobby group—whether it's liberal or conservative—agrees that Dick Clark is about as liberal as you can get. Just look at the brochure I've enclosed for you.

Big Labor will be pouring thousands of campaign dollars into Iowa for Dick Clark. They want Clark to be reelected because he votes with Big Labor 90 percent of the time. But most of their money will probably be spent on expensive radio and television advertising.

To expose Clark's ultra-liberal voting record Roger Jepsen will use a different method: letters to voters.

Certainly he will have to use some of the very, very expensive radio, television and newspaper advertising. But primarily he will conduct his low-budget people-to-people campaign with letters sent directly to voters in their homes.

By writing letters, better than 95 percent of each dollar will be used to personally explain to voters exactly why they should vote against Dick Clark and for Roger Jepsen.

You see, conservatives have proven over and over again they can win elections by writing to voters and convincing them that their opponents vote for big government, big bureaucracy and big spending.

But it still takes money to buy stamps, envelopes and stationery. To reach 650,000 voters with personal letters will cost $90,500 for stamps alone.

Roger called me last week and said he must raise $134,975 by May 24th to keep his voter letter campaign on schedule.

So I hope you'll do me a personal favor by sending the largest check you can personally afford—whether it's $500, $100, $50, $25 or even $15—to help my friend, Roger Jepsen.

Think of it this way: with a contribution of $13 you can help Roger buy stamps to reach 100 voters. $39 will help reach 300 voters. $130 will help reach 1,000 voters.

The important thing is this: Roger Jepsen needs to know where he stands financially as soon as possible. If he has to cut back on his campaign he has to know that now. So if you can help, please fill out the "Yes" card and send it to him today, along with your contribution.

However, even if you can't help now for whatever reason, please send the "No" card to Roger so he can plan his campaign schedule with this in mind.

Remember, this is our best chance to defeat an ultra-liberal who voted to give away our Panama Canal. But in order for Roger Jepsen to win he needs help from conservatives like you.

I told Roger I'll do everything I can to help him win. I hope you will too.

                                        Sincerely,
                                        Meldrim Thomson Jr.
                                        Governor of New
                                        Hampshire

P.S. Please note that the big well-heeled special interest groups are hoping you'll ignore my letter to you so Dick Clark can breeze into re-election. Please don't. Please help Roger Jepsen defeat ultra-liberal Senator Dick Clark by sending your contribution today.

The Thomson fund-raising letter came into the possession of the *Cedar Rapids Gazette* when a California couple, visiting relatives in Iowa, made a copy of the letter they received available to the paper. The *Gazette* broke the story on May 24.

On May 26 the *Des Moines Register* featured an article headlined "Right Wing Support Grows Nationally for Jepsen."

> In his June 6 primary contest with State Commerce Commissioner Maurice Van Nostrand and Indianola lawyer Joseph Bertroche, Jepsen has been endorsed by:
> - A controversial senior citizens' group with a history of endorsing candidates on the basis of issues not connected with the problems of old people.
> - New Hampshire Gov. Meldrim Thomson Jr. who mailed 100,000 letters—with Jepsen paying the $13,000 for stamps—asking conservatives across the country to send money to Jepsen. Thomson is secretary of state in the third party Conservative Caucus' "shadow cabinet."
>
> Earlier Jepsen was endorsed by the Gun Owners of America, a conservative organization connected with direct-mail expert Richard Viguerie, who has been retained by Jepsen's campaign.
>
> Both organizations, the Gun Owners and the National Alliance of Senior Citizens, endorsed Jepsen without talking to, or submitting questions to, Van Nostrand and Bertroche.

The *Register* article noted that the National Alliance of Senior Citizens had been denounced as a "sham" operation by the National Council of Senior Citizens. And with some reason. In 1976 the National Alliance of Senior Citizens had given Iowa Democratic Congressman Edward Mezvinsky a zero rating, which his opponent (and successor) Republican James A.S. Leach advertised. At that time, the *Register* investigated the National Alliance and learned that it was operated by a young South Carolinian, Curt Clinkscales Jr., out of the back of a tailor shop. When the operation was exposed for what it was, Leach apologized to Mezvinsky.

When the Alliance surfaced again in the Jepsen campaign, endorsing Jepsen and saying Senator Clark voted in the best interests of senior citizens only 11 percent of the time in 1977, the *Register* checked on the Alliance's current address and modus operandi. The newspaper discovered that Clinkscales was still in charge (but was out of town) and that the Alliance now operated "out of a sparsely furnished room in a suite shared with the manager of an uptown office building."

The *Register* also reported that the Alliance does not have a political action committee, but, instead, recommends contributions be given to the political committee of the conservative American Physicians and Surgeons—"Our United Republic Political Action Committee (OURPAC)"—in Oak Brook, Ill., reportedly a group of doctor members of the John Birch Society who broke from the American Medical Association because it was too liberal.

The National Alliance for Senior Citizens lists itself as having "either 16,500 or 21,000 members," the newspaper noted, in contrast with the 3.5 million members of the National Council of Senior Citizens, which, incidentally, rated Senator Clark's voting record in behalf of senior citizens at 100 percent in 1977.

But it was the fund-raising letter signed by Thomson that drew the most press attention.

On June 1 a United Press International story in the *Fort Dodge Messenger* reported:

> The [Thomson] letter has touched off a swirl of controversy in a campaign already marked by sharp attacks on Jepsen's conservative allegiances. Jepsen has insisted the letter was just a vehicle for raising money. Thomson has said he wants it known that he's behind Jepsen 100 percent and Jepsen's chief rival says Thomson should keep his nose out of Iowa politics.

The UPI release goes on to quote Maurice Van Nostrand, Jepsen's chief rival for the nomination, as charging Jepsen with enlisting the support of "alien forces whose goals are extremely questionable."

Other Iowa journalists, notably *Cedar Rapids Gazette* political columnist Frank Nye, called attention to two errors of fact in the Thomson letter in behalf of Jepsen and raised the question of whether Thomson had actually signed or even read the letter that was sent out through Viguerie. On May 28 Nye noted that the Thomson letter was wrong when it said Jepsen was re-elected lieutenant governor in 1970 "with the highest plurality of any Republican in Iowa's history," pointing out that greater pluralities were achieved by a number of other Republican candidates in prior elections.

The *Gazette* columnist also rejected the letter's claim that Clark concealed his liberal record from Iowa voters. "Of course that item, like the first, is utterly false. It is non-factual and pure nonsense. Clark talks the same way in Iowa that he talks in Washington. . . . Moreover, his votes—together with those of the other members of the Iowa congressional delegation, Democratic or Republican—are well-publicized by the media in Iowa."

Nye's June 1 column recounted how he had called Concord, New Hampshire, to ask Thomson's press secretary, Buddy Jenkins, about the errors in the letter. "When I read them to him, Jenkins broke in to say that Thomson 'doesn't know about those specifics.' What he does know about, Jenkins continued, is the Panama Canal 'giveaway' and all the Senators who voted for the Panama Canal treaties."

The columnist then posed the rhetorical question, "So where did Governor Thomson pick up this false information?" He answered his own question: "My guess is that he never saw the letter that went out over his name; that it was written for him by the Richard Viguerie Company of Washington, D.C., which is conducting an important part of Jepsen's letter-writing campaign."

The candidate himself denied seeing the letter.

> Roger Jepsen says he didn't see the letter Governor Meldrim Thomson of New Hampshire sent to 100,000 conservatives across the nation before it was mailed last May 8. If he'd seen it in time, Jepsen told the *Gazette* in a telephone interview . . . , he'd have corrected the errors it contained.
>
> Only last week, Thomson's press secretary, Buddy Jenkins, told the *Gazette* he was certain the governor had not seen the letter before it was mailed either. The letter was prepared by the Richard Viguerie Company of Falls Church, Virginia, a firm that specializes in raising funds for conservative political candidates. Bill Rhatigan, who handles public affairs for the Viguerie firm, told the *Gazette* by telephone this morning that he would find out who wrote the letter and call back. He had not called back by noon.[4]

Van Nostrand, who had the implicit but not active support of Iowa's most popular political figure—Republican Governor Robert D. Ray—concentrated his rhetoric on the Far Right in the closing days of the campaign, charging, as the *Des Moines Tribune* of May 26 reported, that "extremists should not make Iowa a battleground. . . . Splinter extremists like those in Jepsen's campaign cannot" win against incumbent Democratic Senator Dick Clark. "The strange, outside forces now involved will do great harm to our state."

The *Tribune* quoted Van Nostrand as asking Jepsen whether

he was a supporter "of the Viguerie announced efforts to destroy the Republican party and replace it with a coalition dedicated only to the promotion of its emotionally-divisive causes?" And: "For what purpose does the right-wing governor of New Hampshire put out 100,000 error-filled letters for Roger Jepsen all over America? What does he want? What will he get?"

Answers to these questions were forthcoming. "Campaign finance disclosure statements filed for the period April 1 to May 22 show that Van Nostrand raised only $20,184 compared to $121,443 taken in by Jepsen. In that same period, Van Nostrand spent only $22,247 to Jepsen's $95,839."[5]

On June 6, Republican primary voters went to the polls and nominated Roger Jepsen, who got 57 percent of the vote to Van Nostrand's 35 and Bertroche's 8 percent.

If the Bell victory in New Jersey and the Jepsen win in Iowa gladdened the hearts of the New Right, the overwhelming victory of Proposition 13 in California left the movement ecstatic . . . and sent shock waves through every level of government, from city hall to White House.

Proposition 13, also known as the Jarvis-Gann initiative, won two-to-one voter approval, even though polls taken just weeks before the June 6 vote indicated the outcome would be closer. The initiative gained incredible momentum in the closing days of the campaign, despite many dire forecasts by Governor Jerry Brown, labor and business leaders, and public employees of what its adoption would mean to government services in California.

Proposition 13 mandates a slash of about 60 percent, or $7 billion, in property taxes in California, leaving more than five hundred cities, over one thousand school districts, and hundreds of special taxing districts with the agonizing dilemma of which services to cut or eliminate, which employees to retain and which to discharge, and where to turn for funding help. "For some communities and school districts that depend heavily upon the property tax, it reduced income by as much as 70 percent."[6] The cut in property taxes was to go into effect July 1, creating a crisis atmosphere in city halls and in school board meetings throughout the state.

The California tax revolt of June 6 was not the first in recent times, nor was it the only manifestation on that particular day.

For example, on June 6 Ohio voters refused to approve higher tax levies to keep schools operating on full schedules. Other states had moved against rising taxes long before the spring of 1978; some have tax-cutting or tax-limiting options under serious consideration.

What distinguished Proposition 13 was its drastic nature and its colossal and immediate consequences.

> Some students of the Federal system said they believed that a number of other initiatives that many states have been exercising for tax relief would be much less disruptive, both in Federal and local programs, than California's radical approach.
>
> About 30 states now have some form of "circuit breakers" on the property tax. First enacted in Wisconsin in 1964, the circuit breaker prevents real estate taxes from exceeding a percentage of an individual's income. So far it has largely helped the elderly and low-income families. A stronger circuit breaker than one already enacted in California was offered to the voters by Governor Edmund G. Brown, Jr., in an effort to head off Proposition 13.[7]

The reference was to Proposition 8, a more modest property tax-cutting and tax-limiting initiative that would have concentrated tax relief among homeowners and renters. Proposition 13, in contrast, gives commercial and industrial propertyowners two thirds of the immediate tax-cut benefits.

Circuit breaker tax-relief mechanisms are not the only more responsible measures enacted in recent days.

> The state legislatures this year have been beehives of activity on tax relief, with a number of them approving "super circuit breakers" which extended relief to a greater number of property owners and to renters. In Oregon, for example, homeowners and renters with yearly incomes of less than $16,000 receive substantial refunds from the state.[8]

The New York Times of June 11, 1978 listed examples of enactments and proposals pegging future state spending to past levels, to percentages of personal income, or to growth of the state economy. It noted instances of such measures in New Jersey, Tennessee, Colorado, Massachusetts, and Michigan.

Why, then, the far more drastic action approved by the voters of California? The answer would appear to lie in the general and in the specific. With reference to the latter, a number of analysts have pointed out that California is unique in several respects. First, its overall tax burden is about 20 percent above that of the average state, and its property taxes have risen at a faster rate than most other states in the last ten years. (It should be noted, however, that California's property tax rate per $1,000 of personal income ranked sixth highest in 1976, trailing, in order, Alaska, Massachusetts, New Jersey, New Hampshire, and Montana.[9])

Second, California had a surplus of almost $5 billion in its state treasury at the time Proposition 13 was adopted, a fact that angered a great many tax-pressed citizens. None of the other high-property-tax states has a surplus remotely approximating California's.

Third, California's system of assessing property values is regarded as the most efficient in the nation. This means that as the value of residential property soared, the tax assessor did not delay in assessing higher taxes. In other states, tax bills are slow in catching up to property value increases.

Fourth, Californians had an opportunity, through a direct vote on the initiative, to express their resentment in uniquely dramatic fashion. Few other states have such mechanisms. However, Californians are not unique in their resentment toward taxes, as taxes reflect the inflated cost of government that they perceive as being bloated, inefficient, and skewed to serving nonproducers at the expense of producers.

In its lead editorial June 11, the *Washington Post* put it this way:

> A revolt is running among the voters, but it is not, we think, against taxes in themselves. It is against the unthinking automatic effects of continuous inflation on the tax structure. It is a revolt against paying steadily higher shares of income, not to meet any demonstrated and urgent public need, but merely because the blind mathematics of inflation and the tax tables work out that way.

On the same day Thomas E. Mullaney, "The Economic Scene" columnist for *The New York Times,* fleshed out the *Post*'s observation on the effects of inflation on taxes.

> The effects of rising Federal taxes and inflation on family budgets during the last two decades were detailed vividly in a recent analysis by the Conference Board. It found that the average American family of four persons would have had to increase its pre-tax income by at least two-thirds last year just to maintain the same standard of living it had in 1970.
> In a typical case, the family that had a total income of $13,220 in 1970

paid $1,896 in Federal taxes that year and had a loss of $2,686 in purchasing power because of inflation over the previous 10 years. That left it with a 1970 income, after taxes, of $8,638 in terms of 1960 dollars, the reference year. To arrive at the same after-tax income last year, however, the family income would have had to reach $21,210 before Federal taxes took a bite of $3,537 and before $9,035 were subtracted because of the ravages of inflation since 1960.

The tax bite, which did not include state and local taxes, was bad enough, but the inflation impact was much worse. Since the Consumer Price Index rose by 56 percent between 1970 and 1977 and is expected to advance by at least another 6 percent this year, the Conference Board estimates that $1 in 1978 will have only 60 percent of the purchasing power of $1 in 1970 and only 46 percent of the purchasing power it had in 1960.

(There is an important economic effect of this concern about inflation and taxes as another section of the Conference Board analysis and government estimates revealed. The Conference Board found that Americans' confidence in government's ability to cope with inflation deteriorated sharply in May, "with buying plans declining precipitously." At the same time, it was believed that business capital spending was running about $100 billion under the Administration's target.)

These are some of the explanations offered for Californians' enthusiastically adopting Proposition 13, but they do not supply the whole answer. Only five years ago the same state resoundingly rejected an initiative to put a legal limit on the amount the state could collect in state taxes, despite the strong support the measure had from then-governor Ronald Reagan. It is possible, of course, that cumulative resentment over taxes and unhappiness over government tipped the sentiment scales in the intervening years.

Writing in the business section of the *Washington Post* five days after the California election, Art Pine observed:

> To many analysts, the protest represents a fundamental shift in the national outlook over the past several years—the end of the share-the-wealth philosophy of the late 1960's and its willingness to enact new social programs that redistribute income, cut taxes for the poor, and close tax "loopholes" that allow wealthy taxpayers to escape payment of taxes.
> The new revolution is a revolt of middle-income and upper-middle-income taxpayers—for the moment, those in the $17,000 to $35,000 a year bracket—who seem to be saying they think we have done enough —that income distribution has gone about as far as it should, that the tax

system is as progressive as it ought to be, and that now it is time to provide relief for them as well. Part of it obviously is the squeeze of inflation and rising tax burdens. The increase in prices has prompted wage boosts that push taxpayers into higher income brackets, leaving them with proportionately less take-home pay than they had at the end of the 1960's. And while Congress has cut taxes almost annually in recent years, most [of the tax saving] has gone to the lower income brackets.

Pine and other analysts believe President Carter may have badly misread public sentiment about taxes and that this is why his tax reform proposals are getting such a cool reception in Congress. People contend that they do not want tax reform to close loopholes or to redistribute income; they want tax *relief.* And whatever reform is enacted ought to help the middle- and upper-middle-income level, not the bottom of the income scale.

Point 4 and the parenthetical observation point up one more factor to consider in analyzing why Proposition 13 rolled up such an astonishing victory. Pine makes this further distinction:

> The revolt is more complex than simply a matter of taxes. Surveys by almost every major polling organization show it also is a protest against the performance of government—frustration that the "bureaucracy" isn't delivering what it promised for the tax money. In effect, voters are deeply distrustful of government—and the tax issue is one way to fight back.[10]

A wide range of resentments and frustrations, many of them legitimate, did indeed accumulate in the five years intervening between the summary rejection of Proposition 1 and the overwhelming adoption of Proposition 13. But it took more than that to turn the tide: It took a campaign to tie all those resentments and frustrations into one package, to articulate them, and to exploit them, and the right wing played a crucial role in packaging the product.

The key figure in the Proposition 13 fight was Howard Jarvis, a seventy-five-year-old chronic gadfly on the California scene. A lobbyist for the Apartment Association of Los Angeles, an organization made up of apartment house owners (who will surely benefit from Proposition 13), Jarvis has run unsuccessfully for offices ranging from county assessor to U.S. senator. For the past fifteen years, however, much of his effort has been directed toward getting property taxes cut in California. In the Proposition 13 campaign he parlayed a determined debating style, a colorful and gutsy public image, earthy humor, and a gift for oversimplifying the issue into a big victory for his long-time obsession.

What isn't widely known about Howard Jarvis is his association with right-wing causes. *Group Research Report* of May 30, 1978, says of Jarvis, "The driving force there is Howard Jarvis, a veteran property-owners' lobbyist and foe of bond issues. Jarvis has long been active in the right wing and has participated in at least two tax protest meetings sponsored by the far-right Liberty Lobby."

Jarvis' campaign was generally supported by the conservative National Tax Limitation Committee, which was organized in 1976 "to impose constitutional tax limitation on the taxing and spending power of government" and focused on the states.

> Its chairman is William Rickenbacker, a conservative writer and money expert; its President is Lewis K. Uhler, an early member of the John Birch Society who became head of California's Office of Economic Opportunity for Ronald Reagan. Richard Viguerie has helped the organization raise money, and its letterhead includes well-known conservatives.[11]

The campaign for Proposition 13 provides a classic example of how the New Right functions. Taking a set of legitimate grievances—the high level and soaring rate of property taxes; the presence of a five-billion-dollar budget surplus the state did not use for tax relief; and what surely appeared to be governmental insensitivity to rapidly accumulating taxpayer unhappiness—Jarvis and company made quantum leaps in judgment and reached conclusions clearly not justified by the facts of the case. The campaign then employed the kind of oversimplified, hyperfervid rhetoric (illustrated by the Jarvis quote at the beginning of this chapter) to tar the full range of public employees, to bulldoze aside thoughtful warnings that a property tax cut of that size and immediacy would certainly slash sinew as well as fat in human services (how could taking away 70 percent of the Los Angeles school district's revenue *not* affect essential school services?), and to obscure the undeniable fact that Proposition 8 was fairer and more responsible than Proposition 13.

What is more, the kind of rhetoric employed by Jarvis and certain other advocates of Proposition 13—whether it was meant to be or not—surely appealed to the less noble aspects of human nature.

Syndicated columnist Joseph Kraft made this observation:

> Behind that legitimate cause, however, there lurks a cloven hoof self-indulgence by the relatively comfortable majority at the expense of the poor minorities. The *Los Angeles Times* and CBS, in that connection, published a highly revealing poll that identified the reasons moving people who voted for Proposition 13. One of the questions asked was what services voters felt could most usefully be curtailed. A huge number (69 percent) cited welfare payments to the poor. A fairly large number (21 percent) named a service chiefly beneficial to the black and Chicano minorities—mass transit. But when it came to services useful to the middle class, the willingness to make sacrifice disappeared. Only 1 percent thought cuts should come in the fire department. Only 4 percent were prepared to see reductions in the amount spent for police.[12]

And Haynes Johnson said of the success of Proposition 13: "The current fed-up-with-government-and-taxes mood severely challenges political leadership at every level from the White House down. It also offers a classic opportunity for political demagoguery and an exhibition of widespread public mean-spiritedness."[13]

The ramifications of Proposition 13 extend even farther. Many leaders of the initiative displayed another facet of the New Right mind-set: *blind indifference to the ultimate consequences of their achievement, even when those consequences fly directly counter to what the New Right professes to believe.*

Examples:

1. The New Right poses as a populist movement that eschews the traditional conservative alignment with big business and industry. Yet, by defeating Proposition 8, which would have limited property tax relief to homeowners and renters, and passing Proposition 13, the New Right actually contributed to helping commercial and industrial propertyowners *more* than the average homeowner. As noted before, only a third of the immediate benefits will go to homeowners, the other two thirds to commercial and industrial propertyowners. Moreover,

> that portion [to homeowners] is likely to decline over time, thanks to the wrinkle in the plan opponents failed to make clear to the voters. Under Jarvis-Gann, assessments can only rise 2 percent a year, until a piece of property is sold, when it is reassessed at market value. Homes change hands every seven years, on the average; commercial and industrial property much less often. Over time, the homeowners will see their share of the property tax burden increasing, while commercial and industrial property owners benefit.[14]

2. The New Right ostensibly believes, as former Treasury Secretary William E. Simon says he believes, that "the best government is the least government." Yet, passage of Proposition 13 seems destined to shift governmental responsibility from the local level to the state and even the federal levels as local units are deprived of the locally generated property tax revenue and control over the spending of that revenue. Money to provide essential services must come from *somewhere*. What the state cannot provide because of restrictions placed on the legislature in voting new taxes or increased rates for existing taxes may have to come from the federal government.

3. In the same regard, although the New Right cites the federal government as the prime target of its campaign to reduce the size and the income of government, passage of Proposition 13 will, in at least one respect, help swell the coffers of the federal government. Because California taxpayers can deduct local property taxes from federal income tax returns, cutting property taxes by 60 percent might increase the federal government's tax take in California by several billion dollars.

4. The intertwine of federal, state, and local programs makes Proposition 13 results even more perplexing. There are now 215 federal grants-in-aid programs going to California, at a cost of $4.1 billion. Because state and local governments have matching requirements to secure these funds, it now appears that California could lose as much as $3 billion of that federal money. Although the federal government provides 90 percent of the funding for such facilities as highways and mass transit, it requires 50 percent in local matching funds for administering food stamps, medical assistance, and other such programs, and 25 percent matching funds for water treatment plants.

5. A seeming target of some Proposition 13 advocates—the cutting of welfare benefits—might also be frustrated by federal-state-local relationships. State officials say that federal law prohibits them from actually reducing the $4.9 billion spent on welfare, so any cuts in government costs will have to come from other areas.

6. Still another consequence may be damage to California's bond rating, for such a sharp blow to the state's income-outgo balance sheet would raise doubts about the state's capacity to

proceed—at least for the immediate future—on a sound, businesslike, orderly basis.

All this, of course, does not even touch upon the biggest question of all—how deeply essential services may have to be cut to meet the economizing mandate imposed by Proposition 13. No one knows for certain. The five-billion-dollar surplus will be used to help cushion immediate cuts, but when the surplus is gone what happens next year? Only one thing seems evident at this point: The constituencies of those human services that have the least political influence will suffer first and most.

It's estimated that Federal funds account for one dollar of every three received by state and local governments today. That's $73 billion, ten times the Federal aid level in 1960. You don't hear any states clamoring to reject that money, but you do hear the argument that Washington, not the state house, largely determines how that money is spent. That, and something else—the actions of the Federal government—are a prime cause in inflation; and it's inflation that forces more and more people into higher income brackets forcing them to pay higher and higher taxes, including higher taxes on the inflated values of their homes.

The familiar villain, Washington, rises again. But the latest explosion of public resentment at the local level has the ironic effect of forcing greater reliance on central authority—first, from the California capital for emergency funds to operate such essential services as schools, fire and police, and then from California to you know where. And who suffers most? As always, those who have the least of everything, including political clout. The frustration and anger are understandable enough, but the result—a furious and selfish lashing out at all forms of government services—tragically sets the stage for even uglier days to come.[15]

The defeat of liberal Republican Clifford Case, the nomination of conservative Roger Jepsen in Iowa, and the overwhelming approval of Proposition 13 in California delighted the New Right and frightened liberals and moderates.

Was June 6, 1978 a temporary high-water mark for the New Right that will quickly recede, or did it signal the beginning of an ultraconservative flood tide that will crest in the Presidential election of 1980?

Liberal columnist Marquis Childs saw the latter as a distinct possibility.

It has long been the conventional wisdom that no one too far to the left of center or too far to the right can be elected president. On the left, Senator George McGovern, the Democratic candidate, proved that in 1972. He carried Massachusetts and the District of Columbia against Richard Nixon.

As the Republican nominee in 1980, Reagan would test the other end of the spectrum. It is hard to believe that anyone holding such consistently conservative views in both foreign and domestic policy can become president. But the tide is moving to the right so rapidly that the wisdom of the past may no longer prevail.[16]

The surface evidence is that political leaders of both parties either enthusiastically or reluctantly agree with Childs. California Governor Jerry Brown campaigned on a platform of "lowered expectations," but once in office he discovered that distinguishing between unjustified demands for government services and legitimate needs for such services was easier said than done. He gambled his Presidential aspirations when he elected to oppose Proposition 13 but then had to scramble—with seeming success—to put a positive face on the outcome of the vote.

On the Republican side, Senate Minority Leader Howard Baker, a Presidential hopeful in 1980, says Republicans would be foolish not to embrace the tax issue, and another potential Presidential candidate, American Conservative Union Chairman Philip Crane, was so inspired by Proposition 13 that he promptly introduced a proposed constitutional amendment to limit federal government spending to one third the national income.

The most significant evidence of the impact of Proposition 13 is the tax bill finally passed in the waning hours of the second session of the 95th Congress.

After rejecting by a margin of nearly two to one the Roth-Kemp tax cut bill, which called for a tax reduction of approximately 30 percent over three years—for a total of $100 billion or more—the Senate voted a tax cut of 20 percent, or $140 billion, over four years if the government met stringent spending targets.

In the House-Senate conference on the tax bill, however, the reduction was limited to a one-year cut of $18.7 billion, a level believed acceptable to the President, and perhaps more prudent with regard to the uncertainties of economic recovery beyond that time period.

But while the Kemp-Roth approach was rejected, the tax revolt of 1978 made an unmistakable impact on the tax cuts that were finally voted into law.

A Congress with a top-heavy Democratic majority clearly shifted away from the historical Democratic pattern of voting tax relief.

As the *Washington Post* of October 16, 1978 noted, this Congress voted a tax reduction bill that gave 79 percent of the benefits to those making more than $15,000 a year, while those making less than $15,000 a year—50 percent of all taxpayers—got only 21 percent of the benefits of the tax cut.

The *Post* noted the day before that

> in the 95th Congress, the concerns of the middle class and American business clearly displaced the agenda of social and economic issues that has dominated Congressional politics since the inauguration of the New Deal 45 years ago. This overwhelmingly Democratic Congress chose to raise Social Security taxes while cutting the tax on capital gains. It rejected virtually every proposal put forward by organized labor; on many issues it gave ground to business. It gave the oil companies a natural gas price deregulation bill they had sought unsuccessfully for 25 years. It willingly voted large increases in defense spending, but shied away from expensive domestic initiatives and concentrated on cutting the Federal budget deficit.

These actions, the *Post* said, represented Congress' collective belief that middle-class Americans—home-owning, employed, and relatively prosperous—would no longer vote for politicians whose principal concern appeared to be the have-nots rather than the haves.

Veteran Democratic Congressman Richard Bolling of Missouri looked at the record of what was an active and productive Congress, but a Congress which nevertheless had little taste for new government programs yet some reluctance to abandon old ones, as a Congress that was "caught between eras, uncertain as to what to do and uncomfortable in its uncertainty."

CHAPTER 9

The Psyche of the Radical Right

Quisling-Traitor Senator McIntyre: Conservative Republicans have added your despicable name to the list of TRAITORS *in our stench-producing Senate dominated by those on the Radical Left and representing your ilk. Your refusal to be swayed by either reason or eloquence indicates your leftist orientation.* HEMISPHERIC SECURITY AND DEFENSE *will be threatened by Castro's Communistic allies and your ideological cohorts. An awesomely large mass of information can be mobilized to invalidate your fuzzy left-wing thinking.* TRAITORS *of your gutter orientation abound in our corrupt Senate dominated by the scum and vermin of the Marxist Democrats. Rest assured, Commissar McIntyre, that you will be classified as insidious and corrupt. Americans who care to stand up in your Marxist behalf are to be sledge-hammered as* QUISLINGS *and odious incendiaries. We will concentrate on your vicious leftist* VOTING RECORD *and your excessive loyalty*

> *to the liberal pig in the tainted* WHITE HOUSE. *My*
> *qualifications: Washington University*
> *postgraduate and honor student. You are*
> *unquestionably one of the most* DISHONEST AND
> VICIOUSLY CORRUPT *hucksters and charlatans in*
> *our thieving Senate controlled by vermin of your*
> FAR LEFT *views. We will work assiduously to*
> *damn you in scathing terms.* YOU ARE AIDING AND
> ABETTING your beloved COMMUNIST CAUSE.
> CONSERVATIVES *are being enlisted to stomp our*
> *way through your Communizing Senate which*
> *dares to stand up to its* CONSERVATIVE BETTERS.
> *Rest assured that we deem you to be on the same*
> *plane as the* COMMUNISTS. *You are vermin.*
> —Letter I received
> following Senate vote on
> Panama Canal treaties

One letter of this sort may be sadly amusing in its absurdity, but when similar sentiments are expressed by hundreds of correspondents, what at first seems absurd begins to appear ominous.

In all fairness, I cannot charge the organizations that make up the New Right with directly soliciting a mail campaign of this kind. Neither can I totally exonerate the movement. From the outset, it was obvious that the very nature of the New Right's effort to defeat the Panama Canal treaties was more likely to prime the pump of paranoid hatred than it was to encourage reasoned and civil opposition to the documents.

This chapter deals with the psychology of the extremist and aims to distinguish between those Americans who are already lost to reason and those who—because of legitimate anxieties—are subject to the blandishments of the New Right yet could still be reached by the voice of moderation.

I have drawn upon the insights of Richard Hofstadter's *The Paranoid Style in American Politics*, which provides, in my judgment, the definitive analysis of modern-day right-wing extremism. Although Hofstadter's book was published nearly a decade before the emergence of the New Right, the mind-set, techniques, and goals of the movement and of its zealous fol-

lowers closely resemble the characteristics of the pseudoconservative Hofstadter described. To highlight this correspondence, excerpts from Hofstadter's analysis have been paralleled
with contemporary quotations from New Right leaders, of
whom few, if any, were widely known when Hofstadter's book
was written.

> There is . . . a dynamic of dissent in America today. Representing no
> more than a modest fraction of the electorate, it is not so powerful as the
> liberal dissent of the New Deal era, but it is powerful enough to set the
> tone of our political life and to establish throughout the country a kind of
> punitive reaction.[1]

> *We're going to look very carefully at the votes when all this is over
> and do an awful lot of punishing next election.*
> —*Richard Viguerie*

> *We must prove our ability to get revenge on people who go against us.*
> —*Howard Phillips*

Hofstadter noted that unlike most of the liberal dissent of the
past, the new right-wing dissent is based upon a relentless demand for conformity.

> It can most accurately be called pseudo-conservative . . . because its
> exponents, although they believe themselves to be conservatives and
> usually employ the rhetoric of conservatism, show signs of a serious and
> restless dissatisfaction with American life, traditions, and institutions.
> They have little in common with the temperate and compromising spirit
> of true conservatism in the classical sense of the word, and they are far
> from pleased with the dominant practical conservatism of the moment.[2]

> *We are different from previous generations of conservatives. We are
> no longer working to preserve the status quo. We are radicals, working
> to overturn the present power structure of this country.*
> —*Paul Weyrich*

After discussing nineteenth-century manifestations of extremism, Hofstadter noted some important differences with the contemporary right wing.

> The spokesmen for those earlier movements felt that they stood for
> causes and personal types that were still in possession of their country—
> that they were fending off threats to a still well-established way of life in
> which they played an important part. But the modern right
> wing . . . feels dispossessed: America has been largely taken away
> from them and their kind, though they are determined to try to repossess
> it and to prevent the final destructive act of subversion. The old Ameri-

can virtues have already been eaten away by cosmopolitans and intellectuals; and old competitive capitalism has been gradually undermined by
socialist and communist schemers.[3]

Our enemies are not encroaching socialists [who are] taking away
what's there. They have already succeeded. We are not in power. They
are.

—Paul Weyrich

Hofstadter noted still another feature distinguishing contemporary Rightists from their predecessors: a bold disposition to
broaden the old foreign conspiracy theories to include betrayal
of national security and independence by "major statesmen
seated at the very centers of American power." When he wrote
this particular segment of *The Paranoid Style in American Poli-*
tics, Hofstadter may have been thinking particularly of Robert
H. Welch Jr., founder of the John Birch Society. Early editions of
Welch's book, *The Politician*, published in 1963, reportedly described Dwight Eisenhower as "a dedicated, conscious agent of
the Communist conspiracy." *

Today's New Right further exploits the "betrayal at home"
theory, at times exhibiting the same recklessness in impugning
the loyalty and patriotism of prominent American leaders. Witness these excerpts from a speech National Conservative Caucus Chairman Meldrim Thomson Jr. delivered at a regional
meeting of the John Birch Society in Los Angeles, California on
March 8, 1978:

Why, I ask, should we turn over to appeasers and compromisers with
Communism—men like Kissinger and Brzezinski whose commitment to
the high ideals of America's founding fathers is as cavalier as the wiles of
an alley cat—the direction of the sacred homeland of Washington, Lin-
coln and Teddy Roosevelt. . . . We tolerate at our own peril men in pub-
lic office such as Kissinger, Brzezinski and Andrew Young—co-con-
spirators in the establishment of one-world government.

Carter's foreign policy is based on an accommodation with commu-
nism. It would homogenize the freedom precepts of our founding fa-
thers with the tyranny of the Soviets and the inhumanity of Red China
to produce the horror show of one-world government. Carter would
lead us beside the communist path to national suicide.

* Later editions of *The Politician* muted the charge to some degree, saying
Eisenhower was "either a willing agent, or an integral and important part of a
conspiracy of gangsters determined to rule the world at any cost."

President Kennedy gutted the Monroe Doctrine when he through evil purpose *or* by miserable cowardice *pulled out of the Bay of Pigs commitment and thereby placed the stamp of approval on Castro's murderous and inhuman regime.*

(This kind of inflammatory language—by the national chairman of the New Right's largest grass-roots political action organization—makes it impossible for me to exonerate the movement of priming the pump of hatred.)

As Hofstadter makes clear, the obsession with conspiracy that inspires such rhetoric is linked closely to two other common characteristics of extremist reasoning: apocalypticism and absolutism. Those who are locked into this mind-set, he contended, believe history *is* a conspiracy, set in motion by demonic forces of almost transcendental power. They believe that nothing short of an all-out crusade is necessary to defeat it.

These people, Hofstadter said, see the fate of this conspiracy in apocalyptic terms, so they traffic in the birth and death of whole worlds, whole political orders, whole systems of human values. They are always "manning the barricades of civilization." He described them as "a secular and demonic version of adventism."

I work twelve hours a day "to save the western world."
—Richard Viguerie

The Canal issue is the last chance we Americans shall have to preserve our freedom, short of catastrophic war.
—Meldrim Thomson Jr.

Considering the absolutist tendencies in this kind of extremist, Hofstadter wrote:

He does not see social conflict in the manner of the working politician. Since what is at stake is always a conflict between absolute good and absolute evil, the quality needed is not a willingness to compromise but the will to fight things out to a finish. Nothing but complete victory will do. Since the enemy is thought of as being totally evil and totally unappeasable, he must be totally eliminated—if not from the world, at least from the theater of operations.[4]

Every Senator up for reelection who fails to vote against the treaties must be swept from office as though he were a Benedict Arnold. You and I must not stop there. We must mount the greatest electoral revolution in the history of our nation by sending only Americans to Congress, and to our State Houses and Legislatures. Yes, and on that great tide of public resentment we shall ride the crest of the storm until Carter and all of his one-worlders and international bankers are driven from office in 1980.

— *Meldrim Thomson Jr.*

Thomson's allusion to "international bankers" is in the pattern of a fourth and perhaps the most distinctive feature of extremist reasoning. Hofstadter considered this especial characteristic when he wrote about "a curious leap in the imagination that is always made at some critical point in the recitation of events."

He said that the surface plausibility of typical pseudoconservative conspiracy theories

> lies, in good measure, in this appearance of the most careful, conscientious, and seemingly coherent application to detail, the laborious accumulation of what can be taken as convincing evidence for the most fantastic conclusions, the careful preparation for the big leap from the undeniable to the unbelievable.[5]

The list of banking creditors of the Panama Canal reads like the International Bankers Who's Who. It includes the Narody Bank of Moscow, the London Branch of the Chase Manhattan Bank, Citicorp International Bank of London, International American Development Bank, Continental Bank of Chicago, the Export-Import Bank of Washington, the Marine Midland Bank, and the Agency for International Development. All of these banks are vitally interested in the success of the proposed [Panama Canal] treaty. They see the American taxpayer as eventually picking up the tab for bailing Torrijos out of hock. . . . Businessmen with whom I talked [in Panama] suggested that their American companies would lobby for a new treaty with Panama. I hope that if they do, the taxpayers and working people of this nation will mount the biggest boycott in the history of America against all companies that place pride above principle.

— *Meldrim Thomson Jr.*[6]

We have discovered that the executive branch of our government is now totally controlled by David Rockefeller's Tri-lateral Commission. Approximately 65 members are elite bankers, multinational businessmen and politicians here in the United States. In excess of 20 are allegedly involved in the executive branch of our government. They have negotiated, drafted, signed and are about to have the Panama Canal treaties ratified. Through interlocking directorships and bureaucratic control, they have been able to silence the media.

— *Mail-o-gram sent to all members of the U.S. Senate and the Supreme Court on March 14, 1978 by the "Committee of the Silent Majority"*

> *The Panama Canal treaties are "the product of incompetent negotia-*
> *tion influenced by corruption and ineptitude at the highest level leading*
> *to surrender of effectively American territory to a hostile authoritarian*
> *dictator who at least winks at narcotics trafficking, buttressed by im-*
> *mense and probably partly illegal lobbying expenditures by the Execu-*
> *tive branch."*
>
> —Charles A. Moser
> Treasurer, Committee for the
> Survival of a Free Congress,
> March 10, 1978

Thus, in the instance of the Panama Canal treaties, that "curious leap in imagination" Hofstadter described took a few unrelated facts—six consecutive Presidents favoring modernization of the canal treaty and several banks overextending credit to Panama—and wove them into a detailed syllogism with a conclusion so preposterous it even drew the scorn of that paradigm of conservatism, William F. Buckley Jr.

Buckley, who, to the dismay of the New Right, supported ratification of the Panama Canal treaties, concluded a column he wrote at the time of the treaties debate with this cutting observation:

> There are people going around—I mean grown people—saying that
> the whole Panama Canal treaty revision is a plot comprehending Presi
> dents Eisenhower, Kennedy, Johnson, Nixon, Ford and Carter, the State
> Department, the Joint Chiefs of Staff and the majority of the Senate to
> bail out a couple of U.S. banks that lent too much money to Panama.
> That's the right wing's Grassy Knoll.

Grassy Knoll it would seem to be, but judging from the letters I received concerning the Panama Canal treaties many Americans were able to make that "curious leap in imagination," going on for page after page with alleged documentation to sustain that bizarre theory. Many of these messages also exhibited the previously described characteristics of apocalypticism, absolutism, and obsession with other alleged conspiracies.

If liberals and moderates are to understand the impetus behind the New Right and why the tenets of the movement seem plausible to so many Americans, it is necessary first to consider the factors that may contribute to the mind-set of the pseudoconservative. Hofstadter posed questions and then offered answers.

> All of us have reason to fear the power of international communism,
> and all our lives are profoundly affected by it. Why do some Americans

try to face this threat for what it is, a problem that exists in a world-wide theater of action, while others try to reduce it largely to a matter of domestic conformity? Why do some of us prefer to look for allies in the democratic world, while others seem to prefer authoritarian allies or none at all? Why do the pseudo-conservatives express such a persistent fear and suspicion of *their own government* . . . ? Why is the pseudo-conservative impelled to go beyond the more or less routine partisan argument that we have been the victims of considerable misgovernment . . . to the disquieting accusation that we have actually been the victims of persistent conspiracy and betrayal?[7]

A speculative hypothesis to answer these questions is offered, a hypothesis that my experience with the Radical Right persuades me may be valid.

Pseudoconservatism, Hofstadter said, might be "in good part a product of the rootlessness and heterogeneity of American life and, above all, of its peculiar scramble for status and its peculiar search for secure identity."[8] In this country, he said, a person's status, defined as his relative place in the prestige hierarchy of his community, and his rudimentary sense of belonging to the community, defined as his "Americanism," have been closely joined. There is a special poignancy and urgency to our status strivings, Hofstadter conjectured, "because, as a people extremely democratic in our social institutions, we have had no clear, consistent, and recognizable system of status" and "because we no longer have the relative ethnic homogeneity we had up to about eighty years ago, our sense of belonging has long had about it a high degree of uncertainty."[9]

Hofstadter noted that status concerns of present-day politics are shared by two groups of Americans, who arrive at them from opposite directions. The first group are the old-family, Anglo-Saxon Protestants, and the second group those who are found among descendants of latter-day immigrants, many of them Catholic. The Anglo-Saxon old families, he said, are most disposed toward pseudoconservatism when they are losing caste, the newer Americans when they are gaining caste. The first group claims status by descent, but their stocks are not as dominant today as they once were. In consequence, he said, "some of the old-family Americans have turned to find new objects for their resentment among liberals, left-wingers, intellectuals, and the like."[10]

Even more important in any consideration of today's New Right is Hofstadter's hypothesis as it relates to the second group

—the new-family Americans—for it is them to whom the New Right devotes so much attention.

Nearly nine million immigrants arrived here between 1881 and 1900 and another fourteen and a half million in the next twenty years. Indeed, immigrants and their descendants make up such a large portion of the population that Margaret Mead contends the characteristc American outlook is now a third-generation point of view.

Rebuffed and made to feel inferior by "native stock," long denied better jobs, often treated as second-class citizens, many immigrants grew insecure over their social status and unsure of their identity and sense of belonging. Thus, "achieving a better type of job or a better social status and becoming 'more American'" became "practically synonymous, and the passions that ordinarily attach to social position have been vastly heightened by being associated with the need to belong."[11]

Earlier I noted how, as an Irish-Catholic in a state long dominated by old-family WASPS, my own early attitudes and value systems were influenced by these strivings. The fact that my father had achieved economic standing in our home community did mitigate our new-family insecurity over status and identity, however. Thus, I was never subjected to the secondary, but crucial, pressures described by Hofstadter.

Social changes and variation in life-styles strain the relationships within both old and new families, Hofstadter said. Old families see these changes as threats to their inherited social position and to traditional imperatives of character and personal conduct deriving from nineteenth-century Yankee-Protestant-rural ethos. New families see these modifications as making it more difficult to hold the respect of their children, to discipline them to conform, to be respectable and to succeed, and to protect economic and social status won through great sacrifice. The accelerated pace and intensity of these social and life-style changes that have occurred in the thirteen years since Hofstadter wrote *The Paranoid Style* have, in turn, sharply increased these intrafamily strains. I have seen the results in ethnic-Catholic families in New Hampshire and in old-line Yankee families as well.

"The relations between generations," Hofstadter wrote, "being cast in no stable mold, have been disordered, and the

status anxieties of parents have been inflicted upon children."
By putting inordinate pressure on their children to conform and
be respectable in order to realize the ambitions denied them,
parents unconsciously create great hostility to authority. But
because of the child-parent relationship this hostility cannot
even be admitted to consciousness, much less expressed. As a
result, Hofstadter hypothesized, it sometimes manifests itself
in precisely the opposite manner—"a massive overcompensa-
tion . . . in the form of extravagant submissiveness to strong
power."[12]

Hofstadter called attention to studies showing that among
people who "have strong ethnic prejudices and pseudoconservative tendencies, there is a high proportion of persons who
have been unable to develop the capacity to criticize justly and
in moderation the failings of parents and who are profoundly in-
tolerant of the ambiguities of thought and feeling that one is so
likely to find in real-life situations."[13]

He contended that among other things, pseudoconservatism
is a disorder in relation to authority that is characterized by an
inability to find means other than by domination or by submis-
sion to relate to other humans.

> The pseudo-conservative always imagines himself to be dominated
> and imposed upon because he feels that he is not dominant, and knows
> of no other way of interpreting his position. He imagines that his own
> government and his own leaders are engaged in a more or less contin-
> uous conspiracy against him because he has come to think of authority
> only as something that aims to manipulate and deprive him. It is for this
> reason, among others, that he enjoys seeing outstanding generals, distin-
> guished Secretaries of State, and prominent scholars browbeaten.[14]

The letter quoted at the beginning of this chapter reveals
this characteristic. It also reflects another trait that Hofstadter
links to the pseudoconservative—superpatriotism.

Since so many Americans' forebears voluntarily left one country to come to this land, they cannot, as people in their native
land do, think of nationality as coming with birth. Nationality
becomes for them an object of striving.

> This is one reason why problems of "loyalty" arouse such an emo-
> tional response in many Americans and why it is so hard in the American
> climate of opinion to make any clear distinction between the problem of
> national security and the question of personal loyalty. Of course, there is

no real reason to doubt the loyalty to America of the immigrants and
their descendants, or their willingness to serve the country as fully as if
their ancestors had lived here for three centuries. Nonetheless, they
have been thrown on the defensive by those who have in the past cast
doubts upon the fullness of their Americanism.[15]

Hofstadter pointed out, for example, that people in other
lands do not find it necessary to speak of themselves as "100
percent" French or English or Italian, nor to call one another
"un-English" or "un-French" or "un-Italian" when they disagree over national policies. And, he asked, what other country
finds it necessary to create institutional rituals for the sole purpose of guaranteeing to its people the genuineness of their nationality?

It is in these uniquely American attitudes, Hofstadter said,
that we find the primary value that patriotic societies and antisubversive ideologies have for their exponents: They provide
reassurance to the old-family American and to the new-family
American.

Hofstadter also conjectured that the typical prejudiced person
and the typical pseudoconservative are often one and the same,
and that it is merely the expediencies and the strategy of the situation that cause groups that once emphasized racial discrimination to find other scapegoats. Both the old-American type and
the new ethnic elements are

> so desperately eager for reassurance of their fundamental Americanism
> [that they] can conveniently converge upon liberals, critics, and noncon-
> formists of various sorts, as well as Communists and suspected Commu-
> nists. To proclaim themselves vigilant in the pursuit of those who are
> even so much as accused of "disloyalty" to the United States is a way not
> only of reasserting but of advertising their own loyalty—and one of the
> chief characteristics of American super-patriotism is its constant inner
> urge toward self-advertisement.[16]

Hofstadter said that the modern-day superpatriotic pseudoconservative is much happier to have as objects of hatred the
Eastern Establishment and the Ivy League intellectuals rather
than Julius and Ethel Rosenberg. In the minds of the
status-driven, he contended, it is no special virtue to be more
American than the Rosenbergs, but it is rewarding indeed to be
more American than the powerful leaders of the nation—Presidents and secretaries of state, for example. This is why, he im-

plied, that in the ideology of the authoritarian right wing, anti-Semitism and other blatant forms of prejudice "have been recently soft-pedaled."

> Anti-Semitism, it has been said, is the poor man's snobbery. We Americans are always trying to raise the standard of living, and the same principle now seems to apply to standards of hating. So during the past fifteen years or so, the authoritarians have moved on from anti-Negroism and anti-Semitism to anti-Achesonianism, anti-intellectualism, anti-nonconformism, and other variants of the same idea.[17]*

Toward the conclusion of this examination of the characteristics that define the pseudoconservative, Hofstadter contended that the rise of the Radical Right is not a momentary mood, but one of the long waves of twentieth-century America. He could not foresee it plunging this country into a totalitarian nightmare, but he closed on this prescient note:

> In a populistic culture like ours, which seems to lack a responsible elite with political and moral autonomy, and in which it is possible to exploit the wildest currents of public sentiment for private purposes, *it is at least conceivable that a highly organized, vocal, active, and well-financed minority could create a political climate in which the rational pursuit of our well-being and safety would become impossible.*[18]

---

* Evidence of this is in the letter cited at the beginning of this chapter. For instance, the President is called "the liberal pig in the tainted White House."

CHAPTER 10

Why Now?

The success of the "New Right" is due not only to its own ingenuity and luck, but also to the present defensiveness and confusion within the progressive community. While the "New Right" displays a boisterous elan, the progressive community is questioning most of its assumptions, including such basic ones as the value of political activism.
—SCOTT WOLF
The Democratic Viewpoint,
February 1978

When Richard Hofstadter acknowledged the possibility that a movement like the New Right could evolve in American politics and have the effect he envisioned, he may not have foreseen how swiftly this could come about. In the past two years the organizations that make up the New Right, at times working only with one another and at other times working with old-line conservative organizations, have indeed succeeded in creating "a political climate in which the rational pursuit of our well-being

166

and safety"* has become considerably more difficult, if not impossible.

We have already recounted some of the movement's electoral successes, but the evidence transcends that.

In terms of party organization and structure, two prominent leaders of the New Right have risen to powerful positions within the national Republican party. Charles R. Black, former chairman of the National Conservative Political Action Committee, is now the political director of the Republican National Committee. He, in turn, has placed former NCPAC personnel in key positions with the RNC; for example, J. Kenneth Klingle and David Nickles now both serve as regional RNC directors. And Roger Stone, who once worked for the Viguerie-connected Public Service Research Council and was treasurer of the National Conservative Political Action Committee, is now chairman of the Young Republican National Federation.[1] Moreover, the New Right also has succeeded in installing their people in dozens of key local and state party positions.*

Beyond this, we have already seen how the New Right has created a potent meld of single-issue constituencies; how it worked with veterans and with patriotic organizations to keep the new Panama Canal treaties hostage for months; how it worked with a variety of taxpayer groups to push Proposition 13 and other tax-limiting referenda to victory; how it worked with the U.S. Chamber of Commerce and the National Association of Manufacturers to stymie passage of labor law reform; how in the 95th Congress it beat back new voter-registration legislation, public financing of elections, the Consumer Protection Agency, a number of other important pieces of progressive legislation, and made its impact felt in the tax bill voted by that Congress; and how it is now launching a campaign to kill SALT II.

One could survey these early accomplishments and the move-

* See chapter 9.
* The *Washington Post* of August 7, 1978 provided an example: "Oregon Republicans, who blocked the comeback of liberal former governor Tom McCall, saw their party organization taken over by a right-wing faction last week as Walter Huss, a fundamentalist minister, won the state party chairmanship. . . . Huss, whose candidacy was opposed by virtually all Republican officials and candidates in the state, conducted an intensive effort, recruiting conservative supporters at the precinct level."

ment's organizational, communicating, and financing skills and draw the reasonable conclusion that the New Right might well control the 1980 Republican national convention and nominate its own candidates to head the ticket.

The question, then, is why has the New Right evolved at this particular time . . . and why has it been so effective?

The obvious reasons have been previously examined. The leaders of the New Right are, for the most part, young and vigorous political activists who have been turned off by the traditional parties, who are well organized, work well in concert, and have become skilled in the use of computer technology, direct mail lobbying, and fund-raising. Moreover, the New Right allows each member group of the organizational network to function in a highly focused manner, confident that the overall goal is being pursued in different channels by other members. This serves to limit duplication of effort and conserves and sharply focuses the impact of energy and money.

Then, too, the New Right is not hobbled by old-line political loyalties. Its leaders do not hesitate to challenge Republican candidates and officeholders who do not measure up to their rigid standards of conservatism.

Linked to these assets is the freedom this tightly knit handful of political leaders has in deciding just what issues to exploit. They do not have to win consensus from a caucus, much less a political party. Over a cup of coffee they can decide what kind of campaign in behalf of what kind of subject can generate maximum emotion and political return, be it the Panama Canal, abortion, women's rights, gay rights, gun control, pornography, or other issues involved in status politics.

Earlier I discussed the social forces at work in our time to bring those status issues to the forefront of the political process and how the pressures of inflation and taxation have now begun to merge status politics with interest politics . . . again to the advantage of the New Right. Columnist George C. Will, one of the more thoughtful and responsible of today's intellectual conservatives, summed up the political importance of inflation in just five words: "Inflation is a great conservatizer."

Not only are more and more Americans caught up hard in inflation's squeeze—approaching double digit dimensions in the summer of 1978—but they are becoming more aware of and discouraged by the intransigence of the inflation problem and more disenchanted with their government's seeming inability to bring it under control.

Tied closely to inflation is the inflated tax bite taken from wage earners' wallets and from small businesses. Both groups share with many other Americans the chronic suspicion that because of unfair tax laws they pay more than their share of the load. And they suspect that their tax dollars are going to support an ever-larger, ever-more-intrusive, yet ever-more-remote federal bureaucracy.

Under the twin pressures of inflation and taxation, a shift in emphasis has taken place in interest politics. The overriding consideration now seems to be what government is doing *to* me, not what government is doing *for* me. The New Right is ably and assiduously encouraging this shift, in part, by exploiting the thrift ethic so commonplace among home-town Americans from old-line families and new-family urban ethnics. In order to be a good citizen, one must pull one's own weight. One does not "go on the town," as it is said in parts of New England. Thus, living within one's budget, saving for the future, bequeathing to one's children the means for an even more independent life is both goal and norm. Although Keynesians can make a case that there are times when government deficit spending will prove cost-effective in the long run, this notion runs completely counter to the thrift ethic. For many years loyalty to what the New Deal had meant in terms of economic well-being served to cover up this ideological conflict. But as the era of deficit spending, unbalanced budgets, and increasing national debt was extended under both Democratic and Republican administrations, the contradiction between government practice and the familial thrift ethic invited politicizing.

Moreover, the incongruity serves to encourage other resentments, not the least of which is the ill will that "producer" citizens feel when they measure their way of life against what they perceive to be the way of life of "nonproducers"—those on welfare, for example. While the producers caught in the inflation-tax bite are shopping carefully and doing without in order to stay within their budgets, they may see food stamp recipients shopping without restraint. As they struggle to meet doctor bills, dental bills, and health insurance premiums, producers see nonproducers getting health care through Medicaid that they, the producers, pay for with their tax dollars.

Coupled with this, and especially relevant in the case of low- and moderate-income citizens, is the fact that it is most often their families and neighborhoods that have been thrust out on the cutting edge of government's efforts to amend the wrongs of racial discrimination. It is the Middle American, especially the blue-collar Middle American, whose children are bused across school district lines to achieve racial balance in classrooms, and it is in his or her neighborhood that the effect of fair housing legislation is felt.

Underlying these specific resentments and frustrations is a more general anxiety, a fear that much that is held near and dear is under assault; that America is losing its direction, purpose, status, and power; and that its adversaries abroad are, in contrast, growing more powerful and threatening by the day. The notion that the Soviet Union now enjoys a decided military advantage over us and that, in partnership with Cuba, it is taking over Africa seems to be accepted by a number of Americans.

Even taking into account the youth, vigor, organization money, and computer skills of the New Right and the chance coalescing of a wide range of issues made to order for its exploitation, we still do not have the complete answer to why the movement emerged when it did or has succeeded as it has. The answer may lie in the relative absence of inspired opposition.

If we check the record closely, we will find that the successes of the New Right have been achieved by enlisting a relatively small number of highly motivated people to vote, to serve as convention delegates, to elect party officers, to lobby, and to spread the movement's gospel at a time when so many other Americans have withdrawn from politics out of apathy, preoccupation with self, or cynicism . . . *and* at a time when the New Right's natural opposition seems in a state of disarray.

Voter apathy is not a new phenomenon. Participation in the election process has been in decline for a number of years. In 1960, 63 percent of those eligible voted for President; by 1976 that figure was down to 54 percent. The same decline is evident in voter registration, despite the easing of requirements. In 1968, 77 percent registered to vote; eight years later that percentage dropped to 66.7. Moreover, the largest bloc of non-voters is the young—those under thirty-five.

What may be accelerating this disengagement from the political process in current times are the same conditions, ironically, that encouraged the rise of the New Right. Just as periods of peace and relative prosperity are the times when discontent traditionally surfaces on the political Right, they are also the times when many Americans turn away from social and political responsibilities and turn inward upon themselves. There is a reason why sociologists and psychologists call this generation the "Me Generation."

Columnist Haynes Johnson declared that "we are selfish, vain, narcissistic, insecure, overweight, ugly—and we don't give a damn about politics. Self-improvement is our preoccupation, hedonism our philosophy, looking out for No. 1 our theme. That last trait specifically speaks to what passes for the politics of the moment." For example, he noted, best-seller lists are dominated by self-improvement books like Robert J. Ringer's *Looking Out for Number One*.[2]

Accompanying the apathetic and the self-absorbed in the drift away from the political process are the cynical. A number of reasons why so many Americans have become cynical about their government have already been considered. What is important here is the set of consequences that flow from cynicism.

In midsummer 1978 Haynes Johnson wrote: "We are in a season of cynicism, and selfishness, that makes the task of anyone, at any level of government, increasingly difficult. Pity not Jimmy Carter, in Washington, but worry about the political process itself, across the country."[3]

Detachment from the political process, whether through apathy or hedonism, plays directly into the hands of the New Right. So does massive public cynicism. It was noted earlier that only 10 percent of the registered Republicans voted in the New Jersey primary in June 1978, thus making it possible for a New Right candidate to capture the Senate nomination with only a fraction of the vote. It has been pointed out, too, that the voter turnout for the celebrated Proposition 13 election in California was *lower* than it was for the previous primary, when no such nationally controversial issue was on the ballot.

Widespread cynicism at the same time inspires a "pox on both your houses" attitude toward the traditional political parties and the political process itself. It also makes the cynical citizen susceptible to the New Right's array of single-issue appeals and supportive of the kind of negative and punitive politics it practices.

All this is happening at the very time when, as David Broder puts it, the center of our political consensus is shattered. Not only are traditional coalitions for social legislation less united and less potent than they were, but individual liberals and moderates have retreated to the sidelines to rethink old assumptions.

Mention has also been made of the emergence of the "neoconservatives," that cluster of former intellectual leaders in the Democratic party who now publicly question the validity of federal programs they once supported. They are not unique among Democrats these days. Because a great many erstwhile bona fide liberals and moderates are doing their individual reassessments, columnist Ellen Goodman has called this the "ambidextrous age of political opinion."

> The New Ambidexters believe that welfare mothers should get off the dole and go to work, and that mothers of small children should stay home with them. They believe that we've all become far too selfish, too "me-first," but that individuals have the right to lead their lives as they choose. The Ambidexters simply hold on to a wide range of opinions simultaneously, without always seeing them as contradictory. They want government to provide more and cost less. They want security and independence. They believe in responsibility and freedom.
>
> They have lived long enough to see the cost accounting of change. They have seen that change, with the solutions, comes with a full attachment of new problems. When the government sets up a program to help those who can't work, they end up also helping those who won't work. When the government helps the aged who don't have families to depend on, they end up with more aged depending on the government instead of families. . . .
>
> The Ambidexters don't want to go back to the '30's and the '50's. Few people want to remove the Social Security System or take away compensation for unemployment. They have no interest in returning to desperation. But when they look ahead to the future they weigh the issues in both hands. The Ambidexters are aware that there are still serious social problems. They believe the government should Do Something. National Health Care. Day Care. Welfare Reform. But there are other problems. Big Government. Family Responsibility. Taxes.[4]

Ellen Goodman said it for a lot of us. We *are* puzzling. We *are* reassessing. I do not see this as bad; I see it as a mature, responsible facing-up to new realities. Out of it I hope will come a new consensus among liberals and moderates. Goodman sees this happening; she described it as "a regrouping by caring, activist people . . . who are . . . under few illusions about the problems of government, who are cautious about master plans to overhaul society, but who still want to help. People who are willing to work within the ceiling of 'lowered expectations' and within the structure of 'cost-effective' planning."[5]

Unfortunately, we moderates and liberals are taking this hiatus for introspection and the search for new consensus precisely at the time when events and developments are encouraging the New Right to become more aggressive in espousing their dangerous certainties and bolder in their punishing tactics.

This has a significance beyond the obvious. Indeed, it provides another and crucially important dimension to consider in gauging the potency of today's Radical Rightist movement. If we were to limit our assessment to the amount of money raised and spent, the number of candidates nominated and elected, the number of party offices captured, the legislation passed or stymied, perhaps the New Right would not appear as powerful a political force as I believe it to be. But when we factor in the political temper of the times, notably the movement's increasing dominance of the public dialogue, we can begin to appreciate the potency of the New Right in full measure.

Admittedly, this is more a matter of subjective judgment than statistical analysis, but I believe the evidence sustains my judgment.

When Howard Jarvis comes to Washington fresh from his Proposition 13 victory, he is lionized not only by conservatives and the press; he is surrounded by liberals who find his views repugnant and dangerous but who still want to be photographed with him. This is partly motivated by the instinct for political survival. Politicians do not want to be perceived by their constituents as bucking the trend or out of step with an alleged majority.

But there is another fundamental human tendency at work here—the impetus to conform in order to appear respectable and credible. Given the range and tenor of the New Right's issues, this means fewer and fewer political leaders are willing to say or do anything that the Rightists could portray as improvident, irreverent, or unpatriotic. As a result, too many of us skirt such issues or obfuscate them or even, to our great discredit, echo or emulate the New Right in order to minimize political damage.

This is not unique to our times. Harry Truman ostensibly hated McCarthyism, but his public denunciations of the man and the movement—although bolder than those by Dwight Eisenhower—were nevertheless not as vigorous or as consistent as some of Truman's supporters were urging. Instead, he accepted certain antisubversive measures that outraged civil libertarians.

On another level, one could cite the politicians' perennial skittishness over abortion. Few politicians, myself included, have been definitive about this issue. Most of us know that we ought to speak out on the issue, if for nothing more than to cool its heated divisiveness—but few of us have done so.

And now fate has handed the New Right a basketful of issues to exploit in one-dimensional terms. What concerns me—indeed what inspired me to write this book—is the growing reluctance of so many of us to risk bucking the tide by insisting that these matters be discussed in *full* dimension. If no one tries to bring balance and perspective to the public dialogue, how can reason prevail when the nation must make political and policy decisions that can determine not only its well-being but its very survival?

In the fevered atmosphere of the tax revolution, for example, who is going to tell the people that while their total taxes are high, they are *lower* than in all but one other major country—Japan? Who dares remind them that federal income taxes have been cut in each of the previous three years and in 1978 were cut again by $18.7 billion? Who dares to tell the people that federal taxes as a percentage of the gross national product have scarcely varied a percentage point in the past quarter century? Or that the same is true of the federal budget and the ratio of citizens who work for the federal government?

In the outcry over welfare, who has the courage to point out that 90 percent of all welfare recipients are children or mothers who have to take care of those children? That analysts in the past three administrations—Republican as well as Democratic —found welfare cheating to be far less significant statistically than notorious individual instances would indicate? That cheating by providers of some of these programs—doctors and medical laboratories serving Medicaid and Medicare recipients— had become so flagrant Congress had to legislate to control it?

In the backlash over school busing, who will insist that we recognize that disparity in educational and in economic opportunity still exists? That it is this disparity that helps keep black teenage unemployment hovering between 40 and 50 percent in some areas?

In the haranguing over "feeding at the public trough," who is pointing out to the people that among those feeding at the trough are a number of American industries and countless colleges and universities—all dependent for survival on federal contracts, loans, grants, and research awards?

Against the false and calculated propaganda that the women's movement is made up of lesbians and radicals, who is going to insist that the public keep its collective eye on the basic legitimacy of the Equal Rights Amendment? How many are calling attention to the continued inequality in male-female pay for the same job or, for that matter, in hiring consideration for the same job? How many are reminding the public that while women constitute more than half the population, they hold less than 7 percent of all elected offices; that in the past two hundred years only twelve women, as compared with 1,715 men, have served in the U.S. Senate; that only eighteen of the 435 members of the House of Representatives are women (the same number that were there forty years ago); and that no woman has ever served on the Supreme Court?

In the face of Rightist-conservative certainty that government spending and wage hikes are the only reasons for inflation, who is cautioning that this is a dangerous oversimplification? That it does not take into account the enormous impact of poor harvests, cold winters, cartel energy pricing, third-party reimbursement in the medical sector? That food price hikes in 1978 could be laid to the reduced supply stage of the beef cycle, poor harvests of certain vegetables, and the earlier and excessive world demand for feed grain? That the greatest increases in housing costs have not been labor, but land and monthly financing costs and lumber and insulation shortages? How many are pointing out that wage settlements in major labor agreements have been *decelerating*—not accelerating—in recent years, and that workers' real spendable weekly earnings are *still* below 1972 levels?

Sensitized to the public anxiety building up over Soviet arms and intentions, how many political leaders still have the courage to tell the people how our own defense budget—necessary though it may be—contributes to inflation? It is true that as a percentage of the overall budget, defense spending declined in recent years. But it is on the rise again (the 95th Congress enacted a record-high military appropriations bill), and we must remember that military goods are neither consumer goods nor investment goods. There is only one market for them—government. Consequently, the money that is paid to workers and to firms under defense contracts is free money in the marketplace. None of it goes to buy the product it produces. It therefore adds a tremendous amount of buying power to bid up the price of *other* goods and services.*

This is not an apologia for big governments or high taxes, nor is it an appeal for more social spending or a drastic slash in the defense budget. It is an attempt to bring perspective to some issues the Right is exploiting in one-dimensional terms—and with diminishing challenge from the responsible liberal-center. Under these circumstances, the public is denied the full spectrum of information and opinion it needs to make valid political judgments.

Nowhere is this more apparent or potentially dangerous than in the New Right's campaign to discourage détente, kill an arms limitation agreement with the Soviets before it is finalized and ready for consideration, heat up the arms race, and bring back the Cold War.

The buildup of Soviet arms is undeniable. As a long-time member of the Senate Armed Services Committee and as chairman of the Senate subcommittee on research and development for the past fourteen years, I know how strong the Soviet Union

---

* For a fuller consideration of this point—and the impact of defense spending on the imbalance of payments—see chapter 19.

has become in recent years. This manifest growth in military power, aggression in Africa, suppression of dissidents, harassment of American business representatives and of journalists in Moscow all have worked to the political advantage of the Radical Right. Not only have Rightists used these developments to fan the anti-Communist fervor of their followers, but they have utilized them to intimidate those who understand the need for diplomatic restraint and a cooling of rhetoric but who are reluctant to say so for fear of being labeled appeasers.

Moreover, the New Right is thundering down those who know that the Soviets are not invincible; who know that Russian leadership is old, ailing, and divided; that the Russian economy is more strained by military spending than ours; that Russian agriculture cannot feed the people; that Russia must import some of its technology; that the adventuring in African countries could entrap the Soviets in the same kind of situation in which we found ourselves in Vietnam; that, with the independence shown by Western European Communists, the monolithic power once exerted from the Kremlin is not what it was—and who know, above all, how Red China's presence on the Soviet border frightens the Soviets and by necessity disperses its military force.

From my position on the Senate Armed Services Committee, I know that America has *not* lost the capacity to defend itself successfully against attack. Our country is much stronger than the New Right would have the American people believe— strong enough to negotiate with the Soviets for a mutual reduction in the level of arms.

The endless and constantly accelerating arms race the New Right seems to countenance is a certain blueprint for disaster, not only for us, not only for the Soviet Union, but for the entire world. But we will never be able to achieve a meaningful arms control agreement until we are mature enough to recognize this all important fact. *Neither* side will negotiate so long as it believes the other side has a decided advantage in military strength. A meaningful agreement can only be achieved when *both* sides are convinced that near-parity in armed strength exists. That time is now. We must not let the strident rhetoric and the punishing politics of the New Right force us to abandon reason and abort an opportunity that may never come again.

PART II

Introduction

> *The pseudo-conservative is a man who, in the name of upholding traditional American values and institutions and defending them against more or less fictitious dangers, consciously or unconsciously aims at their abolition.*
> —THEODORE W. ADORNO[1]

Part I examined the psyche of the Radical Right, the composition, goals, and techniques of the New Right, the reasons for the movement's quick rise and early accomplishments, and its potential for further success in the meld of status politics and interest politics—two hitherto contradictory forces that kept conservative-minded citizens within the Democratic fold because they could clearly perceive economic and quality-of-life benefits from New Deal-type programs. The catalyst now joining status politics and interest politics is the inexorable pressure of continuing inflation and rising taxes.

For a long time the appeal of economic self-interest was enough to keep people of widely divergent social views under the broad umbrella of progressive politics. But the inherent strain of those differences was beginning to tell even before inflation and taxation increased the stress factor.

Everett Carll Ladd's article in the October 1977 issue of *For-*

181

tune magazine featured an attitude profile drawn up by the Social Science Data Center of the University of Connecticut that pointed up dramatic differences in how "New Class Democrats" and "Old Class Democrats" viewed certain social issues. (For this purpose, "New Class Democrats" were defined as young, college-trained Democrats in professional and/or managerial jobs; "Old Class Democrats" as older [over 50], noncollege, blue collar.)

Fifty-nine percent of the New Class Democrats favored making divorce easier, but only 21 percent of the Old Class Democrats shared that view. Seventy-three percent of the New Class Democrats thought a pregnant woman should be able to obtain a legal abortion if she is married and does not want more children; only 32 percent of the Old Class Democrats felt that way.

Only 38 percent of the New Class Democrats thought premarital sex was always wrong, but 80 percent of the Old Class Democrats considered this to be true. The same split occurred on the question of homosexuality; here only 27 percent of the New Class Democrats felt such a relationship was always wrong, while 89 percent of the Old Class Democrats believed it was.

Concerning the environment, 85 percent of the New Class Democrats were of the opinion that too little was being spent to protect the air, water, and soil, while just under half the Old Class Democrats expressed the same sentiment.

Although only 5 percent of the New Class Democrats thought there ought to be laws against miscegenation, 67 percent of the Old Class Democrats believed that marriages between Blacks and Whites should be prohibited. On the issue of fair housing laws, 33 percent of the New Class Democrats thought homeowners should be allowed to decide whether or not they want to sell their houses to Blacks, but 78 percent of the Old Class Democrats favored that option.

These comparisons further illustrate the striking attitudinal differences between those Joseph Gusfield called the "cultural fundamentalists" and the "cultural modernists."

Part I examined how successful the New Right has been in exploiting these differences by concentrating on highly personal and emotional issues, and how it has used this technique in combination with an appeal to the strong patriotic impulses of third- and fourth-generation Americans.

Its success is measured in the degree to which it has taken over the Republican party and in its growing appeal to erstwhile Democratic voters. Writing for the Knight-Ridder newspapers in September 1977, Saul Friedman said:

> In legislative battles in Congress, in political fund-raising, in mobilizing support on controversial issues throughout the country, in winning key off-year elections, and in sheer intellectual energy and talent, the "New Right" has overwhelmed the traditional Republican Establishment.

In the February 1978 edition of *The Democratic Viewpoint*, Scott Wolf stated:

> The success of the "New Right" is due not only to its own ingenuity and luck, but also to the present defensiveness and confusion within the progressive community. While the "New Right" displays a boisterous elan, the progressive community is questioning most of its assumptions, including such basic ones as the value of political activism.

In Part I an appeal was made to the progressive community to make every effort to understand the anxieties of the cultural fundamentalists—especially the blue-collar, white Middle American of low to moderate income—and to try to reach common ground with them before the New Right wins them to its cause. I discussed how the pressures of inflation and taxation were beginning to erode the "interest" base that once kept these people within the progressive community.

It is important to note that the New Right now recognizes this development. It has added inflation and taxes to its list of highly exploitable issues in the months to come, and it will argue that government spending for social programs must be drastically cut in order to cool inflation and ease the tax bite.

If the New Right is as successful in exploiting interest politics as it has been already in exploiting status politics, the purge of moderates and liberals from the Republican party and the decline of Middle American support for the Democratic party seem certain to accelerate.

What this could portend for the national political scene—and the course of government—is the subject of Part II and the reason why this book was written.

In its examination of the New Right, the *National Journal* posed a series of questions.[2] For my purpose, the most relevant was, What would this country be like if they [the New Right] succeeded in mobilizing a conservative majority?

In an attempt to answer this question, I turn to my home state of New Hampshire as an example, in microcosm, of what can happen when the Radical Right captures power and influence.

The ensuing chapters illustrate how the understandable yearnings of many Americans for a restoration of traditional values and standards, for conformity and order, for frugality in government, for minimal taxation, and for reaffirmation of "Americanism" can be met by the Radical Right—but at a price a free people cannot afford. When these yearnings are put in the trust of the fear brokers, traditional values and standards are distorted and bastardized to their purposes.

The following chapters also show how the desire for conformity and order can lead to suppression of dissent, to assaults on freedom of expression, academic freedom, women's rights, and the social gospel of the churches; how selective frugality in government further victimizes the least among us; how Americanism is translated into the most reckless kind of jingoism, the wholesale and slanderous impugning of other people's loyalty . . . yes, and even into something disturbingly remindful of that most un-American of concepts—the master race theory.

Part II points out how the politics of threat and reprisal practiced by the Radical Right will, in time, weaken the entire structure of government by discouraging the best among the citizenry from seeking public office for fear of the savage attacks that may be leveled against them or their families.

What has happened in New Hampshire proves that, once in power, the Radical Right does not give the people order and social tranquillity, but instead constant conflict, political uproar, and the heavy hand of authoritarianism. Because of this, Raymond Brighton, editor of the *Portsmouth* (N.H.) *Herald,* was inspired to suggest that it might be time for "The Granite State" to change its name to "The State of Paranoia."

CHAPTER 11

King of the Epithet*

*I honor every other candidate who seeks the
Presidency of the United States. In his or her own
way each has already made a significant
contribution to their state or their country or
they wouldn't be candidates. So let's honor them
for what they've done and then listen to what
they've got to say. But in the process let's not try
to undermine their credibility by any recourse to
character assassination. . . . Newspapers and the
press of this country ought to try to contribute to
that kind of campaign . . . instead of the stuff
this man [Loeb] prints in his newspapers. . . .
This man doesn't walk, he crawls.*
—U.S. SENATOR
EDMUND S. MUSKIE,
standing opposite the
*Manchester
Union Leader* building,
February 25, 1972

* *Time* magazine, January 31, 1972, called Loeb "King of the Epithet."

185

For many years, indeed from the time he burst upon the New Hampshire publishing scene in 1946, the Radical Right in my home state has been represented most visibly by William Loeb and his *Manchester Union Leader* and *New Hampshire Sunday News*. Although he has also owned newspapers in Saint Albans and Burlington, Vermont, in Haverhill, Massachusetts, and in Bridgeport, Connecticut, the flagship of his modest publishing empire has always been the *Union Leader*.

Even though it is small in comparison with major dailies in many other states, the *Union Leader* dominates New Hampshire's media scene. In a state with 820,000 residents, its morning edition has a circulation of 64,000, more than three times the total of its nearest competitor. (Readership, of course, is larger than circulation by a factor of three or four; it is possible that Loeb's daily editions are read by a quarter of the state's population.) Moreover, Loeb's is the only statewide daily and the only morning daily (it publishes morning and early afternoon editions), and his *New Hampshire Sunday News* is the only statewide Sunday newspaper.

The other daily newspapers in New Hampshire—the *Concord Monitor*, the *Portsmouth Herald*, the *Nashua Telegraph*, *The Claremont Daily Eagle*, the *Laconia Evening Citizen*, *Foster's Daily Democrat* (Dover), the *Keene Evening Sentinel*, the *Lebanon Valley News*—are politically moderate and are frequently at editorial odds with Loeb.

Not only does Loeb enjoy a marked circulation advantage over his newspaper competition, but he also benefits from the relative absence of television competition. Northern New Hampshire gets its television reception from stations in Maine and Vermont. New Hampshire's only commercial station is an ABC affiliate in Manchester that is hard-put to compete for viewers with higher-budget commercial stations beaming their signal out of Boston.

The question asks itself: If Loeb's policies and practices are repugnant to a significant portion of New Hampshire's residents, why has his dominance of the state's media scene gone unchallenged? Because it takes a great deal of money to challenge any well-established newspaper, and the *Union Leader* is well established in the largest city of the state. Several attempts have been made to come up with the financial backing required to start a new statewide daily or to convert an existing local daily to a statewide publication. None has gone much beyond the talking stage, even though on at least one occasion several prominent national journalists were reportedly involved. It is generally conceded that any such challenge to Loeb must carry with it a willingness to lose a great deal of money for the first few years, with no guarantee that the venture would ultimately succeed. Making the challenge more difficult is the undeniable fact that Loeb's newspapers are controversial and entertaining and have thorough local and state news coverage, at least when political considerations or Loeb's personal views do not intervene. Also undeniable is the addiction factor; many people who are outraged by Loeb's editorials line up at newsstands side by side with Loeb supporters.

Mention must be made here of the *New Hampshire Times,* a relatively recent but invaluable addition to the state's roster of publications. The *New Hampshire Times,* a weekly published in Concord, concentrates on in-depth reporting and analysis of state government, politics, energy and environment, and social and cultural matters. Although its circulation does not yet compare with that of the *Union Leader,* it is growing. More importantly, the *Times'* readership includes key opinion-makers who amplify its impact.

However, it is not relevant to the primary purpose of this chapter to discuss the New Hampshire media in detail. Rather, my aim is to show how publisher Loeb's mind-set and tactics foreshadowed today's New Right and how he represents a bridging between the Old Right and the New Right.

It is said of Loeb that he is an anachronism, a throwback to the days of highly personal journalism. He has been called "the merchant of venom" and the "king of the epithet," his newspaper a "journal of abuse," his brand of journalism "gut-cutting." Twenty-four hours before he was elected President, John F. Kennedy returned to Manchester, where he had launched his campaign, mounted a platform set up in a park opposite the *Union Leader* building, and said: "I believe there is probably a more irresponsible newspaper than that one right over there somewhere in the United States, but I've been through forty states and I haven't found it yet. I believe there is a publisher who has less regard for the truth, but I can't think of his name."

More given to exercising his considerable wit than to venting indignation in public, Kennedy was the epitomization of "cool." If he had thought Loeb's papers were irresponsible but insignificant to the future of his candidacy, he would have brushed off the publisher's attacks with a wisecrack. That he chose, instead, to denounce him in the way he did suggests that Kennedy knew, as others have had occasion to learn, that Loeb can make a telling and far-reaching impact on the American political process.

Every four years Loeb surfaces as a national figure when reporters and camera crews from all over the country swarm into New Hampshire for the nation's first Presidential preference primary election. There are other states that elect many more delegates to the national conventions than does the small state of New Hampshire, but New Hampshire's primary *is* the first, and the national press convenes there for the initial test of how political winds are blowing.

Much has been written about the validity of the New Hampshire primary, with many observers contending that the state is too small and too unlike mainstream America to provide a true reading. But except for its very low percentage of Blacks, the state is not that atypical. On the contrary, once the absence of a black minority is allowed for, the state is quite representative of the nation as a whole. Indeed, since 1952 no President has been elected who did not first win in the New Hampshire primary.

There is another factor to consider, however, and that is William Loeb's influence on who *survives* that first primary to go on to other testing grounds. When the national press packs its suitcases, typewriters, and camera cases and moves out of New Hampshire's snow and cold, it leaves bemused over what Loeb has said in his signed front-page editorials about the various primary candidates and outraged at how the news columns of his paper flak some candidates and bury others. No doubt some of the press corps take smug pride in the fact their journalistic ethics are not Bill Loeb's ethics.

What they tend to play down is the *effect* of what they have seen. By general consensus, it was Loeb and Loeb alone who caused the Presidential hopes of Edmund Muskie of Maine to self-destruct on the "launching pad" (in this case a flatbed truck parked outside the *Union Leader* building). Journalists who focus on the present and the future forget that it was Loeb and

Loeb alone who nipped George Romney's aspirations in the bud; that it was Loeb and Loeb alone who started Richard Nixon on the Presidential comeback trail after his gubernatorial campaign debacle of 1962 in California; that it is *always* Loeb who dominates and sets the parameters of the primary's public dialogue and who makes the ad hominem argument its centerpiece.

Examples abound, but the best may be found in Jules Witcover's exhaustive analysis of the *Union Leader*'s coverage of the 1972 primary. Witcover's account leads off with this paragraph by James Doyle, taken from the March 10, 1972 issue of the *Washington Star:*

> It was a dirty, mudslinging campaign, one in which the battle was for the votes of the poorly paid mill workers. In an important measure, it was won by neither Muskie nor his principal opponent, Sen. George S. McGovern of South Dakota. It was won by William Loeb, publisher of the Manchester *Union Leader,* whose unproven charges against Muskie seem to have cut deeply into the Senator's vote in the area where Loeb's paper circulates.[1]

Witcover's article ticks off some classic Loeb epithets to illustrate the "lash of his [Loeb's] editorial whip": Dwight D. Eisenhower—"Dopey Dwight" and "that stinking hypocrite"; Nelson A. Rockefeller—"home wrecker"; Margaret Chase Smith—"Moscow Maggie"; John F. Kennedy—"The Number One threat to America"; Eleanor Roosevelt—"Ellie and her belly-crawling liberal friends"; Eugene J. McCarthy—"skunk."* It is not surprising that, as Witcover notes, "within New Hampshire, Loeb's actions over the years have generated chagrin, amusement, and—above all—fear."[2]

Jules Witcover analyzed the 1972 Presidential primary in New Hampshire.

> It seemed clear from the stance Loeb took that his main object in the campaign was to destroy Edmund Muskie's chances for the Democratic nomination. The most evident reason was that Muskie had by that time abandoned his support of the Vietnam war and had become a powerful

---

* Witcover's list of Loeb epithets could be extended to include Gerald Ford —"a jerk"; Jimmy Carter—"that dope in the White House"; the Congress— "stupid, treasonous jackals"; Martin Luther King Jr.—"a pious, pompous fraud"; and Tom McIntyre—"a cheap political chiseler," "a socialist," "ballot bagman," "second story man," and so on.

critic of American involvement. After looking about for a candidate to whom he could throw his support, the publisher settled on Mayor Sam Yorty of Los Angeles, who, like Loeb, remained an unrelenting hawk. In truth, Loeb would have preferred a more impressive national figure than Yorty, but when Senator Henry M. Jackson (D-Wash.) elected not to enter the primary, reportedly because he believed Loeb's support would make him look like an ultra-conservative rather than a centrist, the *Union Leader* had to make do with Yorty. (Loeb denounced Jackson as a turncoat who "decided there were more votes among the peaceniks than the patriots.")*

Yorty was, by all odds, a poor substitute for Jackson against Muskie. The Los Angeles mayor was a rambling oversimplifier of the issues who had a national identification problem as well. But Loeb served him up to voters as if he were a major, serious candidate, meanwhile setting his editorial sights on Muskie. Two other national candidates on the Democratic ballot, Senators George McGovern of South Dakota and Vance Hartke of Indiana—both strongly anti-war liberals who ideologically might have drawn even more fire from Loeb than did Muskie—received remarkably benign treatment, and Hartke at times seemed to be Loeb's candidate.†

Loeb always has maintained, as do most publishers, that, in the best tradition of American journalism, he fights his battles in his editorial columns, reserving the news columns to tell readers what has been happening. The tradition, while noble, sometimes is compromised even in the best newspapers. In the *Manchester Union Leader*, the tradition is not compromised, it is shattered—and seldom more glaringly than during presidential primaries.[3]

Witcover offered an analysis of the news coverage accorded the Democratic field of candidates which showed that Yorty not only got twice the column inches of coverage Muskie got, and more than the other four Democratic candidates combined, but that almost without exception the Yorty copy was favorable and the overwhelming bulk of the Muskie copy was unfavorable.‡

* Bill Kovach, "Nixon's Too Left-Wing for William Loeb," *The New York Times Magazine*, December 12, 1971.

† In the 1968 primary Loeb concentrated his attacks on President Johnson and gave the same kind of benign treatment to Eugene McCarthy. After Johnson announced he would not seek reelection, Loeb went after McCarthy, calling him "a skunk's skunk," among other terms.

‡ *Time* magazine, January 31, 1972, noted that Yorty's "announcement of plans to visit the state rated a three-column headline on Page One, while Edmund Muskie's formal declaration of candidacy was reported on Page 12. A note from Chiang Kai-shek to Yorty, acknowledging the mayor's birthday greetings to the generalissimo, got front-page play."

Yorty stories went on at length about where he spoke and what he said. A head shot of Muskie taken some years ago was used several times; Yorty, meanwhile, was shown meeting with New Hampshire high school students, with nuns, with Francis Cardinal James McIntyre of Los Angeles, and—twice—holding a rifle. The caption under the photo with Cardinal McIntyre told Manchester's heavily Roman Catholic population that "the Cardinal and Yorty have been strong advocates of a Constitutional amendment restoring the right of school children to pray in the public schools." The rifle picture—published twice, on Feb. 6 and again on Feb. 8, with the same caption both days, told gun fanciers and shooting sportsmen that Yorty had visited a Newport, N.H. rifle manufacturer "while on the campaign trail for the Democratic presidential nomination. Yorty, a staunch opponent of gun control measures, is a life member of the National Rifle Association."[4]

Witcover noted that beyond the biased ratio in column inches of news coverage, Muskie was also victimized by the *Union Leader*'s failure to report the details of his campaign speeches.

And always there was the constant barrage of editorials, backed up by anti-Muskie commentary by the *Union Leader*'s stable of ultraconservative columnists—Ralph de Toledano, Victor Lasky, Kevin Phillips, Paul Scott, Holmes Alexander, and David Lawrence. On several occasions Loeb even took the trouble to resurrect columns by Lawrence, Alexander, and de Toledano that had been written and first published up to a year before just because they were critical of Muskie.

Loeb's editorials called Muskie "Senator Flip-Flop," "the Vietnam War dove-chicken," and a "phony." They accused him of "taking New Hampshire for granted." On one occasion the *Union Leader* published a cartoon showing North Vietnamese leaders wearing "Muskie for President" buttons, with one saying, "Well, Comrades, I know who I'm voting for!"

The tenor of Loeb's attacks can be gauged by this line from one of his editorials: "Watch those eyes of Muskie as they shift back and forth in the unguarded moment . . . keep YOUR eye on Moscow Muskie!"

It remained for Loeb to exploit two more issues before the Muskie campaign ran into trouble. On the morning of February 24, 1972 Loeb published a front-page editorial entitled "Senator Muskie Insults Franco-Americans."

Loeb reported that Muskie, campaigning in Florida, had—at least by inference—blasphemed one of New Hampshire's largest minority groups. One Paul Morrison, identified as from Florida, had charged in a letter—reproduced on the editorial page—that he had overheard a Muskie aide at a drug rehabilitation center in Fort Lauderdale say Maine did not have many black citizens, "but we have Cannocks (sic)." The writer said he had asked Muskie what the man meant, and "Mr. Muskie laughed and said come to New England and see."[5]

Loeb's editorial, in bold-faced capital letters, read:

IF PAUL MORRISON, THE AUTHOR OF THE LETTER, HADN'T TAKEN THE TROUBLE TO WRITE ABOUT HIS EXPERIENCE WITH SENATOR MUSKIE IN FLORIDA, NO ONE IN NEW HAMPSHIRE WOULD KNOW OF THE DEROGATORY REMARKS EMANATING FROM THE MUSKIE CAMP ABOUT THE FRANCO-AMERICANS IN NEW HAMPSHIRE AND MAINE—REMARKS WHICH THE SENATOR FOUND AMUSING. . . . WE HAVE ALWAYS KNOWN THAT SENATOR MUSKIE WAS A HYPOCRITE, BUT WE NEVER EXPECTED TO HAVE IT SO CLEARLY REVEALED AS IN THIS LETTER SENT TO US FROM FLORIDA.

A few days later Loeb's paper ran a four-column "news" story which began, "Mayor [Sam] Yorty is an old and loyal friend of France." Then, on the Saturday before the primary election, the *Union Leader* published a second letter on the front page. This letter, allegedly from Harold W. Eldredge of Fort Lauderdale, stated that "I was the person that asked Mr. Muskie the question about his knowledge of blacks," and went on to say Paul Morrison's story was true, that he, Eldredge, had read about the whole matter in the *Fort Lauderdale Press* (sic) and thought he should offer corroboration. The Eldredge letter was published in the *Union Leader* with a caption that read: "Senator Muskie has, in effect, called the Morrison letter a fraud. Readers may be interested in weighing this additional evidence of what was said by Senator Muskie in Florida."

Major newspapers sent out reporters to find "Paul Morrison" after Loeb published the first letter, but no such person could be located. When interviewed days before the election, Loeb said he had additional evidence but wanted to keep the "scoop" for his own paper.

Witcover's article, however, contains this interesting paragraph:

The Eldredge letter, coming on the campaign's final weekend, caused little stir locally. But in Fort Lauderdale, where the first letter had prompted a reporter from the *Fort Lauderdale News* (not *"Press"*) to look for Morrison, a search for Eldredge was made. According to the reporter, Jim Kerr, no trace of either letter writer was found. During the search, Kerr said later, a man calling himself R. Warren Pease came into the paper looking for references to Eldredge in the files: the man said he was from the *Union Leader*, but refused to show any identification. Before the man left town, according to Kerr, he placed a Page 1 advertisement in the *News* urgently asking Harold Eldredge to call "Warren." Kerr said he checked with the paper's advertising department and was told the ad had been billed to the *Union Leader*.[6]

The Morrison letter remains a mystery. Loeb never produced additional evidence that either it or the Eldredge letter was genuine, and no one has ever been able to track down either of the alleged writers.

Moreover, Muskie produced the director of the Fort Lauderdale drug rehabilitation center to attest that no remarks such as the Morrison letter had described had been made.

Months later an article in the *Washington Post* reported that a ranking Nixon White House aide had told the reporter he had written the Canuck letter, but it was not clear whether he was joking or whether the letter had indeed been part of the "dirty tricks" campaign. One of my staff members, to satisfy his own curiosity, phoned the reporter and asked if there would be a follow-up story. "We're not allowed to talk about stories or sources," the reporter answered, "but if you're asking me if he said it . . . he *said* it."

The Morrison and the Eldredge letters furnished the TNT for one of two blockbusters to hit Muskie at the close of the primary campaign. The other was the *Union Leader*'s reprinting of a short item from the December 27, 1971 issue of *Newsweek*, which, in turn, had been taken from a *Women's Wear Daily* article on Muskie's wife, Jane, that had appeared ten days earlier.

James McCartney, national correspondent for the Knight Newspapers, based in Washington, described this incident in a piece titled "What Really Happened in Manchester?" He said the original *Women's Wear Daily* article, written by Kandy Stroud, was a "rollicking" account of Jane Muskie's first political campaign trip of the 1972 primary season.[7]

Stroud's story began, "Bedford, N.H.—'Put your notebooks away, girls, Momma's going to sing tonight.' With that, Jane Gray Muskie lit another filter tip cigaret and invited members of her traveling press corps for cheese and drinks in her room and dinner at the Steak House in her motel."

The next few paragraphs of Stroud's article portrayed a free-spirited Jane Muskie, but taken as a whole, McCartney said, "it portrayed Mrs. Muskie as a reasonably intelligent and thoughtful woman—free-spirited though she may be. That is not, however, the kind of person Mrs. Muskie appeared to be in extracts from Kandy Stroud's story which showed up ten days later in *Newsweek*." *Newsweek* "prepared a six-sentence item . . ." which caught "all the breezy quotes" but totally missed any other dimension to Kandy Stroud's story.[8]

Stroud later claimed that "*Newsweek* picked up the sensational parts of the story. You can lift anything out of its setting and it isn't accurate." And according to McCartney, four days after Loeb reprinted the two-month-old item under the headline "Big Daddy's Jane," the editor in chief and president of *Newsweek* wrote Senator Muskie a letter:

> I cannot tell you how distressed I was to discover that a rather innocuous item in *Newsweek* had been thrust so unfairly into your campaign. . . . Let me assure you that there was no intention whatsoever to reflect discredit on Mrs. Muskie—only to suggest, in a good-natured way, that she is a person who brings a refreshing candor and sense of humor to public life. . . . That this little item should be used so scurrilously against you and Mrs. Muskie is, in my view, deplorable.

On Friday, February 25, Edmund Muskie took his campaign to the doorsteps of the *Union Leader*. Standing on the back of a flatbed truck amid falling snow, he angrily denounced Loeb's use of the Morrison and the Eldredge letters, produced a witness to prove he had never made the remark the letters charged, and then broke down when he came to Loeb's references to his wife, Jane.

Witcover's account quotes the senator: "This man [Loeb] doesn't walk, he crawls. . . . He's talking about my wife. . . . It's fortunate for him he's not on the platform beside me!" For a moment Muskie could not go on. "Reporters at the scene said tears ran down his face and some heard him say, 'A good woman . . .' and then stop, unable to continue."[9]

Those of us who love Ed and Jane Muskie and who know William Loeb for what he is watched the network news that night, and our hearts went out to the tall man standing head down, eyes closed, tears streaming down his cheeks. We could understand the hurt and the frustration. We could appreciate his courage.

To watch this scene on the evening news was especially painful for me. Ed Muskie was not only a dear personal friend, but he was a friend to the Democratic party of New Hampshire. Indeed, the man from Maine had done more than any other out-of-state Democrat to help build the party in New Hampshire. As Loeb's assaults on Muskie grew more and more vicious, I chafed to get into the primary fray, to go back home, stand by Ed Muskie, defend him, and extol him, but I had given my word I would not. In the 1968 New Hampshire primary campaign Governor John King and I had loyally toiled for President Johnson, much to the bitter resentment of Eugene McCarthy supporters within the party. It took a long time to close the party wounds after that campaign, and I promised I would never again take an active role in a Presidential primary. At the outset of the 1972 primary I announced that I would vote for Edmund Muskie but beyond that simple declaration would play no part in his campaign.

Not only was it painful to watch that scene unfold on the televised news, it was deceptive. I reacted as the *Lebanon Valley News* reacted in a March 1 editorial:

> Senator Edmund Muskie did more to commend himself to the presidency with his courageous stand in Manchester Saturday than anything else he has done in New Hampshire to date. For Muskie to stand in front of the *Union Leader* building and tell it like it is took courage, something that's often lacking among campaigners in New Hampshire. Most thinking people in the state could tell Muskie most of what he has learned himself about the Loeb influence here—that it is the work of a crank publisher who chooses to inflict his 19th century brand of yellow journalism on the public from afar. Muskie could have ignored Loeb's vicious attacks on him, his candidacy, even his wife, but he didn't, and he has shown himself to be a stronger figure as a consequence.

But we natives who reacted as the *Valley News* reacted did not realize how badly Muskie had been hurt. Many viewers across the nation who did not know what had driven the senator to this dramatically emotional moment mistakenly saw it as evidence of weakness, not of strength.

Nor did we friends and admirers of Ed Muskie realize at the time how much Loeb's sustained attacks had eroded Franco-American support. Although many leaders of the Franco-American community had openly denounced Loeb for exploiting the Canuck letter issue, the attacks took a toll—especially in *Union*

Leader-saturated Manchester—that was not evident until primary election day.

Loeb, however, sensed he had scored a damaging hit and
moved quickly to follow up. On March 1 his front-page, signed
editorial "Hysterical—and Deceptive" said, in part:

> Thus, if ever a man stood convicted of telling a bald-faced lie, that man
> is Senator Muskie! The one thing they [the people] noticed—and it
> stood out like a worm crawling out of a bad apple—was that Senator
> Muskie has such a short fuse, and such an hysterical response to criti-
> cism, that he certainly would NOT be the man to be in the White House
> and have his finger on the nuclear button.

On March 5, Loeb's *New Hampshire Sunday News* expressed
editorial doubt that "the use of the term Canucks"—which no
one had accused Muskie of using—"was the real reason" for
Muskie's drop-off in preelection polls. "No," the editorial continued, "what the Franco-Americans were really upset about
was the Muskie camp's insistence that the French are the
North's equivalent of our negro problem down south. . . .
Franco-Americans are by no means the only ethnic group who
would regard this as a slur."

This, after repeated attempts had failed to turn up *either* of
the letter writers who reported the alleged Canuck incident, a
flat denial by the director of the institute where the incident allegedly took place that it ever happened, and the fact that Ed
Muskie's sisters are married to men of French descent.

On February 29 reporters from the *Washington Star,* the *Philadelphia Bulletin,* and Britain's *Manchester Guardian* went to
Prides Crossing, Massachusetts to interview Loeb about the
propriety of publishing the Morrison and the Eldredge letters
and of using the *Newsweek* column about Jane Muskie in the
way it was used.

After saying he was "quite" satisfied with his handling of the
Canuck letters, Loeb was asked about Jane Muskie. "Would you
like that in the White House? That type of person?" he responded.

When asked what he meant, Loeb answered:

> The general behavior, the vulgarity of the whole thing. Now look,
> gentlemen, I am agreeable to discussing things. I am not agreeable to
> being the subject of a Star Chamber court examination. And I get the im-
> pression that you are not a reporter, you are a partisan. I think you are a

Muskie supporter. You came down here with a preconceived idea about Bill Loeb, and you're, by God, going to prove it in your story, and I don't give a Goddamn what you write in your story. Because it doesn't affect me one way or another, and that's right on the tape right there. I'm damned tired of stupid publishers hiring left-wing reporters, of which I would say you are a pretty good sample, who write their stories from a predisposed angle, and don't give a Goddamn about the truth.[16]

Washington Star reporter James Doyle, one of the three reporters who interviewed Loeb that day, added further detail in a separate account.

Manchester, N.H.—The publisher of this city's only newspaper has once again turned the Democratic primary into a bitter, name-calling free-for-all, and the fortunes of the front runner, Senator Edmund S. Muskie of neighboring Maine, may well depend on how he has responded to the challenge. The publisher is William Loeb, a heavy-fisted advocate of personal journalism whose editorials refer to Muskie as "Moscow Muskie" and "a phony." In recent days he has printed an as yet unsubstantiated charge that Muskie laughed at ethnic slurs made toward Franco-Americans, who represent 40 percent of the Democratic vote here. He has also published unflattering articles about Muskie's wife, claiming she is "too vulgar" to live in the White House.

Yesterday in a stormy hour-long interview, Loeb promised more such attacks in the days ahead and threatened to throw a reporter off his guarded Massachusetts estate because of the newsman's testy questions. At one point, in answer to a query, Loeb pulled a gun from beneath his jacket and leveled it at one of three reporters to show that he does, indeed, always carry a pistol.[11]

From the beginning of that year's primary, Ed Muskie had two problems to surmount: one was Loeb's intense determination to destroy his candidacy; the other was the national press' widely held and openly expressed notion that Muskie had to take at least 65 percent of the Democratic vote in the New Hampshire primary in order to claim a substantial victory. Both proved too much to overcome.

Final returns on primary election day gave Muskie 47.8 percent of the vote, enough to win, but not enough—by the media's predetermined and arbitrary standards—to claim a convincing victory.

Witcover summed it up in these words:

This [disappointing] showing was attributed by the Muskie camp largely to a very poor vote in Manchester, bailiwick of the *Union Leader*. Although Muskie ran strongly in the state's other cities and working-

class wards, in industrial Manchester where Loeb's words carry the most
weight and where about 40 percent of the vote was cast, Muskie barely
beat McGovern, 36.4 percent to 33.4 percent, with 11.9 for Yorty.
McGovern carried two predominantly Franco-American wards and lost a
third by only one vote.[12]

As for the candidates Loeb endorsed—Sam Yorty on the
Democratic ticket and ultraconservative Congressman John
Ashbrook of Ohio on the Republican side—neither made a political ripple, Yorty taking only 6 percent of the Democratic vote
and Ashbrook but a handful of ballots away from Nixon. But
making Yorty and Ashbrook winners could not have been
Loeb's goal; he must have known that was impossible. His goal
was to wreck Ed Muskie's chances for the Democratic nomination, because he feared, and rightly in my judgment, that Muskie stood the best chance of taking the White House from the
Republicans that November.

I chose to single out the 1972 Presidential primary in New
Hampshire as a detailed example of Loeb at work because it
offers many illustrations of how his mind-set and tactics foreshadowed the New Right's debut on the American political
scene just a few years later.

First, Loeb made intensive and effective use of firsthand communication with the voter. Just as the New Right has perfected
computerized direct mailing, Loeb pumped a steady drumfire of
inflammatory editorials directly into the homes of every sub-
scriber for a period of months.

Second, Loeb chose the issues on which the campaign would
be waged. Like the New Right, which can decide on these matters
at a meeting of a handful of leaders without having to win consensus at caucuses or conventions, Loeb sat down and determined which issues he could best exploit—patriotism, anti-
Communism, the war, ethnicity, gun control, frugality in government, school prayer, the alleged character and personality of
the primary's principals—and he made those the topics to monopolize the voters' attention.

Third, he did not let old political loyalties get in his way.
Like the New Right, which will move as readily against moderate Republicans as it will against Democrats, Loeb sets his own
standards, and woe be to any candidate of either party who
doesn't measure up. Moreover, he is consistent in his inconsistency.

Example: Loeb long had beaten the editorial drum for Richard Nixon's election as President. As mentioned earlier, he started Nixon on the comeback trail in the 1968 Presidential primary in New Hampshire and exulted in his ultimate election that year. But in 1971 Loeb abruptly turned on Nixon, denouncing his trip to Peking as a policy that was "immoral, indecent, insane and fraught with danger for the survival of the United States." When Nixon arrived in Manchester on August 6, 1971, he was greeted by a Loeb front-page editorial entitled "A Sad Good-bye to an Old Friend."

In the editorial Loeb castigated Nixon and Secretary of State Kissinger for trying to improve relations with the Peoples' Republic of China.

> This newspaper and its publisher therefore regretfully announce that if the Democrats—or any other political party with a prospect of capturing the White House—nominate a presidential candidate who is dedicated to the restoration of our national defense and who is prepared to support a foreign policy designed to preserve the security and honor of the United States, we will support the candidate against President Nixon in the 1972 elections.

For all the bluff and bluster of that editorial, which some suspect really had a purpose other than trying to change Nixon's foreign policy, Loeb did support Nixon over McGovern in the general election that year, just as he supported former Republican Governor Wesley Powell in his campaign against me. Loeb had helped Powell to become governor and to get reelected, but when Powell refused to appoint Doloris Bridges (widow of Styles Bridges) to her late husband's seat in the U.S. Senate in 1961, Loeb wrote, "It is not easy to confess a mistake or to say that one is wrong, but this newspaper frankly wasted 11 years of effort on behalf of Governor Powell." In that editorial, published December 7, 1961, Loeb called Powell "vindictive," "egotistical," and "an ingrate," and when Powell later announced that he would seek a third term, Loeb said he had "evidenced the truth of the old saying that power frequently corrupts and makes arrogant those who hold it." He then successfully set about to defeat Powell in the Republican primary of 1962 by backing another candidate—John Pillsbury.

Ten years later Powell challenged me for my Senate seat. Suddenly, Loeb no longer looked upon him as "vindictive," "egotistical," "an ingrate," or "corrupted" by power. Powell was now a born-again Loeb favorite, whom the publisher described as "a firm believer in God and country and strong national defense and the right of citizens to bear arms" and as a person "who is not afraid to call a spade a spade and to stand firmly for his principles." After Powell lost the election, Loeb had a final comment. He said the people who supported Powell were "people who believe also in the eternal verities of religious faith, of patriotism, and decent morals." I leave it to the reader to interpret what this says about the New Hampshire people who voted for me.

Loeb long antedated the New Right in his effective use of direct communication, in handpicking emotional and divisive issues in order to exploit honest—if misplaced or exaggerated—fears and anxieties, and in his ruthless willingness to threaten and punish candidates and officeholders who do not hew to his ideological line.

CHAPTER 12

Rule or Ruin

The people in New Hampshire have never supported or liked me.
—WILLIAM LOEB[1]

There is a long-standing myth to the effect that William Loeb's newspapers so dominate New Hampshire that they can make a difference of fifteen percentage points in the vote accorded candidates Loeb supports or opposes.

No study confirms this conjecture. The most detailed and scholarly examination of Loeb's influence on New Hampshire politics was done by Eric Veblen; some of his conclusions are worth noting. Veblen claims the impact of the *Union Leader* is considerable in terms of the campaign strategy of the candidates, but that the actual effect of the newspaper on the electorate is much more subtle and difficult to measure. He suspects that, at the most, the papers may sway only 3 or 4 percent of the voters, although this is enough to swing a close election one way or the other.[2]

In general elections for the U.S. Senate, Loeb's track record is not impressive. From 1960 to 1975 the *Union Leader* endorsed three victors and four losers. When one considers Loeb's endorsement of elder statesman Norris Cotton in 1960 and in 1966, the overall record becomes even less impressive, because Cotton almost certainly would have won regardless of the newspaper's stand on his candidacy.

In general elections for governor from 1960 to 1975, Loeb endorsed candidates four times and remained neutral five times. Loeb-endorsed candidates won in 1960—Wesley Powell—and in 1972, 1974, and 1976—Meldrim Thomson. The last three elections in particular point up the melding of status politics with interest politics, for the victories were largely due to the successful exploitation of widespread opposition to direct, broad-based taxing of New Hampshire citizens, a tactic Loeb has vigorously pursued over the years.*

Loeb has been more successful in backing primary election winners than in controlling general elections. The eight Loeb-endorsed candidates in the nine Republican gubernatorial primaries from 1960 to 1976 inclusive won six times. The two exceptions were in 1968 and in 1970, when main-line Republican Walter Peterson defeated then lesser-known Meldrim Thomson by three percentage points on both occasions. In Republican senatorial primaries Loeb has succeeded in nominating his candidates in six of the seven contests between 1960 and 1976, the one exception being 1962, when his corrosive meddling in the nominating process so divided the Republican party that I became the first Democrat in thirty years to be elected to the U.S. Senate.

That election year is worth considering in some detail, because it illustrates Loeb's determination to rule or ruin, a characteristic of extremism on both the Right and the Left, and his antipathy toward the regular Republican Establishment, especially the old-family Republicans of prominent status.

The last is a phenomenon that would intrigue the psychohistorian, for Loeb, the most vehement of anti-elitists, was himself born to status. The son of Theodore Roosevelt's personal secretary and influential adviser, Loeb was christened an Episcopalian in the famed Washington Cathedral—with Roosevelt as his godfather—grew up in an atmosphere of power and influence, attended the best schools, inherited money, and today lives in

* See chapter 13.

palatial comfort at his Reno, Nevada ranch or at his fortresslike home in Prides Crossing, Massachusetts.

He has never seemed to find peer acceptance in New Hampshire. There is endless speculation why this is so. Some point out that he is an outlander; he was neither born nor has ever lived in New Hampshire. Some allege that while he is soft-spoken and mannerly in person, his editorial utterances are so tasteless and offensive that status families are reluctant to associate with him. Still others theorize that he has been rejected by the main-line and the old-family Republicans of New Hampshire because his idea of America and of Americanism is contradictory to theirs.

My problems with status politics, the pressures to measure up to what I felt were old-family standards of respectability and manifest love of country, have already been discussed, but over the years, and especially in political competition with Yankee Republicans, I have learned that these pressures were more imagined than real. I discovered that the main-line Republicans of New Hampshire, including the patricians, more often than not are people of decency, honor, and social conscience. They cling to genuinely American values and traditions: respect for freedom of expression, of dissent, of civil rights and civil liberties, of due process of law, of the Constitution. They wear their patriotism in their hearts, not on their sleeves. Many of them are committed to making up for what some of their forebears did to latter-day French and Irish Catholic families who worked for slave wages in the mills of New Hampshire. My political differences with Bill Loeb are differences in kind. My political differences with main-line New Hampshire Republicans are differences in degree, primarily over the proper role of the federal government in meeting social needs and in our respective attitudes about the rights of organized labor.

For whatever of countless possible reasons, Loeb seems to despise the New Hampshire Republican Establishment and has waged war on it for a quarter century. "*The* people in New Hampshire," he once said, "have never supported or liked me." Never was his antagonism toward *the* people in New Hampshire more bitterly expressed than in the 1962 elections. Ironically, I was the political beneficiary of that animosity.

When Styles Bridges, a Republican fixture in the Senate and a long-time Loeb favorite, died suddenly on November 26, 1961, Loeb immediately suggested that Governor Wesley Powell (whom Loeb backed in 1958 and again in 1960) "put aside his own ambitions" and name Doloris Bridges to replace her husband until an election for the remainder of his term could be held the following November. To his credit, Powell did not give in to Loeb's wishes; instead, he named his newly appointed attorney general, Maurice Murphy, as interim U.S. senator.*

In the September 1962 primary, Loeb's candidate for governor, John Pillsbury, succeeded in knocking incumbent Wesley Powell out of the running. But Loeb stumbled in the senatorial primary, when he chose to back Doloris Bridges over the competition of Second District Congressman Perkins Bass, First District Congressman Chester Merrow (who ten years later would try for his old House seat as a Democrat), and caretaker senator Maurice Murphy. Bass led the field in the primary, defeating Mrs. Bridges by 1,700 votes and running away from the other two candidates.

Doloris Bridges first demanded a recount, which resulted in a net gain of ten votes for Bass, and then brought Bass to court for allegedly spending more than the legal limit on his campaign. The Supreme Court threw out the charges, and Loeb's front-page editorial of October 12, 1962 stated:

> It is quite clear to this newspaper that Mrs. Bridges was overwhelmed by a minority of eggheads and left-wingers in the state, supported by the Bass fortune. This confirmation was determined that Mrs. Bridges' conservative and patriotic ideas should not be heard in Washington.

So bitter was the Republican primary that Governor Wesley Powell refused to endorse his party's gubernatorial nominee, John Pillsbury, and threw his support to the Democratic nominee, John King. Doloris Bridges refused to back Bass for senator. On election day John King was elected governor and I was elected U.S. senator. My margin of victory was 10,413 votes. Two days after the primary Loeb exploded over the results (and incidentally paid me a gratuitous insult by implying that there would not even be a contest in the general election).

* Loeb's response to this action is discussed in chapter 11.

The fact that Perkins Bass is to fill out the unexpired term of Styles Bridges is, of course, nothing less than an insult to the memory of Styles Bridges and to everything for which the Bridges' name stood. Bass belongs to the group of World Federalist, international-minded Republicans, who together with their counterparts in the Democratic party, have brought this nation to its present deadly peril in the field of international affairs. The millionaire Bass, born with a gold spoon in his mouth, no more represents the hard-working people of the 2nd District than President Kennedy would.

It is worth noting here that Loeb's opposition to Perkins Bass reflects his seeming intense dislike for main-line, particularly old-family, Republicans. Perkins Bass is the archetypical Yankee patrician. He was born in 1912, when his father, the late Robert P. Bass, was the governor of New Hampshire. Even though the elder Bass served only one term, he is credited with being one of the most enlightened governors the state has ever had, battling the hold the Boston & Maine Railroad then had on the state, pioneering significant conservation measures, persuading the legislature to pass a factory inspection law to improve worker safety in the mills, and establishing the first commission to regulate utilities.

Perkins Bass attended Dartmouth College and Harvard Law School and practiced law until he became an Air Force Intelligence officer during World War II. After duty in China, Bass returned home and entered state politics, serving in both the New Hampshire Senate and the House before running for Congress. He served two terms in the U.S. House of Representatives before entering the Senate race in 1962.

In December 1977 Bass reminisced about the 1962 campaign in an interview in the *Keene Evening Sentinel*, recalling that Loeb had called him "an international-minded millionaire" and "an insult to the memory of Styles Bridges." He makes clear in this interview that he is discouraged by the current state of the Republican party, saying "the moderate view has been pretty well thrown out."

I hold Perkins Bass in considerable esteem. He is a gentleman of the first order, and he and his family have served New Hampshire honorably and well. I admit to drawing considerable satisfaction from his appraisal of my performance on the job over the past fifteen years. At the close of his *Keene Evening*

Sentinel interview, Perkins Bass said, "In my opinion, he [McIntyre] hasn't done a bad job at all. His judgment has been fairly sound all along."

But Perkins Bass was not the only main-line Republican who felt the sting of Loeb's editorial lash in that campaign year of 1962. Another was James C. Cleveland, an attorney who was elected Second District congressman despite Loeb's stinging attacks, holds the office to this day, and has been in and out of favor with the publisher in the ensuing years. Cleveland incurred Loeb's enmity before the election, and the instances deserve retelling because they point up several dramatic attitudinal differences between Loeb and main-line Republicans.

On May 2, 1957 Joseph R. McCarthy died at the Bethesda Naval Medical Center in Maryland. Loeb's editorial the next day, bordered in black, covering nearly two full columns, and titled "Murdered," declared that "Joe McCarthy was murdered by the Communists as surely as if he had been put up before a wall and shot." Loeb went on to name others who were allegedly party to the deed, among them Senator Ralph Flanders (R-Vt.) and a newspaper publisher in Las Vegas, both of whom Loeb charged with portraying McCarthy as a homosexual. He castigated other newspapers.

> Then of course the piously hypocritical newspapers, such as *The New York Times*, the *Providence Journal* and many others, ran slanted reports against McCarthy and heaped abuse and lies on his head through their editorial columns.
> FINALLY, WE COME TO THAT STINKING HYPOCRITE IN THE WHITE HOUSE WHO RECENTLY BECAME SO SMALL THAT HE ASKED EVERY OTHER SENATOR AND REPRESENTATIVE TO HIS RECEPTION EXCEPT JOE McCARTHY.

That was too much for James P. Rogers, a state senator from my hometown of Laconia. On May 7 he introduced a resolution in the New Hampshire Senate that was supported by then State Senator James Cleveland.

> Whereas, the publisher of the *Manchester Union Leader* has on many occasions referred to the President of the United States in terms which are not consistent with good ethics or common decency; and
> Whereas the right of free speech and free press does not grant the privilege of degrading the highest elective office in the land, and
> Whereas, the repeated and malicious abuse of the President is an unhealthy influence, akin to subversion, and

Whereas, on page 3 of the *Union Leader* of Friday, May 3, the said publisher, William Loeb, has referred to the Chief Executive in a manner which is repulsive to all good citizens; now therefore,

Be It Resolved, that the New Hampshire Senate condemns the unbridled use of such vicious and irresponsible language in the public press.

On the third and final reading the resolution lost by a sixteen-to-seven vote, but Rogers and Cleveland stuck with it to the end.

Loeb did not forget Cleveland's effrontery, and when the New Londoner announced that he would seek the Second District congressional seat, the *Union Leader* and the *New Hampshire Sunday News* began to attack, calling Cleveland, among other things, a "One Worlder" with "left-wing economic inclinations." But that was only the beginning.

He [Loeb] turned his fire towards Cleveland for the remainder of the month, harping on the fact that, as an attorney, Cleveland had defended a man who had a record of membership in the Communist Party and that Cleveland had defended the Supreme Court decision on prayer in the public schools. Loeb went so far as to say it would be an "everlasting shame" to elect the New London man. McQuaid joined in and assailed Cleveland as an "inveterate egghead and liberal" on July 29 in the *Sunday News*. Cleveland responded in a Keene speech that Loeb was a "malignant growth" on the New Hampshire scene and a "cancer" among New Hampshire newspapers, to which Loeb replied that Cleveland had libeled him on August 2.

By August 6, Cleveland had had enough and, in a speech at Colby Junior College in his home town, Cleveland said: "Mr. Loeb, I did not crawl out of a foxhole in the Pacific theatre to come back home and crawl on my belly before a junior grade Goebbels whose combat experience has been chiefly confined to law suits and character assassinations. . . . Far too long, New Hampshire has suffered the blighting, corroding and malignant influence of the Loeb papers. Mr. Loeb implies that a lawyer who represents a Communist is a Communist. The logic has devastating implications. The Constitution of the United States emphatically guarantees the right to counsel and it is my position that Mr. Loeb is taking a position that undermines the right. More bluntly stated, Mr. Loeb's position is dangerously subversive of important and hard-won Constitutional rights.

"Again, Mr. Loeb has not only implied that I am an atheist for simply stating that I thought the Supreme Court of the United States' decision was correct, he has openly accused the Court itself of being atheistic by referring to its recent decision as an atheistic one. This unbelievable attack on the Supreme Court is also subversive.

"In addition, I am also campaigning for an end to the reign of terror with which Mr. Loeb seeks to dominate our state by desecrating those who differ with his opinions."

The newsmen who covered the Cleveland outburst must have informed Loeb in Prides Crossing because, in larger type, alongside the story of Cleveland's attack on Loeb was Loeb's two-column answer titled: "Not a Communist, Not an Atheist—Just Confused." He said Cleveland had "very, very bad judgment" and, "We suggest that you take it easy or you will have to be checking with your doctor on your blood pressure every other day."[3]

Cleveland survived Loeb's onslaughts in 1962, winning the Republican nomination by a scant seven-hundred-vote margin in the primary and then going on to victory in the November general election. He has been reelected every two years since, and Loeb long ago reconciled himself to the fact that the New Londoner would be around for years to come.

Cleveland's counterattack in 1962 and his subsequent victories at the polls illustrate the other side of the Loeb-influence coin. Some candidates have been successful by meeting Loeb head-on and making him and his newspapers the issue in a campaign. Cleveland did it in 1962, and I have done it in every one of my own campaigns. And my junior colleague, spirited Senator John A. Durkin, made Loeb eat his words in a celebrated runoff election victory over Louis Wyman in 1975.

The fact that Democrats—Senator Durkin, First District Congressman Norman D'Amours, and I—held three of New Hampshire's four congressional offices in recent years attests to the growth of the Democratic party within the state and to Loeb's inability to control the outcome of elections for federal office.

Nevertheless, we have seen the influence he wields in primary elections, particularly Presidential primaries, and in ensuing chapters his influence on specific issues, starting with the matter of state tax policy, is discussed.

CHAPTER 13

Growing Pains

The beauty of sin taxes is that not only does New Hampshire live on sin, but on other *people's sin, at that. Our biggest liquor sales are at the Massachusetts border and 80 percent of our racetrack clients come from Massachusetts.*
—WILLIAM LOEB[1]

The state is in the gambling business—horseracing, sweepstakes tickets, the 50-cent numbers game. All that has crept like the elm disease, destroying some of the old virtues the Puritans handed down.
—Former New Hampshire Governor SHERMAN ADAMS[2]

We mortgage the state's future so we can boast of current low taxes. . . . We are going to have the lowest taxes plus the fastest growing taxes, an anomalous situation that will end in disaster. . . . Once Thomson finishes being governor, his successor will inherit catastrophe.
—New Hampshire State Representative JOSEPH EATON (R-Hillsboro)[3]

The major reason why Loeb has not been as effective in influencing or controlling federal elections in New Hampshire is the absence or irrelevance of his most effective issue—state spending and state taxes—in those campaigns. This is the issue Loeb has used to influence gubernatorial primaries and general elections and to distort the entire character of one state campaign after another.

Loeb is either credited or blamed as the single most important reason why New Hampshire is still the only state in the Union with neither an income tax nor a sales tax.

Moreover, he has made the broad-based tax so potent an issue that it takes a very strong candidate indeed to reject Loeb's demand that a "no broad-base tax pledge" be taken at the outset of the campaign. The last candidate to tell Loeb what he could do with his pledge was Harry Spanos, a lawyer from Newport and for many years a powerful leader in the State Senate. When Spanos challenged incumbent Governor Meldrim Thomson in 1976, Loeb pulled out all the stops, painting him as a flaming Ivy League liberal as well as a broad-base taxer.

The impact of this all-out assault can be measured by the polls and the results. In the first week of October polls were forecasting a close race, but on election day Thomson won a third term by a record margin, taking 57 percent of the votes.

A month after the election Spanos said in an interview that he believed "William Loeb more than any other single factor was the reason I lost the election. The only time I think my name was ever mentioned on the front page of that paper is when I won the primary, when I was being attacked by Loeb, or when I was responding to the allegations and misrepresentations he had made the day before."

For many years there has been debate over why New Hampshire has such an antipathy to direct taxation. Some have explained it as a relic of the Puritan ethic. Their reading is that many New Englanders still believe virtue is rewarded and vice punished in the temporal as well as the eternal realm; from this it follows, among other things, that spending tax money to help the poor contradicts God's will. I find that reasoning dubious indeed. If there were still people clinging to such a self-righteous ethic, I would have met them on the campaign trail. For all the complaints about taxing and spending that have come directly

to my ears, the notion that the poor are being deservedly punished by God has never been expressed.

Another explanation points to the state's long tradition of frugality, and here I believe there is validity. I think it is likely that
the old regional ethic of "use it up, make it do, or do without"
has been reinforced by the impact of inflation, the energy crisis,
and environmental awareness.

Former Governor Sherman Adams spoke to the question of
New Hampshire frugality, spending, and taxation in a interview
for a series on "New England Perspectives."

> In the middle of the 19th century French Canadians had come down
> into New Hampshire in great numbers to man the looms in the cotton
> mills. Many of them were not of French ancestry at all, but were Irish.
> You could trace their forebears back to the potato famine of 1845 in Ire-
> land. People were faced with starvation, and instead of taking care of
> them, the Crown yarded them wholesale into ships and took them to
> Canada or the West Indies.
>
> On those little farms in Canada, they survived on what they could
> raise—saw almost no money at all. So those who emigrated down into
> New Hampshire to man the woolen mills hated any kind of taxation.
> New Hampshire, in some respects, may be the most illiberal state in the
> union in the sense of being unwilling to follow the communal instinct of
> taxing itself to support services for the benefit of others. Many people in
> this state are still, by virtue of their lineage and family philosophies, ex-
> tremely parsimonious. They are afraid of "going on the town." . . . And
> they think what they earn they should have the use of.
>
> It is an irony in New Hampshire that the principal reason we don't
> have either income or sales taxes is our reliance on what I, when I was
> Governor, labeled "sin taxes." We do a remarkably fine business selling
> liquor to people from Massachusetts. The state is in the gambling busi-
> ness—horseracing, sweepstakes tickets, the 50-cent numbers game. All
> that has crept like the elm disease, destroying some of the old virtues the
> Puritans handed down.[4]*

Adams, unfortunately, is more remembered for having been
Eisenhower's ill-fated chief of staff than for having been one of
New Hampshire's strongest governors.

Still other reasons are advanced for the absence of a broad-
based tax in New Hampshire. One is the absence of an organized, potent, and highly visible constituency for social ser-

* While there is merit in this analysis, I would question that the Irish and
the French newcomers to the state were solely responsible for "illiberal" attitudes in New Hampshire. Yankee traditions also played a part.

vices. New Hampshire's poor, for instance, are not ghettoed, but scattered, largely out of sight and out of mind.

Another is the size and the makeup of the New Hampshire legislature, with 433 members, the third largest legislative body in the English-speaking world. Each legislator represents about 2,000 constituents, and each is paid only $100 a year. Historically, the legislature has been made up, for the most part, of conservative independent businesspeople or retirees who could afford the time without concern for remuneration. In recent years, however, the legislature's complexion has changed, with liberals making significant inroads. Young men and women, some still in college, have run for the legislature either to exercise their idealism or to gain political experience and establish a base for future endeavor. In company with older liberals and moderates of both parties, these newcomers are beginning to give the statehouse a more progressive image—much to Loeb's displeasure.

Spending and taxes remain the all-absorbing issue because Loeb makes them the all-absorbing issue. To explain how they became the issue, a quick review is in order.

New Hampshire has always been a frugal state, an admirable characteristic in terms of sound fiscal management, if not so admirable in terms of human services.

The growth of all government activities and spending during the latter part of the New Deal years offers an example of New Hampshire's care with public money. In his 1939 budget message Governor Francis P. Murphy noted that "since June 30, 1934, the cost of government advanced in our state by $2,658,-000 or 14.5 percent. During the same period in the state of Maine such costs expanded by . . . 46 percent; in Vermont by . . . 43 percent; in Massachusetts by . . . 58 percent; in Rhode Island by . . . 49 percent; and in Connecticut by . . . 42 percent."

Why the difference? According to Murphy, it was New Hampshire's "good legislative control, effective administration supervision, wise financial policies, frugal expenditures, a minimum of overhead, and an avoidance of unnecessary functions."

Toward the end of Murphy's tenure, however, the state began to change its sources of revenue, starting with a tobacco tax in 1939 and the conversion of the state liquor control commission from monitor to revenue-raiser, with liquor taxes thereafter going into the general fund, the depository of tax money that can be used for any purpose. A state lottery—the first in the nation —was introduced in 1963. From then on, as the *New Hampshire Times* noted on May 25, 1977, "New Hampshire was headed down the road toward a reliance on sin taxes—liquor sales, ciga- rette sales, and betting. Today sarcastic legislators call these money-making taxes the state's reliance on 'bets, butts, booze, beds and bellies,' referring to racing revenues, tobacco taxes, li- quor sales and the room and meals tax."

Coupled with these are three other taxes. Two—the property tax and the residence tax (the last vestigial head tax)—are con- sidered highly regressive by many tax authorities; the third is a business profits tax, enacted in 1970.

As early as 1949, former Governor Sherman Adams warned that existing sources of revenue could no longer meet the state's needs. He made a moral judgment, saying it was time "to trans- fer the present dependence on sin to the more secure founda- tion of virtue," and proposed a gross income tax. The State Su- preme Court ruled such a tax unconstitutional. Undaunted, Adams then proposed a combined sales and income tax, which the legislature rejected. The governor made one more attempt, a one percent income tax, which was also turned down.

Adams made a last try in 1950. After succeeding in getting through a major reorganization of state government, he sug- gested that a sales tax be considered. Again he lost, and that set the pattern that has continued to the present. The next two gov- ernors, Hugh Gregg and Lane Dwinell, Republicans like Adams, kept resolutely away from the subject of broad-based taxation, Dwinell opining in 1955 that "the only way to retard the mounting costs of government is to refuse additional reve- nue. . . . A little stinginess can be a good thing." Republican Governor Wesley Powell did not ask for new taxes, nor did his successor, John King, the first Democratic governor in thirty- eight years.

But the issue was drawn again in 1969, when incoming Re- publican Governor Walter R. Peterson Jr. appointed a Citizens Task Force made up of business and government leaders to study possible reorganization of state government and new sources of state income. The task force recommended implementation of a business profits tax and dropped some strong hints that the day was not far off when New Hampshire would have to consider either an income tax or a sales tax. At about the same time, the New Hampshire League of Women Voters published a state action program calling for property tax relief, a total restructuring of the state's tax system, and a broad-based tax to provide needed services.

The legislature did nothing with the recommendations in 1969, but in 1970 it did repeal a stock-in-trade tax, implement a business profits tax, and enact a commuter income tax, which was later to be ruled unconstitutional by the U.S. Supreme Court.

What happened in the political lists that year provides one of the more repugnant examples of Loeb's ruthlessness. The target was not only Governor Peterson—a person whom I respect for his civility, his decency, and his sense of social responsibility— but his family as well.

As he embarked upon his campaign for reelection, Walter Peterson said:

> I will not exaggerate the problems facing us in 1971 and 1972. I will let the facts speak for themselves. I think you should know that we who have boasted of our frugality also preside over the lowest paid state police force in New England, over state employees whose salaries are below the New England average, and whose retirement and other benefits are of an earlier time. Our young people pay the highest tuition in the region to attend their state university. In the helter-skelter of last-minute budget cutting, we have authorized programs without people, people without desks, and offices without people.
>
> We have rarely taken a hard look at the philosophy behind our programs, but instead have been content to cut part or all of what is new, almost invariably leaving what is old. We have not succeeded in cleaning up a single major river basin despite 24 years of trying. We have not succeeded in preventing the drift toward pollution of our priceless lakes.
>
> We must look to the day when we can assure that our young people achieve something like their maximum potential and not be left by the wayside of a society which places too much value on the fortunate few who complete higher education.
>
> We must encourage growth of new industry, but do so selectively. We must encourage tourism, but not be overcome by it.
>
> We must have the courage to withstand the destructive powers of the Loeb press and tell the public what it does not seem to understand—that our tax structure is, and always has been, a reflection of the wishes of the well-to-do.

Loeb responded to the challenge, inciting such intense political pressure on Peterson that he had to promise no new taxes. Once into his second term, however, he did indeed have to make that recommendation. Loeb immediately told his readers, "Peterson spits in your faces."

But that was only the beginning. A *New York Times Magazine* article by Bill Kovach described what happened.

> Loeb once picked up an innocent remark by Peterson's daughter, Meg, and turned it into a running front page attack on the governor. At a White House conference on drugs, Meg said she knew some young people smoked marijuana but thought it was their own business. Picturing Meg as the victim of misguided parents and part of a generation destroyed by drugs, the attack continued until Governor Peterson bought space on the front page of the paper to say: "I am fair game, Mr. Loeb, but I must ask you to stop picking on my 15-year-old daughter, who, after all, is only a young girl with many years of life ahead."[5]

Long before the 1968 election, William Loeb was on the prowl for a candidate that could beat Walter Peterson. He found him in the person of Meldrim Thomson Jr., a law book publisher located in the small town of Orford, New Hampshire.

Thomson, it is said, first came to Loeb's attention and favor when, as a member of the Orford school board, he protested the acceptance of federal funds for the remedial reading program. Before long the buildup began. Articles and pictures about Thomson began to appear in the Loeb press, and when filing time rolled around in 1968, Loeb had his candidate.

But Loeb could not quite sell the little-known Thomson to the electorate that year or two years later. Each time the Republican voters opted in the primary for Walter Peterson, who was not only the incumbent, but who was well known before that as the president of the New Hampshire Senate. In 1970 Thomson was so stung by losing another primary to Peterson, and again by a margin of only 3 percent, that he filed as candidate in the general election on George Wallace's American party ticket, declaring at the time, "I have severed my affiliation with the Republican party forever."[6]

Peterson was reelected, and later Thomson said his decision to file on the Wallace ticket "was a mistake." But, he added, "I had to do it. I either had to give up trying, or stick up for the principles I fought for in the primary."[7]

He may have been sorrier because his mentor, William Loeb, chastised him for the first of very few times in their relationship. It is widely believed that Loeb did not chastise Thomson for running as a Wallaceite (after all, Loeb is a long-time admirer of the Alabaman), but for possibly alienating Republican support he would need when Loeb ran him again in 1972.

Whatever the case, the alienation was not severe enough to cost him another loss. This time around Thomson won the primary and went on to a 41-percent plurality victory in the general election, when a late-filing independent, Malcolm McLane, split the progressive vote with Democratic candidate Roger Crowley. McLane, bearer of another well-known Republican name, is a moderate of the Walter Peterson mold and has since become a persistent thorn in Thomson's side as a member of the Governor's Council.

Thomson's triumph in 1972 put in the governor's chair someone who, in virtually every respect, is an ideological mirror image of William Loeb. Thomson won the governorship by campaigning on two slogans: "Axe the Tax" and "People Above Politics." He has neither axed taxes nor has kept people above politics. Yet, he has been reelected twice, with ever larger margins of victory.

The reasons are fairly described in a profile of the governor written by Patricia Burstein for *People* magazine, for they pointedly illustrate Thomson's skillful blending of status politics and interest politics.

> While critics view Thomson as a right-wing curmudgeon, he also symbolizes to many an earlier, simpler America—a man who favors law-and-order and prayer in the schools, while endorsing a few-holds-barred foreign policy. He has publicly mourned U.S. failure to invade China during the war in Korea, and has asked that the New Hampshire National Guard be trained in the use of nuclear weapons. . . .
>
> The governor has also benefited from his hand-in-glove alliance with William Loeb, the sulfurous right-wing publisher of New Hampshire's only statewide newspaper, the *Manchester Union Leader*. During one 18-month period, in fact, phone records indicated Thomson had called Loeb 256 times—proof, according to his critics, that he was playing Charlie McCarthy to Loeb's Edgar Bergen. . . .
>
> It is Thomson's opposition to taxes, however, that is the key to his political success. New Hampshire is the only state without either a personal income or sales tax; 50 percent of its revenues come from so-called "sin taxes" on liquor, beer, cigarettes and horse and dog racing. Voters

appear to approve, having sent Thomson to the statehouse in Concord
three times.[8]

The last point merits closer examination, for opposition to a
state sales or income tax has been Loeb's trademark for nearly
thirty years, and Thomson gave it his vigorous embrace and his
firm promise to veto any broad-based tax bill that comes across
his desk.

Both men point to a set of undeniable facts to support their
claim that the state has benefited greatly in the absence of a
sales or income tax. Surely the image of New Hampshire as
being relatively tax free—plus the demonstrated aesthetic appeal of its lakes, mountains, seashore, clean air, and essentially
small-town, rural nature—has been largely responsible for the
state's astonishing growth in recent years.

Fastest growing of all northeastern states and among the ten
fastest growing of all states, New Hampshire gained nearly 200,-
000 people between 1960 and 1970, going from 737,681 to 825,-
500. Seventy percent of the new residents are from other states;
40 percent are from Massachusetts alone. In March 1978 it was
reported that another 100,000 people had moved across the
Massachusetts border since 1970, along with scores of corporations. In 1977 alone, sixty-eight industries opened new operations or administrative facilities in New Hampshire, most of
them in the already-crowded southern tier of counties.

As a result of this growth spurt, much of which has taken place
in the past six years, New Hampshire leads the Northeast in
capital investment, increases in real income, and in the creation
of new jobs, has the lowest public indebtedness, the highest
bond rating, the lowest rate of unemployment, and the only unemployment fund in the region that does not show a deficit.

Moreover, new projections show that while the growth in
population nationwide is expected to be 7 percent by 1985,
New Hampshire's growth rate for the same period of time may
reach 19 percent, the fourth highest in the nation. The same
projections indicate that New Hampshire will be ninth among
all states in the rate of increased earnings.

This has not gone unnoticed. *U.S. News & World Report* and
the *Wall Street Journal* have lauded the state's record at a time
when the rest of the nation is feeling the economic crunch and

have praised the state for rolling out the red carpet for business and industry.

Nor have Loeb and Thomson been restrained in their crowing. Loeb, for instance, takes special glee in pointing out that it has been nearly twenty years since Sherman Adams said the state must have a sales or an income tax in order to survive; yet here is New Hampshire in 1978, ostensibly a model of economic growth and fiscal stability.

Both men can point to the political rewards of their antitax stance. As the *Washington Star* noted on March 30, 1978,

> the voting statistics, especially in the counties on the border [with Massachusetts] tell the story succinctly. More than 70 percent of voters registered since 1972 listed themselves as Democrats and in 1976 voted for Democratic candidates at the Federal and local levels. But district by district, they voted for Thomson, returning him to office by a 53,000 vote plurality.

Statistics like those bolster the governor's political confidence. When it was first rumored that he was considering challenging me for the Senate seat in 1978, he was asked how his state antitax theme could work against a federal office incumbent. The *New Hampshire Times* of January 19, 1977 reported his response: "It would be a different kettle of fish, but I think you could use pretty much the same hooks to catch the fish with, and as for bait, you couldn't have finer bait than taxes."

At this writing Meldrim Thomson—after months of vacillation—has announced he will not challenge me for the Senate seat but will seek a fourth term as governor. Since most observers consider him a shoo-in, the question is why did he hesitate over running again? It could be a natural desire to return to his farm and business in Orford after six busy, trying years in the statehouse. Some say it could be something else—the fear that a day of economic reckoning will arrive *before* he completes a fourth term.

Thus far, Thomson has eluded a devastating crisis because he inherited a twenty-four-million-dollar budget surplus when he took office in 1973, a surplus built up under the moderate Republican governor he and Loeb scorned—Walter Peterson; because of the millions of dollars pumped into the state through revenue sharing by another institution they hold in scorn—the

federal government; by dint of increasing a wide range of existing taxes, which Thomson, by implication, had said he would
hold down; and by restricting the level of services.

With each passing year in office, however, the crisis has come
closer to reality. In 1977 the *New Hampshire Times* summed up
the situation for the third-term governor.

> Thomson . . . is finding the going tough. Despite his economy
> moves and his efforts to keep taxes down, the budget of New Hampshire
> continues to grow at an ever increasing rate. This year the governor
> placed before the legislature the state's first billion dollar budget for a
> two-year period, and that was only the beginning.
>
> Before the present legislative session began, a $24 million surplus,
> placed on the books four years ago, disappeared and the state seemed
> headed for a deficit by the end of the present fiscal year. Some immedi-
> ate cuts in state spending headed off the deficit, but the legislature will
> no doubt be working until the final minutes of the session trying to find
> the money to meet what has been called the bare minimum of services
> for the next two years. Broad-based taxes are once again out of the ques-
> tion—Thomson is standing by his pledge to veto any such bill that
> should reach his desk.
>
> The question that perplexes is this: how could a state that has prac-
> ticed such financial restraint end up in such a fiscal mess? After years of
> getting by, and even doing well enough to feel self-satisfied on occasion,
> New Hampshire now seems to have run out of time. . . . Thomson said
> if his advice were followed the result would be a balanced budget, but
> balancing the budget involved such things as firing ten percent of the
> state workers, increasing some existing taxes, across-the-board cuts in
> departmental spending, and the resultant loss of many state services.[9]

When the *New Hampshire Times* turned to state Senate Finance Chairman C. Robertson Trowbridge for an explanation of
how this situation came about, Trowbridge attributed it to a
combination of inflation, soaring energy costs, and an increasing
demand for state services.

Besides, the federal revenue sharing money that looked at
first like money from heaven turned out to have a painful quid
pro quo.

> The Federal government has involved the state in a number of pro-
> grams which cost the state increasing sums of money annually, and the
> threat of a loss of Federal funds hangs over New Hampshire if it does not
> comply with Federal rules. Welfare payments are a good example. . . .
> The state's share of payments in the Aid to Families with Dependent
> Children program was $1,088,953 in 1968. Today it costs the state a total

of $7,314,000 to participate in the same program and the total Federal
and state dollars spent comes to more than $19 million. That figure is
more than the entire General Fund appropriation for the year 1958.

The constantly increasing rate of spending in New Hampshire, coupled with the absence of a revenue source that can keep pace with inflation, has put the state in a bind of monumental proportion. Should the
legislature find a way to balance the budget this year, it will be following
in the footsteps of previous sessions where legislators have usually
opted to let the next session worry about it and have gone home. New
Hampshire may not be able to put it off for two years this time.[10]

By late fall of 1977 one of the state's top fiscal experts, Representative Joseph Eaton (R-Hillsboro), told the Associated Press
that New Hampshire was courting financial chaos unless it puts
its budget in order. Eaton said the proposed new budget was a
"fallacy," that it was not a "money saver." "Temporary crisis
budgeting," he said, "promotes future deficits. A one-shot advance of $5 million in the business profits tax will begin the
1979 spending pattern but will not be in 1979 income. Bor-
rowed retirement funds, delayed purchases of equipment, back-
logs of work, will be concealed burdens for future taxpayers."[11]

Eaton then noted that in 1950, New Hampshire and four other
states of about the same size—Idaho, Montana, and the Da-
kotas—

had about the same bonded debt. . . . New Hampshire now owes as
much as the other four states combined. We mortgage the state's future
so we can boast of current low taxes. . . . We are going to have the
lowest taxes plus the fastest-growing taxes, an anomalous situation that
will end in disaster. Once Thomson finishes being governor, his successor will inherit catastrophe.[12]

The *Valley News* of Lebanon, New Hampshire commented
on the governor's approach to handling the state budget
problem.

The governor has proposed budget slashing that would hurt state programs for the blind, the elderly and sick, the mentally ill and prisoners,
all the while proposing more money for state troopers and race horse
breeding. The governor would cut funds for the Laconia State School,
for the state prison, for the training and development division of the
Mental Health Division, for community and mental health services and
centers for the retarded. The governor is quite willing to propose short-
changing the human services the state provides, but doesn't favor approval of revenue-raising proposals approved by the House, including a
2 percent increase in the rooms and meals tax and a 1 percent rise in the

business profits tax. The business profits tax shouldn't be increased, the governor told the Senate Finance Committee, because of the bad publicity such a move would get outside the state. The needs of the sick and the elderly don't have a chance when weighed against the possibility of bad publicity.[13]

Other state newspapers turned their editorial guns on the revenue side of the problem. In January 1978 the *Derry News* published this commentary:

Okay, some people will say, so there has been no patronage for Derry. At least Governor Thomson has fulfilled his promise to fight taxes. Wrong; more double talk. Here's the Thomson record on taxes taken just from this last session: Thomson initiated the one percent increase in the Rooms and Meals Tax; Thomson initiated the three-quarter percent increase in the Interest and Dividends Tax; Thomson initiated the 10 cents increase in the Land Sale Tax; Thomson initiated the move to make business pay five quarterly installments on their Business Profits Tax this year instead of four—to raise more money; Thomson initiated the increase in the horse wagering tax; Thomson initiated the increase in highway tolls from 25 cents to 40 cents; Thomson also tried but failed to get an increase in the Resident (Head) tax from $10 to $20; Thomson tried but failed to get a two-percent tax on Blue Cross-Blue Shield premiums. The state was broke last year and the governor did what he had to do. The only difference between Meldrim Thomson and some other governor is the doubletalk. Thomson says he won't raise taxes; but he does. The honest guy comes clean from the beginning.[14]

Nor did New Hampshire's skyrocketing property taxes escape media attention. The latest figures (1975) showed that New Hampshire's per capita property taxes are now the sixth highest in the nation, prompting the *Nashua* (N.H.) *Telegraph* to comment:

Governor Meldrim Thomson has been quoted as saying, "New Hampshire is 50th in the nation in state aid to education and we are proud of it. New Hampshire is proud of being the 50th state because it means we are first in the nation in contributions to the public schools at the same local level."

Who's this "we" the governor is talking about? Is he using "we" in the editorial sense, or is he walking around with a rock in his pocket? . . . It must be concluded . . . that he is proud of the fact that the quality of public school education in New Hampshire varies with the wealth of different communities. It must then be true that he is proud of the fact that children in one community have a better opportunity for quality education than their counterparts in a neighboring community. Speaking of pride, is the governor proud of the fact that people on fixed incomes—including those who have worked all their lives to own their homes outright—are faced with constantly rising property taxes to pay for the added cost of education? Now, there's something to be proud of, governor. State aid to education is something which the Thomson administration and its zealous supporters will never recognize as a priority. Such people would prefer an illiterate low and middle income class to the alternative of meaningful tax reform. Only in the administration of Meldrim Thomson can last be considered first.[15]

An editorial titled "The Low Tax Myth" appeared in the *Lebanon Valley News.*

New Hampshire's vaunted standing as a haven of refuge for the oppressed taxpayer has been exposed as a myth. *Money,* the authoritative magazine on the subject published by Time, Inc., revealed in its February issue that New Hampshire, instead of being a nearly tax-free haven, ranks 19th from the *top* among the 50 states in the amount of state and local taxes its residents pay. It is, in fact, a rather nice place for the rich. For those with adjusted gross incomes between $25,000 and $100,000, it ranks about 40th, but for those with adjusted gross incomes of $10,000 to $20,000 it is 19th. *Money's* statistics come from the Internal Revenue Service. They were based on tax returns of 26 million taxpayers who itemized their deductions on their 1975 returns, and thus reported what they paid in state and local taxes. . . . It should be clear from these figures that New Hampshire's stubborn adherence to its sock-the-homeowner taxation favors the rich and penalizes the less rich.[16]

This is precisely what Walter Peterson said when he launched his ill-fated reelection campaign in 1971.

In view of the lengthy, intense indoctrination New Hampshire voters have had on the subject, a politician dependent on their favor has to take a long breath before venturing any opinion favoring introduction of broad-based taxes. There are other (and better) reasons for hesitating than political prudence. Introduction of sales taxes or income taxes does not necessarily bring relief from existing taxes or the reform of a regressive tax system—sometimes it is simply the layering on of still *another* tax.

Further, these taxes—so relatively easy to collect, so readily adjusted upward—do have a way of growing and do tend to encourage bureaucratic proliferation. During my years in Washington I have developed a healthy skepticism about the ultimate effectiveness of throwing more and more tax dollars at problems that require something in addition to fiscal attention.

(I acknowledge that this phrasing is associated with Richard Nixon, but Nixon wasn't *always* wrong.)

When respected experts on state finance, such as Republican State Senator C. Robertson Trowbridge, say the state is heading for economic chaos without meaningful tax reform and a broad-based source of new revenue, I am impressed. And I am impressed that, just as draft-deferred college students led the war protest movement in the sixties, some of the same people who benefit most from New Hampshire's skewed tax structure are in the vanguard of the move to reduce their own privilege and make state taxes fairer to the lower-income citizen. That, I believe, is not only the road toward greater justice, but it is also a decision that can be defended in the name of enlightened self-interest.

It is not my purpose here, however, to argue the case for or against a broad-based tax. People more expert than I on the subject of state financing obviously disagree on this point. In the context of this book the issue here is how Loeb and Thomson have roped off the arena of debate over state financing. Their politics of threat and reprisal have prevented the people of New Hampshire from hearing a full-scale discussion of the issue. When state candidates and state officials are so fearful of the consequences that they dare not even suggest *discussion* of a broad-based tax, the political dialogue is distorted, the reasoning process is short-changed, and the people are denied their right to all the information they deserve in order to make a fair judgment.

The inequities of the present tax structure cannot be ignored; property taxes are high and extremely regressive. Nor can the hypocrisies in the system be denied; the state already has sales and income taxes. Excise taxes on rooms and meals, cigarettes, liquor, and gasoline are sales taxes, and the tax on interest and dividends and the business profits tax on proprietors and corporations are income taxes.

Loeb and Thomson are not impressed. They are still betting the state will be able to skim by on sin taxes, industrialization, and population growth. So determined are the two to ward off anything that smacks of meaningful tax reform that they reach to lengths that are sometimes ludicrous . . . and sometimes alarming. Witness the governor's proposal in June 1977 for a 5-percent tax on bingo and beano games as a new source of revenue, a proposal that quickly raised the ire of churches, religious organizations, and fraternal and ethnic groups. Or consider the clutching-at-straws editorial in the *Union Leader* of December 15, 1976.

> With the state's coffers facing increased demands from government services, it is obviously all the more important that New Hampshire realize maximum revenues from its present sources. It has long been a pet peeve of this newspaper that untold thousands of dollars in Sweepstakes revenue is [sic] being lost to the state, thereby adding to the burdens borne by the taxpayers, because of the failure of many state liquor store clerks to enthusiastically promote the sale of Sweepstakes tickets. . . . It is to be hoped that the next session of the legislature will produce legislation to provide the sort of incentive plan that will encourage liquor store clerks to promote Sweeps ticket sales with some semblance of enthusiasm.

In the same clutching-at-straws category there was the governor's abortive attempt to keep state liquor stores open later on Christmas Eve in order to reap every possible dollar from last-minute shoppers.

Much more serious, however, is the backing these two zealous guardians of public morals give to casino gambling, which both see as a potential rich, new source of sin revenue. Loeb called legalized gambling "voluntary taxation of the *best* variety." In the same February 9, 1977 editorial he said:

> Former Attorney General [Warren] Rudman . . . says he has 15 important people in the state who are joining him and former Governor Sherman Adams to fight legalized state-owned gambling. Well, this newspaper has news for Mr. Rudman. We do not believe the overwhelming majority of citizens in the state of New Hampshire are about to fall all over themselves being impressed by what 15 carefully selected so-called superior individuals think about legalized gambling! . . . It would be interesting to know who is paying Attorney Rudman's fee, and who are the real parties of interest that the former attorney general is representing. . . . Certainly there are the pro-sales and income taxers who are always infuriated by the fact that the state of New Hampshire has done so well without these burdensome taxes. They are always eager to kill any money project, such as legalized gambling, which would bring in more money to the state and thus allow the state to avoid such regressive taxes. The former attorney general's scare tactics and his predictions about all the dreadful people that legalized gambling will bring into the state are just so much silly twaddle.

Two months earlier, on December 6, 1976, a Loeb editorial proclaimed in capital letters: "THIS NEWSPAPER BELIEVES THAT WERE GAMBLING ALLOWED IN THE STATE OF NEW HAMPSHIRE, IT WOULD BE A TREMENDOUS SOURCE OF REVENUE."*

Rudman, who served under Walter Peterson and, for a time, under Governor Thomson, incurred a new burst of Loeb's wrath when he prepared a detailed and persuasive case against legalized gambling in New Hampshire. The thrust of the Rudman report and of a subsequent statement made by Rudman's successor, former Attorney General David Souter, was that no matter how carefully supervised, legalized state-owned and operated gambling casinos would encourage an undesirable element to invade New Hampshire society.

The gambling issue marked one of the rare occasions when John Durkin and I involved ourselves in an exclusively state government matter. Both of us publicly supported the Rudman antigambling faction.

Thomson's role and the outcome of the question were described in the *New Hampshire Times.*

> Proposals to institute various new types of gambling in the state had been aired in years past, but the issue bloomed in 1977 as a result of the looming fiscal crisis. Legalized gambling was seen in some quarters as a way to raise additional needed revenue without having to resort to the use of a sales or income tax.
>
> Early in the year, Gov. Meldrim Thomson, Jr., promised to sign any gambling bill that reached his desk, lending encouragement to the Bally Manufacturing Co. of Chicago, according to a company spokesman. Bally, the world's largest makers of slot machines . . . sent a representative to the state and bankrolled the House lobbying effort in support of legalized gambling to the tune of $10,000. Restaurant and hotel operators, organized in support of casino gambling bills as the Four Seasons Resort Association, set up shop in Concord with Bally cash and mounted a pro-gambling campaign in the State House corridors and the media. Opposition to legalized gambling rose quickly from sources as diverse as former New Hampshire governor Sherman Adams, ex-Attorney General Warren Rudman, city police chiefs, a county sheriff, and senators and

* The nation's most famous oddsmaker and former gambler takes a different view of legalized gambling. The *Washington Post Magazine* of July 9, 1978 quoted James Synodinas, Jimmy the Greek, as saying, "If you think dope addiction is bad, a guy who gets hooked on gambling goes all the way. . . . God forbid if they legalize gambling."

representatives from both political parties. On April 20, a bill to legalize slot machines and gambling casinos was defeated by a 330 to 22 vote in the House.

Many gambling supporters, including Sen. Robert Monier (R-Goffs-town), saw a conspiracy of broad-based taxers behind opposition to the betting bills. On the Senate floor, Monier repeatedly charged that pro-taxers were systematically resisting all non-tax revenue alternatives, and asked that legalized gambling be reconsidered in the Senate. By this time, however, the Four Seasons organization had closed up shop in the wake of the House defeat, and Attorney General David Souter had publicly denounced any plan to introduce further gambling into New Hampshire, citing the probability of luring criminal elements into the state. With further support of casino gambling considered "impractical" by pro-gambling interests, their focus turned to support of a House bill which would legalize only slot machines. Other gambling bills offered the alternatives of legalized gambling only in New Hampshire's non-profit social clubs, legalized betting on jai alai games and legalized sports betting cards. Long before the legislative session drew to a close, however, all of the gambling bills had been defeated, leaving the state's legislators with the task of looking elsewhere for needed operating revenues.[17]

Frustrated by their defeat on the casino gambling proposal, Thomson and Loeb had to fall back to their basic pitch—New Hampshire's favorable tax climate for business and industry—and redoubled their efforts to expand the commercial base to meet the state's money needs. "It is to the business community that we look for creation of wealth," Thomson said in his inaugural address following his reelection in 1976. "Prosperity flourishes where management and labor work in harmony, as they do here in New Hampshire, to create the goods that mankind needs or wants."

Obviously, industrial expansion has been the key to Thomson's politics for the past six years. He has spread the red carpet for new business by publicizing the absence of a state income tax or sales tax, relatively inexpensive land, a diligent and reliable labor force, tax-exempt industrial bonds, low crime rate, and the life-style offered by a state with an abundance of natural beauty and recreational opportunities. A brochure promoting the state is titled "New Hampshire Is What America Was," and along with the enticements cited above boasts that the state has the lowest rate of unemployment in New England, the lowest gross debt, and the highest bond rating.

This unblushing testimony to the state's alleged prosperity

omits the fact that New Hampshire production workers still earn almost a dollar less per hour than production workers average across the nation; that New Hampshire has the highest percentage of workingwomen with preschool children of any state in the country; and that the percentage of New Hampshire people over sixty-five who have incomes below the federally designated poverty level is double the national average.

The brochure also ignores the social, environmental, and dollar costs of rampant population and industrial expansion. In its April 15, 1977 issue *Forbes* magazine, the respected business journal, took a hard look at the positive and the negative results of the state's growth policy under Meldrim Thomson. The conclusions drawn are evident in the article's title: "The Wrong Road Taken."

As long as he was riding high on the favorable pieces that appeared in the *Wall Street Journal* and other conservative publications, Meldrim Thomson could ignore an occasional critique from a *Forbes* magazine and could continue to pretend that the only people who objected to his policy of unbridled industrial growth were the "eco-freaks," as Loeb described them. Environmentalists have long been pictured by both men as the archenemies of jobs and economic progress. In April 1976, for instance, Thomson said, "America is in full retreat before a tiny band of environmental terrorists who would stop all human progress to multiply the coyote or foster the love life of the mud worm."[18]

However, Loeb and Thomson are learning that environmentalists are not the only people in New Hampshire who are becoming deeply concerned over the consequences of pell-mell, unplanned growth. Local governments, who feel the pinch the most, are hoisting the warning flag throughout the state. In a special report on "The State of the State," the *New Hampshire Times* cited the experiences of the fastest-growing county, city, and town.[19]

Rockingham County, the fastest-growing county in New Hampshire, is also one of the fastest-growing counties in the United States. In 1970 it already had a population of 138,950. By 1977, 33,500 more people had arrived. Because of this amazing growth, the county had to hire Patricia Harry, a public relations specialist, to handle requests for information. The *Times* quoted Harry as follows:

These are some of the things growth has meant to us. Within the last five years the number of criminal cases pending before the Superior Court has increased 400 percent. The county is now building a new jail because a lot of the people who are convicted in court are not being sentenced because of the lack of prison facilities. Juvenile crime accounted for 40 percent of all crime in the county five years ago; now that figure is 90 percent.

In some places first graders go to school from 6:15 a.m. until noon because the schools are on double sessions. In other places the kids go to school on triple session, all year 'round. They have color coded cards to tell which session they're in, and the schools try to arrange it so that the kids in the same family have the same color cards, so they'll all have vacations at the same time. The waiting list of senior citizens for the Rockingham County home is longer today than it was before the new addition was built just three years ago.

Of Nashua, the state's fastest-growing city, the *New Hampshire Times* said:

The Gate City's population increased by 18.1 percent from 1970 to 1977, adding some 11,000 people, for a total of 65,900 who now reside within the city limits. Nashua's allocated budget has jumped from $14,769,882 to $33,879,271 during the seven-year period, while the property tax rate has soared from $32.40 to $52.50 per thousand—even though new industry has shouldered a large portion of the tax burden. The city maintained a force of 90 policemen and 106 firemen in 1970; it scrapes by with 129 policemen and 121 firemen today.[20]

Assessing the impact of runaway growth on the town of Raymond, the *Times* reported:

In the town of Raymond . . . 453 building permits for mobile homes were issued from 1970 to 1976, as compared to only 250 permits for permanent homes during the same period. Of the 1,600 dwellings in Raymond today, 700 are mobile homes. The town's population has increased 50.2 percent . . . in the last seven years. At town meeting this year, Raymond residents "threw some water on the fire" by voting to impose a total moratorium on house building permits while town planners began work on a comprehensive master plan.[21]

But Raymond is not the fastest-growing town in the state. That distinction belongs to Londonderry, which has watched its population increase by an incredible 123.5 percent in the past seven years. "What this has meant in pocketbook terms is the doubling of the town budget . . . and a rise in the tax rate from $29.80 to $45.50 per thousand."[22] In the past six years this small town has had to triple the size of its police force and its fire department.

In an earlier report the *New Hampshire Times* noted that "at least three formal groups are considering various impacts that rapid growth may have on New Hampshire and the quality of its environment."[23] The last may appear to be an observation of modest significance, until it is noted that one of those groups— Forum on New Hampshire's Future—is the brainchild of one of Meldrim Thomson's Republican predecessors, Hugh Gregg, and includes in its blue-ribbon list of fifty members Walter Peterson, prominent business leaders, industrialists, lawyers, academicians, Democrats, and yes, some close friends and associates of Thomson himself.

Forum on New Hampshire's Future grew out of a series of speeches Gregg made several years ago that expressed his concern about the lasting and devastating impact runaway growth would have on the state. Forum is pledged not to *stopping* growth, but to helping *plan* growth.

Temporary president of Forum is David F. Putnam of Keene, who says the group intends to be a private fact-gathering organization that will serve "all the people concerned with rapid growth and change in New Hampshire." Putnam said Forum will be nonpolitical, nonpartisan, and nonprofit, will *not* promote legislation, but *will* act as an information resource and will publish a newsletter and sponsor forums and seminars.

The significance of the Forum's development is not so much its modest aspirations, but rather what it is. The Forum represents the respected Establishment. Thomson cannot shrug it off as a collection of eco-freaks. He knows that there are indeed many thoughtful, responsible citizens who are genuinely alarmed at what unrestrained growth policy portends for New Hampshire.

Stimulus for growth planning is coming from inside the state legislature as well. State Representative Barbara Ganley heads a Subcommittee on Growth within the House Committee on Resources, Recreation and Development. This subcommittee has a sweeping mandate to explore the effects of population increases on the quality of life and the costs of living. According to the *New Hampshire Times*, the subcommittee's ultimate goal is to write a policy statement on growth and to possibly recommend legislation to the House.

Thomson has been made to respond to these and other manifestations of public concern, along with pressure from the federal government. In June 1977 he appointed a Governor's Advisory Committee on New Hampshire's Future, headed by John Sununu, his adviser on science and technology. Not the least of the factors that inspired the governor to set up this advisory committee were demands made by the U.S. Department of Housing and Urban Development that the public be brought into the state's comprehensive planning process.

> Without a vehicle for participating by those affected by government action, Thomson would automatically lose Federal funds for the Office of Comprehensive Planning. These statewide planning grants amounted to $76,000 last year, a sum representing a substantial part of the executive planning department's revenues.[24]

Theoretically, the three new groups concerned with growth— one privately based, one based in the legislature, one based in the executive department—should work together and supplement one another's resources and expertise. Perhaps this will occur. But there is a basic philosophical difference between Thomson and the first two groups that may be difficult to overcome. Thomson's commitment to growth and his authoritarian bent seem unlikely to accommodate the desires and goals of the Hugh Greggs, the Walter Petersons, and the Barbara Ganleys of New Hampshire.

The governor's executive order creating his Advisory Committee on New Hampshire's Future points up that difference, for it instructs that "plans and policies shall address ways to *encourage* growth but *not* discourage it."[25]

Thoughtful people in New Hampshire, people who revere its beauty and its character, look at projections that show Salem growing by 500% in the next fifty years, Exeter-Portsmouth by 350%, Nashua by 300%, Manchester by 300%, and so on. They observe the soaring land values—and soaring property taxes. They see around them the phenomenon of urban sprawl, unplanned strip developments, paving over of farmland. They examine figures that show the state's water supply is only "one third of what will be needed 30 years from now—if the present rate of growth continues"; other figures indicate that "Exeter's industrial employees cost the town more than they contribute in taxes." Seeing all this, they ask how a state the size of New Hampshire can survive the impact and retain its beauty or its character.[26]

Meldrim Thomson once worked for a law book publishing firm in Brooklyn, New York. In 1944 he moved his wife and children out to Stony Brook, a fifty-five-mile commute from Brooklyn, because he "wanted to get out of Brooklyn and move to a rural atmosphere." Later he bought a farm and 1,400 acres of land on the side of Mount Cube in Orford, New Hampshire, a town of 800 people.[27]

From that lovely, isolated rural oasis perhaps it is difficult for Meldrim Thomson to empathize with the growth pains of New Hampshire's southern tier of municipalities. But perhaps it won't be long before he witnesses those growing pains closer to home. Donnella Meadows, of the Environmental Studies Department of Dartmouth College in Hanover—only seventeen miles south of Meldrim Thomson's farm—says:"You ought to see what they're doing up here in the Hanover area. Of the land around here 80 percent is woods and ledge—20 percent is beautiful open farm land. Now *which* do you suppose they're developing? What was once a beautiful corn field is now the Lebanon Plaza, with four fast-food operations."[28]

Thus far, however, Meldrim Thomson is unmoved. *Yankee* magazine quoted him to this effect:

> New Hampshire is running second to Florida in population growth— east of the Mississippi, that is. But I don't think there's a problem here in New Hampshire. In Taiwan, where I visited recently, there are 17 million people boldly improving their position in the world in an area no larger than New Hampshire and Vermont combined.[29]

In New Hampshire an ever-growing number of people believe there *is* a problem. Unlike Meldrim Thomson, they're beginning to appreciate that there is indeed no such thing as a free lunch . . . in private life or in the life of an entire state.

In time, maybe enough people will understand the consequences of Thomson's policies and tactics to retire him from public life. Unfortunately, his long tenure in office will have residual influence for years to come. Thus, the process of reorientation will itself be difficult and protracted, and, I fear, the state's recovery to true economic health may take even longer.

The moral expresses itself: People throughout the nation who find appeal in the agenda of the New Right should look first at the New Hampshire experience before they commit themselves to the Rightists' cause.

CHAPTER 14

The Cloning of William Loeb

> *[Meldrim Thomson is] a remarkable citizen-politician. . . . Underneath beats the heart of a man who is so principled, so genuinely American that even his admirers can scarcely believe he is for real.*
> —Conservative Digest[1]

> *The Republican establishment has no use for me.*
> —MELDRIM THOMSON[2]

> *Thomson is a crafty, shrewd, tremendously perceptive politician. He has an uncanny ability to find little tiny issues and make huge events out of them.*
> —TOM GERBER[3]
> Editor, Concord (N.H.)
> Monitor

> *The guy's [Thomson] a disaster. Everything he touches turns to bitterness. . . . The man has polarized the state. . . . He creates a negative*

atmosphere. His principle seems to be control by
negation. It's a screwy kind of anti-force.
—C. ROBERTSON
TROWBRIDGE[4]
Chairman, New
Hampshire State Senate
Finance Committee;
publisher of *Yankee*
magazine, *The Farmers*
Almanac, and the *New*
Englander business
journal

Crucial to the Thomson/Loeb goal of rapid industrial development for New Hampshire is a plentiful and reliable source of energy. This is why both men pushed so hard in 1974 for what would have been the world's largest oil refinery, near Durham, New Hampshire, and why—when the refinery could not win approval—they turned their promotional attention to winning the battle over building twin giant nuclear power plants at Seabrook, New Hampshire, a controversy that continues to this day.

New England always has been plagued with energy supply and price problems. Because it gets cold early and stays cold late in New England winters, home heating fuel is consumed in great quantity. Because of the distance from oil- and gas-producing states and from coal mines, the rates paid for it are among the highest in the country.

During my years in the Senate I have spent more time on energy policy than on any other subject, with the possible exception of defense matters. Over the years I fought hard, and with some success, to ease oil import quotas to allow more of what was then lower-priced foreign oil to be imported into this country. Because of the quotas, American consumers were paying up to $5 billion a year more for oil supplies than they would have had to pay in the absence of such quotas. Moreover, by keeping lower-priced foreign oil out of the American market, we were paying another price: the rapid depletion of domestic sources of supply.

Since the oil embargo of 1973 the world price of oil has

skyrocketed, to the marked detriment of the economy of every nation that is in part or totally dependent upon imported oil. In the intervening years I have studied alternative sources of energy, with a particular eye on their possible benefits to New England, and have been persuaded that the benefits can be significant indeed; it *is* possible for us to develop energy sources that will not pollute, cannot be exhausted, cannot be made subject to manipulation of international cartels and thus will not contribute to world tensions. Accordingly, I have introduced a number of bills encouraging research and development and fostering the creation of a mass market for solar and other alternative energy devices in order to bring prices down.

Realistically, it will be years before these new sources can meet even a substantial part of our energy needs. Thus, long ago I reluctantly concluded that New England might have to accept oil refineries and/or nuclear power in order to survive until the promise of Sun Day is realized. In principle, I, too, favored an oil refinery—although I selfishly hoped it would *not* have to be located on the abbreviated coastline of New Hampshire. And I favored the nuclear power plants at Seabrook, provided they met every test for safety, security, and environmental soundness.

Many New Hampshire people felt the way I did; they did not oppose the oil refinery or the nuclear power plants per se, but they *did* object to the way both were being promoted by Loeb and Thomson. The techniques the publisher and the governor used provide case studies of extremism at work and illuminate a number of points: their shared attitude (and that of the New Right generally) toward dissent, toward the powers of the courts and the regulatory agencies, toward restraints on the use of executive power; their views on the nature of progress and purpose of government; their readiness to bend the rules, trample on individual rights, and violate civility in order to get whatever they want at the moment.

In 1974 what they wanted most was a refinery; in the ensuing years, nuclear power. The refinery issue began to crest in December 1973, when Aristotle Onassis flew into New Hampshire in a private jet and announced that he wanted to build the world's largest refinery at Durham. Even though Onassis made it clear he was not "a Greek bearing presents for New Hampshire," Thomson and Loeb welcomed him as though he had arrived on a well-laden sleigh drawn by reindeer.

Onassis outlined plans for a six-hundred-million-dollar refinery that would process up to 400,000 barrels of oil a day, compared with 55,000 barrels a day processed by an average U.S. refinery. Had the refinery been built, it would have made New Hampshire second only to Texas in total oil refinery capacity and would have given Onassis mastery over a fifth of the entire energy consumed in the United States.

Actually, before Onassis arrived his agents had been at work for months obtaining options on land near Durham Point, the site of the proposed refinery. Some residents who signed options to sell their land claimed they were never told it was to be used for a refinery. By one count, some forty Durham Pointers sold options on more than 3,200 acres. Had the property actually been sold, it is estimated that the payments would have totaled more than $5 million.

The refinery plan called for a complex covering more than 3,000 acres of Durham Point, a town of about 5,500 residents that jumps to a population of 15,000 when nearby University of New Hampshire is in session. The refinery complex would have dwarfed both the town and the university and would have included some fifty storage tanks. An off-loading terminal for tankers would have been located six miles out to sea, in the Isles of Shoals. A fifteen-mile pipeline was planned, to carry the imported crude oil over or under the beaches at the small nearby ocean town of Rye, then overland to the Great Bay estuary, under the bay, and on to Durham.

Loeb and Thomson heralded the refinery as the salvation of the state, welcomed Onassis with a joint press conference, and took the prominent visitor on a tour of the *Manchester Union Leader,* which later published large pictures of all three men.

Thomson cited a "close working relationship" between the state and "well-known petroleum refinery and shipping firms" and threw his energies into getting the refinery located in Durham.[5]

But, as Daniel Yergin noted in *Boston Magazine,* opposition quickly developed on two fronts:

Thomson would not cooperate with New England's other governors in working out a comprehensive regional plan. Other governors agreed that New England, most vulnerable of all regions in the energy crisis, needs its own refining capacity, but they generally go along with Vermont Governor Thomas P. Salmon, who declared that such a facility should only be built after close scrutiny and on a rational basis.[6]

Salmon was supported by John McGlennon, New England regional administrator for the Environmental Protection Agency. In mid-January 1974, McGlennon stated: "There can be no doubt that there are strong arguments for refineries in New England. However, we must not let this need panic us into hastily conceived development." A detailed study of petroleum development in New England should be prepared, he said, before major refinery construction is begun.

Meanwhile, the planned refinery was generating a huge environmental outcry from Durham-area residents.

A good deal of New Hampshire's scant 15 miles of coastline is already closed off by Air Force and Navy bases and by what is planned to be one of the largest nuclear plants in the world. The refinery's oil storage tanks —each one six acres in size, four in a row, 16 rows—would stretch for two miles along the coast. That would place one billion gallons of inflammable material within one mile of a major flight path of the Air Force base. The refinery would have transformed the entire region, developing satellite industries of all kinds, and turning rural New Hampshire into something like Perth Amboy, New Jersey.[7]

The local fight against the refinery was led by Dudley W. Dudley, a native of Durham Point and the first Democrat the community had sent to the state legislature in fifty years. Her campaign stressed these points: Southeast New Hampshire is not economically depressed; the resulting oil products from the refinery would, according to federal allocation rules, be distributed evenly across the nation, rather than concentrated locally; Durham uses about a million gallons of water a day, whereas the refinery alone would need between five and nine million gallons per day; the Isles of Shoals, used for marine studies, would be turned into an oil terminal, and there would be environmental damage.

Loeb responded to Dudley Dudley in typical style. In *Union Leader* editorials she became "Dum-dum Dudley," and she and her supporters were branded "eco-freaks" who stood in the way of New Hampshire progress.

But other voices were also calling for caution on the refinery plan. The *Keene Evening Sentinel* of March 4, 1974 editorialized: "New England needs an oil refinery—perhaps more than one. But New Hampshire does not need one of the world's largest on its very short, ecologically-fragile seacoast." The *Sentinel* argued that the refinery would not guarantee New Hampshire adequate fuel; that the skilled people needed to operate the refinery would be hired from out-state, not in-state; that while New Hampshire could earn considerable revenue over the refinery's lifetime by taxing its finished products, that fiscal bonanza would be offset significantly by new burdens placed on state services brought on by accelerating development in the state's already urbanizing southeast quadrant; and that neither Durham nor surrounding towns affected by corollary development would fare favorably in terms of taxes because, in time, additional development spawned by the refinery could raise demand for public services and drive the tax rate sharply upward.

Loeb, Thomson, and Onassis' Olympic Refineries met every criticism with accelerated promotion. The campaign climaxed in March 1974, when the promoters placed eight-page, prorefinery supplements in the state's newspapers, presented nine hundred radio spots in one week, and televised public meetings about the refinery, only to be sharply rebuffed by New England's most respected and venerable institution—the town meeting.

Although Loeb had conducted a write-in poll that indicated the vast majority of the state's residents were in favor of the Onassis plan, the town of Durham met in annual meeting and voted to reject the refinery proposal.

The *Union Leader* bellowed in outrage, and Meldrim Thomson, alleged champion of decentralized government and home rule, moved to circumvent the Durham town meeting decision. He tried to ram a bill through the state legislature that would give a state commission the power to overturn local rejection of a refinery site. This time Thomson, the outlander, ran head-on into New Hampshire natives who revere home rule even when it goes against their wishes. The legislature, including some of Thomson's ultraconservative allies, voted a resounding "No."

Olympic Refineries made overtures to other New Hampshire communities, but the steam had gone out of the refinery steam-

roller, and in the weeks that followed, Onassis turned his attention to other states. When he began courting Rhode Island, Governor Phillip W. Noel took note of Thomson's role in the New
Hampshire refinery campaign and said, "There's no way we
will run through the New Hampshire exercise where one man
decides this is good for the whole state."[8]

There is an interesting footnote to the refinery story. William
Loeb has said he champions Israel because "it stands as a bul-
wark against the heathen, non-Christian world." At the time of
the oil embargo, he called Arab leaders "heathen swine" and
said they should be asked, "How would you like to have us
bomb your holy cities of Mecca and Medina out of existence?"
At the time of Jacqueline Kennedy's marriage to Onassis, Loeb
said Onassis was "a foreigner, an Argentine citizen whose career with women such as Maria Callas and with strange business practices has not been exactly as exemplary as that of Lan-
celot."[9] Yet, when Onassis put forward the refinery proposal,
Loeb fell all over himself welcoming the man—and this despite
published reports that Onassis probably would "offer part ownership in his planned New Hampshire refinery to Saudi Arabia
or another Persian Gulf nation in return for an assured supply of
crude oil."[10]

The bid for the oil refinery lost, Loeb and Thomson turned
their endeavors to the proposed twin nuclear power plants for
Seabrook. This 2.3-billion-dollar-plus project by the New
Hampshire Public Service Company, in collaboration with util-
ity firms in other northeastern states, has been in the works for a
number of years. If ever completed, Seabrook Station would be
the nation's largest nuclear power installation. Progress has
been hampered by delays and ambiguities in regulatory commission rulings, challenges to regulatory decisions, challenges
in the courts, financing problems, and vigorous opposition by
several environmental groups.

Essentially, the debate over the Seabrook nuclear plants is
the same as the one over the Durham refinery. On the one side,
Publisher Loeb, Governor Thomson, the Public Service Company, and other ardent advocates of nuclear power are promis-
ing abundant energy supply at reasonable cost, construction and
operational jobs at the plant site, more vigorous industrial and
commercial growth because of the anticipated energy supply

and allied and supportive businesses, and a tax bonanza from the new plant. Opponents argue that nuclear power is not necessary; is hazardous to life, health, and the environment; may not prove more economical than fossil fuel power generation; will degrade the ambience of the coastal region; will cost more in demand for increased services than it will generate in taxes; and will prove an employment boon only through the construction period.

My readings tell me that the majority of New Hampshire citizens favor construction of the Seabrook plants. However, the degree of enthusiasm varies. There are a number of state residents who feel, as I do, that nuclear power is, at best, a necessary evil that should be replaced as quickly as possible with safer, more abundant, alternative energy sources. These people have deep-seated reservations about the vulnerability of nuclear power plants to sabotage and acts of terrorism and are very much concerned about the still-unsolved problem of nuclear waste disposal, even though they are not paranoid about catastrophic nuclear plant accidents.

Nevertheless, Loeb and Thomson chose to ignore responsible skepticism about nuclear power. They defined the issue as one pitting those who stand for progress against those who, as Loeb put it, want to go back to "oil lamps and outhouses."

In the spring of 1976 Thomson declared that it was official state policy to support the Seabrook plants. In May he had 30,000 copies printed of a tabloid promoting nuclear power in order to counter what an aide called "a bunch of nuts" waging a campaign against the proposed nuclear power plant at Seabrook.

The *Nashua Telegraph* of May 28, 1976 reported that Marshall Cobleigh, the governor's chief legislative lobbyist, said the Administration published the tabloid *Energy Profile* because there is "misinformation" being circulated by opponents of the Public Service Company of New Hampshire's proposed Seabrook plant. The story quoted Cobleigh as saying the Administration had no qualms about printing and circulating the tabloid, which he estimated would cost about $700, and said the money for the publication came from Thomson's federally funded Governor's Council on Energy. Headlines in the brochure included "Granite Staters Back Seabrook," "Labor Backs

Nuclear Plant," and "Seabrook Plant Cheaper Than Coal." Cobleigh believed that the brochure would help usher in nuclear power for New Hampshire: "We know we're going to get it, but a bunch of nuts have it in their head they're going to stop it."

The Clamshell Alliance, an antinuclear group, held a peaceful protest at the Seabrook site in the spring of 1976 and incurred the wrath of both the governor and Publisher Loeb.

Early the following year, with another protest slated that spring, Thomson escalated the campaign for Seabrook. He ordered pro-Seabrook petitions printed at state expense and asked state liquor store employees to solicit customer signatures. His goal was to collect 100,000 signatures to be sent on to Washington as a message to the federal bureaucracy.[11]

When Cobleigh was asked if the same avenue of petition solicitation was open to groups opposing the Seabrook plant, the *Nashua Telegraph* reported that Cobleigh answered: "It would have to be approved by the governor. . . . It's not likely that it would, either, since the other view is not in the state or national interest."

Robert Backus of Manchester, a lawyer for the New Hampshire Audubon Society and the Seacoast Anti-Pollution League, called the use of state employees to solicit signatures on the petitions "improper." He said the governor's efforts were "unfair to thousands of citizens, including the majority of Seabrook voters, who do not favor the plant, but cannot call upon government resources for a similar petition on the other side."

At several locations throughout the state, opponents of the nuclear power plant attempted to place anti-petitions in state liquor stores, next to the petitions favoring Seabrook construction. When permission was denied, they retreated to the stores' parking lots and sought signatures there.

In Nashua, police ordered the petition-circulators to leave the liquor store parking lot. When they refused, they were arrested, jailed overnight, and arraigned on charges of criminal trespass, with bail set at $200 each.

But at the state liquor store parking lot in Portsmouth, petitioners were allowed to demonstrate. The city attorney there declared that the liquor store was public property and that demonstrators "had every right to be there as long as they were peacefully demonstrating."

The *Nashua Telegraph,* which supported the Seabrook plant, strongly criticized the arrest of six petition-circulators at that city's state liquor store parking lot.

> The right of petition is guaranteed by the First Amendment of the U.S. Constitution. We view with disbelief the realization that the right of petition has been denied; and on public property at that.
>
> It has now been learned that employees of state liquor stores have been warned that signing of anti-nuclear plant petitions would be met with "repercussions." According to one state employee—who understandably wished to remain unidentified—a supervisor was overheard verbally reprimanding another employee for signing such a petition. Not only is such action contrary to the letter of the First Amendment, it is clearly a civil rights violation. As for the governor's dictum that any state employee who disagreed with state policy was free to state his disagreement—after quitting, we find it totally repugnant to the guarantee of free speech.[12]

The Clamshell Alliance announced early on that it intended to mount another sit-in, on April 30, 1977, at the site of the Seabrook construction, and for weeks prior to that event the governor and Publisher Loeb railed about the antinuclear element and the alleged threat of violence. The governor's language became so provocative that on April 28 Republican State Senator Trowbridge took the Senate floor to warn that if violence occurred at Seabrook and if state police were not instructed to use restraint, "the [state] administration will be accountable."

After a demonstration at the Seabrook site in the fall of 1976, the Superior Court issued an injunction against trespassing there. But before the 1977 sit-in took place, an agreement reached in court ruled out arrests for contempt of court unless demonstrators crossed a chain link fence that surrounded the construction site.

No one crossed the fence; there was no violence. However, 1,414 objectors were arrested on trespassing charges. After the first demonstrator was convicted and was given a suspended sentence, Attorney General David Souter objected, saying the offense warranted fifteen days in jail. The judge called back the defendant and changed the sentence to a fine and fifteen days in jail.

The problem was where to incarcerate more than 1,400 protesters; local jails could not accommodate such numbers. The demonstrators were held in the armory. Then, faced with the costs of guarding, feeding, and prosecuting so many defendants, the state suddenly realized it was caught in a bind.

Meldrim Thomson made a nationwide appeal for funds to help New Hampshire pay the costs. He called the protesters "a mob whose stated purpose was to illegally occupy the private property of others" and said, "I am hopeful our needs for funds will fall fruitfully upon the ears of corporations, labor unions, and rank and file citizens throughout America."[13]

When it appeared that the total costs might near a half million dollars, Thomson was forced to turn for help from, of all places, the Law Enforcement Assistance Administration of the federal government, one of his favorite scapegoats.

When LEAA rejected the application, pointing out that the agency was not established to help states pay for police or military operations, but rather to help the entire criminal justice system find new methods and facilities for preventing or solving crimes, Thomson filed a second application, this time asking LEAA for $170,000 to help defray the costs of arresting and keeping the demonstrators under confinement.*

Again LEAA rejected the request, and Thomson went into what the *Concord Monitor* called a "paroxysm of histrionics," saying he might try to have Congress abolish LEAA, suggesting that New Hampshire might not accept any more LEAA funds, attacking the Carter Administration for allegedly being "opposed to nuclear energy generally and to the Seabrook plant specifically."

> The governor accused LEAA of spending "millions of taxpayers' dollars for useless studies," but he failed to say that New Hampshire has applied for and received millions of dollars in LEAA program grants in the last four years. . . . The governor's reaction to the denial of LEAA funds was that of a spoiled child who couldn't get his way.[14]

The Clamshell Alliance scheduled another demonstration at Seabrook later in the summer of 1978, and Thomson went off in hot pursuit of federal help. In April he wrote a letter asking the entire New Hampshire congressional delegation to sponsor fed-

---

* The *New Hampshire Times* of May 25, 1977 reported that the total bill for the demonstration was set at $364,349 and that the state expected to receive $143,881 from the Public Service Company. Thomson's nationwide appeal for donations brought in $6,124.

eral legislation that would make it a federal crime to cross state
lines to violate the law. The statement Thomson made in releas-
ing the letter read:

> The announced invasion of this state by a lawless mob on June 24, at
> the expense of New Hampshire taxpayers, is clearly of Federal concern.
> The prior illegal actions of a lawless mob, 85 percent of whom were from
> out of state, has already imposed upon our people an unconscionable fi-
> nancial burden as the result of their illegal actions last May 1. . . . If the
> U.S. attorney finds that Federal Law is either absent or inadequate to
> cope with the announced illegal invasion by the Clamshells on June 25,
> I have requested the New Hampshire Congressional delegation in the
> U.S. Congress to introduce appropriate legislation. The Federal legisla-
> tion should be designed to protect the taxpayers of New Hampshire from
> any such unwarranted and unsolicited mob invasion by the Clamshell
> Alliance or any other lawless minded group that conspires to cross state
> lines for the purpose of violating our laws. The legislation should also
> provide for the Federal government to reimburse the State of New
> Hampshire for any and all financial costs which may accrue as the result
> of any illegal action perpetrated in the course of the inter-state invasion
> by the Clamshell Alliance or any other lawless minded group.

I responded to this request by saying that a quick check by
Thomson would show that it was already a federal crime to cross
state lines to incite a riot or to conspire to commit such an offense. I continued:

> If the governor has evidence to show this is the case, he should imme-
> diately report it to the U.S. Attorney or the FBI. I must conclude that the
> governor has made this request of the Federal government because he
> does not feel capable of carrying out the responsibilities of his office to
> maintain law and order in an intelligent manner. The governor has had a
> whole year to devise a plan to cope with this demonstration. Perhaps if
> he had not spent so much of that year in Taiwan, Panama, South Africa,
> California, Texas, Florida and heaven knows where else, he might have
> found time to face up to this obligation. But he didn't and now he's try-
> ing to pass the buck.

On May 1, 1978 a related event occurred that revealed another facet of the Thomson mind-set. The Clamshell Alliance attempted to rent the National Guard Armory in Portsmouth to
hold a dance commemorating the 1977 Seabrook demonstration.

Thomson's Administration tried to block the rental by demanding a $10,000 surety bond. The governor again called the
alliance a "lawless mob," claimed the dance was an attempt to

raise funds for "lawless acts," and was reported to have said he feared the group might "break into armory vaults and take automatic weapons."[15]

New Hampshire Superior Court Justice John W. King ruled that the Clamshell Alliance was just as entitled to lease the National Guard Armory as any other group of citizens and also denied the state's request that the alliance be forced to post a $10,000 bond. Justice King's ruling was upheld by the New Hampshire Supreme Court. "Once again," said Thomson, "the courts have skewered the rights of the vast majority of law abiding New Hampshire men and women to the spit of legal technicalities—thus placing the so-called rights of a lawless mob above those of the hard-working, tax-paying members of our society."

The *Nashua Telegraph* commented on this remark.

> It is obviously the governor's belief that only those groups which agree with his rather strange political philosophy are entitled to the same rights and privileges guaranteed the citizens of the nation and state. In that he sees those who favor construction of the Seabrook plant as the majority, he apparently feels that it is his prerogative to trample on the rights of the minority. . . . There's a frightening tone to the philosophy of New Hampshire's executive branch of government; a tone which is alien to the principles of a democratic republic.[16]

Thomson's alarums over the Clamshell Alliance dance and the ensuing protest demonstration at the Seabrook plant June 24–27, 1978 proved unwarranted. The *Boston Globe* reported that the dance ended "peacefully at midnight, having had all the turmoil of a high school sock hop." As this chapter was written, what may have been the largest antinuclear power demonstration in history had just been concluded at Seabrook. Newsreporters estimated the turnout for the three-day demonstration at upward of 20,000 people. There were few incidents to mar the peaceful atmosphere of the demonstration and no arrests. Steve Hilgartner of the Clamshell Alliance pronounced the demonstration "a success beyond our wildest dreams." Meldrim Thomson said the alliance "has experienced what must be to them a very distinct and humiliating defeat."[17]

Although occasioned by the Seabrook issue, the *Nashua Telegraph* editorial about the "frightening tone" of Thomson's Administration referred to a consistent pattern, not an isolated incident.* Only nineteen days after first taking office as governor, Thomson demonstrated his very special notions about the rights of citizens vis-à-vis his own prerogatives.

As the story was told by Daniel Yergin in *Boston Magazine*, on that day Thomson sent his administrative assistant, Fred Goode, to the State Tax Commission with the mission of obtaining the confidential tax returns of a number of businesses run by certain of his opponents. On the same day he himself slipped secretly out of state and turned up at the offices of the New England Organized Crime Intelligence System in Wellesley, Massachusetts, where he demanded to see any files that might exist on certain people—among them myself and former Governor Wesley Powell.

No such files were provided. Moreover, when the stories about the "fishing expeditions" came out, they created a furor; Thomson was charged with "police-state tactics," scandal mongering, and seeking information for political blackmail. But the governor was undismayed.

> He self-righteously declared that the search by his assistant Fred Goode was prompted by unnamed rumors about improper activities in the awarding of some racing concessions.
>
> When the Supreme Court declared that Goode's search was illegal, the governor responded that the ruling was meaningless. He would interpret the Constitution as he understood it *and "not as it is understood by others."*
>
> He developed an even more ingenious explanation for his foray into Massachusetts: he was checking to see if files were kept on New Hampshire politicians. Further, he charged that he had discovered that secu-

---

* On August 17, 1978 the Associated Press led off an article with this paragraph: "Gov. Meldrim Thomson Jr. says he has 'irrefutable proof' that communists were involved in the June 24 anti-nuclear power demonstration at the Seabrook atomic power plant construction site. He urged 'members of Congress who share our views on the importance of Seabrook and nuclear energy . . . to look carefully into the question of communist influence in nuclear staged demonstrations.' Regarding the communist charge, Thomson said he has a copy of a leaflet from the June 24 demonstration 'where the communists circulated literature which attacked the American free enterprise system in general and nuclear power in particular.'"

William Loeb's *Manchester Union Leader* of August 18, 1978 backed the governor's allegation of "irrefutable proof." Loeb wrote: "Make no mistake about it: Seabrook is in the front line of the Communist fight to take over the United States."

rity was lax at the anti-crime center—not because he wasn't shown any files, but because word of his secret visit had leaked out.[18]

On April 16, 1973 Thomson went on television to comment on the issue, saying, among other things, that the Supreme Court's opinion was "a poor opinion and bad law."[19] He went on: "There is nothing sacrosanct about our courts and judges. In fact we might hope for better justice if they were frequently subjected to the bright light of constructive criticism."*

An editorial in the *Keene Evening Sentinel* typified the reaction.

> For a man who professes the highest respect for law and order, Governor Meldrim Thomson has embraced the astounding philosophy that every public servant must guide his official actions according to his own interpretation of the constitution. . . . Thomson has argued that the state constitution allows him, as "supreme executive magistrate," to override such safeguards if necessary to his enforcement of state law.

Despite the mauling Thomson took over such incidents, this one did not serve as a growth experience. A UPI wire story dated February 18, 1976, out of Washington, reported on a Thomson speech.

> Gov. Meldrim Thomson of New Hampshire says Federal courts should be stripped of their power over prayer, busing, capital punishment and many other matters. The life tenure also should be removed from all but Supreme Court judges and reduced to eight-year terms, Thomson stated Saturday to the Conservative Union. The Republican governor chairs the national Conservative Caucus.
> "Instead of stemming the onrushing tide of power that daily drains from our states to the vast flood plain of Washington, I have witnessed the last erosions of state sovereignty," he said.
> Thomson repeated his call to amend the 14th Amendment of the Constitution which guarantees equal protection under the law, "so that the residual powers of sovereignty are restored to the states. The due proc-

---

* As several papers noted, there was a paradox here. At the same time Thomson was defying the court ruling, one of his assistants was testifying on his behalf before a legislative committee, arguing against amnesty for draft evaders. *Foster's Daily Democrat* observed on that June 18, "at the same time as Mr. Thomson was telling the state he no longer believed in the separation of powers and the need for him to obey New Hampshire law, his aide was appearing before a legislative committee saying that the 'destiny of America is guided by laws rather than by the will-of-the-wisp whims of men who would turn those laws aside for the benefit of their own advantages of the moment.' What hypocrisy!"

ess clauses also ought to go," he said. "It is highly significant that no single constitution framed for English speaking countries since the 14th Amendment has embodied its provisions."

Needless to say, at every point in these controversial incidents, Loeb's *Union Leader* was in Thomson's corner. Commenting, for example, on the editorial attacks occasioned by the governor's effort to raid tax commission and police agency files, Loeb wrote:

> The citizens of New Hampshire KNOW that the left-wing, anti-Thomson, pro-sales tax daily newspapers of the state are not telling the truth about Governor Thomson and his administration. . . . As a result, the screams of fury and frustration of the anti-Thomson politicians and the special interests are being drowned out by the other cheers of the people. The latter are saying with one voice: "GO TO IT, MEL! YOU'VE GOT THE SO AND SO'S ON THE RUN. KEEP IT UP!"

Loeb, of course, was still euphoric about having elected Thomson, for Thomson was a governor tailor-made to Loeb's philosophy and purpose. They are not only in close harmony but in close contact. As indicated earlier, *People* magazine reported that "during one 18-month period . . . phone records indicated that Thomson had called Loeb 256 times—proof, according to his critics, that he was playing Charlie McCarthy to Loeb's Edgar Bergen."[20]

Like Loeb, Thomson is vehemently anti-gun control, anti-amnesty, anti-Panama Canal treaties, anti-Equal Rights Amendment, anti-Gay Rights, anti-United Nations, anti-American Civil Liberties Union, anti-Martin Luther King Jr. and Andrew Young, and fervently pro-prayer in the public schools, pro-death penalty, pro-Taiwan and South Africa, pro-military, pro-oil refineries, offshore oil drilling, and nuclear power.

He has proclaimed "America Before UN" Week, saying "America's emphasis for world peace must be for America first in all things"; he has recommended that the National Guard be trained in the use of nuclear weapons; he has flown the flag at half-staff to commemorate Good Friday (until a court ruling let stand by the Supreme Court forced him to do otherwise); he has lowered the flag to half-staff to protest President Carter's declaration of amnesty and has flown it at half-staff to protest the signing of the Panama Canal treaties; he has invited Nantucket and Martha's Vineyard to become part of New Hampshire by seceding from Massachusetts; he has engaged in vitriolic battles with the State of Maine over lobster-fishing boundaries, with the State of Massachusetts over liquor purchases in New Hampshire, with the State of New York over New Hampshire people who allegedly did not pay New York traffic tickets; he has said of those who would proceed with caution in offshore oil drilling that their "dilatory tactics will be viewed in retrospect as sheer treason" and has said of environmentalists, "This great country has been brought to a screeching halt by a small band of highly vocal environmentalists who have no regard or concern about the future civilization of this great nation."

According to Patricia Burstein, writing in *People* magazine,

> His [Thomson's] enthusiasm for capital punishment is so great that when he signed a bill reinstating the death penalty in New Hampshire last September he announced proudly, "I feel like John Hancock when he finished putting his signature on the Declaration of Independence."[21]

On April 30, 1974, the *Concord Monitor* quoted Thomson as saying Richard Nixon had laid to rest the Watergate issue in his nationwide address. Nixon, Thomson said, "for almost two years carried his cross of abuse. He has come out of the ordeal as one of America's great statesmen." Thomson added that "not since Lincoln has any man suffered so much in maintaining so resolutely his faith in a Constitution" which he preserved by insisting on Presidential privilege.

Before he even took office, he made it clear that welfare would be a favorite scapegoat, even though New Hampshire's welfare program is modest and stringently regulated. In like manner, he has been harshly critical of many other social programs and turns to them as the first avenue of economizing in state expenditures. In 1977, he recommended such "economy" measures as eliminating several staff positions and cutting $250,000 from the budget for the state mental hospital (shortly after the hospital finally regained the accreditation it had lost through years of neglect); eliminating the state's 2.8-million-dollar contribution for medical aid to the needy; cutting educational aid to the handicapped by $3 million, state grants to community mental health centers by $822,000, and grants to centers for the mentally retarded by $354,000.

Thomson set a record by vetoing forty-two bills passed by the legislature in 1977. Included were vetoes of a measure that would have allowed terminally ill patients to order life-support systems disconnected when they no longer could stand the suffering; a bill that would have required hearing aid dealers to register with the state, would have banned door-to-door hearing aid sales, and forced rebates to those who were talked into buying hearing aids even though they did not need them; a bill to provide up to $5,000 compensation to victims of violent crime; a measure that would have funded state search-and-rescue operations; a bill requiring restaurants to post instructions on how to save persons choking on food; a bill to give state aid to victims of hemophilia. Of the last the *Concord Monitor* said, "Even the governor's patsies in the Senate couldn't stomach [that] veto. . . . The veto was one of three the legislature voted to override."

In the same session, however, the governor vetoed a bill that would have required electricity suppliers to offer customers rates based upon off-peak power use; another that would have prevented utilities from including the cost of institutional advertising in charges to customers; and yet another that would have banned the storage of high-level nuclear wastes in New Hampshire. His Senate supporters killed another bill banning utilities from charging customers for the costs of power plant work in progress. (Note: In their support of the utilities, Thomson and Loeb are somewhat out of step with other New Rightists. *Group Research Report* has noted that a number of New Right candidates are campaigning against utilities.)

Where Loeb and Thomson resemble each other most closely is in their mutual intolerance of opposition and dissent. Take the case of George and Maxine Maynard of Claremont, New Hampshire. George and Maxine are members of Jehovah's Witnesses, and in 1974 George decided that the motto on the New Hampshire license plates—"Live Free or Die"—was against his religion. He taped over the motto and was arrested. The first time the fine was suspended, but when he refused to pay the fine the second time, he was arrested and sent to the County House of Corrections for fifteen days.

George then decided to take the police to U.S. District Court in Concord, where he won an injunction preventing further arrest on plate-taping charges, at least until the court had had an opportunity to rule on the constitutionality of the law. A three-judge panel ruled the law unconstitutional, but Meldrim Thomson's Administration appealed all the way to the U.S. Supreme Court and lost.

As the *New Hampshire Times* noted, "The Maynard case cost the state in a number of ways: The motto law was nullified, the state's reputation suffered during the case, and the legal fees in the pursuit of George and Maxine Maynard will total about $55,000."[22]

In governmental administration the duties of many officials are spelled out in statutes, so that even though they serve under higher officials such as a governor, they do not serve as messengers or robots but have their own responsibilities to the law and to the citizenry. But that is not Meldrim Thomson's view of the matter, as a long list of New Hampshire administrators have learned. That list already includes New Hampshire State Hospital Superintendent Major Wheelock, State Game and Fish Director Bernard W. "Buck" Corson, State Police Director Paul Doyon, Economic Development Director Edward J. Bennett, University of New Hampshire President Thomas O. Bonner, State Prison Warden Raymond G. Helgemoe, and State Welfare Director Thomas L. Hooker.

Major Wheelock came to New Hampshire on loan from Richard Nixon's Office of Management and Budget, in 1972, to help Walter Peterson modernize the state's budget operations. Subsequently, Governor Thomson named him administrator of the New Hampshire State Hospital.

Wheelock accomplished the mission he had been assigned. He succeeded in getting the state hospital re-accredited in 1977 and drew many deserved plaudits for the achievement. He did it by wheedling funds for improvements and more staffing, despite harassment from the governor.

When Wheelock's term expired in March of 1977, the governor refused to reappoint him, and he served as a holdover director, with the support of the governor's Executive Council, until he resigned in October.

A UPI story dated August 2, 1977 reported Wheelock's announcement he would resign and quoted him as saying that his troubles with Thomson over budgets, access to patient records, and other items had been like exposure to "guerilla tactics."

State Game and Fish Director Buck Corson had been director

of the division for nine years and an employee for thirty years. He was generally regarded as one of the most professional and dedicated fish and game directors in the nation. A few years ago Corson informed the Public Service Company of New Hampshire that the temperature of the water pumped back into the Merrimack River from its Bow generating plant exceeded standards established by the U.S. Environmental Protection Agency. In the presence of two Public Service Company executives, Thomson admonished Corson to never again write such a letter, even though the fish and game director is required by law to do so.

Corson also ran afoul of the governor by expressing environmental concerns about the proposed Olympic oil refinery in Durham, and for the next two years he was pressured by the governor and the Fish and Game Commission (all ten members are Thomson appointees) to leave his post before his December 31, 1977 retirement date. Corson fought back by taking his case to the state Supreme Court and successfully held his job until he chose to retire.

State Police Director Paul Doyon resigned his post during 1977, ending a twenty-two-year career with the force. His performance as director was considered a model of independence and integrity.

Colonel Doyon was first nominated by Walter Peterson to head the state police and was later reappointed by Thomson, but Thomson reportedly extracted from Doyon an undated letter of resignation. After that time Doyon and Thomson went head-to-head on several occasions but never with the impact that was generated when Doyon testified before the House Judiciary Committee in favor of a bill to decriminalize marijuana.

"Marijuana use is not a criminal problem but a social problem," Doyon told the committee. "No good end is served by processing occasional marijuana users through the criminal justice system." Doyon alluded to the burden the marijuana laws placed on the state police as well as to the ineffectiveness of the current laws deterring marijuana use, but the situation looked quite different on the front page of the *Manchester Union Leader* the next day. In a front-page editorial Publisher William Loeb called for Doyon's resignation, while castigating his "softheadedness," and in an accompanying interview, Thomson declared that a person who held such views was not fit to head the state police.

Economic Development Director Edward J. Bennett had the effrontery to tell a service club audience, in response to a question, that he thought a pulp mill project the governor was trying to lure to Walpole "stinks," and the governor asked for his resignation. Bennett took his case to the courts but lost and has since moved to Vermont. A postscript: The people of Walpole reached essentially the same judgment Bennett did, for they elected not to invite the pulp mill to their community.

However, the person who came under the heaviest pressure and the most scathing attacks before he was forced to leave his job was former University of New Hampshire President Thomas Bonner. That was not surprising, for institutions of higher learning have long been a favorite Loeb target—and, in more recent years, a favorite Thomson target as well.

Loeb protested repeatedly and vehemently when a student group invited James Jackson, editor of *The Worker*, to speak at the university in April 1964. Later Loeb gave strong editorial support to the Feldman Bill, a measure that would have prevented Communists from speaking on campus. The bill was defeated in the legislature in 1965. (Loeb has a convenient double standard with regard to the First Amendment. Although he was adamantly opposed to Jackson being allowed to speak at the university, he denounced students at Dartmouth College in scathing terms for shouting down a lecture by William Shockley, a proponent of the theory that Blacks are genetically inferior to Whites, and equally excoriated antiwar Yale students for drowning out a speech by Gen. William Westmoreland.)

In 1970 the *Union Leader* portrayed the University of New Hampshire as a campus under siege and a hotbed of violent radicalism after "Chicago 7" figures David T. Dellinger, Abbie Hoffman, and Rennie C. Davis were invited to the campus. In truth, demonstrations at UNH were mild compared with antiwar activities on many other campuses.

In later years Loeb and Thomson have delivered stinging attacks on the university for allowing a Gay Rights student organization on campus and for a university study of the oil refinery proposal for Durham. When the report, which proved to be unfavorable to the refinery, was issued in April 1974, the *Union*

Leader described it as a product of "Durham kookdom" and said, "There really ought to be an open season on professors." Thomson claimed the authors of the report had done "a disservice" to the university.

There have been a number of other attacks over the years, but the most dramatic was that leveled against Tom Bonner. Dr. Bonner, who once worked for Senator McGovern and who once ran unsuccessfully for Congress from Nebraska, came to the UNH presidency from the University of Connecticut. When university trustees selected Bonner for the presidency, Walter Peterson commended the selection. But on April 22, 1971 Meldrim Thomson was quoted in newspaper articles as saying that Bonner's selection was political, that it would be an issue in the campaign the following year, and predicted that Bonner's stay at UNH would be unhappy and unsuccessful. "In selecting Bonner," Thomson reportedly said, "the University Board of Trustees has performed a miserable miracle. It has made [former] President McConnell look like a conservative."

Thomson then asked the legislature to pass a resolution condemning the trustees for picking Bonner, urging that the selection be withdrawn and suggesting that the university's appropriation should be tied up until the Bonner selection was rescinded.

An article by Bill Kovach in *The New York Times Magazine* noted how Loeb and the *Union Leader* reacted to the Bonner selection.

> Dr. Bonner . . . learned first-hand of Loeb's power shortly after the announcement of his appointment last summer. Loeb assigned an investigative reporter to study Bonner's background. In a six-part 25,000 word series filled with innuendo, unsupported charges and brazen editorializing, the *Union Leader* concluded that Bonner was a leftist threat who would "destroy your most precious possession—your children." Bonner reacted in anger, denouncing the work as "garbage." He toured the State seeking support and learned what most people in public life in New Hampshire already knew; the fear of Loeb's power and the lack of restraint in his attacks keep opponents quiet for years.
>
> "I would hesitate to say anything in public about Loeb," one businessman told a reporter covering Bonner. "It's not a question of my speaking out; it's a question of what he will do in the paper to my family. He has no sense of decency. If there's anything he can publish against you, he will."
>
> "I discovered," Bonner said later, "that there is just no vehicle for an-

THE FEAR BROKERS

other view. Everything is so fragmented it is always a fight on his terms and in his field. Every day I opposed him gave him more fodder to sustain the attack, and in the end it was the university that suffered. I had to, under the circumstances, withdraw."[23]

But Bonner tried one more tack; he asked to meet with Loeb and his executives and reporters. Loeb did not attend. In writing of that meeting later, Bonner said:

As I sat with his top executives and reporters in the . . . summer of 1971, the words that occurred to me over and over again was Hannah Arendt's phrase—"The banality of evil." Surrounded by these well-mannered and friendly men—they might well have been a group of Baptist clergymen—I realized that so commonplace, so banal had become the monstrous evil they do daily to hundreds of human beings that they regard it as of no more moral consequence than studying a dinner menu or driving to work each day.

In the spring of 1974 Tom Bonner announced his resignation.

Colleges and universities, representing as they do citadels of intellectual and academic freedom, are both irritant and threat to the authoritarian mentality, and recently there have been indications that the liberated woman is also both irritant and threat.

Loeb's reaction to the famous CBS interview of Betty Ford by Morley Safer offers some examples.* One *Union Leader* editorial commented:

We're willing to concede that Mrs. Betty Ford, the President's vocal mate, is a "liberated woman," as she claims—liberated from common sense, a sense of what the nation's moral standards should be, and any sense of her responsibilities as the wife of the President of the United States. . . . Mrs. Ford's views can at least be said to range consistently between immoral and amoral. . . . There are times when even the gentle Gerald Ford must wonder whether wife beating doesn't occasionally have its good points.

In another editorial, published August 13, 1975 and titled "Unfit for the White House," the *Union Leader* said:

* Betty Ford told Safer she would not have been surprised if her children had experimented with marijuana, because so many young people had. She also said she hoped that if her daughter were contemplating a premarital affair she would discuss it with her first. Nothing in her remarks connoted approval of either marijuana experimentation or premarital sex. She merely acknowledged the prevalence of both in today's world.

The immorality of Mrs. Ford's remarks is almost exceeded by their utter stupidity. Involving ANY prominent individual, this would be a disgusting spectacle. Coming from the First Lady in the White House, it disgraces the nation. IS IT ANY WONDER THAT OUR YOUNG PEOPLE FEEL THEY HAVE NO GUIDELINES AND NO STANDARDS TO WHICH THEY CAN ADHERE WHEN THIS KIND OF IMMORALITY AND NONSENSE COMES OUT OF THE MOUTH OF THE WIFE OF THE PRESIDENT OF THE UNITED STATES? Mrs. Ford has made a statement as stupid as it is immoral.

In the March 20, 1978 *Congressional Record*, Representative Newton I. Steers Jr. (R-Md.) inserted an exchange of letters between Publisher Loeb and genteel, capable, and delightfully liberated Representative Millicent H. Fenwick (R-N.J.). The letter from Loeb to Congresswoman Fenwick read:

You will not like the enclosed front page editorial, but this is how I see it. Regarding the situation on the Panama Canal, you know what the polls indicate and you are not only voting against it but you are also throwing away a great political issue and are handing it to the Democrats on a silver platter. Stupider than that you couldn't be.

Representative Fenwick responded:

Thank you very much for your letter. I was impressed by your bannerline: "There is nothing so powerful as truth."

There is nothing so convincing as accuracy. There is nothing so winning as courtesy. There is nothing more desirable in our plural society, under our Constitution, than the practice of dissent with civility.

Each one of us is entitled to his or her opinion, and you may be surprised to know that I was delighted—though not surprised—to learn about yours.

In New Hampshire, women make up 51.2 percent of the population. More than half the women over sixteen are in the labor force and the number is steadily rising. At the time of the 1970 census, New Hampshire had the highest proportion of working mothers with preschoolers in the country—31.9 percent.

Educated women outnumber educated men in New Hampshire, in numbers of high school graduates and college attendance. Yet, New Hampshire workingwomen take home an average of two thirds the pay of men.

New Hampshire's Commission on the Status of Women was created by the 1969 state legislature to exist for four years. Later, however, the legislature made the commission permanent and increased the number of commissioners from ten to fifteen, serving three-year terms.

When the commission was first established, Walter Peterson appointed women of differing politics to be commissioners, saying, "If you pick people who represent only one viewpoint, it's a mistake. You don't get the dialogue you need when you appoint people who all think the same way."

Yet, that is precisely what Governor Meldrim Thomson has done, and because the commission so reflects his own views, it has drawn heavy criticism from such established women's groups as the Association of Business and Professional Women's Clubs and the YWCA and has had its funding terminated by the legislature.

But Thomson, ever resourceful, succeeded in getting his executive council to approve the transfer of $7,800 in federal funds from Title 2 of the Employment Act to the commission, thus keeping it alive for another four years.

When the commission was first established in 1969, it set about to define and focus attention on the problems facing working and nonworking women and held hearings throughout the state covering thirty-two areas of possible sex discrimination. But the Thomson-appointed commissioners, in time, turned the emphasis away from these objectives and toward Thomson's philosophy.

Even though the New Hampshire legislature had ratified the Equal Rights Amendment before Thomson became governor, had passed its own Equal Rights Amendment, and in 1977 had beaten back an attempt to rescind confirmation of the state ERA, Thomson's Commission on the Status of Women pleaded with the legislature to abolish ERA.

In an article titled "Don't Call Me Ms." M. Eileen McEachern of Hampton, New Hampshire quoted Thomson as saying, "Women don't need ERA." She also cited a statement he made at an October 1977 press conference in Boston, prior to his addressing the fifteenth annual convention of Women for Constitutional Government, a women's group strongly opposed to ERA: "Women are very special, they are better than men, they are Wonder Women."

McEachern went on to write: "Believing supporters of the amendment [ERA] 'could be a danger to our constitutional government and civilization,' Thomson stated that 'the same ones who backed the ERA amendment in my state also support lesbianism. I fear them as enemies of every decent society.' "[24]

There was a big uproar over the Commission on the Status of Women that same fall, the article notes, when the commission refused to support a federal plan to aid battered wives. Reportedly, the commission's consensus was that "it is not the role of government to enter into the affairs of private lives" and that "the feminist movement is afoot to make women dissatisfied." One commission member felt that "these women libbers irritate hell out of their husbands," and another observed that "mothers operate bulldozers and fathers change diapers. Children are left free to become full-blown savages." Still another warned, "Before it is too late, we girls had best restore Father as 'King of the Castle' or we are about to lose our crown as 'Queen.' "[25]

McEachern noted that the commission had held a series of rape symposia throughout the state and then had issued a report that listed mode of dress and "more freedom for females, therefore less protected" as among the causes of rape. The commission also urged society "to be aware that homosexuality is playing a tremendous role in the increase in sex crimes" and claimed that "it is highly possible there is a direct relationship between sex education in the schools and the increase in sex crimes."[26]

Indeed, the commission introduced House Bill 146 to prohibit sex education in the public schools and to require a public hearing prior to adoption of major changes in any educational program. The education committee ruled the bill "inexpedient to legislate," McEachern reported, and its recommendation was upheld by the legislature.

Former commissioner Sandra Smith, who is legislative coordinator of the National Organization of Women, commented: "The commission is so hung up with the word 'sex' that they don't even know what it means. Making people feel comfortable just being human beings is what the women's movement is all about." Nevertheless, Smith believes there is a positive effect resulting from the Thomson-dominated commission. "The consciousness of women has never been raised as much as it has with the asinine statements and stands coming from this commission. When you have traditional groups like the YWCA and the Business and Professional Women's Club chastising the commission, that's great. That's just what we need."[27]

The Commission on the Status of Women points up what is certain to be a problem in New Hampshire for years to come: Meldrim Thomson, after three terms as governor, has been able to fill a great many appointive posts with people who reflect his political philosophy. And some of them will be around long after he has left the governor's office.

For all the bizarre incidents, for all the heavy criticism from the responsible press in New Hampshire, for all the national ridicule his antics have provoked, Meldrim Thomson, with William Loeb's press agentry, has been able to survive.

Somehow he has put together a blend of status politics and interest politics that attracts supporters few would imagine he could attract. Not the least of these are some of the state's labor leaders. They have looked upon his efforts to locate a refinery in New Hampshire, to build a nuclear power plant in New Hampshire, to lure new industry to New Hampshire in the single dimension of jobs. But they have not measured the man and his philosophy against the full criteria of what constitutes a friend of labor.

Thomson's Conservative Caucus is allied with a New Right movement that embraces a number of anti-union organizations, and its leadership certainly does not reflect pro-union sentiment.

On March 10, 1978 the *Manchester Union Leader* featured a story about a speech Thomson delivered before an insurance company gathering, in which the governor was quoted as saying: "Social Security, were it not so serious, would be a joke. . . . Far better had we left this tinkering with our economic and social requirements with private industry. . . . Medicare and Medicaid have really created more problems than they have solved."

Social Security, Medicare, and Medicaid are dear to the hearts of organized labor.

When a group of New Hampshire supporters of Cesar Chavez's labor movement asked that the state discontinue sale of Gallo wines because of a two-year labor dispute with the Gallo company, Thomson, according to the *Union Leader,* urged the State Liquor Commission to *expand* their sales of Gallo wines;

served notice that the Cesar Chavez labor movement was not needed in New Hampshire; had his picture taken while he purchased a half gallon of Gallo Chianti; and sent an aide to tell the liquor commission that the governor knew the American people liked "baseball, hot dogs, apple pie—and Gallo wine."

The *Union Leader* praised him to the skies.

This has been a portrait of Meldrim Thomson Jr. pursuing the tenets of the Conservative Caucus in his role as governor of the State of New Hampshire.

Following chapters profile Thomson and his mentor, William Loeb, against the national backdrop of some elemental social and political issues.

CHAPTER 15

Some of My Best Friends . . .

I was raised in the South and yet some of my warmest friends are colored people.
—MELDRIM THOMSON,[1]
denying that racism
drew him to the
American Independent
party in 1970

This newspaper is not anti-black, it is not racist.
—WILLIAM LOEB[2]

Americans may differ on the specifics of advancing the cause of human rights, questioning, for example, whether cross-district busing to achieve racial balance in classrooms does more harm to race relations than good, or whether the national commitment to human rights ought to be linked to trade, aid, and arms sales abroad. But it is clearly evident that the vast majority of people accept the basic principles underlying America's commitment to civil rights and civil liberties. Indeed, despite the

260

injustices of past and present and despite remaining prejudices, this commitment is the bedrock upon which the nation was founded.

There remains, however, a small group of Americans who pay lip service to human rights but at the same time manifest reservations at the least and deep resentment at the most over granting these rights and liberties to certain groups within the society. These same people are likely to resist the use of our national influence to ease repression by authoritarian regimes abroad.

There has never been much question about William Loeb's feelings on race, black leaders, and civil rights legislation.

Loeb is a supporter of William Shockley, Nobel prize-winning professor of engineering science at Stanford University and coinventor of the transistor. Dr. Shockley is not controversial in engineering science; he is decidedly controversial in the conclusion he draws from his avocational studies in the field of genetics.

The New York Times of December 11, 1977 quoted Shockley as saying in a telephone interview a few days earlier that he had reached "the inescapable opinion that a major cause of American Negroes' intellectual and social deficits is hereditary and racially genetic in origin." Shockley was further quoted to the effect that this "is not remediable in a major degree by practical improvements in environment" such as better schools, jobs, or living conditions.

Shockley's comments were included in an article about The Pioneer Fund, which the *Times* described as a private trust fund based in New York that has for more than twenty years supported highly controversial research by a dozen scientists "who believe that blacks are genetically less intelligent than whites." Shockley reportedly got $179,000 from the fund over a period of ten years. Looking into The Pioneer Fund, the *Times* discovered that the founder of the trust was Wycliffe P. Draper, who died in 1972. Draper was described as the reclusive heir to a Massachusetts textile machinery fortune who left $1.4 million to The Pioneer Fund.

Among two men listed as directors of The Pioneer Fund in 1975, the most recent year for which Internal Revenue Service records are available, is John B. Trevor of New York, a founder of the American Coalition of Patriotic Societies, adviser to Billy James Hargis' Christian Crusade and author of an article on South Africa that appeared in *The Citizen,* a publication of the White Citizens Council. Testifying against more liberal immigration laws in 1965, Mr. Trevor warned against "a conglomeration of racial and ethnic elements" that he said led to "a serious culture decline."

The other Pioneer director is Thomas F. Ellis of Raleigh, North Carolina, manager of Jesse Helms' 1972 campaign for Senator and an important backer of Ronald Reagan's 1976 Presidential campaign.[3]

The *Times* article reported that Wycliffe Draper also gave money to right-wing political candidates, including the late Representative Donald Bruce of Indiana and the late Representative Francis E. Walter, onetime controversial chairman of the House Un-American Activities Committee.

Walter, according to the *Times,* served as a director on two now defunct committees supported financially by Draper that gave grants for genetics research. "When it was disclosed in 1960 that Richard Arens, staff director for the Un-American Activities Committee, was also a paid consultant to the Draper-financed committees, Mr. Arens was forced to leave his congressional job."[4]

When the *Times* tried to interview the president of The Pioneer Fund, New York lawyer Harry F. Weyher, Weyher described the fund as "a client," said, "I am not going to talk to you any more," and hung up. The *Times* described Weyher as having had "long standing connections with conservative causes or political candidates, although no one has suggested that the conservatives in question shared [his] interest in eugenics or hereditary research."[5]

Shockley and others who share his theory of the genetic inferiority of Blacks are in the distinct minority among professional geneticists. The *Times* noted that the Genetics Society of America, a leading professional organization, published a statement of its committee on genetics, race, and intelligence that was endorsed by nearly 1,400 members. The statement said, in part:

> In our views there is no convincing evidence as to whether there is or is not an appreciable genetic difference between races. Well designed research . . . may yield valid and socially useful results and should not be discouraged. We feel that geneticists can and must also speak out against the misuse of genetics for political purposes and the drawing of social conclusions from inadequate data.

Theories of racial inferiority sustained a sharp setback in recent years because data developed by Cyril Burt, a British scientist who had underpinned the theory, are now described by leading geneticists as being without scientific value.

Anyone who follows discussions among geneticists knows of the enormous difficulty attending any effort to separate heredity from cultural and environmental influences. Anyone who has read the novels of Ralph Ellison and of James Baldwin, who has observed the work of such international figures as Ralph Bunche, Julius Nyerere, and Kenneth Kaunda, or who has worked, as I have, with Senator Edward Brooke on the most complex and sophisticated defense issues will look with vast skepticism (or perhaps with amusement) on any effort to establish "black inferiority." And anyone with any sense of history will recall the truly horrible human consequences that can follow from sensationalized exploitation of shoddy "research" that attempts to show the superiority of one race over another. Group egotism of the kind that Hitler fed with his insane theories of Aryan superiority is a sleeping force that, once awakened, is capable of the most shocking evils. A generation that has experienced the gas chambers of Auschwitz ought never to forget that the essential unity of the human race is both a sacred religious truth and a practical political principle that we abandon only at our own great peril.

Yet, Loeb persists in championing Shockley. In the March 1973 edition of *The Citizen*, which the *Times* described as the publication of the Citizens Council (one of the most vehement and vigorous foes of desegregation), appeared an article titled "Newsmen Back Doctor Shockley."

> Publisher William Loeb, whose address was one of the highlights of the 17th National Leadership Conference of the Citizens Councils of America in New Orleans last September and who is a long-time supporter of Doctor Shockley . . . wrote and published on the front page of his newspaper an editorial entitled: "Dr. Shockley Battles for the Facts" which is reprinted as an accompaniment to this article.

In that editorial Loeb said one apparent reason for Shockley's rebuff by the scientific community was that "U.S. cultural life has been so entranced by the 'we are all equal' theory, or 'we all can be made equal given the right schooling or the right environment' that no other idea must ever be considered, especially one that might involve the question of black v. white mental capacity."

What is chilling is Loeb's hint at what might be another "idea" to be considered. After calling black students at Dartmouth "black savages" for clapping down Shockley's words in a lecture, Loeb engaged in some fascinating sophistry. "Dr. Shockley is NOT a racist. Dr. Shockley's inquiry is NOT designed to show that any race is SUPERIOR to another. Dr. Shockley is simply interested in the DIFFERENT CAPACITIES of various groups in our society."[6]

Loeb then goes on to this ominous comment:

> And in one step farther, Dr. Shockley raises the problem that our society must somehow devise a method by which the incompetent and less gifted, and those with serious physical inherited defects, can be prevented from breeding and reproducing their kind—and thus considerably lowering the quality of mankind.[7]

Shades of the Third Reich!

Is it any wonder that Loeb is a northern darling of the Citizens Councils of America (popularly called the "white citizens council") and of its propaganda organ, *The Citizen?*

The issue of civil rights and racial discrimination pitted me directly against William Loeb early on. While I was serving as the late Senator Hubert H. Humphrey's deputy whip in the eighty-three-day marathon effort to pass the Civil Rights Act of 1963, Loeb was serving as national chairman of the Coordinating Committee for Fundamental American Freedoms. This was a group of prominent citizens organized to defeat proposed civil rights legislation by distributing pamphlets and newspaper advertisements in key states and by directly lobbying the Congress from a headquarters established directly across the street from the Senate office buildings.

But when Loeb testified before the Senate Committee on Commerce in opposition to the public accommodations features of the pending civil rights legislation, he did not mention the new organization in his testimony.

His comments were predictable, for long before he had tipped his hand as to how he stood on civil rights legislation. In August 1960 he wrote of the civil rights plank adopted by the Democratic national convention:

The so-called "civil rights" plank . . . is misnamed. If the program were carried out as the Democrats urge, it would really enslave the majority of the American people and deprive them of their rights in favor of some noisy minorities who have scared the politicians half to death.

In June 1961 he wrote:

There are, of course, educated Negroes in the South. But there are many primitive, almost half-savage Negroes in both Africa and the South. They can be easily aroused and stirred into wild, uncontrollable emotions. When this occurs, it naturally creates equally strong emotions on the part of Southern white men and women who rise to defend their homes and their women and children.

When testifying before the commerce committee on the 1963 civil rights bill, Loeb identified himself as "one of the few Americans who ever penetrated the Communist Party without becoming either a Communist or acting as an FBI agent" and said he therefore knew "what the policy of the Party was in the late 30's on the subject of racial agitation, and their plans to use it to bring about revolution in the United States." He had no reason to believe that this "policy" had changed.

Loeb contended that passage of the civil rights bill would "be like pouring gasoline on this blaze of racial hatred. The searing flames from this conflagration will not only consume the vast majority of patriotic and law-abiding colored and white citizens . . . but finally it could very well consume the United States, itself."

Throughout 1963 and up to passage of the civil rights legislation in 1964 Loeb's newspapers bellowed opposition. Not only in its editorial columns, but in the news play accorded stories about black unrest, black demonstrations, and black crime, and in cribbed commentary about the alleged genetic differences between Blacks and Whites, the *Union Leader* and the *New Hampshire Sunday News* fanned the flames of conflict.

Late summer and autumn of 1963 saw an almost daily barrage. A few examples will indicate the character and the scope of Loeb's individual compaign: On August 16, 1963 his front-page, signed editorial was titled "The Gray House." It was an attack on miscegenation.

Will some future administration decide that the White House would look better, not white, but light gray or light brown? It makes one won-

der whether the nation will some day be light brown, not white. There is
so very little intermarriage in the North that many Northerners think the
South's preoccupation with fear of intermarriage between Negro and
white is unrealistic. However the other day a distinguished citizen of
this country, back from Brazil, said he had changed his previous broad-
mindedness on the subject of marriage between black and white since
he had seen the results in Brazil of intermarriage between the races.
What he said he found was a vast number of mongrels, without the good
characteristics of EITHER black or white. He attributed much of Brazil's
chaotic political conditions to the instability of this vast section of Brazil's population. . . . So let's keep the White House white and let us
keep the United States the way it is now—nine-tenths white.

On August 2 the *Union Leader* criticized the NAACP and on
August 16 an editorial attacked the black culture of Washington,
D.C.* On September 9 Loeb's front-page editorial said the civil
rights march on Washington included a number of phony clergy
dressed in rented clerical garb. That same issue featured an
over-the-masthead eight-column headline titled "Starts Political Career on Boner"—a continuation of the *Union Leader*'s ex-
cerpting from Victor Lasky's book *JFK: The Man and the Myth*
—and an under-the-masthead eight-column headline on the Alabama schools desegregation conflict.

On September 14 the *Union Leader* ran an eight-column
headline titled "Gap Between Negroes and Whites" above an
article on the alleged mental inferiority of Blacks, reprinted
from *Our Southern Observer.*

The issue of September 17 banner headlined: "Birmingham
Seeks Troops."

An editorial on September 26 said:

> But although the civil rights movement is not Communist in origin, it
> IS A FACT that Communists and their fellow travelers have infiltrated the
> movement and that their goal is, not to solve the problem, but to create
> chaos at a time when national unity is all important. It also is true that
> many "liberals" including those who, in the past, aligned themselves
> with Communist front organizations, are playing important roles in the
> civil rights movement.

---

* On August 18, 1978, as New Right leaders were trying to block Senate passage of a Constitutional amendment granting the District of Columbia full
Congressional representation, Loeb's *Union Leader* called Washington "our
national disgrace," "a veritable jungle," and said, "It is quite evident that
blacks do not know how to run a city properly."

The *Sunday News* of September 29 featured a lead editorial that lashed out at the NAACP and praised Louise Day Hicks, head of the Boston school board.

The barrage continued through the autumn, culminating with an article reprinted from the *Charleston* (S.C.) *Post* on the eve of Christmas week and banner headlined: "Negro Filled with Lifetime Hate."

In the spring, as the vote on the civil rights bill neared, Loeb picked up the tempo. On April 13, 1964 his front-page editorial, "Fire Starting in the North," opened on this note: "The surprisingly strong showing of Governor George C. Wallace in the Wisconsin presidential primary on the same day of the race riots in Cleveland indicates that even in the far North the white people are becoming tired of being shoved around by the black minority."

On April 28 his editorial, "Red Faces Among the Black," opened with this comment:

> Last summer when this writer testified before the Commerce Committee of the United States Senate that there were Communists in the civil rights movement stirring up black against white, there was the usual cry of "McCarthyism." It is interesting, therefore, to note the recent complete confirmation of the charge of Communists in the civil rights movement by none other than J. Edgar Hoover, head of the Federal Bureau of Investigation.

Loeb's April 30 editorial castigated the elderly mother of Massachusetts Governor Endicott Peabody for taking part in civil rights marches and demonstrations.

On May 25 the *Union Leader* reported that George Franklin, first vice-president of the NAACP in Manchester, New Hampshire, told a chapter meeting, "We need not concern ourselves with such ranting . . . daily vindictive venom . . . misuse of the press . . . willful distortion of truth." Franklin called an anti-civil rights legislation ad published in the *Union Leader* some weeks before under the auspices of Loeb's national Coordinating Committee for Fundamental American Freedoms and titled "Billion Dollar Blackjack" a "masterpiece of distortion and misrepresentation."

The Coordinating Committee for Fundamental American Freedoms placed anti-civil rights legislation ads in newspapers across the country. In addition to "Billion Dollar Blackjack," others were titled "Civil Rights and Legal Wrongs" and "The Federal Eyes Looking Down Your THROAT!" to cite two examples.

The campaign continued in the *Union Leader*. An April 1, 1964 editorial charged that "Civil Rights Bill Spells Civil Chaos," and a May 13 editorial contended that a provision in the 1963 Civil Rights Act would violate the Thirteenth Amendment by forcing barbers and beauticians to serve black people even if they preferred not to. The front-page Loeb editorial of May 26 was titled "Terror in the Streets" and hammered again at black street crime.

While Loeb was conducting his one-man anti-civil rights campaign in New Hampshire and was spearheading a nationwide campaign by his Coordinating Committee for Fundamental American Freedoms, I was working closely with Senator Humphrey to secure passage of the legislation Loeb was going all-out to defeat.

In the spring of 1964 I decided to take the counterattack directly into New Hampshire. In the first week in April I addressed the State Democratic Women's Spring Conference and told them that the *Union Leader*'s distortion of the civil rights legislation "makes me sick. When you read the papers here in New Hampshire [meaning Loeb's papers], you'd think the passage of this bill would bring us to the end of the world. But don't let any editor tell you the world is going to hell if the civil rights bill is passed."

Loeb, confident the civil rights bill was unpopular in the state, gave front-page banner-headline treatment to my speech, noting in the covering article, "In the Senate, McIntyre has been an all-out advocate of the stiff Civil Rights measure . . . and this is believed by many political observers to have plunged him into hot water with strong elements of the Granite State electorate."

The *Union Leader* followed up with an editorial.

> Senator Tom McIntyre is a highly emotional politician these days. He can brook no criticism. If you disagree with his stand on the civil rights bill, you are a bigot, a racist or worse. . . . He recently boiled over at New Hampshire newspaper critics of the civil rights bill—he meant us —and declared: "It all makes me sick." Well, we are beginning to get a little of that "sick" feeling ourselves, particularly where Senator McIn-

tyre is concerned. We are becoming increasingly sick of his self-righteousness and hypocritical posturing and gesturing on the civil rights issue. . . . We suggest that he is sick because he sees his political future going down the drain in a whirlpool of voter revulsion generated by the civil rights bill.[8]

In late spring of 1964 I did something I had never done before and have not done again. I appealed directly to the clergy of New Hampshire to speak out in behalf of the civil rights bill. Early in April, I sent an open letter to all the Catholic, Jewish, and Protestant clergy in the state. In that letter I stated that the civil rights bill then before the U.S. Senate was "a constitutional issue and nothing else" despite "the railing of opponents."

> Down at bedrock of the fight for civil rights lies a moral issue as great as any in our history. Our Judeo-Christian culture can no more exist half-discriminated against and half-privileged today than it could survive "half-slave, half free" a hundred years ago. . . . There is no question today that the great religions and their leaders have overwhelmingly committed themselves to this fight . . . as a matter of what is morally as well as legally right.

My letter credited the clergy for the work they had already done in combatting the "half truths, the innuendoes and the downright lies" of opponents of the civil rights bill, whose "concept is grounded in ignorance, in intolerance, in hate, in a stubborn refusal to recognize injustice."

I closed with this appeal:

> Because this is a great moral as well as legal issue, I find it not inconsistent with our concept of separation of Church and State for the clergy to make known to the members of their congregations the true facts of this legislation and what it seeks to do—legally, to stamp out inequality wherever it exists in this nation; and morally, to wipe out forever an ugly blot so that we may truly say that "all men are created equal and endowed by their Creator with certain inalienable rights." Believe me when I say that those of us who are waging this fight in the Congress can be sustained in no better way than to know that the respected members of the clergy in our states are fighting with us and praying for the success of this mission.

The positive response I got from this letter, not only from the clergy but from editorials in such highly respected Republican newspapers as William Rotch's *Milford* (N.H.) *Cabinet* and from opinion samplings conducted by friends among Democrats and Republicans in New Hampshire, convinced me that I had done the right thing, not only in working so hard for passage of the Civil Rights Act, but in seeking the support of priests, ministers, and rabbis back home.

A letter from a friend whose business requires an accurate reading of public opinion noted the broad base of support for civil rights legislation among liberals and moderates of both parties. He pointed out that half the membership of the NAACP in New Hampshire was Republican and strongly supportive of my position on the 1964 bill. (It is the absence of such liberal-centrist consensus on many of today's issues that allows the New Right to dominate the public dialogue and affect the political process to a degree far out of proportion to its numerical strength.)

Loeb and his Coordinating Committee for Fundamental American Freedoms lost the battle to defeat the civil rights bill, but he is still fighting the war. His antagonism toward the Kennedy brothers and Martin Luther King Jr. persists to this day, for he blames those three more than any others for the rights advancement he fought so hard to stop.

On June 13, 1963, for example, Loeb's editorial said:

> The Kennedys, by their telephone calls to Mrs. Martin Luther King and by their grandstanding play for votes among the Negroes, have given the Negro rabble the idea that the Kennedys are behind them no matter WHAT they do. . . . The Kennedys have now created an explosive situation which needs just a small spark to bring about one of the most tragic and sorry sights ever to face Americans. . . . The responsibility for this rests, in part, on the Supreme Court, which has interfered with local customs in an unwarranted manner, but it rests PRINCIPALLY on the shoulders of the Kennedy administration, which has created an explosive situation. When that explosion comes the American people will know whom to blame. THIS NEWSPAPER WARNED REPEATEDLY BEFORE THE ELECTION OF THE KENNEDYS, AND HAS WARNED SINCE, THAT THESE YOUNG MEN ARE OF THE STUFF OF WHICH DICTATORS ARE MADE. THEIR IMMEDIATE REACTION TO ANY OPPOSITION IS NOT PERSUASION BUT FORCE. KENNEDY'S FREE USE OF FEDERAL TROOPS IS IN THE COMPLETE PATTERN OF MUSSOLINI, HITLER, STALIN AND KHRUSCHCHEV.

As for Martin Luther King, Loeb did not let up even after the black apostle of nonviolence was assassinated. His editorial on Dr. King's death included these passages:

> The real irony . . . resides in the fact that Dr. King—whatever his motivation—had the ability to stir others to violence. . . . If it is proper for critics of the late Senator Joseph McCarthy to continue to express their hatred for the man as well as his beliefs, it is certainly proper to continue to take issue with Dr. King's tactics.

That same issue, April 6, 1968, prominently displayed a front-page article quoting Loeb's in-house ultraconservative Black, the late George Schuyler (who reviewed books for the *Union Leader* and was on the John Birch Society panel of speakers) as saying Dr. King's assassination was "very unfortunate" . . . but "largely of his own doing."

Loeb's personal feelings about King were expressed many times in many ways, but typical is his assessment of King's qualifications for the Nobel peace prize.

> To give the award to a Negro who has never dealt in international relations at all, but has merely created bad feeling between races inside nations, is, of course, a complete perversion of the purpose for which the Nobel Peace Prize is awarded, and makes the Nobel Peace Prize worthless in the future. AFTER THE AWARD TO MARTIN LUTHER KING, NO SELF-RESPECTING INDIVIDUAL OR RESPONSIBLE LEADER OF A NATION COULD EVER BE INTERESTED IN OR ACCEPT THE NOBEL PEACE PRIZE.[9]

Loeb liked to quote FBI Director J. Edgar Hoover as saying Martin Luther King was "the most notorious liar in the United States," and when Hoover died, in 1972, and Coretta King criticized the FBI files gathered on her late husband, Loeb mounted an all-out assault, ticking off virtually every charge he or anyone else had ever made about Dr. King and referring to Hoover as "this splendid American."

The fact that the years since have been kinder to the memory of King than they have been to Hoover does not daunt Loeb, for he says that the liberal press has protected King by covering up discrediting material while impugning Hoover's record.

Loeb continues to flail the race issue. On October 4, 1973 he used a heinous murder committed by six black youths in Boston as the springboard for an editorial.

> It is . . . in the opinion of this newspaper, typical of the savagery of some of the blacks in this country. They hate whites. They are without any moral restraint. They have no more feeling for a situation like this apparently, than jungle savages from the darkest parts of Africa. It is be-

cause this newspaper wants to avoid this type of thing happening in New Hampshire that we are hopeful that the black population of New Hampshire will never increase from its present minimal figure.

Three days later State Representative Robert Gillmore (R-Manchester) took Loeb to task, labeling the editorial "vicious nonsense." Gillmore said that although some Blacks and, for that matter, some Whites are undoubtedly "savages," it does not follow that it is desirable that no more Blacks whatsoever should live in New Hampshire. "The publisher properly concedes that most Blacks in New Hampshire are 'self-respecting' and 'respectable.' If we must make assumptions about the character of the state's future black population, isn't it more reasonable to suppose that any new Blacks might be rather like those already here?" Gillmore went on to say he resented the implication that "savagery" is common only to "some Blacks." "The number of Blacks lynched by white Southerners was a national disgrace."

Gillmore concluded with this remark:

> Finally, I would urge Mr. Loeb to look with more understanding at his heritage. Both of us admire Teddy Roosevelt and the Republican background from which he came. I would remind Mr. Loeb that Roosevelt's party and mine has a distinguished heritage of pioneering equal protection for Blacks. Ours was the first party of civil rights. I respect and honor that tradition and that of my ancestors and I would hope Mr. Loeb would do the same.

This remonstrance and reminder fell on deaf ears. Loeb reached the apex of absurdity on the race issue in a front-page editorial titled "'Roots': Dangerous Brainwashing." Loeb described the celebrated ABC television drama about slavery in America as a

> wild exaggeration of the unfortunate conditions which existed under slavery. It was . . . an attempt to create a SENSE OF GUILT on the part of the white population of the United States.
>
> The reason for the appearance of "Roots" at this time is that the Russians want to create a sense of guilt on the part of white people as to how black people have been treated. When the Russian Communists lead hordes of black terrorists to slaughter whites in South Africa on a large scale, the American white population will have been so brainwashed that instead of reacting to support their fellow whites in South Africa, they will sit by and do nothing. . . . IN SHORT, THE RUSSIANS ARE PREPARING THE AMERICAN MIND TO ACCEPT THE RUSSIAN

BLACK CONQUEST OF SOUTH AFRICA. IT IS AS SIMPLE AND DIRECT AS THAT.

Loeb then said he was not accusing ABC of being on the payroll of the Russian Communists or of being Communists.

> [But] the United States, as well as the whole world, is full of what Lenin, the father of Russian communism, once called "USEFUL IDIOTS." The individuals in important positions, especially in the communications field, whom the Communists have discovered react in certain ways and in the ways that the Russians want them to react when the right emotional button is pressed. Then all the Communists have to do is press that button and stimulate the action they desire. . . . NOW THAT YOU KNOW HOW THE ASSAULT AGAINST YOUR MIND WORKS, WATCH OUT THE NEXT TIME AND DON'T BE TAKEN IN.

Until Meldrim Thomson Jr. became the governor of New Hampshire most state officeholders either respected Martin Luther King's contributions to the advance of human rights or muted whatever reservations they might have had.

The new tack under Thomson became dramatically apparent in the summer of 1977. The first target was not Dr. King, however, but Andrew Young, the black U.S. ambassador to the United Nations. Young was a close associate of Dr. King, played a leading role in the Poor People's March on Washington in 1968, and later became a congressman from Georgia. Sometime during the summer, Thomson's Conservative Caucus decided to seek the removal of Young as UN ambassador. A caucus mailing, reportedly to 200,000 people, included a letter from Thomson—signed first as governor of New Hampshire and then as chairman of the Conservative Caucus—bearing a seal that recipients might well have assumed was the official State Seal of New Hampshire.

The *Lebanon Valley News* commented:

> Meldrim Thomson Jr. is governor of New Hampshire. The governor of New Hampshire has no business appending his name and title to a letter, written on what appears to be official state stationery, soliciting money for a campaign to oust UN Ambassador Andrew Young.
>
> The letter has been sent to some 200,000 people by the so-called Conservative Caucus. Thomson (besides being national chairman) is secretary of state for the Caucus' "shadow cabinet" formed to monitor policies of President Carter and his administration. The letter itself is written in outrageously bad taste. It accuses Young of supporting "Communist butchers and terrorists" and includes a picture of a burned and maimed

child. The caption says the child was a victim of violence by Black
Power terrorists who, it implies, have the heartfelt support of the UN
ambassador. It is mortifying for everyone in New Hampshire that such
cockamamie slurs are being disseminated by the governor. The state's
citizens deserve an apology from Thomson for implicating them in his
nonsense.[10]

Thomson's message included a contribution pledge card, an
ouster petition card addressed to President Carter, and a
bumper sticker bearing the block lettered words "ANDREW
YOUNG MUST GO."

After a public outcry about the alleged misuse of the New
Hampshire State Seal on the mailings brought about the revelation that the seal Thomson used was not the official seal, but one
made up to resemble it, the *Portsmouth Herald* was moved to
comment:

By designing a seal that looked like the real thing, the governor accomplished his objective of intimating that the whole state of New
Hampshire supported his red-neck views on Young. . . . When a more
devious man comes to New Hampshire politics, he will have been ap-
prenticed to the master craftsman, Governor Thomson, for a generation
or two.[11]

Ambassador Young's spokesman, Tom Offenburger, told
Washington newspeople that Young was aware of the letter but
would not comment on it. "I think it is a pitiful, sick attack on
him," Offenburger said.

The Conservative Caucus was pushing in the Congress, too,
to have Andrew Young impeached, but by October 1977 only
nine conservative House members supported the impeachment
resolution. Eight were Republicans, but the most active was a
Democrat, Congressman Larry McDonald of Georgia, already
identified as a member of the John Birch Society Council. It was
apparent by year's end that the Young impeachment resolution
was going nowhere. In late summer of 1977 another incident
put Meldrim Thomson squarely in William Loeb's corner on a
matter involving civil rights.

UN Ambassador Young, who was chairman of a dinner
planned for that October to raise funds for the Martin Luther
King Jr. Center for Social Change, sent out a pro forma letter to
the governors of all fifty states, asking them to serve as honorary
vice-chairpersons of the event.

Thomson received his letter of invitation, but instead of declining with a personal letter he went public, announcing that he had answered Young's invitation as follows:

> As long as you pursue an advocacy of aid and comfort to Communist interests that is wholly foreign and un-American to the great majority of our citizens, I could never be associated with you in any capacity. Second, I heartily agree with the appraisal of Dr. Martin Luther King, Jr., by the late J. Edgar Hoover and believe that Dr. King did great harm to the American way of life through his association with Communist-inspired organizations. Therefore, I would find it impossible to support a fundraiser for a memorial to such a person.

State Senator C. Robertson Trowbridge took umbrage at Thomson's attack on the memory of Dr. King and on Ambassador Young and refused to appear with the governor at the opening of a new state liquor store in Keene, New Hampshire on August 11. Robertson issued an explanatory press release.

> The governor could perfectly well have declined the invitation, but to give the impression that the State of New Hampshire feels that the Rev. King and Andrew Young are Communist-connected is just too much for me and my only way of showing my personal distaste for his remarks is to not join the governor when he comes to Keene to claim credit for what he considers an accomplishment—a liquor store.

The issue did not fade quickly. An Associated Press story out of Concord on November 2, 1977 read as follows:

> Gov. Meldrim Thomson today labeled as "racist activity" a news conference held by a group of blacks in front of his office to denounce him. The news conference—by the Reverend Ralph Henley (pastor of New Hampshire's only predominantly black church—New Hope Baptist in Portsmouth)—was "an example of the type of racist activity" that New Hampshire has avoided, Mr. Thomson said.

At that news conference Henley described Thomson's statements about Ambassador Young and Dr. King as symptomatic "of his racist tendencies." He said the governor had to understand that "he can't make those kinds of remarks and expect to go unchallenged."

Martin Luther King Jr. paid with his life for his courageous efforts to achieve racial justice in America. Andy Young stood beside him in those efforts and took the same risks. As UN delegate for the United States he has not always been discreet in his public utterances, and I, no less than anyone, regret those indiscretions and their timing. Nevertheless, in the uproar over his candid remarks it is easy to overlook the element of embarrassing truth that lies behind them, his overall record of achievement in the United Nations, and the lingering racism that surely contributes to the vehemence with which he is denounced in some quarters.

A case in point was Young's comment in a Paris newspaper interview that there are "hundreds, maybe even thousands, of people I would call political prisoners" in the United States. That remark was made in midsummer 1978, just when President Carter was leading a protest over the rigged trials of Soviet dissidents.

Some political leaders called for Young's instant ouster as ambassador. Larry McDonald began beating the impeachment drums again. In New Hampshire, Meldrim Thomson went to a Republican "pre-campaign convention" and said, "While we're thinking of articles of impeachment on Mr. Young, we should start thinking the same way about his boss."[12] And William Loeb leaped into print with an offer of $10,000 to Young if the ambassador could prove "that there is one political prisoner in the United States." Wrote Loeb: "Ambassador Young may not be a Communist, but if he were, he could not do any more to help the Communist forces throughout the world. . . . Whomever Ambassador Young is supporting, one thing is clear—he is not a friend of the United States."[13]

I cannot defend the imprecision of Andrew Young's remark. Had he been more specific in what he meant by "political prisoners" or had he put his meaning into historical context, he would have avoided the avalanche of criticism. If he meant that poor people have fewer recourses for staying out of jail than rich people, he should have said so. If he was referring to the "Wilmington 10," he should have said so. If he meant that virtually every major black and native American leader of our time has been imprisoned at one time or another for what was part of a political protest, he should have said so.

Or, he could have taken a candid look back at American history—slavery, the denial of suffrage to women until 1920, persecution of the labor movement by massacres and injunctions and jailings, the long confinement of Indians to reservations, the internment of Japanese-Americans in World War II, what some have called the FBI's persecution of Martin Luther King, and the prosecution of Vietnam dissidents.

That Young was not that precise is regrettable, and I would hope that in the future he will be more definitive and more discreet in his timing. But there is an element of truth in what he said, and what was lost in the confusion over that particular remark was the ambassador's denunciation of Moscow's persecution of dissidents. He said, "I think the current Soviet dissidents could well be the salvation of the Soviet Union. They are a natural development of the Soviet society, but the leadership has not yet realized it."

Most regrettable, however, is the way an incident like this obscures the very real accomplishments of Ambassador Young. When President Carter praised him for his "slow, steady, consistent effort to generate the trust of Africans," that praise was earned and deserved.

Finally, there has been a peculiar and artificial virulence about the attacks that have been made on Andrew Young in the wake of the indiscretions that obscure his contributions. Part of that virulence, I believe, derives from a domestic racism that still plagues us. Part of it can be traced to resentment against the new stance this country has been taking in race-related issues that rise in our dealings with African countries.

This aspect of the matter is considered in that part of the following chapter which recounts the heavy criticism Meldrim Thomson invited from the press and the churches following his visit to South Africa and his extravagant praise of the apartheid government of that country.

CHAPTER 16

The Publisher, the Governor, and the Clergy

While questioning the integrity of nearly all the institutions of American life which most of us have always regarded as essential to the well-being of our nation, Mr. Loeb and his newspapers present only one interpretation of the news, and this interpretation we believe fosters an atmosphere of hatred, bigotry and racism, pronounced under the guise of a simplistic pseudo-religion. We believe Mr. Loeb has failed in his great responsibility of public trust.

—From a display
advertisement in the
*Manchester Union
Leader* of September 17,
1968, paid for and signed
by forty-one Catholic
priests and repeated in a
second ad published
October 24, 1968 that

was paid for and signed
by 107 of the state's
Protestant ministers

*We write together to share our deep continuing
concern for our fellow human beings who suffer
under oppression in South Africa. Governor
Thomson is quoted as having referred to a high
level of freedom in that anguished land. Our
Christian consciences will not allow this
statement to go unanswered.*
—From a communication
addressed to "The
Congregations of God's
People in New
Hampshire," signed by
the bishops and
denominational
executives of the
Catholic Church of New
Hampshire and the
main-line Protestant
denominations, January
1978

Chapter 6 of Part I examined the real or apparent linkage between the rise of the New Right and the politically conservative
element of the evangelical movement. This chapter considers
the phenomenon as it manifests itself in the political life of New
Hampshire. Both Publisher Loeb and Governor Thomson follow a Far Right evangelical approach to political issues and do
so with obvious effect, even though evangelical church affiliation in the state is miniscule.

In 1976 the National Council of Churches reported that 50.3
percent of New Hampshire's people are church-affiliated. Of
that 50.3 percent, 71.5 percent are Roman Catholics. Catholics
make up 36 percent of the entire population of the state.

The next highest percentage is the United Church of Christ,
with 34,899 members, or 4.7 percent of the total population. Of
the other major denominations, American Baptists number

16,482; Episcopalians, 18,316; United Methodists, 17,437; Unitarians, 3,248. No other denomination comprises as much as one percent of the total population.

Publisher Loeb's willingness to clash with the main-line religious leaders of the state and to take his argument directly to their parishioners by way of his newspapers is evidence of his righteous certainty. But it is also a practical device, for it is the only way he can counter the liberalizing influence of the social gospel of the main-line churches.

A Baptist by conversion, Loeb shows little tolerance for the variety of political and social views that exists within that faith. Read what he wrote about fellow Baptist Jimmy Carter in an editorial titled "That Dope in the White House":

> As a Baptist, this writer can say he considers President Carter a disgrace to the Baptist denomination, and if encouraging traitors to this nation by pardoning the scum who deserted the nation in times of war, and wanting to be friends with the Communist slave masters in Cuba and China, and now wanting to encourage the use of marijuana by lowering the penalties against it represents born-again Christianity, then this writer can only say that it's too bad Carter was born in the first place.

In his profile of Meldrim Thomson, Daniel Yergin wrote: "Thomson, a devout Baptist of strong fundamentalist convictions, accords money a central role in his personal ethic. If you want money, you must work hard and struggle to get it, but once you have gotten it, it should be yours."[1] If Yergin's analysis is correct, it does much to explain, in a few words, why Thomson is so opposed to taxes, and particularly to high levels of tax money used to finance human services.

The governor is not reluctant to wear his religiosity on his sleeve—or to impose it on the state. In the spring of 1978 he attracted some national attention by lowering the state flags to half-staff to commemorate Christ's death on Good Friday. Enjoined from doing so by a court order sought by four Protestant ministers and a rabbi through the American Civil Liberties Union, Thomson took the issue to the Court of Appeals of the First District. The appeals court set aside the injunction on the grounds that there had not been a full hearing on the merits of the case, but the U.S. Supreme Court decided on a five-to-four vote to let the injunction stand.

The *Manchester Union Leader* then provided Thomson with

space in two editions to make his case for lowering the flags. Claiming that the legal dispute in the issue is based on misinterpretation of the "establishment clause" of the First Amendment of the Constitution, Thomson said in part:

> The Federal judiciary, at the prompting of a few shrill liberal leaders, have moved America to the brink of utter indifference to its great heritage of religious faith. While such action 150 years ago would have created universal disapproval and indignation among our people, most citizens today are numb and frustrated by the actions of their officeholders and the decisions of their judges. The hypocrisy of their position and the tortured reasoning of their decisions, which inevitably exclude God and with Him morality from the people's places, will, unless corrected, lead this nation to destruction.

As if to buttress the governor's self-image as constitutional and theological authority, the *Union Leader* provided considerable space in its issues of March 27 and 28, 1978 for a long, two-part article on "The Trial of Christ," written by Thomson thirty-eight years earlier.

Loeb's editorial reaction to the flag-lowering issue climaxed on March 29.

> There is something slightly insane about clergymen objecting to a Governor who wanted to indicate by lowering the flag that Christians in New Hampshire do remember the sacrifice of Our Lord on the Cross and that most sacred of all days, Good Friday. The intrusion of the Civil Liberties Union into the matter is, of course, understandable. This newspaper believes that wherever there is an opportunity to downgrade religion or patriotic love of country, the Civil Liberties Union will always be in the forefront under the argument that someone's liberties are being infringed on. . . . This newspaper considers the action by the three Protestant clergymen as giving offense to all Christians in New Hampshire and is completely incredible. The only good from their act has been to inform the rest of the nation over national television that once again New Hampshire is doing its best to stand up for God as well as country.

Loeb had to acknowledge that a rabbi was also involved, and he did it by putting quote marks around what he claimed was a "thought expressed by many citizens." That quotation read: "I can understand the rabbi being involved although we do not believe he has the approval of most of his fellow rabbis because such action gives an opportunity for the anti-Semites to once again attack the Jews."

The *Portsmouth Herald,* however, looked upon the governor's flag-lowering from a less adulatory viewpoint.

> Thomson's gesture is purely a grandstanding, shoddy piece of poli-
> ticking intended to trap the unwary into believing he is in the forefront
> of true believers. Or, as an acquaintance who practices the Greek Ortho-
> dox faith asked on learning of the flag lowering: "What's he going to do
> for us next week end?" In that church Easter is April 25. People of Jew-
> ish faith might well ask: "What's he ever done for us?"[2]

Loeb's involvement in the Good Friday flag-lowering issue
marks just one chapter in a long book; his clashes with the
clergy go back many years and involve a number of issues. A
quarter century ago, for example, the issue of alleged Communist infiltration of the Protestant clergy was the most sensational
of the day. It came about because of an article titled "Reds in
Our Churches" that appeared in the July 1953 edition of *The
American Mercury.* The article was written by J.B. Matthews,
who was director of the staff of the House Un-American Activities Committee from 1938 to 1945 and who became staff director for the late Senator Joseph R. McCarthy's Senate investigat-
ing subcommittee shortly before "Reds in Our Churches" was
published.

In that article, which led with the flat declaration that "the lar-
gest single group supporting the Communist apparatus in the
United States today is composed of Protestant clergymen,"
Matthews wrote:

> It is . . . nothing short of a monstrous puzzle that some seven thou-
> sand Protestant clergymen have been drawn into the network of the
> Kremlin's conspiracy. Could it be that these pro-Communist clergymen
> have allowed their zeal for social justice to run away with their better
> judgment and patriotism? A partial explanation of these thousands of
> clergymen who have collaborated in one way or another with the Com-
> munist-front apparatus may be found in the "social gospel" which in-
> fected the Protestant theological seminaries more than a generation ago.

Publication of the Matthews article caused an immediate uproar in the press and within the subcommittee itself. The three
Democrats on the McCarthy subcommittee—senators John L.
McClellan of Arkansas, Stuart Symington of Missouri, and
Henry M. Jackson of Washington—denounced the article as a
"shocking and unwarranted attack against the American clergy"
and demanded that appropriate action be taken against

Matthews. Defending Matthews, McCarthy said the article did not constitute an attack on the clergy and added that because Matthews was not a "professional" staff aide as defined by law, he would not bring the issue of Matthews' dismissal up for a subcommittee vote. Senator Jackson said McCarthy served notice he would not recognize any member to make a motion for Matthews' resignation.

Loeb leaped immediately to Matthews' defense. He said in an editorial that he had known Matthews for twenty-one years and described him in capital letters as "ONE OF THE GREAT EXPERTS ON THE SPIDER WEB OF COMMUNISM, A WEB THEY WEAVE IN THEIR USE OF EVERY PART OF AMERICAN LIFE, ESPECIALLY IN THE PRESS, THE RADIO, THE PULPIT AND IN GOVERNMENT OFFICES, FROM WHERE A HANDFUL OF COMMUNISTS CAN TWIST AND DISTORT AMERICAN PUBLIC OPINION."[3]

The publisher said he agreed that the overwhelming proportion of clergy are among the country's most patriotic citizens,

> but there are definitely Communists and pro-Communists in important places among the United States clergy. There are others, like New Hampshire's Episcopal Bishop Hall, who while innocent of any desire to aid the Communists, can be influenced to do what the Communists want. . . . An investigation of the Communist web among the clergy . . . might awaken good church leaders such as Bishop Hall to the true state of affairs. Once awakened, many would become as militant [sic] anti-Communist as this newspaper. They would not then attack this newspaper as Bishop Hall has done in most unchristian fashion.[4]

Loeb's support notwithstanding, J.B. Matthews resigned as staff director of the McCarthy subcommittee on July 9, after President Eisenhower sent a telegram to three clergy—one Protestant, one Catholic, one Jewish, of the National Conference of Christians and Jews—in response to a wire from the clergy that described Matthews' article as "unjustified and deplorable." Without naming Matthews, Eisenhower's telegram made clear whom he meant when he asserted that "generalized and irresponsible attacks that sweepingly condemn the whole of any group of citizens are alien to America. Such attacks betray contempt for the principles of freedom and decency." The President added that the nation's churches are its "citadels of our faith in individual freedom and dignity."

Later that month McClellan, Symington, and Jackson quit McCarthy's subcommittee in protest over McCarthy's tactics. McCarthy promptly accused them of quitting because, he said, they did not want to expose communism and corruption in the Democratic party, a familiar McCarthy ploy that McClellan and Jackson immediately denounced.

On July 19 the National Council of the Churches of Christ in the United States of America, which, at that time, included churches with a combined membership of 35 million people, issued a statement publicly criticizing the McCarthy subcommittee's counterpart in the House, the un-American activities committee, for using "certain un-American methods and procedures." "Frankly," the statement said, "some of the procedures of your committee with reference to its files bear too much resemblance to the techniques of J.B. Matthews to satisfy the minds and consciences of a responsible group of clergymen and laymen charged with the duty of studying ways and means of maintaining our cherished freedoms."

Undaunted by the criticism, the House committee voted six to three to give Matthews a chance to "document" his charges of communist activity in the Protestant clergy by appearing before the committee later that fall.

Loeb's *Union Leader* immediately ran an editorial congratulating the House committee and made a rare criticism of Senator McCarthy, saying, "McCarthy showed extremely poor taste in dismissing Matthews without giving him a chance to tell his story in public." The same editorial blasted the National Conference of Christians and Jews for "completely distorting what Matthews said, and then having President Eisenhower wire them a further distortion of what Matthews said, in an obvious attempt to gain votes."

Loeb's obsession with finding communist influence behind so many socially responsible organizations, including main-line Protestantism, is not, of course, the only point that has been at issue between him and religious leaders. Long an ardent advocate of prayer in the public schools, he rarely lets an opportunity go by to vent his spleen on the Supreme Court decision that outlawed the practice and on the clerics who support that decision.

On May 27, 1963 his front-page editorial, titled "Presbyterian Assembly Helps Build a 'Wall,'" attacked the General Assembly of the United Presbyterian Church for going on record in opposition to prayer in public schools, in opposition to Sunday closing laws, and in opposition to tax privileges for churches and clergy. Loeb said he hoped such action "does not reflect the thinking of the majority—or even many—of the 3,200,000 members of that church." He closed on this note: "Incidentally, we understand that Presbyterian churches and churches of all denominations are still guaranteed police and fire protection by the State. Obviously, this is some benefit to religion. Perhaps the General Assembly of the United Presbyterian Church should take up this 'urgent' Church-State issue at their next assembly."

A *Union Leader* editorial on "Prayers and Politics," dated June 23, laid the Supreme Court decision outlawing prayer in public classrooms to Kennedy. Voters, the editorial said, should be reminded that "Mr. Kennedy's" Supreme Court appointments "have been from the same range of Liberal-Leftist, secularist, anti-religious pettifoggers as those which, with few exceptions, marred the previous administrations of Messrs. Truman and Eisenhower."*

Loeb reserves most of his passion on the issue of church and state for the social gospel, with "activist" priests, ministers, and rabbis his particular target—whether it be in urging peace in Vietnam, or civil rights, or any number of other social issues.

On September 17, 1968 his targets struck back. Forty-one New Hampshire Catholic priests paid for and signed their names to a large display ad in the *Manchester Union Leader*. The logo on the ad read "Nothing So Powerful As Truth?" and the text read in full:

> With each issue of the *Manchester Union Leader*, we are assured by William Loeb that "there is nothing so powerful as truth." The time has

* Two days after the court's initial decision, Kennedy said: "We have in this case a very easy remedy and that is to pray ourselves. And I would think that it would be a very welcome reminder to every American family that we can pray a good deal more at home, we can attend our church with a good deal more frequency and we can make the true meaning of prayer much more important in the training of all our children. I would hope that as a result of the decision, all American parents will intensify their efforts at home, and the rest of us will support the Constitution and the responsibility of the Supreme Court in interpreting it."

come when we can no longer sit back and be subjected to Mr. Loeb's idea of "truth."

Mr. Loeb certainly has a right to his ideological stance, but since the *Union Leader* is the only statewide newspaper, the only newspaper read by many New Hampshire citizens, Mr. Loeb has an obligation to present and interpret the news in a much more balanced manner. We believe, however, that Mr. Loeb is more interested in carrying out a program of indoctrination then dissemination of the news.

The *Union Leader* monopoly gives Mr. Loeb and his papers an unopposed opportunity to indoctrinate. To credit them with presenting a responsible conservative point would be an injustice to authentic conservatism. They promote instead a reactionary right-wing philosophy.

The indoctrination involves creating a climate of fear, distrust and suspicion. Mr. Loeb would have us believe that nothing can be trusted. Schools, churches, presidents and high government officials, labor, the Supreme Court, the United Nations, the mass media—all have come under attack. Mr. Loeb writes in an editorial: "In continuing to try to awaken the American people from their slumber, it is most important for all to engage in the crusade to realize that they cannot rely on the communications media—the press, the radio, the TV and its secondary line, the churches and the educational system. It was the infiltration of Communists and left-wingers of the communications media, and of churches and schools which led to the fantastic distortion of what Goldwater stood for."

Whom do we trust? Mr. Loeb? While questioning the integrity of nearly all the institutions of American life which most of us have always regarded as essential to the well-being of our nation, Mr. Loeb and his newspapers present only one interpretation of the news, and this interpretation we believe fosters an atmosphere of hatred, bigotry and racism, pronounced under the guise of a simplistic pseudo-religion. We believe that Mr. Loeb has failed in his great responsibility of public trust.

We can no longer remain silent while he continues to undermine confidence in our leaders and national institutions. We can no longer remain silent while he continues to advance his dangerous and immoral doctrines. The Catholic Bishops of the World Council write in the Decree on the Instruments of Social Communication: "A special need exists for everybody concerned to develop an upright conscience on the use of these instruments, particularly with respect to certain issues which are rather sharply debated in our time. . . . The manner of communication should furthermore be honorable and appropriate; this means that in the gathering and publication of news the norms of morality and the legitimate rights and dignity of a man must be held sacred." We call upon all citizens of New Hampshire to exercise conscience in this matter.

A front-page article in the same edition of the *Union Leader* discussed the ad, pointedly noting that it was signed by less than 10 percent of the state's Catholic priests, implying that those circulating the ad for signatures had difficulty getting even forty-one signers, contending that the prime instigator was Monsignor Phillip Kenney, chairman of the Manchester Diocesan Commission on Human Relations. Monsignor Kenney, a courageous priest with a passionate commitment to social justice, has clashed with Loeb on a number of occasions.*

The news article about the ad provides an example of how straight news can slide into propaganda. One paragraph reads: "Besides accusing the newspapers of promulgating a 'reactionary' philosophy—a term traditionally employed by Communists and left-wingers to describe anything they happen not to like— the ad employs a large number of generalities to express hostility."

In his editorial comment, Loeb chose to go the patronizing route, saying the priests could have saved their money for the ad by simply sending their message in the form of a Letter to the Editor.

> It was therefore silly for the small group of priests . . . to spend $242.21 for the advertisement. . . . This newspaper doesn't feel right about keeping the money the priests paid for this ad, so we are going to apply it as a memorial to a wonderful Catholic girl who owed her education and her early musical training to the tender loving care of the Religious of the Sacred Heart. This day a check for $242.21 has been drawn on the order of the Philippa Schuyler Memorial Fund and sent to Mrs. George Schuyler, Philippa's mother.[5]

Philippa Schuyler, the brilliant and musically talented daughter of the late George Schuyler, the black ultraconservative journalist who did literary reviews for the *Manchester Union Leader,* made her piano debut at Carnegie Hall before she was ten and was also a writer of prominence. She was killed in Vietnam while covering the war for the *Manchester Union Leader.*

After noting that Francis Cardinal Spellman presided over Philippa's funeral at St. Patrick's Cathedral in New York, Loeb concluded his editorial on this note:

> If ever one individual in this century represented the very BEST of the Catholic faith and the highest ideals of HER faith, it was Philippa Schuyler. It seems, therefore, only proper to this newspaper that the

---

* For other accounts of Loeb's conflicts with Monsignor Kenney and other members of the Catholic clergy, see Kevin Cash, *Who the Hell* Is *William Loeb?* (Manchester, N.H.: Amoskeag Press, 1975).

priests' misspent money be given in the memory of such a girl, whose whole life was an example of the good and the beautiful for which all of us should attempt to strive in this strife-torn and dissension-filled world.[6]

But Loeb had scarcely relaxed, presumably confident that he had routed the forty-one impudent priests by shaming them, when 107 Protestant ministers bought space in the *Union Leader* in support of the ad placed earlier by the priests. The ministers' ad, which appeared on October 24, reprinted virtually the entire text of the priests' ad following this introductory paragraph: "We the undersigned ministers of New Hampshire whole-heartedly support the statement made by 41 Roman Catholic priests in an advertisement entitled 'NOTHING SO POWERFUL AS TRUTH' in the *Manchester Union Leader* on September 17, reprinted in part below."

The ministers' ad closed with these words:

> We too can no longer remain silent in the face of the *Union Leader*'s continual presentation in its editorials of a reactionary right-wing philosophy. At the same time, we believe that if the *Union Leader* presented its readers with a well-reasoned conservatism, it could be a good paper and render a vital service to the state of New Hampshire. We call upon other citizens to exercise conscience in this matter.

Now Loeb realized he had more to contend with than a group of bumptious young activist priests, and his editorial response took up more than two full columns of space.

> These people spend so much time marching at Selma or at Resurrection City or demonstrating and agitating for one political cause or another that this newspaper sometimes wonders whether they have time to preach the glory of God or to take care of the spiritual needs of their churches.* As a matter of fact, in many cases they DON'T. . . . The interesting thing about these political clergy is the narrowness of their political philosophy. They concentrate on wanting the U.S. to surrender in Vietnam, with utter disregard for what would happen to the innocent South Vietnamese people, left to the mercy of the Viet Cong and the Communist killers in the North. These same clergy are all for the negro

---

* Loeb's *Union Leader* took the same tack in editorials on August 16 and August 17, 1978, castigating Catholic nuns who engaged in civil disobedience at the Seabrook nuclear power station. The first editorial opened on this note: "When we were a boy nuns were seen but seldom heard outside the classroom. Now we see the disgusting spectacle of two sisters participating in civil disobedience at the Seabrook Nuclear Station site."

[sic] first, last and always. The negro can do no wrong, according to them, or if he DOES wrong, it is to be explained by his disadvantaged position. The white individual can seldom do any GOOD, according to their philosophy. Yet, you do not hear a single one of these political clergy raise his voice against anything the Russians or other Communists do. . . .

What is fascinating about the moral blinders the political clergymen seem to wear every day is that they can be SILENT on the real moral issues right under their nose. For instance, this newspaper has for many years been carrying on a campaign against obscene literature and obscene movies in the Granite State. This newspaper has turned down thousands of dollars in advertising revenue by refusing to publicize and advertise obscene movies and obscene advertising of movies. Yet never once have we had one of these political clergymen come to our support or to the support of the mothers and fathers of New Hampshire who are trying to block this flood of obscenity that desecrates our state. Apparently, since obscenity does not involve Selma, the negro, Vietnam or the Russians, these clergymen could not care less about it. Perhaps they finally WILL when some member of their family is attacked by a sex-crazed individual who has been driven to his crime by reading or seeing this kind of pornography.[7]

Loeb made another leap in judgment by accusing the clerics of ignoring the drug problem, the divorce problem, and the drinking problem in the state. He noted that the *Union Leader* periodically prints a long list of divorces to call attention to that particular problem. Then he fired what he must have considered the lethal shot:

So the question this newspaper would raise is: What kind of clergymen ARE these political clergymen? The question arises in our minds and in the minds of many OTHER people: Should they BE clergymen or should they abandon their clerical robes and become politicians? They apparently prefer the latter role to the former.

ABOVE ALL, CERTAINLY THEY SHOULD NOT BE USING THEIR PULPITS TO ATTACK INDIVIDUALS, AS SOME OF THE SIGNERS OF THIS ADVERTISEMENT HAVE DONE AGAINST THIS PUBLISHER AND THIS NEWSPAPER. PULPITS ARE NOT PUT THERE FOR THE PURPOSE OF ATTACKING INDIVIDUALS AND THEN TO BE USED AS A HIDING-PLACE WHEN THE NEWSPAPER AND THE INDIVIDUAL RESPOND. Possibly the main difficulties with the political clergy are their arrogance and their VERY limited outlook—which is a polite way of saying they are plain stupid.[8]

Clearly, Loeb appeared stung by the double onslaught of the clergy-backed ads.

In the ensuing years Loeb and the leaders of the church engaged in brief skirmishes, but it was not until the winter of 1978 that another major confrontation occurred. This time the precipitating agent was Meldrim Thomson Jr., in his double role as governor of New Hampshire and as "secretary of state" of the Conservative Caucus' shadow cabinet. By wearing two hats Thomson had become New Hampshire's most peripatetic governor, making forty-three trips out of the state in the single year after he was sworn in for a third term, including two weeks in Taiwan, when he and three members of his family were guests of the Taiwan government, five days in Panama, and eleven days in South Africa.[9]

The *Concord Monitor* noted that travel agents estimated the Taiwan trip would have cost the Thomsons $11,000 if they were paying the bill as private citizens. "If Thomson were a Federal instead of a state official, the gift of the trip would be illegal. This is what the government of South Korea did for several members of Congress, and we now have a national scandal that's called Koreagate."[10]

The *Monitor* noted Thomson's previous indications of support for the Taiwan government by opposing more open relations with the Communist China regime on the mainland and by running the Taiwan flag up and down the statehouse flagpole on three occasions in recent years. "But we doubt whether the value of these 'services' approaches the $11,000 mark," the *Monitor* said.[11]

But Loeb and the *Union Leader* praised Thomson's trip and gave the governor generous space for his own written account of the journey. Strangely missing was mention of the shoes Taiwan exports to the United States, the single issue of direct importance to New Hampshire and to its badly hurting domestic shoe industry.

The Taiwan trip, however, was only a prelude to things to come. Thomson's trip to South Africa in January 1978, reportedly funded by the South African Freedom Foundation, a nonprofit organization with close ties to the South African regime, triggered an unprecedented outburst of editorial comment and direct involvement by the clergy. Throughout his visit to South Africa, Thomson's statements in wire service stories, interviews, press conferences or press handouts made headlines back home. He established himself as the only American leader, in President Carter's view, who, in effect, endorsed South Africa's apartheid policies. (Thomson demanded an apology from the White House for the President's comment; it was never forthcoming.)

Two wire service stories published January 19, 1978 provide some representative quotes from the governor. The United Press International story quotes him to this effect:

> I am convinced that John Vorster [South Africa's former prime minister], who has defied the world opinion of liberals and communists as he moves his nation toward greater opportunities for all of its 25 million inhabitants, is one of the great world statesmen of today.
>
> I was greatly impressed by the constructive manner in which he and his administration are resolving the internal problems of their country with calmness, compassion and courage.

Thomson said Blacks in South Africa "earn five times more than blacks of other African countries." The UPI release pointed out that Thomson did not say what their earnings were compared to those of Whites in their own country.

UPI noted that Thomson's statement was issued on the day thousands of black children in South Africa stayed away from classes on the first day of the new school year, protesting what they say is inferior black education, and also observed that Thomson had left for South Africa shortly after meeting with New Hampshire black leaders who protested his criticisms of Martin Luther King Jr.

The Associated Press story of the same day, which quoted Thomson as saying, "They [South Africans] have a free press, they have free elections," pointedly noted that only Whites are allowed to vote. It reported that "Thomson said he realized that South Africa allows unlimited detention without charge or trial of the person, but said he felt this might be justified under the current threats against South Africa." Also, he continued "to have a very strong feeling that the true story of Africa is not being told in the world press."

The *Union Leader* published Thomson's statement issued from Johannesburg at the conclusion of his South African visit. In that statement Thomson listed "several things that stand out prominently in my mind."

> 1. South Africa recognizes the danger of communism and will never bend or surrender to it whether it flows from such pressure groups as

the World Council of Churches, such militant powers as SWAPO, or the Communist-tainted United Nations.

2. The economy of South Africa is strong and growing stronger despite the stupid attempts of the Carter Administration to discourage the investment of American capital in South Africa.

3. Today South Africa is a leader in the world in successful energy policy. . . .

4. South Africa's health program, for blacks and whites alike, is in some respects superior to what exists today in the United States. . . .

5. The low cost housing I saw in Soweto and Sepokeag is outstanding. Certainly, America with her decaying and near bankrupt major cities could learn a lesson in housing and community planning from South Africa.

6. South Africa is making remarkable progress in election reform. . . .

7. Finally, I am distressed to see the friendly relations that have long existed between the United States and South Africa destroyed by the insane, dangerous and meddlesome foreign policy of the Carter Administration. . . . As one American, I can assure the people of South Africa that there are millions of my fellow citizens back home who bitterly oppose the foreign policy of the Carter, Young and Brzezinski administration. And what is more, we plan to do all we can to correct it in the elections next November.[12]

Thomson may not have appreciated the outrage and the uproar his statements were creating back home, but he must have learned about this before he left Johannesburg, because press reports indicated he changed his plans to land in Manchester, in order to avoid a crowd of protesters gathered there. Instead, he landed at Boston's Logan Airport and proceeded by car directly to his farm at Orford.

For weeks after, Thomson was under sustained attack from most of the daily newspapers in New Hampshire, from the *Boston Globe,* and from both Democratic and Republican leaders in the state. A sampling of commentary follows:

What we'd like to know is what is so compassionate about a government, controlled by one million whites and keeping 19 million blacks in virtual bondage; that won't provide equal opportunities for all people; that kills black leaders such as Steve Biko, who chose to speak up; that shuts down newspapers which criticize the government; that even while Thomson is in the country is tearing down the homes of some 50,000 blacks in an effort to drive them out of the cities in the name of lily-whiteness.[13]

The governor's misrepresentations about South Africa were an embarrassment to the United States, humiliating to New Hampshire and morally inexcusable.[14]

Perhaps the harshest criticism came from the staunchly Republican *Nashua Telegraph*.

> Governor Thomson has brought shame upon the people who elected him to office. It is altogether realistic to expect that had Meldrim Thomson been a public official in the late 1930's, he would have spoken out in defense of Adolph Hitler. Hopefully, New Hampshire will soon be rid of Meldrim Thomson and the immorality which he represents. Until that time, it is incumbent upon the responsible segment of New Hampshire society to speak out in opposition to that immorality.[15]

The most dramatic rebuff was leveled by the leading clergy of New Hampshire. A banner headline above the masthead of the January 30 edition of the *Boston Globe* told the story: "N.H. Churchmen Denounce Thomson's S. Africa Views." The bishops and the denominational executives of the Catholic church of New Hampshire and of the main-line Protestant denominations jointly signed a communication addressed to "The Congregations of God's People in New Hampshire."

> We write together to share our deep continuing concern for our fellow human beings who suffer under oppression in South Africa. Governor Thomson is quoted as having referred to a high level of freedom in that anguished land. Our Christian consciences will not allow this statement to go unanswered.
>
> In our understanding, the situation is quite to the contrary. Religious leaders who are now serving in South Africa, or who have served there before their exile by the Vorster regime, inform us that the injustices and denials of freedom which first caused our concern to focus on that land continue unabated. Therefore, we are united in calling upon the people of several communions to become informed about the situation in South Africa in regard both to the churches and to the nation, to hold the people of South Africa warmly in our prayers, and to take whatever action each considers to be appropriate.

The letter was signed by Catholic bishops Odore J. Gendron and Robert Mulvee; the Rt. Rev. Philip A. Smith, bishop of the Episcopal Diocese of New Hampshire; the Rev. Benjamin R. Andrews Jr., the Rev. Edward D. Brueggemann, the Rev. Robert D. Fiske, and the Rev. Stephen V. Weaver, conference ministers of the United Church of Christ; the Rev. Robert W. Williams, executive minister, and the Rev. Arthur N. Foye, associate executive minister, American Baptist Churches of New Hampshire; the Rev. Eugene A. Brodeen, president of the New England Synod of the Lutheran Church in America; the Rev. James A. Batten, Northern District superintendent, United

Methodist Church; the Rev. James M. Hutchinson, executive secretary of the New Hampshire-Vermont Unitarian-Universalist Association; and the Rev. Eugene Turner, synod executive of the Northeast Synod of the United Presbyterian Church.

In addition, the Catholic diocesan newspaper published the text of a statement strongly condemning South Africa's racial segregation policies that had been issued one year before by the Catholic Bishops' Conference of South Africa: "We again profess our conviction, so often repeated, that the only solution of our racial tensions consists in conceding full citizen and human rights to all persons in the Republic, not by choice on the false grounds of color, but on the grounds of the common humanity of all men, taught by our Lord Jesus Christ."

The clergy's communication drew quick plaudits from a number of New Hampshire dailies. The following comment was typical:

> To its credit, the New Hampshire Council of Churches has chosen to lock horns . . . with Governor Meldrim Thomson Jr., who has come back from a totally unnecessary, freeloading trip to South Africa. . . . There is no such official post in the United States government as "shadow secretary of state," but the right-wing, oppressive governments visited by Thomson choose to overlook that fact and accept Thomson at his own value, which is far more than it's worth. Gov. Thomson, when he goes abroad, doesn't represent the thinking of decent people in New Hampshire. He travels as the representative of 300,000 (out of 200 million population) ultra-right escapists from the 20th Century.[16]

Thomson called a press conference to report on his trip and to respond to his critics. He complained of being misquoted and quoted out of context and said his praise of South Africa's leaders "does not mean that I endorse or have ever believed in apartheid, nor does it mean I approve of laws on terrorism and banning." He did not say his own statement, issued on the eve of his departure from Johannesburg, was a misrepresentation of his feelings about South Africa.

The *Concord Monitor* editorialized:

> The governor's meeting with the press Tuesday was not a news conference. It was a forum for extolling the virtues of South Africa. He would entertain questions on nothing else, including issues in New Hampshire. Thus it was a publicity gimmick on behalf of South Africa— a return favor to the government that picked up the tab for his trip through a foundation it controls.[17]

On clergy criticism of his statements Thomson obfuscated. After saying he was "pleased" to see the statement by the clergy, he added:

> While they disagree with some of my comments, which they have a perfect right to do, they admit that their information is based on hearsay rather than personal experience. What was constructive and important about their statement is that they suggested to their communicants that they should inform themselves about South Africa. And this, I hope, all of their communicants will do, for truth has a way of correcting the myopia of prejudice.

Thomson chose to ignore the statement by the Catholic Bishops' Conference of South Africa, which expressed a viewpoint that was not based on hearsay, but on the direct experience of those Catholic clerics *in* South Africa.

Loeb also chose to ignore the South African bishops' conference, mounting a two-column-long front-page editorial attack on New Hampshire's clergy and New Hampshire's press.

> The governor's Leftist political enemies, particularly the Leftist newspapers of New Hampshire, by distortion and outright lies are attempting to make the governor appear to be a racist because of his recent trip to South Africa and his remarks while there. One result is that 14 members of the clergy have been played for suckers and trapped into a political fight in which they have no business if they believe in separation of church and state. They are being used by the enemies of economical government in New Hampshire. Their idealism and their innocence and almost complete ignorance about South Africa has been taken advantage of. These clergymen most certainly have NOT increased their stature with their congregations.

Loeb's editorial proceeded to describe South Africa as Loeb sees it. "Most of the blacks in South Africa are from right out of the jungle. . . . The South Africans are doing the best they can to bring these blacks out of the jungle and into modern existence and to train them for responsible positions and effective living."

The reader already exposed to the chronicling of Loeb's opposition to civil rights legislation may find some unintended irony in the excerpt from the publisher's editorial on South Africa.

> There is no similarity between the civil rights struggle in the United States and the situation in South Africa. In the United States the civil rights battle is to see to it that the blacks in the nation have the same

rights and privileges as the white people enjoy in this country of ours. The blacks represent only about 13 percent of the population. During the height of the civil rights struggle, the white people in the United States were not being asked to turn over the United States to the black people in this country and to be ruled by them.*

The naive clergy in the State of New Hampshire and other innocent people who are constantly attacking South Africa are doing so because they have swallowed, hook, line and sinker, the Leftist propaganda put out by the news media of the United States. The purpose of this propaganda is to make South Africa a pariah among nations—and the purpose of that is to allow black revolutionaries under Communist control in the rest of Africa to take over the mineral resources of South Africa and Rhodesia. . . . In other words, you have been lied to, you have been stuffed to the gills with false propaganda by people who are using innocent, well-meaning Americans to do their dirty work. The attacks on Governor Thomson since his return are a complete disgrace, but what can you expect from the left-wing news media of New Hampshire, a media [sic] that has no more interest in the truth than the devil does in Sunday school.

Loeb's contention that only liberals and "left-wing" news media were displeased with Thomson's views on South Africa was an obvious distortion of fact. Not only are most of New Hampshire's other newspapers moderate Republican in their editorial views, but conservative political figures as well as liberals objected to Thomson's comments. No better illustration could be found than in this Associated Press wire story of February 3, 1978:

Governor Meldrim Thomson Jr. apparently will have the last word on the withdrawn invitation to speak at a fund-raising dinner for a Massachusetts gubernatorial hopeful.

Conservative Republican Edward King this week withdrew an invitation for New Hampshire's Republican governor to speak at tonight's dinner because of the governor's support for the Vorster regime in South Africa.

It remained for Paul Szep, *Boston Globe*'s Pulitzer prize-winning editorial page cartoonist, to make the most pungent commentary of all. His cartoon depicted a burning cross in the back-

---

* This is not what Loeb was writing in 1960. In August of that year he attacked the civil rights plank of the Democratic national convention, contending that if the plank were carried out "it would really enslave the majority of the American people and deprive them of their rights in favor of some noisy minorities who have scared the politicians half to death."

ground, a long line of sheet-shrouded figures, and Thomson in the foreground, wearing the hooded shroud of what appears to be the Grand Kleagle. The thought, "John Vorster has a dream" is shown coming out of his head. The caption read: "News Item: South Africa. N.H. Gov. Meldrim Thomson described Prime Minister Vorster as a courageous statesman and said grass-roots Americans are opposed to President Carter's policy toward South Africa."

CHAPTER 17

The Armchair Warriors

The military are not only our main defense against the enemy, but they are also the main repository of freedom in this country.
—WILLIAM LOEB[1]

He's a frustrated Army general.
—PETER THOMSON,
speaking of his father,
Meldrim Thomson Jr.[2]

Down the centuries it can be noted that the best chauvinists and jingoists have shared a characteristic: they have been above draft age.
—HUGH MOFFETT,
retired assistant manager
of *Life* magazine[3]

Early in March 1978 editorial cartoonist Paul Szep again targeted Meldrim Thomson, this time in company with William Loeb. The cartoon was captioned "New Hampshire's Right

Brothers—Invincible in Peace . . . Invisible in War" and depicted Thomson and Loeb in rompers, but wearing World War I spiked helmets, gleefully playing with a nurseryful of toy soldiers, tanks, and planes.

The cartoon may have been inspired by a passage in the speech I delivered on the Senate floor on March 1 announcing my intention to vote for ratification of the canal treaties and denouncing the tactics of the New Right in their campaign against the treaties. In that speech I said:

> In all of this nation, there may not be two more recklessly belligerent public figures than Meldrim Thomson and William Loeb. Though neither has ever worn the uniform of his country into battle, they are the first to demand the kind of precipitous action that could plunge young Americans back into combat.

As I've tried to make clear in a number of public pronouncements, I do not consider service in the armed forces the litmus test of patriotism. I know full well that there are countless persons of unquestioned patriotism and courage who, for a variety of legitimate reasons, were never inducted into service. Why William Loeb and Meldrim Thomson did not serve in World War II is their business, not mine.

While I do not object to the fact that neither served, I do object to the way in which they have recklessly impugned the loyalty, patriotism, and courage of those who *did* serve their country in wartime and of others who did not. I deplore their reckless bravado in advocating policies that, I believe, could lead us into *another* war that *others* would have to fight.

As citizens, Loeb and Thomson have every right to state their views on public policy, including matters of war and peace. Nobody would hold that only veterans have earned that right, for such a principle would exclude not only most women, but the youth who would have to serve in any new war. But I do believe that people who have not seen combat should exercise their imaginations about its horrors. Such an exercise should lead them to restrain their appetite for war and to modify their attacks on Americans who see the issue differently than they.

Let me cite examples of what I mean.

In the 1972 Presidential preference primary in New Hampshire, Loeb made Edmund Muskie his prime target and the ultimate Democratic nominee escaped relatively unscathed. But once George McGovern became the Presidential candidate, Loeb's attacks intensified.

His most scurrilous attack came in midsummer of that election year. Using an article from the official publication of the John Birch Society as a starting point, but without identifying it as such, Loeb ran a series of page-one articles that brought into question McGovern's courage on his last mission as a bomber pilot in World War II; the primary article featured the word yellow.

Three members of the crew who served aboard McGovern's *Dakota Queen* immediately condemned the implied accusation that McGovern had taken a milk run on his last mission. Bill Ashlock, the tail gunner, gave this account to the *Washington Post*.

> It was a typical deal that you got a milk run on your last mission, one that wasn't dangerous so you wouldn't get shot down on your last mission. McGovern could have gotten out of it [a dangerous mission], but he left it up to the crew. We voted to go. . . . We were over target. There was heavy flak. We suffered three hits and we didn't deviate from course. We dropped our bombs. We had our hydraulic line shot out and, when we returned to base, we had to hand-crank down the flaps. When McGovern landed the plane, he ordered the crew to release parachutes out the waist windows to act as a drogue and halt the ship. That was the only thing that stopped us.

To lay the question to final rest, McGovern asked the Defense Department to make public that part of his military record that directly responded: "Throughout many combat missions against highly important and strategic enemy installations, [he] . . . demonstrated the highest order of professional skill, heroism, leadership and devotion to duty."

To me, the spectacle of Bill Loeb—who lives behind walls in a fortress home, protected by a small arsenal and by fierce watchdogs, and who rarely ventures forth without being armed —so much as hinting without firm evidence that a combat pilot was "yellow" on his last mission is repugnant.

A further word on this subject: Many well-meaning friends have tried to make me out a war hero in order to defend me against slurs on my courage and patriotism leveled by the likes of Loeb and Thomson. In truth, although I came home from combat with a modest collection of medals and citations, I was no war hero. However, combat left two indelible impressions on me—witnessing true heroism on the part of others and witnessing firsthand the ghastly horror of war itself.

Can war *ever* be justified? This is a question of ethics, approached variously by differing schools of ethicists. My answer is predicated upon the fourth-century teaching of Augustine, whose thinking came out of the necessity to guide Christians confronted with the chaos into which the Roman Empire was falling. Today, Augustine's just war theory is still a useful guide, not only for Catholic and Protestant moralists but for political leaders of any creed. It tells us, in brief, that there are times in history when war is a permissible moral choice—provided there is no other way to defend essential human values, provided there is reasonable chance for success, provided the military means used are as humane as possible and are proportioned to the value of the end that is sought. Given the deadliness of modern weapons, it becomes harder and harder to justify war, but there still may be occasions when conscience defends that choice. But I would add, with equal emphasis, that what I saw in combat convinced me that only a true necessity of defending our national integrity and security is a sufficient rationale for war, and that every other option must be tried first.

For a long time I felt the Vietnam War was a just war, but by mid-1968 I could no longer justify its justness. The arguments I had ritualistically trotted out in behalf of our role in Southeast Asia no longer convinced me. Moreover, there was growing evidence that our involvement was not *preserving* our national integrity, but *destroying* it; not *enhancing* our security, but *weakening* it by eroding confidence in the judgment of the national administration and the defense establishment. It had become clear to me that militarily we had done everything that could be reasonably asked of us without bringing down the wrath of the civilized world. It was equally clear that the one thing we could not give the people of South Vietnam was trust in their own government and belief in their own cause.

In 1969, in a speech before the National Academy of Sciences, I said the only hope for South Vietnam to survive without our endless help was to democratize its government by broadening the base of popular support. I expressed skepticism at the time that this would ever happen. Three years later, in a commencement address at Belknap College in Center Harbor, New Hampshire, I alluded to that speech.

Nothing in the months since has eased my skepticism. We have seen
more repressive purges. We have seen more suppression of newspapers.
We have seen more stifling of criticism and opposition. We have seen a
one-candidate ballot make a mockery of what was supposed to be a democratic election. And for every instance of valor by South Vietnam
troops, we have seen two refusals to stand firm and fight. I say this not to
question the courage of these troops. I say it to question the regime they
are asked to defend.

A year ago this month, a young American soldier fresh back from the
invasion of Laos, called on me in Washington. "Tell me," I said to him,
"did the South Vietnamese troops stage an orderly withdrawal—as we
were told? Or did they turn tail and run when the going got tough?"

"Senator," he said, "it was the damndest rout you ever saw. And I will
tell you something else, sir. I don't blame those guys [the South Vietnamese troops] one bit. Who'd want to fight for what they've got to fight
for?"

In June 1970 Richard Nixon asked me to be part of a White
House fact-finding mission to Vietnam and Cambodia to assess
the effects of our invasion of Cambodia. The mission was made
up of Democratic and Republican senators, congressmen, and
governors, along with key White House personnel. While there
I often struck off on my own to talk directly with diplomats, military officers, members of the "pacification" teams, Vietnamese,
and, most importantly, war correspondents.

What I learned from them did not square with the consensus
report prepared for the President by the leaders of the mission. I
refused to sign the report, instead filing a minority-of-one dissent, which I delivered to Nixon and made available to the
media.

In that report I said that the Cambodian incursion, far from
shortening the war, broadened it and would likely prolong it. In
June 1973 I took the Senate floor to announce that I was supporting and cosponsoring legislation to terminate funds for any
further hostile action by U.S. forces in Indochina, noting that
"here we are—three years later—thirty-six long, bloody months
later—still making war in Cambodia; still locked in debate over
war-making authority; still trying to end the most divisive war
in our history in the face of charges that we are only giving comfort to the enemy."

Later in my floor statement, I elaborated on that point.

As all of us know too well, this long, agonizing, frustrating war has
taken a terrible toll of wounds and scars at home as well as on the battle-

field. Deep, deep wounds have been sustained by those whose patriotism has been impugned because they have spoken out against continuing this senseless war. I was pointedly reminded of this just a few weeks ago when my distinguished senior colleague from New Hampshire, Senator Norris Cotton (a staunch Republican), joined in a unanimous vote in the Appropriations Committee to cut off funds for further bombing. Though many of us hailed his courage and independence, others responded with vicious abuse.

The largest newspaper in our state, the *Manchester Union Leader*, turned on my colleague with an editorial titled: "The Reds Thank You, Senator Cotton." Now no reasonable, rational man could ever question the patriotism of Norris Cotton, and the newspaper's charge that "Communist agents are happy with his remarks" is patently ridiculous. I say that this kind of shopworn, discrediting talk is what helped get us into Vietnam and kept us there far too long. . . . Questioning the patriotism of those who disagree with us is not only grossly unfair to those whom we impugn, it is of itself un-American, and it tears the very fabric of national unity and purpose.

In April 1975 I addressed the American Bankers Association Council at its annual meeting in White Sulphur Springs, West Virginia, but instead of talking about banking issues, I summed up my feelings about the Vietnam War:

The final, ultimate and most reprehensible betrayal of truth in this endless travesty is the misbegotten efforts already under way to dump a load of guilt and anguish upon the American people for the fall of South Vietnam and Cambodia. . . . The American people did not sell out South Vietnam and Cambodia. They gave their dollars. They gave their sons. Fifty-six thousand Americans died in Indochina. But so far as we know not one Soviet or Chinese soldier fought on the side of North Vietnam. The American people gave thirty-four times as much military aid to South Vietnam as the Communist powers gave to North Vietnam. And let the record show that, by the CIA's own estimates, we gave the South Vietnamese $6.6 billion in assistance since the signing of the Paris peace accords, while the Soviets and Chinese were giving $2.7 billion to the North.

I stated that there was an inherent flaw in a foreign policy that allied us with authoritarian regimes whose sole claim to our support was not that they stood for freedom, but that they *spoke* against communism. I concluded: "From beginning to end, paradox, duplicity, and self-delusion have presented us with an endless series of impossible options in Southeast Asia, including the final and agonizing choice of pledging even more aid or risking the lives of those Americans still in Saigon to *South Vietnamese reprisal.*"

In the commencement address at Belknap College mentioned earlier, I closed on a note that, at this point in my life, sums up my feelings about wars of questionable justness.

> The years go by, and to me life becomes ever more precious. Not just *my* life. But *all* life. Especially for those of you who have so much of it ahead of you.
>
> War is the enemy of life. War—and those who *urge* war.
>
> There are four lines from "The Two Sides of War" that I would like to quote, because for me they have taken on a new edge, a cutting sting.
>
> All wars are planned by old men
> In council rooms apart,
> Who plan for greater armament
> And map the battle chart.
>
> Those lines were written many years ago. But nothing has changed. Old men still plan and urge the wars *young* men must fight. I cannot do that any more. I choose to speak for peace. I choose to add my voice to those who ask not only an end to this senseless war—but a pledge never again to commit American lives, American resources, *and the American spirit,* to a war of such dubious merit.

Such thoughts prompted William Loeb and his newspapers to call me a "hawk-turned-dove—turned chicken" and "Senator Cut-and-Run."

A sampling of editorial comment by Loeb and his newspapers over the years should provide some indication of how unrelenting and reckless a "militarist" he has been and remains to this day.

On Vietnam, Loeb was the ultimate hawk, advocating a win-at-any-cost approach that included the use of nuclear weapons. At one point he wrote:

> Of course, what our government would do if it was a government of any guts, and if we still had the fundamental American belief in freedom, would be to inform the North Vietnamese government that it has violated the peace treaty of two years ago and will either pull its troops back beyond the peace line—immediately—or we will obliterate one of their cities by conventional or nuclear weapons, whatever is the handiest. To do anything else is simply to invite eventual attack on our cities and on our own shores.

On the eve of my 1966 Senate election contest with Gen. Harrison Thyng, Loeb pulled out all the stops.

> This newspaper believes that, by training and by his demonstrated courage—which has brought him 57 decorations and medals—this is the man who should be representing New Hampshire in the Senate of the

United States. . . . Thyng is the man who has first-hand knowledge of the most critical issue facing the Nation. . . .

This publisher can only pray, as the decision on Tuesday approaches, that you will not be misled, that you will not be fooled by this mass of left-wing propaganda, but that you will realize that when we are at war, as we are today, we need the voice of a military man in the Senate of the United States because he knows what the score is. He knows how to bring this terrible war to a quick end. . . . May almighty God give New Hampshire men and women the vision to make the right decision on Tuesday.

After the election Loeb said that "in the six long years ahead" the people of New Hampshire

will wake up to the facts of life and be very, very sorry over the unfortunate choice of Sen. McIntyre on Election Day 1966. When you turn down a man such as General Thyng, who has served his country outstandingly in two wars and is the bearer of 57 military decorations, you dishonor those brave Americans whom we are supposed to HONOR on this Veterans Day.

On January 26, 1968 Loeb gave us his formula for handling the *Pueblo* incident (when North Korean ships captured and took into custody the *USS Pueblo*).

There is only one way to solve the present crisis in Korea and that is to demonstrate overwhelming naval power off the North Korean port where the *USS Pueblo* and its crew are being held. Then give the North Koreans a limited number of hours, 4 or 6, in which to release the ship and its crew. If the North Korean government does not comply within that time, then simply obliterate that North Korean town. Unfortunately, this may not save the lives of the American boys on that boat. This, of course, would be a tragedy, but it would be a much WORSE tragedy to allow the Communists in North Korea to get away with this seizure of an American boat on the high seas.

Loeb then applied the same kind of reasoning to the continuing war in Vietnam.

In the same fashion, there is only one way to end the war in Vietnam, and that is to serve notice on North Vietnam that unless they cease their aggression against South Vietnam within a given number of days and come to the conference table ready to agree to no more aggression, we will then obliterate Hanoi, then Haiphong, and then flood the northern part of the country.

Two days later Loeb's associate publisher, B.J. McQuaid, added his own touch.

The best move we could make in this direction [to recover the *Pueblo*]
would be to "escalate" on a major scale the war in Vietnam. . . . For a
starter, pick out just one fat, conspicuous target and blast it to hell. Haiphong Harbor would do well enough. Particularly at a time when it was
full of Soviet shipping.

On October 15, 1969 the *Union Leader* welcomed Vietnam
Moratorium Day with an over-the-masthead banner printed in
red and blue on the white newsprint that read "ATTENTION ALL
PEACE MARCHERS: Hippies, Yippies, Beatniks, Peaceniks, yel-
low-bellies, traitors, commies and their agents and dupes—
HELP KEEP OUR CITY CLEAN! . . . Just by Staying Out of It!"

Loeb's front-page editorial, titled "Hanoi's Little Helpers,"
announced:

It's now official. The peacenuts who are demonstrating today, urging
the United States to "bug out" and run in Vietnam, have the hearty and
complete approval of the Communist government of North Vietnam. If
they could do so, Hanoi would probably send a medal to every confused
and mixed-up supporter of the "peace" marchers today.

Elsewhere on the front page was a UPI story headlined
"Loeb Turns Down Moratorium Ad."

William Loeb, publisher of the *Manchester Union Leader*, said yesterday his newspaper was refusing all advertising supporting the Vietnam
moratorium day. Walter Dunfey of Manchester said more than 300 persons, including clergymen, educators, doctors, lawyers and students,
had collected $1,700 for a front page ad which would have been pub-
lished today.

"We are refusing all advertising that promotes the so-called Vietnam
moratorium. We do this because we are not interested in blood money,"
Loeb said.

Loeb said he considered the efforts of those backing the moratorium,
whether well-intentioned or not, a stab in the back for all those who have
fought in Vietnam. He said it is an insult to those New Hampshire families who have lost "brave sons in Vietnam." In an editorial comment
yesterday, the *Union Leader* . . . called the moratorium "a deliberate
and dishonest play on the emotions of the American people" and said
it would undermine the peace talks in Paris.

That edition also featured an inside editorial titled "Senator
Cut-and-Run," which attacked my change of views on the war.

What the Senator should have added—if he had any intention of being
completely candid, is that the same people who forced [sic] him to
switch from a "hawk" to a "dove" on the Vietnam questions are dedicated to the proposition that ANY war, ANY foreign policy decision, that

hampers Communist aggression will automatically enlist their services in provoking national disunity, and thus will cause the Senator to cut and run. "Senator Cut-and-Run" is not simply proposing that we accede to the Communist demands in Vietnam. What he REALLY is endorsing, whether he realizes it or not, is the proposition that Communist imperialism be permitted to function unchecked all over the world.

To Loeb, any effort to improve the possibilities of peace through overture, accommodation, and compromise constitutes appeasement or treason, and his ire on this count is directed toward Democrat and Republican alike.

Thus it was that in 1971 he broke sharply with Richard Nixon when the President announced he would go to mainland China in the cause of peace. While I was congratulating the President and saying that I hoped this first official contact with the People's Republic would hasten an end to the Indochina conflict, lead the way to disarmament talks with the mainland Chinese, and enhance the chances for peace, the *Union Leader* was printing such charges as: "There are no words in the English language, or in any other language, to describe the utter perfidy, the utter indecency, the utter betrayal of everything for which the United States stands, of what has just been accomplished by Richard Nixon under the thumb of Henry Kissinger." According to Loeb's paper, the Peking trip was "a display of political, military or moral cowardice."

It was obvious that Loeb not only looked upon the Peking trip as an obsequious overture to the hated communists, but as a betrayal of his Nationalist Chinese friends on Taiwan. Indeed, the latter could well have provoked most of his fury.

Meldrim Thomson shares Loeb's global views and his admiration for military power and is no less pungent in expounding both.

In a speech before the Newton, Massachusetts chapter of Young Americans for Freedom, the Eastern Massachusetts chapter of Americans for Congressional Action, and the Nathaniel Hall Forum of Newton, Thomson was quoted by the Associated Press as saying:

When President Truman refused to permit our troops to cross the Yalu River, he committed America to her first disastrous no-win war. He thus signaled to the Communists of the world our irresoluteness and hesitancy to come to grips courageously with adversaries sworn to bury America.

The Associated Press also reported that Thomson said if Barry Goldwater had been elected in 1964, "the Viet Cong would have been driven from Vietnam and the war there brought to its successful end long ago."

Even after the war was over Thomson was unrelenting. Backed by Loeb, the governor found President Carter's declaration of amnesty an invitation to all-out political attack. It is true that many Americans, myself included, had reservations about a general amnesty, believing it might serve to discourage willing persons from fighting a future war that might be just and necessary. Nevertheless, many of us who held such reservations also knew that this was indeed a war of such questionable justness as to mitigate the offenses for which amnesty was sought. Further, we recognized amnesty as a sincere attempt to heal the internal wounds of the war and to turn the nation's attention to the future.

But for Thomson there was no such understanding. He ordered state flags flown at half-staff to protest amnesty as "America's Second Day of Infamy." He held anti-amnesty rallies on the statehouse steps and fanned the flames of amnesty resentment among veterans groups and patriotic organizations. In an open letter to the President, Thomson wrote:

> Your proposed amnesty can only have the effect of destroying forever that great American will that has brought success to American armies in every war for the past century, except the two no-win wars of Korea and Vietnam. I urge you for the sake of our future national security to place the deep concern of millions of American veterans above the opportunism of those who turn their backs on America in her time of need.

What I find most repellent is the way Loeb and Thomson have made "peace" a synonym for weakness or appeasement.

After the 1972 Presidential preference primary in New Hampshire, William Loeb appeared on NBC's *Today* show and announced that he would support any third-party candidate—even George Wallace—if either Edmund Muskie or George McGovern were the Democratic nominee and Richard Nixon was the Republican Presidential candidate. "The peace candidates won last night," he said, "the peace at any price candidates won."[4]

Reluctantly, he supported Richard Nixon in that election, but in 1976 he did indeed endorse George Wallace, in part because of Wallace's views on Vietnam and the military.

In April 1975 columnist David S. Broder quoted Wallace as telling him:

There is going to be a great revulsion in this country against our going in there and not winning that war. The people of this country are going to remember the politicians who were intimidated by the loud noise-makers in the streets. This is an emotional thing. The people can't stomach government that wasted all that money and all those lives for no purpose. . . . We ought to have bombed them out of existence up in North Vietnam.[5]

Sensing that both Loeb and Thomson would exploit Wallace's Vietnam theme in rallying opposition to the Panama Canal treaties, I began, in mid-1977, to prepare for what I knew was going to be an especially difficult political issue.

As the godson of Teddy Roosevelt, William Loeb had been a long-time advocate for retention of full control over the canal. Fourteen years ago Loeb already was in high dudgeon.

Believe it or not, the Panamanian flag is to fly above the Stars and Stripes in the Panama Canal Zone on certain occasions. The trick was sneaked over the American public so quietly that most Americans are probably not aware of this shocking and fantastic order by the State Department. Can you imagine putting the American flag below any other flag on American territory? This gives you some idea of how nearly insane are the people who run our foreign policy. These internationally-minded people, who don't believe in pride or patriotism, probably think there is nothing wrong about this order. . . . But that is not the way the other nations regard the situation. They realize that by such an act they have effectively further nibbled away at United States control of the Panama Canal.[6]

It had been evident since one month after his reelection, in 1976, that Meldrim Thomson, as chairman of the Conservative Caucus, one of the two most active antitreaty organizations in the country, was looking for an issue on which to challenge me for my Senate seat in 1978. As I considered the issue in late summer of 1977, I discovered I was in an uncomfortable predicament. If, after studying the new treaties, I was to decide on the merits that they did not deserve ratification, I would be suspected of knuckling under to pressure from Loeb and Thomson. But if, on the other hand, I was to decide the treaties did deserve ratification, I might be accused of supporting them just to spite Loeb and Thomson.

Aggravating the situation were public announcements by Conservative Caucus National Director Howard Phillips that conservatives should make a "political sitting duck" of Tom McIntyre over the canal treaties, and that the Conservative Caucus could "make it a political impossibility for McIntyre to vote for that treaty."

Then, too, I had an item of personal discomfiture over the issue. In 1975, admittedly without proper forethought or study, I had put my name to Senate Resolution 97, which, in effect, urged retention of undiluted U.S. "sovereignty" over the Canal Zone and held that the power to dispose of U.S. territory or other U.S. property is vested in the Congress, which includes the House of Representatives.

Not only did this prior act appear to commit me to a vote against ratification of the treaties three years later, but it also effectively put me on record that the House as well as the Senate should have a voice in the decision to turn over control of the canal and U.S. property to the Panamanians after the year 2000. As it turned out, six other senators who signed that resolution voted, as I did, for ratification of the treaties. And, as it turned out, the Supreme Court, in the spring of 1978, let stand a ruling that the President and the Senate (contrary to challenges from congressional treaty foes), acting by a self-executing treaty may transfer to another nation property in which the United States has an interest.

By late summer 1977 I knew I had but one recourse: to give the Panama Canal treaties hard attention for the next four or five months. This time I resolved to vote only after I had studied all the provisions, weighed all the possible consequences, sought the counsel of those whose judgment I most respect, and heard out the views of constituents who were speaking dispassionately from facts not emotion.

On September 16, a week after the signing of the treaties but months before ratification would be taken up in the Senate, I addressed the New Hampshire Council on World Affairs in Manchester.

> I am going to talk about the Panama Canal treaties. And I am going to do this because some things have to be said before Bill Loeb and Meldrim Thomson stampede this issue far beyond the reach of reason, common sense and balanced judgment. . . . I have come here to ask the people of New Hampshire to join with me in a thorough study of the issue and a careful weighing of the arguments for and against ratification

of the treaties. I have come here to ask you to read more than the *Union Leader*, to listen to more than Meldrim Thomson, and to avoid succumbing to the emotionalism on both sides of this most difficult question. We owe it to ourselves. We owe it to our country.

At the close of the speech I addressed the political facts impacting upon the issue, noting that Thomson and the Conservative Caucus had seized upon it as the issue to unseat Tom McIntyre.

> They make two rash assumptions. That they already know how I am going to vote; that they are either going to make me change my mind or make me pay the political consequences. Let me make this as clear as I can. The puppet Governor of New Hampshire may dance to Bill Loeb's strings, but I never have and I never will. I do not fear Bill Loeb, because I do not respect him. In my view, he is neither a New Hampshireman—by birth, residence or appreciation of the state—nor a person who understands what this great country of ours is all about. So Mr. Loeb and Mr. Thomson and the Conservative Caucus can take their threats and run them up and down the Governor's flagpole.

I spent as much time as possible in the ensuing months to learn all I could about the canal itself, the original treaty, and the provisions of the new treaties. Despite the fact that I reserved judgment on the treaties for a period of six months and did not announce how I would vote until the morning of March 1, 1978, Loeb, Thomson, and the Conservative Caucus maintained constant pressure on the issue.

The ultimate absurdity came when the Conservative Caucus of New Hampshire passed a resolution of censure on December 4, 1977 and sent it to me like a subpoena. I was "censured" for my September speech on the canal treaties, a speech in which I had merely spelled out the pro and con arguments and had taken no position. This resolution "censured" me for allegedly giving aid to a recognized dictator, one Omar Torrijos; for indicating I was willing to violate the Constitution and my oath of office by even *considering* a vote for treaty ratification; for failing to recognize through my speech and "personal ignorance" that the treaties would provide the communist regimes with a legal beachhead from which they would eventually overpower all nations of Central and South America; for saying in the speech that however I voted I would vote in "good conscience"; for happening to be chairman of the Subcommittee on Financial Institutions when, the resolution said, "it is common knowledge that the financial institutions of the United States have more than a vested interest in the canal treaties."

Not only did the resolution censure me, but it "required" me to appear before the caucus in Wolfeboro, New Hampshire on February 12, 1978 to justify why I should not vote against ratification and/or refute said censure. My nonappearance, the resolution said, would constitute prima facie evidence of my intent to vote for ratification. I did not go before the caucus, so I have to assume I was tried in absentia and found guilty of a decision I had not yet made at that time.

Meanwhile, Thomson was flying about the country lashing out at the treaties in speeches before such groups as the 1977 National American Legion Convention and the John Birch Society. A few paragraphs from the speech he delivered before the Legionnaires will indicate the tenor of his remarks and the direction of his approach to the issue.

> Will America continue [its] flight from greatness, or will we, in the spirit of our Founding Fathers, draw the line of reckoning at the Big Ditch and there stand firm against the rising tide of Communism? Have we become so spineless, so cowardly that we jump when any tiny foreign power bent upon blackmail, snaps its corrupt fingers?
>
> Treaty negotiator Sol Linowitz was recently quoted as saying that the opposition to the treaty is one of emotionalism; it is one of great ignorance on the part of the American public. He sounds much like the group of American businessmen with whom I talked in Panama City early last June. About the many government-instigated instances of Panamanian youth tearing down and desecrating Old Glory these money-hungry merchants said, "They are just kids blowing off steam." Back in 1964 when the Panamanian public desecrations of the American flag began our public officials should have issued an order similar to the one given by John Dix, the New Hampshire-born customs official in New Orleans at the outbreak of our Civil War. Dix said: "If anyone attempts to haul down the American flag, shoot him on the spot."

In his speech before the American Legion, Thomson had to circumvent an uncomfortable fact: The Joint Chiefs of Staff, the highest military officers in the land, had endorsed the new canal treaties. Thomson did it by impugning their professional integrity, saying: "After the Singlaub incident, we all know that the President keeps a headlock on the military. Active commissioned officers will either say what the administration desires or remain silent. Therefore, we must look to our retired officers for the most accurate and honest appraisal of the importance of the canal to our security."

I took particular note of that line in my March 1 floor speech.

What this notorious armchair warrior—and others like him—is telling us, in effect, is that a man like Admiral Holloway, a man who fought for his country at Saipan, the Southern Palau Islands, Tinian, Leyte, and Surigao Straights, Korea and Vietnam, a man who has earned the Bronze Star, the Navy Commendation Medal, the Distinguished Flying Cross, and three Air Medals, a man who rose to top command of our Navy by the age of 54, cannot be trusted when he tells us, as he did, that "the new treaties are in the best national security interest of the United States."

This is a prime example of what I meant when I said radical extremists believe that we would see every issue as they see it—if there was not something sinister in our motivation. In this instance, the National Chairman of the Conservative Caucus—Governor Thomson of New Hampshire—would have us believe that military leaders like Admiral Holloway have compromised their integrity and the nation's security in order to ingratiate themselves with the administration. How insulting. How absurd.*

In the next few days and weeks large blocks of my speech on the treaties and the New Right were reproduced on the op-ed pages of the *Washington Post,* the *Boston Globe,* the *San Francisco Chronicle,* the *St. Louis Post-Dispatch,* the *Hartford Courant,* the *Christian Science Monitor,* and even the *Chicago Tribune.* Editorials on the speech appeared in countless other dailies, and such columnists as James Wechsler in the *New York Post,* Richard Strout in the *Christian Science Monitor,* Marquis Childs in the *Washington Post,* and Hal Gulliver in the *Atlanta Constitution* made favorable comment.

Flattering as the national press attention was, I was most heartened by the support the speech drew from the newspapers back home—the *Portsmouth Herald,* the *Claremont Eagle,* the *Keene Evening Sentinel,* the *Lebanon Valley News,* the *Concord Monitor,* the *Nashua Telegraph,* the *Milford Cabinet,* for example—and by the letters and telegrams and phone calls I received from the people of New Hampshire.

* The Joint Chiefs of Staff have disagreed with administrations over the years, two recent examples being President Carter's decision to abandon the B-1 bomber and his decision to withdraw troops from South Korea over a period of years. The Joint Chiefs opposed both decisions and put their opposition on the record.

From Thomson, Loeb, and the Conservative Caucus the reaction was just what I expected. Thomson called the speech "an unstatesmanlike outburst reminiscent of Muskie's crybaby act in the New Hampshire Presidential primary of six years ago" and said:

> Senator McIntyre refuses to represent the will of the people of New Hampshire. Thus he attacks the very foundations of constitutional government. His decision to support the giveaway treaties in no way changes the facts on the issue so vital to the security and well-being of our people. We have no need for anyone in the Senate who thinks he is smarter than the people, and who refuses to represent their wishes on major national issues.

Gordon Humphrey, former state coordinator for the Conservative Caucus and a candidate in the Republican Senate primary in New Hampshire, said: "The people of New Hampshire have made it crystal clear they oppose giving up our canal in Panama. But Senator McIntyre, displaying the arrogance that comes from sixteen years in Washington, has chosen to ignore the people."

State Republican Chairman Gerald P. Carmen, a Thomson man, called the speech "the most disgraceful performance from any politician the state of New Hampshire has ever elected."

After Loeb had fully gathered his wits, he struck hard ten days later with a front-page editorial and with a column by former Nixon speechwriter and conservative columnist Pat Buchanan spread across the top of the front page. Buchanan's column, published earlier in the *Boston Herald-American,* criticized my speech, praised New Hampshire's economy under Thomson's governorship, and lauded Loeb's coverage of my speech, asking how many liberal publishers would give conservative critics that kind of coverage. Buchanan asked where I had been when the extremist Left was raising political havoc.

When I first read Buchanan's comments in the *Herald-American* I felt I had to respond. In a letter to the editor I chided Buchanan for neglecting to read the full text of my speech before he leaped to the defense of Loeb and Thomson, pointing out that I *had* discussed the excesses of the extremist Left.

> So when Buchanan asks where I was when the ideological left was on the attack, I can answer that there were times when I was in its line of fire. But I want to tell Mr. Buchanan that unhappy as the extremists of the left have been with me at times, they never called me a traitor to my

country or spewed as vile abuse as I am taking from his friends on the Far Right. Example: "McIntyre, you G——D——traitorous s——of a b——. I hope you live 30 years and have terminal cancer every minute of that time."

And now I would like to put a question to Mr. Buchanan: Where were you, sir, when your friend William Loeb was heaping abuse on your boss, President Nixon, for going to Moscow and Peking? I'll tell you where I was. I was in New Hampshire defending your boss and calling his peacemaking efforts "Mr. Nixon's finest hour."

Where were you, Mr. Buchanan, when your friend Mr. Loeb was calling President Ford "Jerry the Jerk"? And suggesting that Mr. Ford reconsider the virtues of wifebeating after Mrs. Ford's candid interview with Morley Safer? Well, I'll tell you where I was. I was in New Hampshire telling my fellow Democrats that while I disagreed with Mr. Ford's politics and policies, he was a good and decent man and an honorable President. And I was in New Hampshire defending Betty Ford's honesty and praising her courage for making breast cancer surgery a topic of public and life-saving discussion. That's where I was, Mr. Buchanan.

P.S.: I do owe this much to Mr. Buchanan. By quoting the UPI dispatch that described my speech as being delivered in the "unemotional Yankee monotone of a man discussing a tax bill" he makes a laugh of the Loeb-Thomson charge that it was an hysterical outburst on the Senate floor.

But Loeb's editorial that day titled "Crying Tom and the New Right" was no laughing matter.

The Senator is apparently completely unaware of the political storm that is gathering against *both* the Democratic leftists and liberals and the Republican do-nothings. This storm is the result of the indignation of the New Right against the failure of *either* party to address itself to the goal of righting the real problems of our day which are disturbing all sensible Americans.

The New Right is something of which you *should* be frightened, Senator, not for the paranoid reasons that you mention but for the reason that once it is through its formative stage of political organization, no political force in the country will be able to stand in its way. You will see, Senator, the biggest political upheaval in this country. There will be more new faces in the Senate and the House of Representatives and in the White House than you, Senator, ever imagined possible.

There were other *Union Leader* editorials and other statements by Thomson in the days that followed, but on March 18 Loeb strained credulity as even he had not strained it before.

Three days earlier Loeb and I had engaged in a five-minute debate on the canal treaties on ABC's *Good Morning, America* show, with Peter Strauss serving as moderator. In that short time span few debating points could be driven home, and at worst I considered the debate a standoff. But on the eighteenth Loeb ran this front-page editorial titled "Perfect Answer to McIntyre":

"Well, I am a Communist, so I would have to support Senator McIntyre's position on the Panama Canal."

The speaker: A New York taxi driver!

Immediately after the "Good Morning, America" program last Wednesday, the ABC management arranged for two taxi cabs to be waiting to take Senator McIntyre and his aide to the airport to return to Washington and this writer to LaGuardia to return to Boston.

When this writer entered the cab, the driver asked, "Were you on the 'Good Morning, America' show?"

I said, "Yes, but you missed the big fish. If you had been first in line, you would have had the honor of driving Senator McIntyre and his aide to the airport."

The cab driver said, "What was your part on the show this morning?"

This writer replied, "I was debating Senator McIntyre on the issue of whether we should give away the Panama Canal."

"Which side were you on?" asked the driver.

"I was *against* giving up the Panama Canal and Senator McIntyre was *for* giving it up," I said.

"Well, I am a Communist, so I would have to support Senator McIntyre's position on the Panama Canal," he answered.

At that moment, to prove his point, the driver lifted from the seat beside him the Communist newspaper *The Worker*. From that point on to LaGuardia, this writer listened to a long sermon on the virtues of communism and the evils of capitalism. The driver actually was trying to gain citizenship in Communist East Germany and give up his U.S. citizenship. So, there was no question about it—this fellow was a 100 percent 14-carat solid gold Communist. He was quite frank in saying that the United States was *stupid* to give away the Canal, that the Communists would move in whenever they felt like doing so and take over the Canal and, thus, control the capitalistic lifeline.

This writer couldn't help wishing that he could have had this taxi driver on the "Face-Off" segment of the "Good Morning, America" program, because it would not have been necessary to argue with Senator McIntyre and the other fool Senators who want to give away the strategic waterway.

I showed this editorial to a friend and asked him what he thought of it. "I think," he said, "that it would be as impossible to find Loeb's commie cabbie as it was to find the guy who wrote the "Canuck" letter about Ed Muskie."*

* See chapter 11.

CHAPTER 18

"Americans" and "Americanism"

Americanism is a question of principle, of idealism, of character; it is not a matter of birthplace, or creed, or line of descent.
—THEODORE ROOSEVELT

In New Hampshire the public and media discussion of my speech on the Panama Canal treaties and the New Right was short-lived. Four days after I spoke, Meldrim Thomson preempted the headlines by delivering a speech quite as controversial as his earlier remarks about South Africa.

Addressing a John Birch Society regional meeting in Los Angeles, Thomson offered views on "Americans," "Americanism," and U.S. foreign policy that drew a vigorous response from persons more sensitive than the governor to the pride of that substantial portion of New Hampshire's population who are naturalized citizens or second-generation descendants of immigrants . . . and more wary than he of reckless innuendo.

Let me cite from the full text of Thomson's speech those paragraphs that aroused the most controversy.

317

318 THE FEAR BROKERS

Friends, no president in the history of our nation ever before devised and pursued a foreign policy so detrimental to the best interest of America—and so un-American to our Great Heritage, as has the man who strode from the peanut fields of Georgia to the White House!

What has happened in recent decades to this once great land of the brave? Why have we Americans allowed the foreign-born Kissinger, tainted with his old-world ideas . . . to fashion America's foreign policy for eight tragic years? Or why do we now suffer foreign-born Brzezinski, naturalized in 1958 . . . to draw us into the maelstrom of world communism? As far as the kind of officials we allow in our State Department is concerned, we should follow the course said to have been ordered by George Washington in posting guard before a battle—put only Americans on guard tonight. Why, I ask, should we turn over to appeasers and compromisers with communism—men like Kissinger and Brzezinski, whose commitment to the high ideals of America's founding father is as cavalier as the wiles of an alley cat—the direction of the sacred homeland of Washington, Lincoln and Teddy Roosevelt?

Carter's foreign policy is based on an accommodation with communism. It would homogenize the freedom precepts of our founding fathers with the tyranny of the soviets and the inhumanity of Red China to produce the horror show of one-world government. Carter would lead us beside the communist path to national suicide. Surely, in succumbing to Carter's leadership he will lead us into the shadows of the Kremlin forever.[1]

Elsewhere in the speech Thomson cited what he described as an "excellent book" by Anthony Sutton "in which by chapter and verse he [Sutton] pointed out that America was committing national suicide by providing military aid to the Soviet Union."

Sutton correctly noted that all presidential administrations, from that of Woodrow Wilson to that of Richard Nixon, have followed a bipartisan foreign policy of building up the Soviet Union. This policy is censored. It is a policy of national suicide. An update of this statement would have to include Presidents Ford and Carter.[2]

Thomson went on to describe the kind of President he thinks America needs, concluding the litany with this description. "Finally, a man who would get rid of the likes of Kissinger, Brzezinski and Andrew Young and who would offer to pay the fares of all one-worlders to any communist nation on the globe providing they took their un-American ideas with them!"

Toward the close of the speech appeared the following passages, which deserve to be read slowly, sentence by sentence:

Finally, the give-away of our American Canal in Panama reveals the deep commitment of the Carter Administration to bring freedom to an end in the United States by accommodation with communism. President Kennedy gutted the Monroe Doctrine when he through evil purpose or miserable cowardice pulled out of the Bay of Pigs commitment and thereby placed the stamp of approval on Castro's murderous and inhuman regime.

Friends, the Canal issue is the last chance we Americans shall have to preserve our freedom short of catastrophic war. Even if Senators, forgetting the lesson of Washington at Valley Forge, and callously ignoring their responsibility to their people, should ratify these infamous treaties we must not cease our efforts. The issue of the Canal must be taken to the polls this November. Every Senator up for reelection who fails to vote against the treaties must be swept from office as though he were a *Benedict Arnold*.

You and I must not stop there. We must mount the greatest electoral revolution in the history of our nation by sending only *Americans* to Congress, and to our State Houses, and Legislatures. Yes, and on the great tide of public resentment we shall ride the crest of the storm until Carter and all his one-worlders and international bankers are driven from office in 1980. Then, for the first time in decades, shall we walk again humbly before God, proud of our great heritage; and grateful that we can pass on to our children our precious liberty, purified by the sacrifice and blood of all American patriots.[3]

Few readers, I suspect, will need help in identifying what is wrong with these remarks. If only for the honor of my state, however, I want to include some of the responses that came from editors and from political figures in New Hampshire.

The *Keene Evening Sentinel,* for example, found in the speech a "hardly veiled" implication that "American citizens born abroad are not to be entirely trusted when it comes to matters of important national policy." The editorial continued:

> State GOP Chairman Gerald Carmen, gamely trying to mute the meaning of Thomson's words to New Hampshire's large number of foreign-born citizens, says the governor "is without equal in the fair and unbiased way he looks at his fellow human beings."
>
> Why then did Thomson feel it necessary to refer to the ancestry of Brzezinski and Kissinger? There is nothing fair or unbiased in such barefaced innuendos. If there is a common denominator among foreign-born Americans, it is an acute appreciation for the entrenched freedoms of their adopted land. Indeed, in our experience, naturalized citizens seem to take these freedoms more seriously than many native-born.
>
> They know, if Thomson does not, that American citizenship is indivisible.

Commenting on Thomson's suggestion that George Washing-

ton distrusted foreigners, *Portsmouth Herald* editor Ray
Brighton offered the governor a lesson in history.

> What would Washington have done without the services of the Mar-
> quis de Lafayette, a Frenchman; Baron DeKalb, a German; Thaddeus
> Kosciusko, a Pole; Baron von Steuben, a Prussian; or Casimir Pulaski, a
> Pole? They weren't Americans of Thomson's persuasion—White Anglo-
> Saxon Protestants.

And the *Sentinel*, in the editorial already quoted, updated the
lesson, commenting on Thomson's remark that senators who
voted for the canal treaties should be swept from office as
though they were Benedict Arnolds.

> By Thomson's definition, apparently, anyone who supports the Canal
> treaties is unpatriotic, perhaps even dangerous. A list of such "danger-
> ous" people, therefore, would have to include the following backers of
> the treaties: Frank Borman, a former astronaut; George Meany, presi-
> dent of the AFL-CIO; General Lauris Norstad of Dublin, N.H., former
> chief of NATO forces; General Matthew Ridgway, retired Army chief of
> staff; General Maxwell Taylor, former Chairman of the joint chiefs of
> staff; Admiral Elmo Zumwalt, former chief of Naval Operations; John
> Wayne, who needs no introduction; and former President Gerald R.
> Ford.
> That's pretty good company for Benedict Arnold to be keeping. Maybe
> he wasn't such a bad guy after all.

It was not surprising that New Hampshire Democrats, like my
spirited young Senate colleague, John Durkin, Congressman
Norman D'Amours, and others, responded angrily to the
speech. Some Republicans also were appalled, among them
George Roberts, Speaker of the New Hampshire House of Representatives, and House Majority Leader Marshall French. Of
all the comments that made the public record, however, perhaps the most telling was offered by State Representative James
Burchell of Rochester, New Hampshire.

> We must not look upon those with whom we disagree on important
> issues such as the Panama Canal, taxes, nuclear power, or foreign policy
> as incompetent fools, as unpatriotic and certainly not as "un-American,"
> as Thomson would have us do, for his kind of behavior could only lead to
> a destruction of our country's social and political fabric, a fabric in which
> people cooperate with each other, respect the views of others, and ad-
> here to the constitutional policies of the majority.
> As I listen to Governor Thomson's words, I hear faint echoes of a time
> in another country where men of a narrow ideology castigated public of-
> ficials with whom they differed on matters of public policy as traitors and
> unpatriotic; where the virtues of a master race were extolled to the deni-

gration of all who didn't fit into the official concept of a true citizen; where people became so polarized and the social fabric so weakened that they could accept an emerging totalitarian regime. . . . I can only say this to the people of New Hampshire. Please do not allow others to determine for you what is "un-American" and who, by their policies, will "destroy America." For the very people who are so busy telling you these purported great truths are the ones we all have much to fear from.[4]

I have no reason to believe that Meldrim Thomson changed any of his views about Americanism as a result of the drubbing he took over the John Birch Society speech, although he must have sensed that permitting his opinions to become known to non-Birchers had been a mistake.

Indeed, there is a sense in which the speech is unrepresentative of contemporary Rightist rhetoric about Americanism. It is too crude, too nakedly revealing, a throwback, as it were, to the harsh fuming of Far Right splinter groups of an earlier era. Most other New Right leaders would not let the essential arrogance of claiming to speak for America—and to grade the Americanism of others—be seen so clearly. They may be as willing to cultivate the politics of suspicion, but, generally speaking, their tactics are subtler and their language less brazen.

In the present context, however, there is a special usefulness in examining a Birchite speech given by the highest officeholder of a staid New England state. For here the fangs were bared; the passion that infuses New Right chauvinism was on open display. Yes, Thomson's ideas are absurd and his language offensive. *But all evidence indicates that Thomson meant what he said.* There are some who think of the Meldrim Thomsons of our time as calculating, cynical politicians who simply put into practice the counsel of Warren G. Harding: "I don't know much about Americanism, but it's a damned good word with which to carry elections." That judgment is wrong. Today's generation of hyperpatriots are not mere political charlatans; they are bold, resourceful, well-organized, and well-financed, and they are also deadly serious, true and passionate believers.

This is one reason their aspirations are so frightening. The other is the strength of their appeal. The instinct they tap is not just a regional or passing aberration, but a timeless, universal human failing. It is a disease that is latent in nearly all of us; or, more accurately, a vice to which any of us can be tempted.

I speak of chauvinism, of course. In moments of detachment

we all recognize what it is and the tragedies it has wrought in human history. It may have been Napoleon's personal megalomania, for example, that goaded him into his insane march on Moscow, but it was the force of chauvinism that persuaded the soldiers and the people of France to support his endless, bloody adventuring. Early in this century it was the superheated nationalism rampant in Europe that prepared the way for the mass slaughter of the Great War. Then, too, Hitler's talk of Aryan supremacy appealed as strongly to nationalist pride as it did to racial hatred, and it worked its evil consequences in a nation as sophisticated and theretofore civilized as any in previous history. And sadly, it must be added, it was an uncritical, unreflective, push-button chauvinism that helped launch our own misoriented crusade in Vietnam and then to prolong it past all reason.

One must ask why it is that chauvinism still flourishes even though we know the agonies it has brought and the still greater horrors it could bring about today. One reason is that it draws its force from elements that are seemingly natural to human beings, or that are, at least, deeply rooted in our cultural heritage.

Almost without exception, we are all subject—to a greater or lesser extent—to xenophobia: the *unreasoning* suspicion, fear, and hatred of strangers (and, by extension, of different customs or contrasting ideas). Xenophobia differs not only in intensity, but even in kind from prudent caution. Of all human emotions it may be the one most easily roused by purposeful demagogues.

We are subject also to the appeal of group egotism. In our culture it is not thought seemly to believe (much less to assert) one's *personal* superiority. Only a free spirit like Muhammad Ali can boast openly, "I am *the* Greatest!"—and even Ali does it with a twinkle in his eye. Group egotism is a way, then, to disguise personal egotism and make it acceptable. "Americans are the greatest, strongest, richest, cleverest people of all time." Not said, but meant: "I just happen to be one of them."

Group egotism, to be sure, has its relatively harmless and/or amusing forms: the rivalry between Yale and Harvard (from my point of view the less-famous rivalry between Dartmouth and Harvard is the more pertinent), between Eastsiders and Westsiders in Manhattan, between New York and the rest of the country, between the life-styles of, say, California and New England.

But group egotism has its virulent, poisonous side as well. In a realistic view of human nature, that is not surprising; it is, after all, a way by which to meet real needs of the deprived ego. As the experience of the human race demonstrates, such needs go unsatisfied among great numbers of people, in this culture and this country as in any other. The human quest for personal reassurance and recognized status is a force as powerful in its sphere as nuclear energy is in the realm of physics.

The political relevance of all this is clear. Xenophobes—people who *need* enemies—and people who can assure themselves of their own worth only by exaggerating it are the natural targets of professional chauvinists who are themselves victims of the same failings and are therefore willing to feed and channel factionalism, distrust, strife, and polarization. I hope this book has shown that the skillful agitators who comprise the leadership of the New Right are engaged in precisely these kinds of activities.

What is to be done about it? How can liberals and moderates —and, for that matter, genuine conservatives—counter the powerful appeal of New Right chauvinism? What is to be said about Americanism? I offer not a program, and I hope not mere pious preachment. I offer only warnings—and a principle.

The first warning is a repetition of a thought expressed previously: This is a deadly serious matter. It is precisely because we truly are a rich and powerful nation that we can't *afford* to be chauvinists. More directly, we have weapons in our arsenal that can blow up the world; our potential enemies have a matching set. In this circumstance, reckless efforts to stir up nationalist fervor not only endanger our national interests, *they betray humanity.*

The second warning is directed to those who share my distaste and distrust of New Right flag-waving. Chauvinism, it must be remembered, is a vice that looks like a virtue, or, more precisely, it is (like many other vices) an exaggeration of a virtue. We are not cosmic spirits. We are flesh and blood human beings with natural, unbreakable ties to familiar places, customs, faces—to our families, our ethnic "clans," our native land. Granted, personal, ethnic, and national loyalties are readily abused. But in themselves they are cohesive and creative forces. Surely no people, including Americans, should make their nation into icon or idol. But, just as surely, it is *not* corny to love America.

As for Americanism, the principle I suggest is simple: the less said the better. Instead of competing with the New Right in defining what it is, we would be better advised to define America as a land where no doctrinaire political "isms" of *any* breed are comfortably at home. The best elements of our political heritage do not constitute an ideology, much less an orthodoxy.[5] The founders of this nation did not concoct a new religion; on the contrary, they avoided even the semblance of such an effort. Our Constitution is not a creed; it is only a set of (admirably balanced) working rules for effective, but limited government. It contains no definition of Americanism—and no Johnny-come-lately has the authority to impose one now.

CHAPTER 19

Conclusion

*There will always be dissident voices heard in the
land, pressing opposition without alternatives,
finding fault but never favor, perceiving gloom on
every side and seeking influence without
responsibility. These voices are inevitable. But
today other voices are heard in the land—voices
preaching doctrines wholly unrelated to
reality . . . doctrines which apparently assume
that words will suffice without weapons, that
vituperation is as good as victory and that peace
is a sign of weakness. . . . We cannot expect that
everyone, to use a phrase of a decade ago, will
"talk sense to the American people." But we can
hope that fewer Americans will listen to
nonsense. And the notion that this nation is
headed for defeat through deficit, or that strength
is a matter of slogans, is nothing but just plain
nonsense.*

—From the speech JOHN
F. KENNEDY was to
deliver in Dallas the day
he was assassinated

325

It seems appropriate to begin this concluding chapter with some reflections about my own role and posture in this struggle.

The office of U.S. senator confers power, perquisites, and privileges. This combination also creates certain occupational hazards, not the least of which is the temptation to take oneself too seriously. In constitutional terms, one senator commands exactly one one-hundredth of the power of the Senate, but majority votes are made by adding one to one to one to one, until fifty-plus-one "Ayes" or "Nays" have been gathered to enact or defeat a given legislative proposal.

This means that in certain dramatic circumstances the vote of one senator can determine the spending or the withholding of tens of billions of dollars; can approve or strike down bills affecting crucial issues of foreign policy; can affect the prices everyone must pay for bread and toasters, for gasoline and automobiles, for roof shingles and whole houses; can influence the way in which a police officer on a beat and the President in the Oval Office carry on their jobs.

Less dramatically but more importantly, senators help shape legislation at earlier stages of the process, in caucuses and in committees, on these and other issues, and they defend the rights and explain the needs of constituents in everyday relations with the executive branch.

One consequence of all this is that senators get a great deal of attention, much of it meant to be flattering, and as a result are tempted to take a somewhat too solemn view of their own significance in the affairs of humanity.

My awareness of this temptation does not at all mean that I have successfully resisted it in writing this book; the Senate is no place to develop a spare prose style, devoid of inflated rhetoric. If there are passages that offend on these grounds, I beg the reader's indulgence.

I ask to be judged on substance. I am convinced that in this book I have not been "viewing with alarm" out of professional habit; I believe I am talking about something real. There *are* "fear brokers" among us, and it is important that they be recognized for what they are.

There is a paradox here, of course. This book attacks alarmists and suspicion-mongers. In response it can easily be said (and will be said) that I have engaged in the very practices I condemn—that I am myself a broker of fear.

Although I can anticipate that charge, there is no way I can rebut it on my own behalf. It will be for the reader to examine the weight of the evidence, to judge the reliability of the sources, to measure the validity and persuasiveness of the argument—always, I hope, balancing these qualities against those exhibited in the generous samplings from New Right materials contained in these pages.

But let me complicate the task a little further.

In politics—considered here not as the tactics of winning elections, but rather as the art of governance—there are no mathematical certainties, no axioms that can be demonstrated with the clarity of a principle from Euclidean geometry. Even in the natural sciences the most rigorous experiment can establish the truth of a theory only with a certain tentativeness, for it is always possible that one day another theory will be devised that will explain the data better. It is important to understand that there is no true science of politics that offers either mathematical precision or even the tentative certitude of chemistry and physics. Always one is dealing with too many factual unknowns and too many human variables.

That makes all of us fallible. If fifty million Frenchmen *can* be wrong, so can two hundred million Americans; and so can sixty-seven senators. The senators who voted to ratify the canal treaties, then, cannot *prove* that they acted in the best interests of the country, any more than they can *demonstrate* their subjective intention to do so.

These considerations may appear to undermine my own thesis. Not so. Consider this too-familiar analogy for the precarious situation of the American people in the late twentieth century: We are all passengers in a lifeboat on a stormy sea. Nobody *knows* how to reach land and safety. None of us even has a sure *method* of setting the best course.

In that situation the presence of a faction willing to factionalize the rest of us—willing, out of fanatical confidence in its own solution, to heighten our fears and play upon our temptation toward panic—is a great danger to all. Our best resources are reason, mutual trust, determined calm, and disciplined following of our inherited, tested processes for accommodating differences and pulling together. Such methods don't always work, but they work better than fright-mongering and harassment.

The analogy fails in one respect: Most people in a tiny vessel on a tossing ocean would gladly put their trust in a single, knowledgeable authority figure. That's not appropriate, desirable, or workable in a democratic nation. The very point of America is that our system lets all of us have a voice in shaping our personal and national destinies.

It follows that everybody, bar none, has a right to be heard. That right can be abused, as I believe it has been by the leadership of the New Right. But abuses of free speech should not (with very limited exceptions) abrogate its continued exercise. If I want no Americanist orthodoxy interpreted and enforced by the New Right, neither do I support any other exclusionary version of democracy.

Oliver Wendell Holmes properly cautioned that "if there is any principle of the Constitution that more imperatively calls for attachment than any other, it is the principle of free thought —*not* free thought for those who *agree* with us—but freedom for the thought that we hate." Thomas Jefferson put it another way: "For God's sake let us freely hear both sides."

Any attempt to muzzle the New Right, to coerce its silence, would be to emulate its own practices, to flout the First Amendment, and to commit, in my view, a costly political error.

What, then, is to be done? There are two broad necessities. One is a project of political education of a kind that is implicit in the very purpose of this book. The other is concerted action against those conditions in our society that most favor the growth of the New Right.

In very large part, political awareness and sophistication mean the ability to make distinctions, to see differences that are really there. Republican Senator Mark Hatfield made a contribution to that kind of awareness when he took the floor just moments after I concluded my speech on the Panama Canal treaties and the New Right. He acknowledged that on certain issues—abortion, common-situs picketing, public financing of senatorial elections—he had adopted positions very unpopular with liberals, and that on other issues he had offended the Radical Left—people who identified themselves as Communists, Socialists, or Marxists. These critics, he implied, had made their displeasure known in vigorous terms. And yet, he said, "in all of my communications on these and other subjects I have seldom received letters that spew forth such a venom of hatred as I have received from within this group now called the Radical Right who so violently oppose the Panama Canal treaties."

Along with venom came hyperpatriotism: "They want to have the American flag wrapped around their viewpoint. I have a few letters with me today which are replete with phrases like, 'A vote for support of the treaty is an act of treason.' 'You are a traitor for having indicated your support of the treaty.' 'You are not an American.'"

Besides identifying their own views with Americanism, the senator noted, the Radical Rightists tend to "baptize" their own judgments by making them a test of religious orthodoxy: "'I thought you were a born-again Christian.'" Such people, he said, "do not bother to ask my view of Jesus Christ in an effort to reach some determination of my salvation. Instead, they chose to make a judgment on my religious salvation on the basis of my position regarding the Panama Canal treaty."

Finally, Senator Hatfield registered his concern over another "unsettling" characteristic of the mail he had received: "This horrible cancerous disease of anti-Semitism. . . . Here is a letter: 'Vote against the Panama Canal Treaty. The Jew bankers in New York can go to hell. . . . Don't bail out the Rockefellers and Kike bankers. I am tired of Jew interests.'"

I have already acknowledged that some of today's Radical Right leaders appear to be personally free of the virus of anti-Semitism, and I have mentioned that in much of my own mail from persons clearly associated with the Far Right the note of anti-Semitism either is not present at all or else is muted through the use of such code phrases as "international bankers."

With that understood, I conclude on the basis of my own experience, Senator Hatfield's, and that of others that although anti-Semitism is not an essential ingredient of today's Radical Right in America, neither is it truly antithetical to the spirit of the movement. My research for this book did not uncover evidence that the New Right is building its crusade on hatred of Jews. But neither did it find evidence of any concerted effort *against* anti-Semitism. And there are abundant signs that people who are attracted to anti-Semitism are comfortably at home with other New Right manifestations—with its fanatic chauvinism, its inflammatory rhetoric, its divisive tactics.

Thirty-five years ago a man who wrote under the pseudonym

John Roy Carlson published *Under Cover*, a book about the four years he spent in the Nazi underworld of America. It became a best-seller.[1] On the basis of his experience, Carlson constructed a list of checkpoints to test the inherent fascism of a given political movement. One of these criteria was the presence of anti-Semitism, used as a sort of lye to help dissolve the social fabric. Others were superpatriotism to arouse emotion; a perverted brand of nationalism, using such slogans as "America First" and "America for Americans"; an unrelenting effort to undermine confidence in government, couched in hostile, accusatory terms; defamation of democracy by exaggerating its failings; the pitting of group against group to break down national unity; the use of half-truths to gain the support of the politically ignorant.

Such criteria are not applied with the ease or precision of a yardstick laid against a piece of lumber. Over a generation, styles change, skills grow, seemingly novel issues rise. Is the New Right a new native fascism? If one considers that overt and virulent anti-Semitism is of the essence of fascism, the answer would seem to be "No." But perhaps the label doesn't matter all that much. What Carlson was talking about was not merely a word; he was identifying a dangerously destructive political philosophy that can take many forms. I think that philosophy persists and—for all the reasons given in this book I believe it has a perennial appeal in this country.*

Since we are engaged in the making of political distinctions, it will be useful to note here some reasons why Left-leaning radicalism, in contrast with the Far Right, has not sunk deep roots in the American body politic.

As noted before, until I entered public life my own personal apprehensions about domestic political extremism were focused on the Left. As a Catholic and as a product of the cultural fundamentalism of home-town America, fear of Communism and socialism came naturally and was reinforced by the tensions of the Cold War.

This mind-set, common among millions of Americans of my time, not only tended to blind me to the threat from the political Right, but also to obscure the essential reality that the threat from the Left was far more *external* than *internal*.

---

* See especially chapter 9.

Historically, Communism and socialism have not made deep inroads into the American system.

> Historians have suggested a welter of reasons for the fact that social-ism has been a failure in America: the mainstream of American labor saw radicalism as a threat, not an ally; the large Catholic bloc in America's immigrant working class regarded radicalism as a breach of religious faith; the government made periodic repressive moves against radicals —the strike-breaking troops in 1877, the Palmer raids of 1919, the jailing of communists after World War II, the harassing of radicals with Con-gressional investigations. There are simpler explanations as well; the endless sectarian battles on the Left, the repellent subservience of too many radicals to the Soviet Union, the adaptability of the two-party sys-tem in America, the high standard of living available to most Americans.[2]

But the biggest hurdle for the Left to overcome in America—and the reason it has not succeeded—lies in Americans' basic attitude about America itself. "A nation believing itself limit-lessly rich has no need of collective or communal enterprise, much less government nurturing of scarce resources."[3]

These brief comments, both my own and those I have bor-rowed from others, do not of themselves constitute an adequate kit of tools for the testing of political movements. I hope, how-ever, that they will prove helpful to readers and that they will encourage others to pursue the analysis further.

We do need help. Early in this book I said I did not share the fear that the growth of our problems had outstripped our capac-ity to solve them, but that I am alarmed by our fading capacity to cope with one another. Obviously the two are linked. Even though I do not believe the New Right will ever prevail in America, I do fear its rising influence. Its inflammatory practices and simplistic appeals can delay or obstruct the resolution of issues that can spell the life or death of this nation, and—I speak without hyperbole—of our civilization.

As a member of the Senate Armed Services Committee, for example, I am privy to the most professional assessments of our nation's capacity to defend itself . . . and the capacity of our adversaries to destroy us. Maintaining security while seeking every honorable means of reaching an arms limitation agree-ment will require the most demanding level of reason, pru-dence, restraint, and diplomacy, especially under the psychic pressure of the Soviet arms buildup and adventuring in Africa.

It is one thing for the New Right to exploit highly emotional, but essentially personal, issues. The gathering signs that the movement will now begin to exploit issues like SALT II in the same reckless manner fills me with dread.

The same critical need for intense application of intelligence, for respecting facts, and for public restraint is evident in the entire field of foreign affairs from Western Europe to the Middle East, from Africa to Korea—and in the resolution of our stubborn domestic problems of energy, employment, and the economy.

It is disturbing that even while we apply ourselves to these matters, we must also guard our flanks, as it were, against assaults that undermine the very process in which we are engaged. Yet, it is necessary.

I said earlier that besides persistent efforts toward public identification and refutation of the New Right ideas, we must also take substantive action against conditions that especially favor the growth of the New Right.

It may be surprising that my choice of the first order of business in this realm has to do not with political principle (not, at least, on the surface), but with economics. If we are to combat the frustration and anxiety upon which the New Right feeds, we must mount an *effective* program against inflation. I am not an economist, and in any case, this is not the place to argue the merits of specific anti-inflationary measures. I want only to make two points:

First, that inflation has vastly dangerous social and political effects, beyond the suffering it inflicts on individuals; and second, that resisting inflation is not only or even primarily a matter of making correct technical choices. It also demands moral courage and political wisdom—not only from the President and the Congress, but from every person and group whose decisions and attitudes affect the economy: union leaders and members, management executives, merchants, bankers, environmentalist and consumer advocates, financiers, shareholders—all of us who buy and sell, who rent or own, who live off pensions or interest or dividends, or who earn wages and salaries.

In *The Enemies of Society* Paul Johnson has brilliantly spelled out the profound effects of "hyperinflation," which he describes as "a voracious moral corruption eating out the heart of society."

It [inflation] is the very antithesis of the communal ideal. Where social morality teaches us to see ourselves as part of a whole, members of a human society based on comradeship, mutual help, friendliness, trust, magnanimity and hope in the future, inflation sets group against group and makes self-interest the guiding principle of life. It makes money seem the only social nexus and the only criterion of well-being. It forces on all of us the aggressive posture of comparative envy. It turns money and its ever-changing value into the chief preoccupation not only of the miser and the banker but of every human being, the dominant topic of conversation, the source of all anecdotes, the ever-present nagging worry behind every plan and move.[4]

In a briefer treatment of a similar theme, Henry C. Wallich, a member of the Board of Governors of the Federal Reserve Board, said:

Inflation has ended the dollar's role as a trustworthy measure of values. Dealings and contracts based on the dollar have become deceptive. This is not simply a cause of economic injury. It is a moral as well as an economic issue. Without honest money our economic dealings will be neither efficient nor even honest. . . .

Inflation is like a country where nobody speaks the truth. It introduces an element of deceit into all our economic dealings. . . . Inflation is a means by which the strong can more effectively exploit the weak. The strategically positioned and well-organized can gain at the expense of the unorganized and the aged.[5]

I have said that inflation is an enormous *moral* challenge. The reasons are evident. Successful measures against inflation will ask a degree of enlightened self-interest that is difficult to summon up in our intensely competitive society, in which the interests of so many and diverse economic blocs at least *appear* to be pitted against one another. Inflation is a drama in which we all have roles, in which we see all other characters as villains, ourselves the only heroes. Almost everybody wants inflation to go away; almost nobody is willing to take any blame for its ravages or to fall behind in the race against it or to suffer the pains of dislocation that may be necessary to defeat it. And all this is true not only within our own economy, but in relations with other nations.

For the sake of concreteness, I will consider briefly—without passing judgment on its merits—the thesis argued for some years by Seymour Melman of Columbia University, who finds the economic effects of the arms race a primary source of inflation. The reason is not only the sheer size of the defense budget and the contribution it makes to the federal deficit, nor is it only the effect on our balance of payments of the sums spent for defense overseas. There are other factors at work.

First, Melman argues, the military goods, like tanks or missiles, we produce—apart from the relatively small proportion sold abroad—are simply withdrawn from the U.S. economy. They are not properly considered consumer goods, nor are they productive of new wealth, like machine tools or steel mills. None of the tax money spent to produce military goods is spent to buy the goods produced; it is simply freed in the marketplace to bid up the price of *other* goods and services.

Second, there is the mode of production. In practice, and despite safeguards, most defense contracts turn out to be cost-plus. The military economy is unlike the civilian economy in that the one customer for military hardware, the Pentagon, is far more concerned with performance than with cost, and to assure high-quality performance, costs are allowed to creep up (or zoom up) inexorably. This has powerful inflationary effects on the *civilian* economy, for the makers of consumer goods are in competition with the hundreds upon thousands of defense contractors for supplies and for the services of engineers, technicians, and administrators. Their costs (and therefore their prices) zoom upward accordingly.

The final effect Melman cites is related to the previous one. Because between a third and a half of all American engineers and applied scientists (Melman's estimate) are engaged in military research, this country is falling behind in technological innovations that improve either the quality of civilian products or the productivity of the labor force or both. (Melman believes the spillover effect of military research on civilian production is overrated.) American ingenuity has not diminished, but so much of it is devoted to research and development of weapons that we no longer compete on favorable terms with other industrial nations, such as Japan and West Germany, in producing for the consumer or in the manufacture of machine goods.

For the sake of the larger argument, let us suppose (without examining it more closely) that Melman's thesis is accurate— that the size and character of our defense spending are principal factors in inflation. Or, better, imagine that Melman and his associates, debating the issue before a panel of disinterested and competent judges, could establish the truth of their analysis.

Here is the point: What I have just suggested is not possible. Quite apart from the foreign-policy implications of the Melman program—in other words, considering only the economic aspects and not the need for adequate weaponry—there simply *is* no such panel. All of us, including the most distinguished academic analysts residing in ivory towers, have interests at stake in any debate about inflation.

That becomes painfully clear in every congressional action on the defense budget, for example, when it often seems that the need for defense-related jobs in localities across the land has at least as much effect on the final decision as do the requests from the Department of Defense. Even the most gradual and carefully planned conversion to civilian production imposes dislocations on workers and management alike and creates uncertainties for lenders and investors that few would welcome.

This is but one illustration, chosen almost at random, of how the "truth" about inflation, if it is available, will be resisted when it is translated into a program. To acknowledge this immense difficulty, however, is not in the least to diminish the importance of facing up to it courageously, cooperatively, and with real commitment. Inflation is truly the enemy of our society.

> It makes the young predatory, the middle-aged mean and acquisitive, the old fearful. It penalizes not just the poor, the old, the sick and the weak, but the decent, the diffident, the unselfish, the reasonable, the temperate, the fair-minded, the loyal and the generous. It allows the social mood to be determined by the rapacious, the unscrupulous, the antisocial and the bully. Uncontrolled inflation creates a world of blind materialism, where ideals cannot be realized, where force, power and selfishness are the only dynamics, and where charity is dead.[6]

One could hardly prepare a better soil for the growth of the New Right.

If dampening the flames of inflation is the first priority in weakening the appeal of the New Right, then, in my judgment, strengthening the two major political parties is the second.

In John Roy Carlson's words, written thirty-five years ago: "I would dread to see in America the victory of a force either from the extreme Left or extreme Right. I hope Americans will remain middle-of-the-road Democrats and Republicans, and that these two parties will keep fighting bitterly at election time and become firm friends after the battle."[7]

In my speech on the canal treaties and the New Right, I addressed the debilitation of the two-party system.

> More and more Americans appear unwilling to abide by the essential ethic of the party system—that willingness to tolerate differing views within the party, and to accept the party platform however unpalatable some of its provisions, in order to advance a general political philosophy. As a result, the traditional role of the parties is slowly being usurped by a thousand and one passionately committed special interest, splinter faction, and single-issue constituencies.

In this kind of balkanized political milieu, the electorate is not only left confused, but the purposeful course of government is disrupted by distraction.

This appeal must be directed, of course, not only to the general public, but to practicing politicians of both parties, whether in office or in the party apparatus or in other positions of influence. Both parties can be (and have been) faulted for recent failures of courage—the Democrats particularly on Vietnam, the Republicans on Watergate. In both cases the fault was in part a failure of true party loyalty, for instead of remaining faithful to principles of party there was an inclination to substitute loyalty to persons in power. When that happens, the usefulness of the party system is eroded; the parties exist to serve the country and not the other way around.

The two-party system, while it is not of the essence of constitutional government in this country, has served us long and well, and we must attend to its preservation. That requires both discipline and intelligence, and it also depends on that same comity of which I have spoken. David Broder wrote in his classic study of the decline of the two major parties:

> The party system is essentially a device for making choices between candidates and programs, and for enabling those who prevail at the polls to seek to put their policies into action. It is a way of expressing choice; and choice implies division, which will be ever present in a large and diverse nation like ours. But, for the two-party system to work, there must be not only division but large areas of agreement. There must be agreement on the rules of the game, so that losers accept defeat and winners do not attempt to abuse the advantage of victory. There must also be a high degree of agreement on the values and goals the society cherishes, so that political defeat does not seem to carry intolerable penalties for the losers. A party system must reflect the political community it serves, and when that community loses its sense of identity, the party system cannot fabricate one for it.

> Whether we Americans still retain a vision of ourselves as one people, one continent-sized community, is the ultimate question. And that is a question beyond politics.[8]

I believe we *do* retain that vision. There is evidence of that inherent unity and good will in the "brief and shining moment" of the Bicentennial Celebration and in the universal tribute paid to Hubert Humphrey at the time of his passing.

I therefore believe that we can have our political differences and still retain our unity, and that is why I make what appears on the surface to be a paradoxical appeal for more political partisanship *and* more political civility.

I have written much about the abusive and divisive politics practiced by the Radical Right in my home state of New Hampshire, but there is another side to this picture that may serve to resolve the seeming paradox alluded to in the previous paragraph.

For many years my senior colleague from New Hampshire was Senator Norris Cotton, a conservative Republican. We differed on virtually every major political issue of our time, yet we worked in close and compatible harness for New Hampshire and we became fast friends.

One warm, sunny day in the summer of 1977, Norris Cotton, by then retired, performed an act of friendship and political grace so unusual it caught the attention of *The New York Times*.

> Norris Cotton, the retired Senator from New Hampshire, is one of the staunchest Republicans extant, but he values his friendship with Senator Thomas J. McIntyre, a Democrat, so highly that he attended a fund-raising dinner for Mr. McIntyre's reelection campaign. This was in spite of the fact that Governor Meldrim Thomson had indicated he may try to unseat Mr. McIntyre. Explaining his presence at the fund-raiser, Mr. Cotton paraphrased Thomas Jefferson: "I never considered a difference of opinion in politics, in religion, in philosophy, as cause for withdrawing from a friend. I haven't a better friend, a closer friend, in this world than Tom McIntyre."

That is the way American politics *ought* to be practiced.

I believe we ought to deal directly and intelligently with what is perhaps the principal weapon in the armamentarium of the New Right: its distorted version of patriotism. I have discussed in a previous chapter why chauvinism has a universal and timeless appeal; the more reason why we need to resist it

within ourselves as well as in doing combat with the hyperpatriots. I find it unfortunate when political leaders of liberal or
moderate persuasion, in order to respond to pressure from the
Right, *adopt* New Right slogans instead of exposing their shal-
lowness and explaining the danger they create.

It is altogether too important to some Americans to believe
that we are "the No. 1 nation in the world" and that we are
going to stay that way. But what does the slogan *mean?* Many
nations are "No. 1" in the world in one way or another: Nepal,
for example, in the height of its mountains, Switzerland in the
manufacture of watch movements, Saudi Arabia in oil reserves,
and Idi Amin's Uganda in sheer brainless terror.

It is simply a fact that the United States is economically the
richest and militarily the most powerful nation in the world. It is
a fact so obvious that it hardly needs to be spoken, least of all by
us; that is behavior characteristic of schoolyard bullies constantly in need of reassuring themselves, rather, than of gentle
giants, who are conscious of their strength and equally conscious of the responsibilities it confers.

There is a further consideration. The first necessity of political wisdom is to be in touch with reality. Today's reality is not
that of 1789, when America was a young, struggling nation
largely isolated from the world. Neither is the present reality
that of 1945, when the United States was triumphant in war and
largely untouched by its physical ravages, when virtually every
other major nation was largely in ruins and heavily in debt, and
when this country was the sole possessor of the atom bomb. At
that time neither any single power nor any possible combination of powers could have challenged us.

We live now in a vastly different reality, a truly multipolar
world. That need not be a disaster for us. Is it not a more nearly
normal state of affairs than the one it replaced? To be an impe-
rial power ought not be our national goal; given our history, our
political principles, and our national character, we should be
uncomfortable in such a role. It may be granted that the present
situation is more dangerous for us; again, the more reason we
should speak softly and hope that one day our big stick can be
laid aside.

Our new situation does not require bluster. Instead it asks
from us a spirit of cooperation with our allies, of responsibility
toward those who depend upon us for aid and/or protection, of

watchfulness toward our potential adversaries—watchfulness not only of the threat they pose, but of any meaningful signals they may give of moving away from the shared insanity of "Mutual Assured Destruction" toward reliable guarantees of peaceful competition.

My final recommendation returns to the main theme of this book: that we must confront the New Right with courage and boldness.

The New Right must *not* be allowed to intimidate responsible citizens. They must *not* be allowed to use their perverted brand of Americanism to frighten other Americans into silence.

They must be confronted and challenged and questioned at every turn. They must be made *accountable.*

For inspiration I suggest we turn to the words of two of the most decent Americans who ever competed for the Presidency —Dwight David Eisenhower and Adlai Ewing Stevenson.

"I don't think the United States needs super-patriots," said Dwight Eisenhower. "We need patriotism, honestly practiced by all of us. And we *don't* need those people who are more 'patriotic' than you or anybody else."

Speaking before a national American Legion Convention in New York City on August 27, 1952, Adlai Stevenson said:

> There are [those] among us who use "patriotism" as a club. . . . What can we say for the self-styled patriot who thinks that a Negro, a Jew, a Catholic or a Japanese-American is *less* an American than he [or she]? That betrays the deepest article of our faith, the belief in individual liberty and equality which has always been at the heart and soul of the American idea.

Had Stevenson delivered this speech in recent years, he would, no doubt, have used more inclusive language. Nevertheless, some of his words are particularly appropriate to the theme of this book:

> It was always accounted a virtue in a man to love his country. With us it is now something more than a virtue. It is a necessity, a condition of survival. When an American says he loves his country, he means not only that he loves the New England hills, the prairies glistening in the sun, the wide and rising plains, the great mountains and the sea.
>
> He means that he loves an inner air, an inner light in which freedom lives and in which a man can draw a breath of self-respect. Men who have offered their lives for their country know that patriotism is not the *fear* of something; it is the *love* of something.

And so it is.

Notes

Author's Note

1. Sinclair Lewis, *It Can't Happen Here* (Garden City, N.Y.: Doubleday, 1935).
2. See Richard Hofstadter, *The Paranoid Style in American Politics and Other Essays* (New York: Knopf, 1965); Daniel Bell, ed., *The Radical Right: The New American Right* (Garden City, N.Y.: Doubleday, 1964); Theodore W. Adorno et al., *The Authoritarian Personality* (New York: W.W. Norton, 1969).

Part I—Introduction

1. Jacob Bronowski, *The Ascent of Man* (Boston: Little, Brown, 1973), p. 367 (italics added).
2. Ibid.

Chapter 1: Target: Home-town America

1. Andrew Kopkind, *New Times*, September 3, 1977.
2. Richard Hofstadter, *The Paranoid Style in American Politics and Other Essays* (New York: Knopf, 1965).
3. Joseph R. Gusfield, *Symbolic Crusade: Status Politics and the American Temperance Movement* (Urbana, Ill.: University of Illinois Press, 1963).
4. Hofstadter, *The Paranoid Style in American Politics*, op. cit., pp. 87–88. Used by permission.
5. Michael Novak, *Washington Star*, October 10, 1976.
6. Magda Denes, *In Necessity and Sorrow: Life and Death in an Abortion Hospital* (New York: Basic Books, 1976).

Chapter 2: Sharp Turn to the Right?

1. Howard Phillips, *Wall Street Journal*, May 29, 1975.
2. Marquis Childs, *Washington Post*, June 15, 1978.
3. Wesley McCune, *Group Research Report*, March 29, 1978.
4. *A Citizens Guide to the Right Wing*, Americans for Democratic Action, Spring 1978.
5. *Washington Post*, April 3, 1978.
6. *Washington Post*, July 3, 1978.

Chapter 3: Something's Stirring

1. David Broder, *Washington Post*, June 21, 1978.
2. Everett Carll Ladd Jr., "The Democrats Have Their Own Two-Party System," *Fortune*, October 1977, pp. 212–26. Courtesy of Fortune Magazine. Used by permission of author.
3. Ibid.
4. Ibid.
5. Ibid.
6. Ibid.
7. Richard Hofstadter, *The Paranoid Style in American Politics and Other Essays* (New York: Knopf, 1965), p. viii. Used by permission.
8. Ibid., p. ix.
9. Lloyd A. Free and Hadley Cantril, *The Political Beliefs of Americans: A Study of Public Opinion* (New Brunswick, N.J.: Rutgers University Press, 1967).
10. "Arch-Conservative's Crusade: Abolish the Republican Party," *Washington Star*, June 24, 1975.
11. Ladd, "The Democrats Have Their Own Two-Party System," op. cit.
12. Ibid.
13. *Washington Star*, June 24, 1975.
14. Broder, *Washington Post*, June 21, 1978.
15. Ibid.
16. Ibid.

Chapter 4: The New Right—Substance and Strategy

1. William J. Lanouette, "The New Right—'Revolutionaries' Out After the 'Lunch-Pail' Vote," *National Journal*, January 21, 1978, pp. 88–92. Used by permission of *National Journal*, copyright owner.
2. Ibid.
3. *Washington Star*, June 23, 1975.
4. Wesley McCune, *Viewpoint*, Vol. 8, No. 2 (2d quarter), 1978. Used by permission.
5. Ibid.
6. Ibid.
7. Seymour Martin Lipset and Earl Raab, *The Politics of Unreason* (New York: Harper & Row, 1970), p. 110.

8. McCune, *Viewpoint,* op. cit.

9. Ibid.

10. Dale Kramer, "The American Fascists," *Harper's Magazine,* September 1940.

11. McCune, *Viewpoint,* op. cit.

12. Ibid.

13. D.W. Brogan, "The Illusion of American Omnipotence," *Harper's Magazine,* December 1952, pp. 21–28.

14. Richard Hofstadter, *The Paranoid Style in American Politics and Other Essays* (New York: Knopf, 1965), pp. 132–33. Used by permission.

15. Ibid., pp. 96–97.

16. Ibid., p. 128.

17. Ibid., p. 129.

18. Ibid., pp. 106–7.

19. Scott Wolf, *Democratic Viewpoint,* February 1978. Used by permission.

20. Ibid.

21. *Ripon Forum,* December 1977.

22. Lanouette, "The New Right," op. cit.

23. *Democratic Congressional Campaign Committee Report,* December 1977.

24. *Group Research Report,* February 28, 1977.

25. *Washington Star,* June 23, 1975.

26. *Democratic Congressional Campaign Committee Report,* December 1977.

27. *Washington Star,* June 23, 1975.

28. *A Citizens Guide to the Right Wing,* Americans for Democratic Action, Spring 1978.

29. *The New York Times,* December 4, 1977.

30. Ibid.

31. Lanouette, "The New Right," op. cit.

32. *A Citizens Guide to the Right Wing,* op. cit.

Chapter 5: Tactics and Techniques

1. From Philip Crane's column, "Chairman's Comment," in the American Conservation Union's magazine *Battle Line,* March 1978.

2. Excerpted by permission from an article by William Schneider in the July/August 1978 issue of *Politics Today.* © 1978 by Politics Today, Inc.

3. Ibid.

4. Ibid.

5. Ibid.

6. *The New York Times,* July 19, 1978.

7. "Viguerie: Into Politics by the 'Back Door,'" *Washington Star,* June 23, 1975.

8. Ibid.

9. William J. Lanouette, "The New Right—'Revolutionaries' Out After the 'Lunch-Pail' Vote," *National Journal*, January 21, 1978, pp. 88–92. Used by permission of *National Journal*, copyright owner.

10. Ibid.

11. Ibid.

12. "The Godfather of the 'New Right' Feels the Torch Is Passing," *Washington Star*, June 23, 1975.

13. Ibid.

14. Jules Witcover, *Marathon* (New York: Viking Press, 1977).

15. Christopher Buchanan, "New Right: 'Many Times More Effective' Now," *Congressional Quarterly*, December 24, 1977, pp. 2649–53.

16. *The New York Times*, December 4, 1977.

17. "The Godfather of the 'New Right,'" op. cit.

18. Ibid.

19. Lanouette, "The New Right," op. cit.

20. "The Godfather of the 'New Right,'" op. cit.

21. Lanouette, "The New Right," op. cit.

22. In William J. Lanouette, "The Panama Canal Treaties—Playing in Peoria and in the Senate," *National Journal*, October 8, 1977, pp. 1556–62. Used by permission of *National Journal*, copyright owner.

Chapter 6: Religion and the Far Right—Salvational vs. Social Gospel Politics

1. Richard Quebedeaux, *The Worldly Evangelicals* (New York: Harper & Row, 1978).

2. *The New York Times*, July 17, 1978.

3. Richard Hofstadter, *The Paranoid Style in American Politics and Other Essays* (New York: Knopf, 1965), p. 73. Used by permission.

4. Ibid., p. 78.

5. Ibid.

6. Ibid.

7. Ibid., p. 80.

8. Ibid., p. 81.

9. Ibid., pp. 81–82.

10. *Des Moines Register*, January 24, 1978.

11. Ibid.

12. Speech delivered by Peggy L. Shriver. Used by permission.

13. Ibid.

14. Ibid.

15. Donald W. Shriver Jr. and Karl Ostrom, *Is There Hope for the City?* (Philadelphia: Westminster Press, 1977).

16. Speech delivered by Peggy L. Shriver.

17. *Washington Post*, September 29, 1977.

18. Dale Kramer, "The American Fascists," *Harper's Magazine*, September 1940.

19. *Sojourners*, April 1976.

20. Ibid.
21. Ibid.
22. *Washington Post*, April 27, 1978.
23. The phrasing is borrowed from John C. Bennett, *Christians and the State* (New York: Scribner's, 1958).

Chapter 7: The Hyperpatriots

1. In William J. Lanouette, "The Panama Canal Treaties—Playing in Peoria and in the Senate," *National Journal*, October 8, 1977, pp. 1556–62.
2. Terence Smith, *The New York Times*, December 4, 1977.
3. *Democratic Congressional Campaign Committee Report*, February 1978.

Chapter 8: June 6, 1978—A Political Benchmark?

1. *Washington Post*, June 8, 1978.
2. *The New York Times*, June 11, 1978. Copyright © 1978 by The New York Times Company. Reprinted by permission.
3. Ibid.
4. Frank T. Nye, *Cedar Rapids Gazette*, June 1, 1978. Used by permission.
5. *Des Moines Tribune*, May 26, 1978.
6. *The New York Times*, June 11, 1978.
7. Ibid.
8. Ibid.
9. Ibid.
10. Art Pine, *Washington Post*, June 11, 1978.
11. *Group Research Report*, May 30, 1978.
12. Joseph Kraft, *Washington Post*, June 11, 1978.
13. Haynes Johnson, *Washington Post*, June 11, 1978.
14. David Broder, *Washington Post*, June 11, 1978.
15. Johnson, *Washington Post*, June 11, 1978.
16. Marquis Childs, *Washington Post*, June 13, 1978.

Chapter 9: The Psyche of the Radical Right

1. Richard Hofstadter, *The Paranoid Style in American Politics and Other Essays* (New York: Knopf, 1965), p. 43. Used by permission.
2. Ibid., pp. 43–44.
3. Ibid., p. 23.
4. Ibid., p. 31.
5. Ibid., pp. 37–38.
6. Speech delivered before the 1977 National Convention of the American Legion.
7. Hofstadter, *The Paranoid Style in American Politics*, op. cit., p. 50.
8. Ibid., p. 51.

9. Ibid.
10. Ibid., p. 56.
11. Ibid.
12. Ibid., p. 58.
13. Ibid.
14. Ibid.
15. Ibid., p. 59.
16. Ibid., pp. 60–61.
17. Ibid., p. 61.
18. Ibid., p. 65 (italics added).

Chapter 10: Why Now?

1. From an article by Julian Gammon, former chairman of the Arlington County (Va.) Young Republicans, in a 1978 issue of *RebElephant,* a Young Republican publication.
2. Haynes Johnson, *Washington Post,* April 5, 1978.
3. *Washington Post,* July 16, 1978.
4. Ellen Goodman, *The Boston Globe,* December 16, 1977. © The Boston Globe Newspaper Company. Reprinted with permission.
5. Ellen Goodman, *The Boston Globe,* July 18, 1978.

Part II—Introduction

1. Theodore W. Adorno, *The Authoritarian Personality* (New York: Harper & Row, 1950).
2. William J. Lanouette, "The New Right—'Revolutionaries' Out After the 'Lunch-Pail' Vote," *National Journal,* January 21, 1978, pp. 88–92. Used by permission of *National Journal,* copyright owner.

Chapter 11: King of the Epithet

1. In Jules Witcover, "William Loeb and the New Hampshire Primary: A Question of Ethics," *Columbia Journalism Review,* May-June, 1972. Reprinted from the *Columbia Journalism Review.* Used by permission.
2. Ibid.
3. Ibid.
4. Ibid.
5. Ibid.
6. Ibid.
7. James McCartney, "What Really Happened in Manchester?" *Columbia Journalism Review,* May-June 1972.
8. Ibid.
9. Witcover, "William Loeb," op. cit.
10. Ibid.
11. James Doyle, *Washington Star,* March 1, 1972.
12. Witcover, "William Loeb," op. cit.

Chapter 12: Rule or Ruin

1. In Bill Kovach, "Nixon's Too Left-Wing for William Loeb," *The New York Times Magazine*, December 12, 1971. Copyright © 1971 by The New York Times Company. Reprinted by permission.

2. Eric Veblen, *The Manchester Union Leader in New Hampshire Elections* (Hanover, N.H.: University Press of New England, 1975).

3. Kevin Cash, *Who the Hell Is William Loeb?* (Manchester, N.H.: Amoskeag Press, 1975). Used by permission.

Chapter 13: Growing Pains

1. In Bill Kovach, "Nixon's Too Left-Wing for William Loeb," *The New York Times Magazine*, December 12, 1971. Copyright © 1971 by The New York Times Company. Reprinted by permission.

2. Sherman Adams, in interview by Richard Meryman, "Sherman Adams: The Quintessential Doer," *Yankee* magazine, April 1978. Used by permission.

3. In Adolph Bernotas, "State Is Courting Financial Chaos," Associated Press story, Concord, New Hampshire, October 17, 1977.

4. Adams in Meryman, "Sherman Adams," op. cit.

5. Kovach, "Nixon's Too Left-Wing," op. cit.

6. *Boston Magazine*, June 1977.

7. *Boston Magazine*, May 1974. Reprinted by permission of *Boston Magazine*.

8. Patricia Burstein, "New Hampshire's Meldrim Thomson Is a Man of His Century—But Which One?" *People*, November 28, 1977.

9. *New Hampshire Times*, May 25, 1977. Used by permission.

10. Ibid.

11. In Bernotas, "State Is Courting," op. cit.

12. Ibid.

13. *Lebanon Valley News*, June 7, 1977.

14. *Derry News*, January 12, 1978.

15. *Nashua Telegraph*, March 11, 1978.

16. *Lebanon Valley News*, March 7, 1978.

17. *New Hampshire Times*, December 28, 1977. Used by permission.

18. *Boston Magazine*, June 1977.

19. *New Hampshire Times*, May 24, 1978. Used by permission.

20. Ibid.

21. Ibid.

22. Ibid.

23. *New Hampshire Times*, December 28, 1977.

24. *New Hampshire Times*, December 14, 1977.

25. Austin Stevens, "Confessions of a Landholder," *Yankee* magazine, March 1978, pp. 108–24. Used by permission.

26. Ibid.

27. *Boston Magazine*, June 1977.

28. Stevens, "Confessions," op. cit.

29. Ibid.

Chapter 14: The Cloning of William Loeb

1. In "Rising Stars on the Right," *Conservative Digest.*

2. In Patricia Burstein, "New Hampshire's Meldrim Thomson Is a Man of His Century—But Which One?" *People,* November 28, 1977.

3. *Boston Magazine,* May 1974.

4. Ibid.

5. Daniel Yergin, *Boston Magazine,* May 1974. Reprinted by permission of *Boston Magazine.*

6. Ibid.

7. Ibid.

8. *Boston Magazine,* May 1974.

9. *Manchester Union Leader,* October 16, 1968.

10. Robert Lenzner, *The Boston Globe,* March 1, 1974. Lenzner attributed the quote to Constantine Gratsos, described as Onassis' "right hand man." Lenzner said he also asked Gratsos about a rumor that Onassis would be using Teamster Union funds to finance the refinery. Lenzner reported that Gratsos scoffed and said, "I have never seen a Teamster."

11. *Nashua Telegraph,* January 2, 1977.

12. Ibid.

13. *New Hampshire Times,* May 18, 1977.

14. *Concord Monitor,* May 31, 1977.

15. *The Boston Globe,* May 2, 1978.

16. *Nashua Telegraph,* May 2, 1978.

17. *Washington Post,* June 27, 1978.

18. Daniel Yergin, *Boston Magazine,* May 1974.

19. *Keene Evening Sentinel,* April 19, 1973.

20. Burstein, "New Hampshire's Meldrim Thomson," op. cit.

21. Ibid.

22. *New Hampshire Times,* December 14, 1977.

23. Bill Kovach, "Nixon's Too Left-Wing for William Loeb," *The New York Times Magazine,* December 12, 1971. Copyright © 1971 by The New York Times Company. Reprinted by permission.

24. M. Eileen McEachern, "Don't Call Me Ms.," *Boston Globe Sunday Magazine,* March 12, 1978.

25. Ibid.

26. Ibid.

27. Ibid.

Chapter 15: Some of My Best Friends . . .

1. *Boston Magazine,* May 1974. Reprinted by permission of *Boston Magazine.*

2. *Manchester Union Leader,* October 4, 1973.

3. *The New York Times*, December 11, 1977.
4. Ibid.
5. Ibid.
6. *Manchester Union Leader*, September 17, 1971.
7. Ibid.
8. *Manchester Union Leader*, April 9, 1964.
9. *Manchester Union Leader*, November 24, 1964.
10. *Lebanon Valley News*, August 1, 1977.
11. *Portsmouth Herald*, August 6, 1977.
12. *Manchester Union Leader*, June 29, 1978.
13. *Manchester Union Leader*, July 14, 1978.

Chapter 16: The Publisher, the Governor, and the Clergy

1. Daniel Yergin, *Boston Magazine*, May 1974. Reprinted by permission of *Boston Magazine*.
2. *Portsmouth Herald*, March 19, 1978.
3. *Manchester Union Leader*, July 9, 1953.
4. Ibid.
5. *Manchester Union Leader*, September 17, 1968.
6. Ibid.
7. *Manchester Union Leader*, October 24, 1968.
8. Ibid.
9. Tom Ferriter, *Lebanon Valley News*, February 2, 1978.
10. *Concord Monitor*, December 7, 1977.
11. Ibid.
12. *Manchester Union Leader*, January 28, 1978.
13. *Claremont Eagle Times*, January 19, 1978.
14. *Concord Monitor*, January 3, 1978.
15. *Nashua Telegraph*, February 1, 1978.
16. *Portsmouth Herald*, January 31, 1978.
17. *Concord Monitor*, February 3, 1978.

Chapter 17: The Armchair Warriors

1. *Manchester Union Leader*, April 6, 1964.
2. *Newsweek*, June 26, 1978.
3. Hugh Moffett, from his weekly newspaper column, "Vermont Life."
4. *Manchester Union Leader*, March 9, 1972.
5. David Broder, "Vietnam: An Issue for Wallace," *Washington Post*, April 1975.
6. *Manchester Union Leader*, May 20, 1964.

Chapter 18: "Americans" and "Americanism"

1. *Concord Monitor*, March 10, 1978.
2. Ibid.
3. Ibid.

4. *Portsmouth Herald,* March 13, 1978.

5.   Cf. John Courtney Murray, S.J., *We Hold These Truths* (New York: Sheed & Ward, 1960), passim.

Chapter 19: Conclusion

1. John Roy Carlson, *Under Cover* (New York: E.P. Dutton, 1943).

2. Jeff Greenfield, *Harper's Magazine,* September 1977.

3. Ibid.

4. Paul Johnson, *The Enemies of Society* (New York: Atheneum, 1977).

5. *The New York Times,* August 3, 1978.

6. Johnson, *The Enemies of Society,* op. cit.

7. Carlson, *Under Cover,* op. cit.

8. David Broder, *The Party's Over* (New York: Harper & Row, 1971).